SPENCE'S ANECDOTES

JOSEPH SPENCE

Engraving by THOMAS COOK, the frontispiece to volume viii of Nichols' *Select Collection of Poems*, 1782

Joseph Spence

OBSERVATIONS, ANECDOTES, AND CHARACTERS OF BOOKS AND MEN

COLLECTED FROM CONVERSATION

— — — *Apis Matinæ*
More modoque
Grata carpentis thyma Horace

EDITED BY
JAMES M. OSBORN

VOLUME II

OXFORD
AT THE CLARENDON PRESS
1966

Oxford University Press, Ely House, London W. 1
GLASGOW NEW YORK TORONTO MELBOURNE WELLINGTON
CAPE TOWN SALISBURY IBADAN NAIROBI LUSAKA ADDIS ABABA
BOMBAY CALCUTTA MADRAS KARACHI LAHORE DACCA
KUALA LUMPUR HONG KONG TOKYO

PRINTED IN GREAT BRITAIN

CONTENTS

Volume I

Volume II

APPENDIXES

LIST OF ILLUSTRATIONS

PART III

ANECDOTES FROM SPENCE'S TRAVELS ON THE CONTINENT

(§§ 1302–1619)

¶ *The following series of conversations occurred in France during Spence's three visits to that country. The first group centre on the learned men he met at Lyons in the summer of 1731 when travelling as companion and tutor to Charles Sackville, the youthful Earl of Middlesex.*

1302. At a convent (I think it was of Benedictines) at Caen, in Normandy, they keep an exact *terrier* of all the lands which formerly belonged to the monks of that order in England, in hopes it may be one day of good use to them.

MR. CLARK, *who saw the writings in their possession 1731*

This was the Abbey of St. Étienne; William I presented them with lands in several counties of southern England. The 'papiers terriers' were preserved in the archives until the present century (C. Hippeau, *L'Abbaye de St-Étienne de Caen, 1066–1790*, Caen, 1855, p. 8). The speaker may have been Thomas Clarke, Esq., who subscribed to *Polymetis*.

1303. 'Tis the general maxim of all *our* colleges to choose a man of management for their head rather than a man of letters.

PÈRE DE COLONIA, *of the Jesuits' College at Lyons May–September 1731*

Dominique de Colonia (1660–1741) was librarian of the Jesuit Collège de la Trinité and a prolific author in both Latin and French, prose and verse. His best known book, *L'Histoire littéraire de la ville de Lyon*, had been published in 1728, only three years before Spence's arrival in Lyons.

1304. The temple or altar (of the sixty nations of Gauls, at Lyons) was dedicated to Augustus ten years before the Christian era and two years before the month of Sextilis was called Augustus in the general reformation of the calendar. The prizes for eloquence [in] Greek and Latin, and the odd punishments, were instituted there afterwards by Caligula.

PÈRE DE COLONIA *May–September 1731*

These subjects are discussed in Père de Colonia's *L'Histoire littéraire de la ville de Lyon*, i (1728), ch. 6. The 'odd punishments' for the losers included being tossed into the Rhône, which washed the walls of the place of assembly.

1305. In speaking of Benedict XIII, he said that he was a good man, a mediocre bishop, and a bad Pope.

PÈRE DE COLONIA *May–September 1731*

Present-day historians agree in this evaluation of Benedict XIII, who occupied the papal throne from 1724 to 1730. He is described as devout, humble, and almost childish in his trustfulness of favourites, but too old and untrained to manage the affairs of his office (L. Pastor, *History of the Popes*, English edition, ed. E. Graf, xxxiv, 1941, 297–9).

1306. Our *religieux* are such ecclesiastics as live in their regular houses, according to their several orders: chanoines, such as serve in particular churches; curés are those who have parishes under their care, and vicaires are their assistants. Our abbés are of two sorts, *grands et petits*: the former are governors of houses, and the latter, ecclesiastics in the world, and without cure.

LÉGRIS *May–September 1731*

Légris, the author of this and the following conversations, is not otherwise identified. Possibly he was a Jesuit priest whom Spence knew at Lyons during the summer of 1731.

1307. One of the greatest liberties of the Gallican church is that no bull, or order whatever, sent by the Pope, is looked upon as any way valid among us, till it has first passed the King and then the Parliament. By this means, for instance, the King of France can never be excommunicated as to his own subjects, and the Parliament can stop anything they dislike. The present Pope sent his bull for a Jubilee on his promotion to the see, with pardon to all except the Jansenists. The Parliament did not like this exception and sent the bull back for amendment. That was refused, and so we had no Jubilee at all. LÉGRIS *May–September 1731*

The 'Declaration of Gallican Liberties' was formulated in 1682 by a synod headed by Bossuet. Légris refers to the jubilee announced by Clement XII in September 1730, two months after his accession.

1308. The ⌜Duke of Savoy, late⌝ King of Sardinia made an absolute act of mortmain some years ago, and was much for humbling the clergy. He took the education of the children, too, out of the hands of the Jesuits, and none but secular priests can teach them in his dominions. Had the late Regent lived a few years longer, I daresay we should have seen as bold steps (at least) taken among us.

LÉGRIS, *at Lyons May–September 1731*

The act of mortmain had been issued by Duke Emmanuel Philibert in 1567; it provided that estates of subjects dying without heirs should revert to the state instead of allowing them to be left to the Church. Victor Amadeus II enforced it and other anti-ecclesiastical measures. His edict depriving the clergy of the right to teach in public schools was the first substantial setback the Jesuits had received in any country.

1309. After the Duke of Villeroy, governor of the town and three provinces, the provost of the merchants is the chief in Lyons, and after him the four écrivains or consuls. All taxes, imposts, and orders from the King are issued by the intendant, who is a sort of viceroy there. There is a presidial for judging of causes, even capital, of several kinds.

LÉGRIS *May–September 1731*

The Dukes of Villeroy were the traditional governors of Lyons. Légris refers to the ninth Duke, Louis-François-Anne de Neufville, the undistinguished son of the notorious François.

1310. They speak in France of Rousseau as one of their best poets. He lives at Brussels. He has published a fine translation of the seven penitential psalms, has wrote some satirical pieces, extremely severe, and is now writing the History of Prince Eugene. He has been in England, and [was] extremely well received there.

LÉGRIS *and* LE CLAIRE *May–September 1731*

Jean-Baptiste Rousseau (1670–1741) published the first volumes of his *Odes Sacrées* in 1712. His satires, which had appeared in 1710, caused him to be banished from France in 1712, when he took up residence in Brussels. Although he benefited from the patronage of Prince Eugene for many years, they became estranged in 1724, and the history of the Prince was never completed.

Rousseau came to London late in December 1722 and remained until the following July, the visit being financed by a subscription edition of his works, published by Tonson. He received a cordial reception from everyone, including the King and court. For the concurrent opinions of Ramsay and the Abbé Boileau of Rousseau's pre-eminence among contemporary French poets see §§ 1294 and 1345.

Le Claire, like Légris, has not been identified; probably Spence met them in the Jesuit library at Lyons.

1311. The French acting [was] half singing till within these fifteen years. Quinault: 'et vous parlez plus bas?'

LOINVILLE *May–September 1731*

The speaker was some acquaintance at Dijon or Lyons, but he does not appear in Spence's travel letters. The dramatist Philippe Quinault (1635–88) wrote libretti for Lulli's operas and influenced the transition from the recitative to the operatic style.

1312. If you can't get *Il Cortegiano* I'd advise you to get a small book entitled *Il Sindicato d'Alessandro Settimo*, or another called *Il Nipotismo*. There are in both some diverting things, and they make one acquainted with the secret history of Popes, cardinals, nephews, nieces, whores, and bawds. If you have patience enough, Davila's *Istoria della guerra civili di Francia*, or Bentivoglio's *Storia delle guerre di Fiandra*. They are both fine in their way and much worth reading.

Perhaps you'll be contented with the *Pastor Fido* of Guarini, or the *Aminta* of Tasso; they are both good, but too much of what the French call *trop recherché*.

Tasso's famous *Jerusalem* is both tedious and what Boileau calls '*clinquant*'. One verse of Virgil's is worth a thousand of his, but 'tis much in fashion in Italy, and a gentleman is almost obliged to read it for conversation's sake.

Father Paul's *History of the Council of Trent* is absolutely the finest book in the Italian language.

MR. GR *to* LORD ROBERT MONTAGU *May–September 1731*

The manuscript shows that in the summer of 1731 Spence was collecting recommendations of books to provide the proper background for his sojourn in Italy (§ 1292 is written on the same piece of paper). Spence had met Lord Robert Montagu (1710–62), later third Duke of Manchester, in Lyons, where, presumably, he recorded this information. 'Mr. Gr', who is called 'Dr. Gr.' in a marginal note, has not been identified.

The first two books are by Gregorio Leti (1630–1701), officially a colourful convert to Calvinism but a libertine in fact. Both books were published in 1667 and the second appeared in an English translation as *The History of the Pope's Nephews* in 1669. 'Father Paul' is Paolo Sarpi (1552–1623), Venetian historian and church reformer, whose *Historia del Concilio Tridentino* was published in London in 1619 and in an English version the following year.

¶ *After several months in Lyons, Spence and Lord Middlesex proceeded up the Rhône valley to Geneva where they arrived on 1 October 1731. As the following conversations show, Spence moved largely in academic circles open to him as Professor of Poetry at Oxford.*

1313. The women at Geneva go into the lake publicly: in one particular like the French ladies.

PENTON *26 July–4 August 1729*

In his travel letters Spence described a bathing scene on the Saône at Lyons. One arch of the bridge was 'full of ladies up to the chin in water . . . they have always something on, like our women at the bath, but they don't at all shriek to have men among them' (10 August 1731, B.M. Egerton MS. 2234, f. 27). The jotting about Geneva ladies, curiously enough, was recorded as a travel hint before Spence left England; for Henry Penton see § 803.

1314. The government of Geneva is partly aristocratic and partly democratic. The liberty of the people is really very considerable: it consists in our having no magistrate over us whom we do not choose ourselves, and no law to which we do not give our consent.

MONSIEUR CRAMER *one of the professors at Geneva October 1731*

Jean Cramer (1701–87) became professor of law in 1723; Spence made notes on 'ye Etat présent du Governement de Geneve' preserved among the Spence Papers, from which he extracted these anecdotes.

1315. The Assembly of Bourgeois, or citizens (about fifteen or sixteen hundred in number) nominate persons out of their own body to supply the vacancies in the Council of two hundred. The Two Hundred nominate twenty-five of their members for the Syndic-ship, or chief office, out of which twenty-five, the assembly of bourgeois again, elect four syndics. CRAMER *October 1731*

1316. We have but one book of laws, so small that you may hide it in your hand, and have not had any new law made these hundred years. CRAMER *October 1731*

After the edicts of 1635 the laws of Geneva were not modified until 1738 (H. Fazy, *Les Constitutions de la République de Genève*, 1890, pp. 89–90, 118).

1317. Law-suits are not common among us, and the trade of quarrelling meets with small encouragement. Our advocates (or pleaders) are tied down to a certain, and very low, pay, yet we have about four score of them, because it is necessary for anyone to have been an advocate in order to qualify him for holding any of the chief posts in the republic. CRAMER *October 1731*

Cramer himself followed this procedure; he resigned his professorship in 1738, became a member of the Council of Two Hundred, and later was elected First Syndic.

1318. There are at present 12,000 of our troops in Ireland, and 19,500 belonging to Great Britain—but then the latter includes the garrison of Gibraltar, about 3,000, Port Mahon, about 2,500, and the Invalides, about 3,000.

MR. SOYER, *Chaplain to a regiment October 1731*

Daniel Soyer (*fl.* 1722–43) served as chaplain to General Gore's Regiment of Dragoons, the 10th Hussars, from 1722 until 1737 (C. Dalton, *George the First's Army*, 1912, ii. 218–19). His reason for being in Geneva at this time is unknown; he may simply have been travelling. The 12,000 troops stationed in Ireland had been a fixed number during the 'no standing army' era, when Walpole had to struggle to keep the strength of the regular forces up to 18,000 men. By 'Invalides' Soyer apparently meant disabled soldiers.

1319. Our ecclesiastical polity in Holland is, in my opinion, preferable to yours in England on several accounts. 1. In the people's having a share in choosing their own teachers for themselves. 2. In the clergy's not being so subject to brigues and rivalship and fawning for preferments, as they are with you. 3. In the greater level of their income, which renders them less subject either to pride or to contempt. No clergyman in the province of Holland has under £40 a year, and no one above £240. 4. In the manner of receiving their income, in settled sums, quarterly, from the magistrates, which lessens their concern about temporals and prevents lawsuits and disputes with their parishioners. 5. In their being wholly unconcerned with the civil government, which keeps them out of party quarrels, and gives them more time to attend to their proper employment.

MR. SOYER, *at Geneva October 1731*

The earliest manuscript names the source, 'From Mons[r] Soyer's account of y[e] Ecclesiastical Polity in Holland, it excells ours perhaps in five articles'. The work apparently did not reach print, though Soyer did help edit the first English edition of Blainville's *Travels through Holland, Germany, but especially Italy* in 1743. Spence's use of 'ours' and 'yours' suggests that Soyer may originally have come from the Low Countries to England.

1320. When there was that great fire in the seraglio at Constantinople about fifty years ago, a great deal of the goods, and among the rest several books, were flung into the street. The secretary of the French ambassador, then at the Porte, happened to be walking that way, and as he was getting as well as he could through the crowd, saw a man with a large folio which he had opened but could not tell what to make of it. The secretary saw 'twas a manuscript of Livy, and on turning over the leaves a little farther, found that it had the second decade as well as the first, and probably might have all that is lost to us. He offered the man a handsome reward if he would keep the book under his long robe and follow him with it to his lodgings. The man agreed to it, and followed him, but the crowd and confusion increasing, they were separated, and so the secretary lost the recovery of so great a treasure as this would have been to the learned world.

SOYER *October 1731*

Livy's immense History of Rome extended to one hundred and forty-two books, of which only Books i–x and xxi–xlv have been preserved, some of them incompletely. Early copyists divided them into 'decads' and the second decad has been lost since the end of the Roman era.

Soyer's story derives from a letter of Pietro Della Valle, dated 27 June 1615 from Constantinople, published in his *Viaggi* (Roma, 1650–63), subsequently translated into several languages. The legends about Livy's lost books were the subject of D. G. Morhof's *De Patavinitate liviana liber*, Kilonii,

1685, which Pierre Bayle reviewed in *Nouvelles de la république des lettres*, iii (1685), 609–25. Modern scholars consider these legends implausible. Soyer apparently transferred the story to one of the three conflagrations that ravaged Constantinople in 1693.

1321. Nicolao Cordato Mauro, Prince of Walachia (formerly interpreter to the Porte, afterwards prisoner in Turkey, and again restored to his principality), in the end of the last century wrote a system of Christian ethics in Greek. The piece is very good, and the style not inferior to that of Lucian. There is an account of it in Le Clerc's *Bibliothèque Ancienne et Moderne* [xiv (1720), 113–131].

SOYER *October 1731*

The Greek, Nicolas Mavrocordato (1670–1730), rose from being grand dragoman to the Divan to become ruler of the Danubian principalities, where he introduced the Greek language and manners. Le Clerc published his account of Mavrocordato's Book of Offices the year following its first printing in Bucharest.

1322–3. Cancelled.

1324. The grandees in Spain are extremely ignorant. There is scarce anything like taste among them. Even in the King's palaces they have cut some of the finest pictures, that they formerly brought out of Italy, only to fit them to the places where they are hung, so that you shall see the upper part of a capital piece, perhaps, over one door, and the remainder of it over another.

The FRENCH GENERAL *that we met upon the Alps, in his passage from Madrid to Rome* *October 1731*

The earliest manuscript describes the speaker as a 'French Brigadier in ye Spanish service'. Spence crossed the Alps during the third week of October 1731.

1325. Gibraltar [is] absolutely impregnable by land.

The same FRENCH GENERAL *October 1731*

The defences of Gibraltar were created in the sixteenth century and strengthened by the British after their capture of the rock in 1704. An unsuccessful siege was attempted in 1726.

1326. The French could fit forty men-of-war in four months' time, says the old Count who is to command the Squadron now fitting out at Toulon and Brest; others say fifty. CAPT. COLE *28–31 May 1733 ?*

A Captain Cole is named in Spence's list of Englishmen met on the Grand Tour; possibly he was the Captain William Cole who died 24 April 1769. This conversation occurred when Spence and Lord Middlesex reached Marseilles on their return to England.

1327. Our religion is not founded upon reason.
The ARCHBISHOP OF ARLES *2 June 1733*

(at Arles, speaking of the religion of the Church of Rome. 'Nôtre religion n'est pas fondée sur les raisonnements,' were his own words.)

That great prelate had the goodness to attempt, in a quarter of an hour's visit, to bring us over to the love of popery and of a popish prince. When he found that we held steady to our old principles all that time, he pitied us very much, and was extremely sorry that such fine and such promising young gentlemen would shut their eyes thus against the light, when it was offered to them. He lamented pathetically over us, and begged us again and again to consider all that he had offered to us. If we did not, he said it shocked him to the last degree to think of the sad consequence that could not but follow from our continuing the way that we were in: 'for you protestants,' added he, 'when you die, fall all down into Hell, as the flakes of snow fall upon the earth in the winter season.' ('Quand vous venez à mourir, vous tombez en enfer, comme les flocs de la neige tombent sur la terre dans le temps d'hiver.') ⌜It seems but too much to be apprehended that our divisions will end in a désolation affreuse.⌝

SPENCE

Spence's Travel Notes record a stop at Arles when he and Lord Middlesex were returning from the Grand Tour. The archbishop was Jacques de Forbin-Janson, who held the office from 1711 until 1741. Spence's French has been left as he wrote it.

The following seven anecdotes record the conversation of the Reverend Robert Milling (d. 1749), since 1716 Minister of the English Church at the Hague. Spence had arrived there in May 1737 with his pupil, John Morley Trevor the younger, and remained for about six weeks before going on to Paris. Spence included these comments in the Travel Notes (B.M. Egerton MS. 2235), and later excerpted them when writing the Folio manuscript of his anecdotes.

1328. The Dutch don't seem to labour hard, but they are constantly doing something. They fix on some aim and follow it steadily. More of their industry (perhaps nineteen parts in twenty) is on the water than on the land, for all the towns are chained to one another by canals, and these again are veined out into the meadows. The mills fling the superfluous waters from the meadows into the larger canals, and these carry off the glut of them into the sea. It would be worth the while to have a print of all the canals and smaller ducts in Holland, without marking anything of the land, like the prints that are made of the veins and arteries in the human body.

MILLING *May–June 1737*

In a letter dated 3 June 1737 Spence echoed the phrase, 'nineteen parts in twenty of the industry of this people lies on the water'. Concerning the maps of Holland, Milling apparently was unfamiliar with the highly developed hydrographical maps then available, which showed the waterways and ditches of the polders, along with other physical features. See S. J. Fockema Andreae and B. van't Hoff, *Geschiedenis der kartografie van Nederland*, 's-Gravenhage, 1947.

1329. The Dutch are extremely taxed. Land in the Province of Holland pays about one-third to the states, and another third toward keeping up the dykes and windmills, so that £300 a year can bring in but £100 to the owner. Houses pay two-twelfths, and consequently a house of £60 a year can bring in but £50. All the necessaries of life are numerously taxed. Soap, for instance, costs more on the account of the tax than its original value, and a dish of water-sookie is said to pay thirty-six several taxes, including everything from its purchase to your rising from the table.

MILLING *May–June 1737*

'Water-sookie' is not listed by lexicographers. It was probably based on sugar or syrup (Dutch *sukade*).

1330. Among the variety of taxes that we have among us, one of the best judged, and the least apt to cause complaints, is that on wills. Whatever is left to strangers, or even relations, if collateral (as brothers, nephews, etc.), pays five per cent to the state, and this tax alone brings in £100,000 a year.

MILLING *May–June 1737*

Spence's Travel Notes, the original source of these anecdotes, add the comment 'There's a great many little taxes for passage; evn walking. You pay for going to Church, & for p——g'. Also, 'Money (& many Estates) are by ye Laws to be divided equally among all ye Children of ye Deceasd'.

1331. Under all their taxes, and the immense debt of the public, the people generally live quiet and satisfied enough, for they are industrious and live under their clear income, and have their liberties preserved to them—and indeed happiness, or at least a sufficiency for happiness, seems to be more diffused here than in any other country.

MILLING *May–June 1737*

1332. There is but little of arable land in this part of Holland. 'Tis generally one meadow as far as you can see. What arable we have is generally made by taking off ten or twelve foot of sand, and there's a good soil under it. This sand is generally carried off as ballast to our trading ships, and sold in other countries, and the best of it will thus clear all the expense of taking it off.

MILLING *May–June 1737*

1333. The Dutch clergy were at first put all on an equal footing, for after breaking from the yoke of Spain, the states took all the church-lands into their hands, and allowed each minister £60 a year, with a house and a garden. This was a great allowance then, three times as much as it is now, considering the different value of money and the price of things. The ministers of the little parishes in the country have still this allowance, but in towns they are often allowed more—sometimes instead of a house, and generally on account of the more expensive way of living in the better towns. Thus the minister at Leyden, for example, has £180 a year, and at Amsterdam £220. Whatever their allowance is, 'tis paid them regularly every half year, at the first demand, and without any manner of deductions.

MILLING (*who has himself the best income of any ecclesiastic in Holland for his church at the Hague*) *May–June 1737*

The Reverend Milling's salary was 500 Flemish pounds per year, paid by the British Ambassador.

1334. Amsterdam is built all upon piles, and 'tis said that there is 9,000 of them under the Statehouse alone. They talk of its being seven or eight miles round, and of its having four or five hundred thousand souls in it, but those accounts must be a great deal too large. It appears by the taxation books that there are not above 26,000 houses in Amsterdam, and consequently, if we go by the rule of seven persons to a house, the number of inhabitants will fall short of 200,000. As to the circumference of the town, I think it can't be above five miles. MILLING *May–June 1737*

Spence had made a week's tour through the principal Dutch cities, and on his return checked the population and other facts with Milling.

¶ *The four anecdotes following report a visit to the Palais Royal to see the pictures collected by the Duc d'Orléans. Spence was in Paris 13–22 July 1737 on his second tour, and recorded many of the same details in his Travel Notes. The pictures may be easily identified by consulting Victor Champier,* Le Palais-Royal d'après des documents inédits (1629–1900), *Paris, 1900.*

1335. The noble collection of pictures in the Palais Royal at Paris cost the Regent above a million of louis d'ors (or guineas). In particular, the St. Joseph, little Jesus, and Virgin cost fifteen thousand livres (or 625 guineas), the little St. John, Jesus, and Virgin thirty thousand livres, and the St. John in the Wilderness, fifty thousand.

The OFFICER *who showed us the Palace 13–22 July 1737*

In his Travel Notes Spence recorded: 'There is no Collection of Pictures in France, nor perhaps on this side the Alps, any ways equal to that at y[e] *Palais Royal.* There are said to be about 500 valuable Pieces in it; & y[e] late Regent of France laid out above *4 Mil[lio]ns* of Livres (*above 163000* Eng[lish]) in less than 20 y[ea]rs in getting them together. A great part of 'em were fro[m] the Q[ueen] of Swedens Coll[ectio]n; tho' bought last from D[uke] Livio Odeschalchis. Antonini has made a list of this (not publish'd)' (B.M. Egerton MS. 2235, f. 68).

After he had made his third tour, Spence added in the margin: 'The person who showd it us in 1739 said the Pictures cost 25 Millions of livres'. The three paintings mentioned by Spence are groups by Raphael; see Champier, op. cit., i. 295, 514, which shows that the guide was exaggerating the purchase prices in order to impress the English visitors.

1336. This gallery was all painted by the best Coypel.

'Sure, they scarce come up to his character?' [said Spence].

That is perhaps from their bad neighbourhood. ('Ils ont des mauvais voisins', were his words.) They might do well in any other palace in Paris, but they must look poor and unaffecting to you, after having conversed with so much better company in the rooms just before it.

'But I think even here, those on the roof are much better than these on the walls?' [suggested Spence.]

That's very true. Coypel painted the roof first, and between the painting of that, and his beginning on the sides he took to dramming, which soon spoiled his hand—and so much the faster, because he before used to drink nothing but water. *The same* [OFFICER] *13–22 July 1737*

Antoine Coypel (1661–1722), son of Noël Coypel, painted the Gallerie d'Enée from 1702–5. The paintings were destroyed at the end of the century, but the fourteen paintings are known from engravings, some of which are reproduced by Champier, op. cit., i. 320–2.

1337. This picture of a muleteer was drawn by Correggio, and served for a good while as a sign to a little public house by the roadside. It has still the marks in the upper corners of its having been doubled in for that purpose. The man who kept the house had been a muleteer, and had on occasion obliged Correggio a good deal on the road. He set him up, and painted his sign for him. The persons who were sent into Italy to collect pictures for the Regent met with this sign and bought it of the innkeeper. It cost 500 guineas.

The same [OFFICER] *13–22 July 1737*

Spence's Travel Notes indicate that the palace officer told a slightly conflicting story of the origin of this famous Correggio when Spence revisited the gallery in 1740 (B.M. Egerton MS. 2235, f. 68). Reports that it had been an inn sign go back at least to the *Mercure de France*, March 1722, when the painting belonged to the Queen of Sweden. After the dispersal of the Orleans collection the picture crossed the Channel in 1792 and entered the collection of the Marquis of Stafford, but has since been owned by his descendants, the Dukes of Sutherland (S. de V. Battaglia, *Correggio, Bibliografia*, Rome, 1934, pp. 20, 270).

1338. My Lord is the best of masters, but alas! he grows very old, and I fear can't last long. I would with all my heart, give ten years out of my own life to prolong his, if it could be done.

The OFFICER *who showed the Count of Toulouse's gallery to us 13–22 July 1737*

He added, upon our being affected with what he had said, that this was no great merit in him, that most of his fellow-servants he believed would be willing to do the same, that the goodness of their master to them, and the greatness of their affection for him, was so remarkable and so well known that a friend of the Count's once was saying to him, 'I don't know what it is that you do to charm all the people thus about you, but though you have two hundred servants, I believe there is scarce any one of them that would not die to save your life.'

'That may be,' replied the Count, 'but I would not have any one of them die to save it.' SPENCE

Spence's visit occurred shortly before the death of Louis-Alexandre de Bourbon, Comte de Toulouse (1678–1737), a son of Louis XIV and Madame de Montespan. Spence described the gallery in his Travel Notes (B.M. Egerton MS. 2235, f. 69).

¶ *From Paris Spence and his pupil, Trevor, went to Blois where they settled down for several months to polish their French, as Addison had done before them* (§ *815*).

1339. The bridge at Blois was designed by Monsieur Imbert, though a person in whose hands it was put (on its being much approved of at Court) was inclined to let it pass for his own. It was begun in 1718 and finished in 1722, and cost near two millions of livres.

''Tis really very handsome, but I could wish the obelisk away' [said Spence].

That, Sir, was not in the original design, but was added afterwards, and had better have been omitted.

MONSIEUR BONVALET *of Blois* (*one of the four undertakers of that work*) *August–November 1737*

The celebrated bridge across the Loire was one of the sights reported by travellers. It was begun in 1716 and opened to the public in March 1724, thirteen years before Spence spent a few months at Blois. The original sketches, preserved in the municipal archives, show the obelisk placed over the central arch. These plans are signed by Gabriel, the royal architect; nothing is now known of Imbert, who was probably an assistant.

A description and engraving of the bridge appeared in the *Gentleman's Magazine* in 1754 (p. 588). The bridge was destroyed by the retreating German Army in August 1944, but it has now been restored, including the obelisk.

1340. We have two millions of religious (taking in men and women of all sorts), and twenty millions of souls in France.

ABBÉ PHILIPPEAU *A very sensible priest of the order of St. Genevieve at Blois August–November 1737*

I had been speaking of our common computation of about two hundred thousand ecclesiastics for France. He laughed at that as extremely short of their number, and by his computation made it one tenth, instead of one hundredth only of the whole body of the people. Whereas our clergy in England is but one four hundredth of the people, if we set the clergy at twenty thousand and the people at eight millions. How much would this single article add toward the enslaving and impoverishing the country, if we should ever happen to have a Popish prince over us, and grow as zealous Catholics as they are in France—by turning so many hands from business and trade to the promoting the superstition of the people and increasing the weight of a foreign ecclesiastical power over us. SPENCE

According to M. Moheau, author of *Recherches et considérations sur la population de la France* (Paris, 1778), the number of ecclesiastics was then about 130,000 in a population of 23,500,000. He remarks that this was a favourite subject for exaggeration, especially by foreigners (pp. 100–3). 'L'ignorance, le préjugé, l'esprit de parti ont exagéré le nombre des Ecclésiastiques François' (p. 100). For the Abbé Philippeau see § 815.

1341. Father Courayer was the most amiable man, and was in fact the most generally beloved of anyone I know in our order. I have heard Abbé Bignon, who is as good a judge of writing as any now living, say, that 'he looked on Courayer as the best pen in France.'

ABBÉ PHILIPPEAU *August–November 1737*

For Father Courayer, who had sought asylum in England in 1728, see §§ 70 and 1265. Jean Paul Bignon (1662–1743), the King's librarian and a prolific author, is remembered today chiefly because the newly found flower, the bignonia, was named in his honour.

1342. Courayer is, as Father Paul was before him, a Catholic by profession, but a Protestant in his particular tenets. (His words were: 'Fra Paolo est comme lui Catholique en gros, et Protestant en détail.')

ABBÉ PHILIPPEAU *August–November 1737*

For the Italian reformer, Paolo Sarpi, see § 1312 n. The year before this conversation occurred Father Courayer had published an English translation of Sarpi's *History of the Council of Trent*.

1343. Old Fontenelle has done a great deal of hurt to our language. ABBÉ BOILEAU *winter 1737–8*

I have often heard Ramsay complain of the same. He used to say that he was the chief corrupter of the French language, by his introducing so many new words and expressions, and by his writing with so much wit. Numbers endeavour to imitate him, take the same liberties, and aim at nothing but to shine. Particular instances of his own faults, and of those of his imitators, are enrolled in the *Memoirs* of the *Calotte*. SPENCE

For Ramsay's opinion of Fontenelle see § 1299. *Memoires ... de la Calotte* (Basle, 1725) was a collection of facetious and satirical verses. In the margin of the Folio manuscript Spence explained 'calotte' as 'The name of the Cap that is given to Fools'.

The Abbé Boileau who supplied Spence with literary conversation has not been identified.

1344. Corneille's middle plays (for, you know, they are published according to the order in which they were written) are his only good ones. He has a greater variety of characters, and those more distinguished, than Racine's. One should set his good plays only against those of the latter, which are, in all, but six, and Corneille has nine or ten good ones.

ABBÉ BOILEAU *winter 1737–8*

For Mallet's rating of Corneille's and Racine's plays, see § 938.

1345. Rousseau is now grown old. He was for a long time our only poet; now Voltaire may share the honour of that name with him, and is next to him both in merit and reputation. ABBÉ BOILEAU, *at Tours winter 1737–8*

During the seven-year interval since Ramsay had told Spence that Rousseau was the best French poet, Voltaire had become the rising star (§ 1294).

1346. Marivaux overflows. He begins well but he does not know where to leave off. ABBÉ COLVIL *late 1737*

Abbé Colvil lived at Tours, where Spence and Trevor spent December 1737. Marivaux had published a succession of plays, novels, and other writings. Colvil probably referred to the 'nouvelle préciosité' of Marivaux's style, but may have had Marivaux's characters in mind. Crébillon described the latter as pouring out not only every thought they had ever had, but also everything that they could persuade themselves that they had thought.

1347. 'Tis the Abbé Prévost who wrote the *Memoirs of a Nobleman*, the *Pour et Contre*, and the *Chevalier de Grieux*.

ABBÉ COLVIL *late 1737*

The Abbé Prévost, while a fugitive from his order, published anonymously his famous romance, *Mémoires d'un homme de qualité* (1728). The seventh volume contained *Manon Lescaut*, published separately in 1731. His periodical, *Le Pour et le Contre*, began in 1733 and continued until 1740. When this conversation took place he had become reconciled with the Benedictines, but was living as almoner to the Prince of Conti.

1348. Monsieur Le Sage writes for bread. He has published *Guzman*, and always keeps to Spanish scenes.

'Has he ever been in that country?' [asked Spence].

Yes, I think he has. He is a very worthy good man, and cheerful, though so extremely deaf—and even gay in company by the help of a *cornette*. ABBÉ COLVIL, *of Tours late 1737*

Le Sage's *Histoire de Guzman d'Alfarache* appeared in 1732. There is no evidence that he ever travelled in Spain. Because his deafness required the use of an ear trumpet Le Sage rarely ventured from home except to his favourite café.

¶ *The following series of conversations took place in October and November 1741, when Spence and Lord Lincoln stopped in Paris on their return from the Grand Tour.*

1349. Monsieur Le Sage lives in a pretty genteel manner, though he has little more now to live on than what his son, Montmenil, gets by the stage. He is the best of sons, and they live together in the greatest harmony.

ABBÉ COLVIL *November 1741*

Le Sage's eldest son, René-André, though he studied for the bar, became a famous actor under the name Montmenil.

1350. Montmenil was the best actor in France at that time for plain, easy comedy. When he was upon the stage he did and said everything so naturally that he seemed to be the very person that he represented, and was almost apt to forget that he was upon a stage. Though he was so excellent an actor, the Abbé said that he did not get above a hundred louis d'ors a year by his profession.

ABBÉ COLVIL *November 1741*

Montmenil specialized in acting the parts of valets and country bumpkins.

1351. Je suis mort. Il n'y a long temps que je vivais, mais tout est fini! LE SAGE *November 1741*

What an air of health and complacency in his looks, and yet to say, *Je suis mort*! What then must an infirm old age be? SPENCE

Despite Le Sage's deafness and age (seventy-three) when Spence called on him shortly before returning to England from the Grand Tour, these anecdotes show that Le Sage exuded good spirits and interest in the affairs of the literary world.

1352. I thank God, I don't wish for any one thing that I could not pray aloud for. LE SAGE *November 1741*

1353. Aye, those were the two first works that ever I risked into the world. ('Ces étoient mes deux enfants perdus' were his words.) LE SAGE *November 1741*

We had been speaking of his *Gil Blas* and *Le Diable Boiteux*. SPENCE

Spence may have misunderstood the irony with which the septuagenarian referred to what were not his earliest works, but his two most notable literary successes. He had done several comedies and translations from the Spanish before *Le Diable Boiteux* in 1707. The first part of *Gil Blas* appeared in 1715.

1354. It was in this room that I wrote most of *Gil Blas*. LE SAGE *November 1741*

And an extreme pretty place to write in it was. His house is at Paris in the suburbs of St. Jaques, and so, open to the country air, and the garden laid out in the prettiest manner that ever I saw for a town garden. It was as pretty as it was small, and when he was in the study part of it he was quite retired from the noise of the street or any interruptions from his own family. The garden was only of the breadth of the house, from which you stepped out into a raised square parterre, planted with a variety of the prettiest flowers. From this you went down by a flight of steps, on each side, into a berceau which led to two rooms, or summerhouses, quite at the end of the garden. These were joined by an open portico, the roof of which was supported with columns so that he could walk from the one to the other, all under cover, in the intervals of writing. The berceaux were covered with vines and honeysuckles, and the space between them was grove-work. It was in the right-hand room as you go down that he wrote *Gil Blas*.

SPENCE

Spence's description is apparently the only source of information about Le Sage's house. Among his gardening papers Spence preserved a drawing of Le Sage's garden layout.

The Huntington manuscript adds a few touches: 'His pretty little Garden: rais'd ground at first; then a Green Cage-Walk, on each side; & a Loggietta, (with a Portico in the midst . . .).'

1355. They have made my Hidalgo a Lord in the English translation and a Burgomaster in the Dutch. I believe that people are much alike in all countries: one can't paint one without painting a thousand. LE SAGE *November 1741*

Gil Blas appeared in English and Dutch translations in 1716, a year after the first French printing.

1356. He abused a man *au dessus de lui* (speaking of Boileau and Quinault). He repeated a passage from Quinault's *Rinalde et Armide*, 'vous allez me quitter', etc., which was really very fine, and said a good deal more in praise of him in general. LE SAGE *November 1741*

Boileau looked down on Quinault as a maker of silly verses, his attitude being similar to that of Pope to 'Namby Pamby' Philips. For Lockier's comment on Boileau's uncharitable disposition see § 721.

Le Sage quoted from Quinault's opera *Armide* (1686), Act V, scene i, which actually reads 'vous m'allez quitter'.

1357. Surely, the people of England are the most unhappy people on the face of the earth—with liberty and property and three meals a day. LE SAGE *November 1741*

Somebody had been describing the perpetual complaints that were, they said, in England, in spite of all their privileges and enjoyments. SPENCE

The 'somebody' was Spence himself, his letters reveal.

1358. Holland would be a good country to live in, if you could only change the four elements and the people. ⌜There's nothing but *Canaux*, *Canards*, et *Canaille*.⌝

LE SAGE *November 1741*

If one considers that the earth there is generally marshy, their waters dead, the air offensive, and that they use peat mostly for firing, one must allow that what is said of the elements there comes but too near the truth. SPENCE

1359. Men are a sort of moving plants, and like trees receive a great part of their nourishment from the air. You were observing the other day how sickly that row of trees in the Tuileries looked, from its being pent up so much between the terrace and the wall. 'Tis the same with men who keep too much at home, and 'tis for the same reason that women in general, who keep more within doors than the men, are more unhealthy than men.

MONSIEUR LE GRAND, *at Paris October 1741*

Because the name is so common it has been impossible to identify the speaker.

1360. A lady who came out of the country this summer to see the Court at Versailles, on her return said, that 'bating the amours and debaucheries that reign there, she never saw so dull a thing in her whole life.' ('Outre la passion, je n'ai jamais vu de chose plus triste.') LE GRAND *October 1741*

¶ *After crossing the Alps in the autumn of 1731 Spence and Lord Middlesex made a leisurely way down the Po valley to Venice. They stopped in Verona for several days where they received a warm welcome from the Marquis Scipione Maffei (1675–1755), the literary and social lion of the city. Spence gave a vivid account of him to his mother—'Here lives the famous Scipio Maffei. He is by title a Marquis, and for learning one of the most eminent men now in Italy' (10 November 1731, B.M. Egerton MS. 2234, f. 40v). He took Spence and Lord Middlesex to a ball, and also showed them the local ruins and antiquities.*

1361. When I was young I published a piece called *Ninfa Fidele*. Was I to write anything of that nature now, it should be *Ninfa Infida*. That title would have been the more just—at least I am sure I have found them so!

MAFFEI *c. 10 November 1731*

⌜He's an old bachelor of above sixty. How gay, among all the dancers, at the *conversazione*!⌝ SPENCE

Maffei's *La Fida Ninfa*, with music by Antonio Vivaldi, opened the newly constructed Teatro Filarmonico at Verona just two months after this conversation took place. Spence's letters describe '. . . how busy & officious the good old Gentleman was among all the Ladies, from ye Eldest to the Youngest. He'd whisper each, as soon as ever she stood still; & was sometimes so entangled in the Ranks that he'd put the whole danse into confusion' (10 November 1731). Spence exaggerated Maffei's age slightly; he was then fifty-six.

1362. The French pretend to rival our [Italian] music, and seem to forget that they were obliged to us for their own. Some of our musicians who resided in their country helped them to the sort of music they have, and found it, not on the true principles of harmony, but so as to hit their particular taste. What music they have, such as it is, is a scion from our tree ('une feuille de nôtre arbre,' were his words).

MAFFEI *c. 10 November 1731*

⌜He has himself wrote an opera formerly.⌝ SPENCE

The eighteenth century carried on a long controversy, known as 'la querelle des bouffons', over the relative merits of French and Italian music, which culminated in Jean-Jacques Rousseau's *Lettre sur la musique française* (1753) in which he championed the Italian. Most Englishmen took the Italian side. Spence refers to Maffei's *Il Sansone, oratorio per musica*, published in Florence, 1699.

1363. 'Tis true the French abound in translations of the Greek and Latin authors, but we abound in them yet more than they. Indeed we began long before them: we in the fourteenth century, and they not till the beginning of the seventeenth. MAFFEI *c. 10 November 1731*

His patriotism led Maffei to exaggerate somewhat; he overlooked the work of the Pléiade in mid-sixteenth-century France.

1364. Pray observe with what ease the passions are expressed in that face! Our statuaries now are forced to distort the features to show a passion, their strokes are all violent and forced. This will help you as much as anything to see the superiority of the best ancient sculptors over the modern. We have no one except Michelangelo that comes near them.

MAFFEI *c. 10 November 1731*

The superiority of Greek sculpture had become a critical commonplace (§ 1386). A letter of Spence's indicates that Maffei made this remark when looking at a Greek female figure at the Bishop's Palace, where he took Spence and Lord Middlesex (Spence to Rolle, 15 February 1732, B.M. Egerton, MS. 2234, f. 45).

¶ *Spence and Lord Middlesex travelled down the Adriatic coast from Venice, arriving in Rome about the middle of March 1732. During the three and a half months spent in Rome they pursued a heavy schedule of sightseeing, led by Francesco de Ficoroni (1664–1747), who, despite his years, was still an active cicerone. Spence described him in a letter as 'one of those people that we call Antiquaries here. Their business is to go about Rome to show strangers the Antiquities, Palaces, Pictures & Statues that are there without number. They have generally old Roman Rings and other pieces of Antiquity to sell to the Gentlemen they conduct about the Town ... Ficoroni ... is so old that he had been Conductor to Mr Addison when at Rome & was so to Ld Middlesex all the time we stayed there' (to his mother, 16 November 1732, B.M. Egerton MS. 2234, f. 70v; for Addison see § 816).*

Twelve years later Ficoroni published his Le Vestigia e Rarità di Roma Antica *(1744) and many of the remarks jotted down by Spence are paralleled in the book, some closely and others less so. They provide an interesting example of the repertory of an eighteenth-century guide, and also confirm Spence's accuracy as a reporter.*

1365. There are about thirty-five thousand houses in Rome, twenty-three thousand of which belong to the religious of one kind or another (aux religieux et religieuses). The Pope can put down any religious society if he pleases, so that all their property is in his power.

His usual way of paying or rewarding people that he is obliged to is by assigning them such a pension on some one or other of these religious societies, and as he can thus tyrannise over them, it often occasions his allowing them to tyrannise over their dependents in their turn, to make amends for any great draughts he may make upon them.

FICORONI *14 March–30 June 1732*

Spence, like other English travellers, was concerned with the quantitative statistics on each new city that he visited. No accurate numeration existed at this time; Thomas Nugent's *Grand Tour Containing a Exact Description of . . . Europe* (1749), for example, gave Rome 'twenty two thousand houses and palaces . . . sixty four religious houses of men, forty of women, and thirty hospitals' (iv. 213).

Ficoroni's tone towards his patron Benedict XIV is noticeably in contrast to that in his published *Vestigia*, which is dedicated to that Pope.

1366. When Henry IV of France was reconciled to the Church of Rome, 'twas expected that he should give some remarkable testimonial of his sincerity in returning to the true faith. He accordingly ordered a cross to be erected at Rome, near the church of Santa Maria Maggiore, with this inscription: 'In hoc signo vinces' on the principal part of it. This passed, at first, as very catholic, till 'twas observed that the part on which the inscription was put is shaped in the form of a cannon, and that he had really attributed only to his artillery what they had taken to be addressed to heaven. FICORONI *14 March–30 June 1732*

Henry IV was a notorious turncoat; after the St. Bartholomew Massacre (1572) he preserved his life by swearing fealty to the Church of Rome. He later became a champion of the Protestants, but in 1593 returned to Roman Catholicism. The monument is now in the small court near the baptismal chapel on the side of Santa Maria Maggiore, and was erected by Clement VIII as a memorial to the end of the civil war in France, signalized by the conversion of Henry IV. Ficoroni describes it and illustrates it with an engraving in *Vestigia*, i. 106.

1367. The Monte di Pietà is a bank for charity established by Gregory XIII, and improved by Sixtus V and other of his successors. They lend money out of it to the indigent on pawns of all sorts, without any interest if the sum be under thirty crowns, and but two percent if it exceed it. Two years are allowed for payment; if the debtor fails them, his pawn is sold and the surplus is given to the proprietors.

FICORONI *14 March–30 June 1732*

Founded under the authority of the Franciscans in Perugia in 1462 as an alternative to the near-monopoly of money-lending Jews, the Monte di Pietà spread to other cities. Leo X and his Papal Council gave it official recognition in 1515, and its headquarters in Rome later became one of the sights for foreign visitors. 'This is certainly the greatest pawnbroker's shop in the world' wrote Lady Pomfret in 1741 (Hertford *Corresp.*, iii. 66–67).

1368. What they point out as the four most celebrated pictures are Raphael's *Transfiguration*, Volterra's *Descent from the Cross*, Domenichino's *St. Jerome*, and Andrea Sacchi's *Romualdo*. FICORONI *14 March–30 June 1732*

The same four paintings are so designated in Ficoroni's *Vestigia*, ii. 39–40. There he calls Raphael's *Transfiguration* (formerly in St. Peter Montorio, now in St. Peter's) perhaps the greatest picture in the world. The *Descent from the Cross* by Daniel de Volterra (1509–56) is the principal picture in a series of frescoes in the Orsini Chapel in the church of Trinità dei Monti. Andrea Sacchi's *Vision of San Romualdo*, painted in 1640, formerly hung in the church dedicated to that Saint, now is in the Vatican. Domenichino's *St. Jerome* is also in the Vatican, but in Spence's day it was in the church of S. Girolamo della Carità.

1369. Domenichino is in as high esteem now as almost any of the modern painters at Rome. When you see any works of his and Guido together, how much superior does he appear? Guido is often more showy, but Domenichino has more spirit as well as more correctness (*più spiritoso* was his word). FICORONI *14 March–30 June 1732*

Both Guido Reni (1575–1642) and Domenichino (Domenico Zampieri, 1581–1641) were eminent pupils of the Caracci, so the public enjoyed comparing their work. Even Warton in his *Essay* relates a long anecdote contrasting the styles of the two painters (i. 86–87).

1370. The resting Venus at the Barberini Palace is the finest of all the old paintings in Rome. Carlo Maratta supplied part of the cupids that attend her, but the Venus herself, they say, was not at all retouched.

FICORONI *14 March–30 June 1732*

The fresco of Venus 'in the ancient manner' was discovered when the foundations of the Barberini Palace were excavated. Some modern critics feel that Carlo Maratta overdid the restoration. The painting impressed Spence so forcibly that he described it at length in *Polymetis* (pp. 73–74), calling it the 'Venus Desidiosa'.

1371. The most promising of Carlo Maratta's scholars was one Berrettoni. He died when he was but two and thirty, and not without suspicion of foul play from his master, who could not bear to have one of his scholars excel himself. That he evidently did so may be seen by comparing both their works in the Palazzo Altieri.

FICORONI *14 March–30 June 1732*

There are two altar pieces too in one of the churches called the Gemelli—just as you enter into Rome—one by Carlo Maratta and the other by this Berrettoni, the latter of which is of a darker, graver, and better manner than that of his master. SPENCE

Niccolò Berrettoni (1637–82) had reached the age of forty-five at his death (Spence erred, or was misinformed). That jealousy existed between master and pupil is known, but Maratta is not thought to have been implicated in Berrettoni's death.

By 'Gemelli' Spence refers to the twin churches in the Piazza del Popolo on either side of the entrance to the Corso. One of them, Santa Maria di Montesanto, contains the two altar pieces.

1372. The four most celebrated works of the modern sculptors in Rome are Michelangelo's *Moses*, Algardi's *Story of Attila*, Fiamingo's *Susanna*, and Bernini's *Bibbiana*.

FICORONI *14 March–30 June 1732*

Michelangelo's famous Moses is in the church of S. Pietro in Vincoli (Jonathan Richardson had described it as having 'much the Air of a Goat' in his *Statues and Pictures in Italy*, p. 295). Bernini's Santa Bibbiana stands in the same church, of which he was also the architect. Alessandro Algardi's alto relievo (sculptured in 1640) showing St. Leo forbidding Attila to enter Rome is in St. Peter's. There also is the St. Susannah of François Duquesnoy (1594–1646), a Flemish sculptor who moved to Rome in 1619, where he became known as Il Fiamingo; earlier it stood in Santa Maria de Loreto (Wright's *Observations*, p. 252).

1373. The fine statue of Jonas in the church of Santa Maria del Popolo was made by Lorenzetto after a design of Raphael's, and 'tis remarkable that Jonas, who seems to have been by much the most hot-headed of all the prophets, is represented as much the youngest of them too. His likeness to Antinous, both in his make and youth, is visible to everybody. FICORONI *14 March–30 June 1732*

In his *Vestigia* (ii. 39) Ficoroni mentions this metal bas-relief in the Chigi Chapel, which he considered so excellent that it seemed to be a Greek masterpiece. Early authors, such as Vasari and De Rossi, do not mention the likeness to the hellenistic statue of Antinous in the Vatican, nor do recent scholars, who consider that it resembles not Antinous but Hermes. Lorenzetto (Lorenzo Lotti, 1490–1541) is remembered principally for his two statues of Elias and Jonas in the corners of the Chigi Chapel.

1374. Domenico Guidi was the last of our very good statuaries; he died about fifteen years ago.

FICORONI *when we were looking on the dead Saviour and Virgin by him at the Monte di Pietà, in Rome. 14 March–30 June 1732*

The mezzo-relievo by Domenico Guidi (1625–1701) is in the oratorium at Monte di Pietà. Ficoroni mentions it without detailed comment in his *Vestigia*, ii. 31.

1375. The arts are greatly fallen among us of late, and there is nothing we excel in so much at present as the works in mosaic. They are in greater perfection than they ever were, even among the ancients. In their works of this kind (as to what we have yet discovered), the design is often good, but the colouring indifferent or rather bad. They used nothing but stones with their natural colour, and we use a paste or composition which does not only represent all the principal colours in a strong and lively manner, but all the different shades and degrees of each, as far as they are wanted.

FICORONI *14 March–30 June 1732*

The new 'art' of mosaic work that began in the eighteenth century aimed at achieving a pictorial effect through the use of a highly polished surface. Copies of famous oil paintings, vastly expanded in scale, were the favourite subjects.

1376. The composition for the mosaic works consists of glass, stannum, and lead, and is formed into little oblong squares and ranged according to their different colours and shades, not unlike our manner of disposing our types for printing. These mosaic types are coloured throughout, and are stuck in their proper places in a sort of soft stucco, spread over a stone (which is cut rough on that side) of the size of a picture. When the types are all set, they can smoothen it to the thinness of a shilling, and this smoothing makes it look all of one piece in a proper light and distance, as much as a picture. They don't want for encouragement in this art, for the price bears a proportion to the excellence of the work. They ask a thousand crowns for that little oval piece of Fame, and are to have fifteen thousand for Domenichino's *St. Jerome*, when finished. Indeed, the work takes up a vast deal of time, for they have been four years about that piece already.

FICORONI *and* CRISTOFARI (*the principal of those artists at that time*) *14 March–30 June 1732*

Pietro Paolo de' Cristofari (1685–1743) served as principal mosaicist at St. Peter's and founded the Vatican school of mosaic art that still exists. One modern critic states that 'the effect is that of some brightly-coloured surface, such as linoleum' (E. W. Anthony, *A History of Mosaics*, Boston, 1935, p. 247).

1377. The Roman matrons of old used to carry their children when ill to the temple of Romulus, which was built on the very spot where he was supposed to be found in his infancy. That temple is now christianized, and the women of Rome still carry their children thither on the same occasions. But the priests now are perhaps more cunning than they were of old, for whenever they offer a child thus to the now saint of the place, they pray that 'he would be so good as either to cure him or to take him to himself', so that the parents must always be obliged to them and their prayer can never be unsuccessful. FICORONI *14 March–30 June 1732*

Ficoroni's *Vestigia* gives a description of the temple of Romulus illustrated with a plate (i. 68–70). But since his book is dedicated to his patron Pope Benedict XIV he omitted this criticism of clerical practice. A similar account occurs in Conyers Middleton's pamphlet, *A Letter from Rome, shewing an Exact Conformity between Popery and Paganism* (1729), written after a period of residence in Rome.

1378. The brass wolf suckling Romulus and Remus, now in the Capitol, was found in the temple of Romulus, and the marks are visible upon it where it has been struck with lightning. Cicero speaks of the same accident happening to such a figure in his time (in his third Oration against Catiline), and this must have been made before his time, by the badness of the work. FICORONI *14 March–30 June 1732*

Ficoroni's *Vestigia* gives a similar account, understandably omitting any reference to the crudeness of the workmanship (i. 46–47). Wright discusses it in some detail (*Observations*, 1730, pp. 324–5). The statue is considered to be the product of a Greek workshop in Italy, probably fifth century B.C. Cicero (*In L. Catilinam Oratio* III. viii) adds no further details.

1379. Caracalla's Baths are the most perfect remains of the kind at Rome, and the most capable of giving us an idea of the ancient thermae. The roofs, where left, consist half of pumice stone for the sake of lightness in such large arches. The niches are very perfect in some squares of it, but in the most perfect parts there is nothing to be seen of windows. The Jesuits begged it for their boys to play in and have since sold a good deal of the stone, and often dig for statues in it. FICORONI *14 March–30 June 1732*

They had been digging the very week before we saw it, and had brought up several broken pieces of statues, etc. SPENCE

Ficoroni's account in *Vestigia*, i. 81–84, adds a few details, none of them important. Among the statues found in the ruins of the Baths are the colossal group of the Farnese Bull and the large statues of Hercules and Flora now in the Museum at Naples.

1380. Most of the statues in the great Farnese Palace were found in Caracalla's Baths, and all the marble of which it is built was brought from the Colosseum in Paul the Third's time, a Pope of that family. FICORONI *at Rome spring 1732*

The Farnese Palace is described in Ficoroni's *Vestigia*, ii. 43–45, but he does not mention that the marble with which it was built was taken from the Colosseum, and also, in fact, from the theatre of Marcellus.

1381. The ichnography of Rome in the same palace ('tis since removed to the noble collection in the Capitol,) was found in the temple of Romulus and Remus—that which is now dedicated to SS. Cosmo and Damiano, two brothers too. Though incomplete, 'tis one of the most useful remains of antiquity. The names of the particular buildings and places are marked upon it, as well as the outlines of the buildings themselves, and 'tis so large that the Horrea Lolliana, for instance, are a foot and a half long—which may serve you as a scale to measure any other of the buildings or places in it. 'Tis published in Graevius's Thesaurus.

FICORONI *14 March–30 June 1732*

These fragments belong to the Forma Vrbis Romae, a marble map of the city of the second century A.D., recovered about 1560. They were moved from the Farnese Palace where Spence saw them in 1732 to the Capitoline Museum in 1741; Ficoroni in his *Vestigia* (i. 57–58) mentions them in the later location. They are discussed by J. P. Bellori in Graevius's *Thesaurus Antiquitatum Romanarum* [Leiden], iv (1697), sect. 10; for a modern study see *Forma Vrbis Romae. La Pianta marmorea di Roma . . .*, ed. G. Carettoni et al., 2 vols. folio, Rome, 1960.

1382. There are 10,600 pieces of ancient sculpture of one sort or other (relievos, statues, and busts) now in Rome, and 6,300 ancient columns of marble. What multitudes of the latter sort have been sawed out for tables or wainscotting chapels, or mixed up with walls and otherwise destroyed! And what multitudes may there yet lie undiscovered underground? When we think of this all together, it may give one some faint idea of the vast magnificence of Rome in all its glory.

FICORONI *14 March–30 June 1732*

As the Pope's antiquary, Ficoroni's estimate is probably as accurate as any could be. Digging for antiquities had by this time become a popular activity, as had the faking of statues, coins, carved gems, and other mementos for the tourist trade.

1383. This large statue of Pompey was probably the very same at the feet of which Caesar fell, for it was found on the very spot where the Senate was held on the fatal Ides of March. They discovered it in clearing away the ground to make some cellars for a house that now stands there. The greatest part of the statue lay under that house, but the head

FRANCESCO DE' FICORONI

Engraved frontispiece to his *Le Vestigia e Rarità di Roma Antica* (1744)

of it reached under the ground belonging to their next neighbour. This occasioned a dispute between the two proprietors which was at last decided by Cardinal Spada. He ordered the head of the statue to be broke off and given to the latter, and the body to the former—and you may now see the mark where they were joined again. This decision was not made out of a whim, but very prudentially. From the first, the Cardinal had a great desire to get the statue into his own possession, and by this means he got it much cheaper than he could otherwise have done, for after this division of it, the whole cost him but five hundred crowns.

FICORONI *at the Palazzo Spada in Rome*
14 March–30 June 1732

This large statue is still in the Palazzo Spada. It was discovered in 1552 or 1553 in the Vicolo dei Lentari, near the Theatre of Pompey, though too far (about 330 yards) to justify identification with Pompey. An outstretched hand holds a globe, signifying a ruler or warrior whose dominion extended over a large part of the world, which does not exclude the identification with Pompey. The head, though ancient, is not the original one, and bears no resemblance to Pompey; it may be an example of the custom in latter days of substituting the head of some other person whom the Roman public wished to honour.

Ficoroni's source was undoubtedly D. De Rossi in *Raccolta di statue antiche e moderne* (Rome, 1704, p. 118) but he erred in attributing the judgement to Cardinal Spada for the incident occurred seventy years before his time. In fact it was Pope Julius III who heard of the judgement, and to prevent its mutilation, bought the statue for five hundred *écus*; he then presented it to Cardinal Capodiferro, owner of the Palazzo Spada at that time. Wright gives the story as told him by Ficoroni in 1721 (*Observations*, pp. 298–9).

1384. That arm behind the Laocoon was begun by Michelangelo and left unfinished 'because', as he said, 'he found he could do nothing worthy to be joined to so admirable a piece.' It lies there as a testimony of the superiority of the best ancient artists over the modern, for of all the modern sculptors Michelangelo is universally allowed to be the best.

FICORONI *at the Belvedere in the Vatican*
14 March–30 June 1732

Although the eighteenth century attributed the sketch-model of an arm, lying on the floor of the Laocoon Cabinet, to Michelangelo, Vasari states clearly that it is the work of his pupil, Giovanni da Montorsoli (*Le Vite de' più eccellenti pittori* . . ., ed. G. C. Sansoni, Firenze, 1906, vi. 633). Michelangelo took Montorsoli to Florence with him in 1533 only a year after calling him to Rome, which may explain why the arm was left unfinished.

1385. When they first discovered the Verospi statue of Hercules killing the Hydra, some parts of it, and particularly that monster itself, were wanting, and were supplied by Bernini. Some years after, in digging farther in the same piece of ground, they found the hydra that originally belonged to it, and which differs very much from Bernini's supplemental one, though that is given in Maffei's statues and other books of prints, as antique.

FICORONI *14 March–30 June 1732*

It is now removed from the Verospi Palace to the Capitol, and the original hydra with a horrid sort of human face, snakes for hair and a serpentine body, is there too in the same little court where Marforio lies. SPENCE

The absent parts of the statue (the left arm, the right arm below the biceps, the left leg and lower part of the right leg, the Hydra, a torch, and the plinth) were supplied not by Bernini but by Alessandro Algardi (1602–54). Sometime afterwards the left leg of Hercules and the Hydra were found and placed beside the restored statue. Modern investigation has shown, however, that they are modern fakes, made between 1620 and 1654.

The statue was moved from the Palazzo Verospi to the Capitoline Museum in 1738, where Spence apparently saw it again when he returned to Rome in the spring of 1741. For Marforio see § 1399. Spence refers to Paolo Alessandro Maffei's illustrations for D. De Rossi's *Raccolta di statue antiche e moderne* . . . (Rome, 1704), p. 127 and pls. cxxxvi–cxxxvii.

1386. You may know that Hercules to be Roman by its being so much over-wrought: the muscles look like lumps of flesh upon it. The Greek artists were more expressive without taking so much pains to express.

FICORONI *at the Palazzo Lancellotti in Rome*
14 March–30 June 1732

This statue is still in the courtyard of the Palazzo Lancellotti. For Maffei's similar opinion of the differences between Greek and Roman workmanship see § 1364. In *Polymetis*, p. 5, Spence pointed out that many of the best Roman pieces were produced by Greek artists imported into Italy, where they modified their style to suit Roman taste.

1387. This group of Arria and Paetus is evidently by a Greek artist. Though the place he has chose to stab himself in be very uncommon, 'twas not ill chosen, for the blow could not but be mortal, most of the blood running down among his vitals.

FICORONI *at the Villa Ludovisi 14 March–30 June 1732*

'Tis a very bold stroke and takes away the false idea one might have got of him from the known epigram in Martial.

SPENCE

This group, formerly in the Villa Ludovisi, was purchased by the Museo delle Terme in 1911. Found in the Orti Sallustiani in the sixteenth century it seems to be a marble copy by a Pergamese sculptor of a contemporary bronze group of about 225–200 B.C., erected as part of a triumphal arch by Attalus I to celebrate his victory over the Galati. The famous 'Dying Gaul', now in the Capitoline Museum, found with it, probably occupied the right-hand corner of the group of statues.

The statues were misnamed: they were thought to represent Caecina Paetus and his wife Arria, whose death is related by Pliny (*Epistles*, III. xvi). The wife, having stabbed herself first, gave the dagger to her husband with the famous words, 'Paete, non dolet'; the statue depicts the husband severing the great artery above his collar bone. Martial's epigram is Book i. 13. Modern authorities reject this literary association and consider the statues to depict conquered Gauls.

1388. The diameter of that part of Augustus's Mausoleum, which is still entire, and which was the largest round of all, is fifty paces. In it were deposited the ashes of Julius Caesar, Augustus himself, Marcellus, and Germanicus.

The tomb of Hadrian, now Castle Sant'Angelo, was built on the opposite side of the Tiber to rival this, and is the largest of our ancient mausoleums. It was richly adorned too with fine statues all round each particular rising—which in the Gothic times were thrown down by the Romans that fortified it to defend themselves and crush their enemies.

FICORONI *14 March–30 June 1732*

Augustus constructed his mausoleum in 28 B.C.; it contained the ashes of a long string of emperors, but not Julius Caesar's, who had died sixteen years earlier. The Colonna family converted it into a fortress which was destroyed in 1167. By the sixteenth century it had become a garden; the external diameter is 87 metres. A description occurs in *Vestigia*, i. 137–8.

Hadrian's tomb is 64 metres in diameter and remains one of the finest monuments in Rome. Most of its statues were hurled down upon the besieging Goths in A.D. 537; they are known from a description by Procopius written a few decades earlier. Ficoroni gives additional details in his printed account in *Vestigia*, i. 139–40.

1389. The floor of the Rotunda is so much raised as to hide all the pedestals of the columns in the inside. There was formerly a round of the imaginary figures of the provinces conquered by the Romans in relievo (one against each pedestal) which were taken away when the floor was raised, and are now dispersed about in the Capitol and other collections at Rome. FICORONI *14 March–30 June 1732*

The Roman Pantheon had been converted into the church of St. Mary and All Saints, but was commonly called the Rotunda. Spence may have been confused on the question of the floor's having been raised, for neither Ficoroni (*Vestigia*, i. 131–3) nor modern authorities mention this point. Indeed, Thomas Nugent's *Grand Tour Containing an Exact Description of . . . Europe* (1749) states: 'This temple was antiently ascended by seven steps, that surrounded the whole building; but now there is a descent of eleven steps to go into it, which shews how much the surface of this city is changed' (iii. 258).

1390. When Marcus Aurelius's triumphal arch was taken down to give more space to the Corso, the relievos on it were carried to the Capitol. These are the six compartments of Marcus Aurelius pardoning the vanquished in his triumphant car, sacrificing, receiving the globe from the genius of Rome, Lucius Verus, haranguing, and Faustina ascending to heaven. FICORONI *14 March–30 June 1732*

Ficoroni was confused on this subject; that it was he and not Spence is shown by Ficoroni's description of the relievos in *Vestigia*, i. 45–46, which concurs with this anecdote.

The Arch of Marcus Aurelius was erected in A.D. 176 to commemorate his victory over the Germans and Sarmatians. Apparently it spanned the Clivus Argentarius at its junction with the Via Lata. When it was taken down appears to be unknown, and the question of whether it bore relievos is equally obscure.

Ficoroni seems to have had the Arco di Portogallo in mind, which stood at the corner of the Piazza in Lucina and spanned the Corso. It was demolished in 1662, and some relievos said to be from it are in the Capitoline Museum (H. S. Jones, *A Catalogue of the Ancient Sculptures preserved in the Municipal Collections of Rome. The Sculptures of the Museo Capitolino*, 1912, pp. 302–3, which reports that these relievos are not shown in any early representations of the arch). These relievos, however, do not correspond to Ficoroni's description; his number (six) cannot be explained.

1391. Trajan's column is composed of twenty-four stones only, cut within the staircase. 'Tis one hundred and twenty-eight Roman feet high, just the height of what was taken from the hill to make room for Trajan's forum, which was one of the most magnificent things in Rome. This column stood in the midst of it, and on that was his statue and (they say) his ashes in an urn. FICORONI *14 March–30 June 1732*

Trajan, a Roman Emperor of Spanish birth, erected his splendid column with its spiral sculptured frieze in A.D. 113, four years before his death. The legend that he built it to show the depth of his excavations, and for his sepulchre, is well established (S. B. Platner, *A Topographical Dictionary of Ancient Rome*, 1929, p. 242). It consists of eighteen blocks, plus a capital. The total height including the pedestal is 38 metres. The statue of Trajan that crowned the column disappeared without any representation remaining: Sixtus V erected the present statue of St. Peter in 1588.

1392. In the Justinian Palace at Rome there is a statue of a woman with much expectation and desire expressed in her face. It was long unknown, and I discovered who it was at last by its resemblance to an intaglio of a woman with twelve very uncommon hieroglyphics standing round her, and inscribed 'To the Invincible Messalina' (MESSALINAE CLAUDII INVICTAE). FICORONI *14 March–30 June 1732*

The Justinian collection was dispersed by auction early in the nineteenth century and the present location of this statue is unknown. Ficoroni described it in *Vestigia*, ii. 47, where he based his identifications on medals that resembled her face and a gem showing the same posture carrying the engraved name of the Princess.

1393. The chief ornaments of Constantine's triumphal arch are spoils from one of Trajan, as it was despoiled itself afterwards of the heads of the statues by Lorenzo de' Medici. There is at least seven foot of it hid by the raising of the ground. FICORONI *14 March–30 June 1732*

They began refitting it afterwards while we were there, and the relievos on the lowest part were very mean—bad victories, etc. SPENCE

In *Vestigia*, i. 33–36, Ficoroni describes this arch in some detail, especially the bas-reliefs, and shows a contemporary engraving of the arch before its restoration. Platner's *Topographical Dictionary of Ancient Rome*, pp. 36–38, suggests that the bas-reliefs came from the enclosure wall of Trajan's Forum. Neither mentions anything about despoliation by Lorenzo de' Medici.

1394. It was Sixtus V that began the palace on Montecavallo and placed the two large equestrian statues there, from whence it has its name. They were found in Constantine's Baths, and were brought originally to Rome from Alexandria. The names of Phidias and Praxiteles on the bases are certainly fictitious, and some of the antiquarians say that they were put there by the people of Alexandria.

FICORONI *14 March–30 June 1732*

The Palazzo del Quirinale, one-time residence of the Pope, later of the King of Italy, and now of the President of the Republic, acquired the nickname of Montecavallo from its site opposite the two gigantic equestrian statues in the centre of the Piazza outside the main gate. They are considered to be Roman copies of Greek originals of the fifth or fourth century B.C. In 1589 they were brought from Constantine's Baths by order of Sixtus V and placed in their present location. The inscriptions were a late addition, probably made in A.D. 450 when Constantine's Baths were restored. There is no historical ground for the early belief that the statues originated in Alexandria; perhaps it derived from the popular identification of one of the statues with Alexander the Great and Bucephalus, which Ficoroni endorsed (*Vestigia*, i. 128).

1395. The boys gathering in the vintage on the sarcophagus of Constantine's daughter (about a mile out of Rome, in the Via Nomentana) is what has made people fancy that there was formerly a temple to Bacchus there.

The sarcophagus of St. Agnes, in the chapel just by, has the head of that Saint in relievo in the middle, and a Cupid and Psyche on each side of it.

This adapting of heathen ornaments and things was so frequent among the primitive Christians that the Jesuits in China made it one of their arguments for mingling Christianity and Confucianism together.

FICORONI *14 March–30 June 1732*

Constantia, the elder daughter of Constantine, died in A.D. 354. Ficoroni discusses her tomb in his *Bolla d'oro* (pp. 16–17) which was published in

1732, the year this conversation with Spence occurred. In his *Vestigia* Ficoroni returned to the subject with a lengthy description and engraving of the tomb (i. 176–8). The sarcophagus of St. Agnes is discussed in his preceding pages.

1396. There are three sorts of Egyptian statues: 1) those that are good without any mixture of their bad taste—and this manner is very ancient, before they were conquered by the Greeks. 2) After they were conquered, and their spirits debased, they made the figures of their deities frightful on purpose to keep the people in awe—and this was the cause of their bad taste, some parts out of nature and some in. 3) As everything is apt to degenerate and grow worse and worse when once fallen, they are at last in many of their figures deserted nature entirely, and made every part monstrous and out of all proportion. FICORONI *14 March–30 June 1732*

Before the Napoleonic era opened up knowledge of Egyptian art and architecture, European awareness of the subject was negligible. Ficoroni's generalization was fairly advanced for its time, though based on the fifty obelisks and the few statues and tablets available for study in Rome (see an engraving in *Vestigia*, opposite p. 80 in vol. i). The Bible-oriented Europeans viewed the Egyptian deities as monsters. For example, Spence himself writes: 'To Anubis, they gave the head of a dog; as that of a hawk, to Osiris' (*Polymetis*, p. 5, n. 8).

1397. The two best Egyptian statues in Rome are the young Hercules, with the lion's skin over his head, in the Capitol, and the richer Zingara at the Villa Borghese. You may know them to be Egyptian by the fullness about their mouths ('per oris luxuriem' were his own words).

KNAPTON *or* FICORONI *14 March–30 June 1732*

Both of these statues are Alexandrian, which made them acceptable to eighteenth-century taste, though they do not qualify as Egyptian art. The crude statue of the infant Hercules is described by Spence in *Polymetis*, p. 117, and pictured in Plate xvii, no. 4. The Zingara is carved from white marble. For George Knapton see § 1402.

1398. I measured the Tarpeian Rock when the Duke of Beaufort was here and found it to be eighty palms high, which just answers to sixty feet English. It goes down perpendicular, as you see, and so was easily measured. I took only the height of the rock itself, exclusive of the building that has been added upon it. FICORONI *spring 1732*

Ficoroni discussed the Tarpeian Rock in *Vestigia*, i. 42, in his chapter on the Capitoline Hill. The visit from the Duke of Beaufort (Henry Somerset, 1707–45) occurred about 1727.

1399. The figure of the famous Pasquin, when entire, was the same with that by the Ponte Vecchio at Florence.
COCCHI *July 1732–April 1733*

Maffei, in his collection of statues, number 42, gives that figure, and calls it an Ajax supported by his brother. Poor Pasquin was like to be confined in the Capitol by the same Pope who sent Marforio thither, but the Marquis to whom he belonged prevented it. His descendant is still obliged to pay a certain fine, if any scandal be found affixed to him. FICORONI

The marble statue called Pasquin dates from the third century B.C.; it was found near the Palazzo Torres and erected on a pedestal at the eastern corner of the Palazzo Corsini in 1501 by Cardinal Carafa. The custom developed of sticking anonymous satires to the statue, called *pasquinate*, many of them ridiculing the papal government. Collections of such satires were published from time to time.

Many of the satires were in dialogue form, between Pasquin and some other statue. A favourite was the gigantic river statue called Marforio (first century A.D.) formerly in the street at the foot of Campidoglio, but late in the sixteenth century it was placed in the Capitoline Museum. Photographs of both statues can be seen in the *Enciclopedia Italiana*.

Spence appears to have raised this topic in the autumn of 1732 when he reached Florence. For Dr. Cocchi see §§ 1469 ff.

1400. The top of the column by which they measure the risings of the Tiber at Rome is twenty-two feet higher than the street, and that is twenty-one feet above the common surface of the water, and yet the water has risen so high as to hide the very top of the column. FICORONI *1741*

These columns were in the Porto di Ripetta, an attractive little harbour built in 1704. They can be seen, together with the Tiber flood markings, in the engraving by Alessandro Specchi, architect of the harbour, printed *c.* 1710. The markings show that they were completely submerged by the great flood of 1598. The columns have now been moved to the Piazza del Porto di Ripetta.

When Spence returned to Rome with Lord Lincoln in December 1740 he found the city inundated. He reported in a letter to his mother, dated 8 December, '. . . when we were got within 3 Mile of this place, we found that the Tiber was overflown; & was got all over the road we were obligd to pass. . . . [at the Ponte Milvio]. We sent our servants over first; & then our Postillions on horseback, to see whether the Road was fordable: & as they return'd their answer, that it was; we pass'd boldly over it . . .' (B.M. Egerton MS. 2234, ff. 227–7v).

1401. I had this piece of marble from Hadrian's villa. It was broke from a marble slab to which it had been joined originally. In the juncture was a leaden medal of Hadrian, put there by his order, as princes now place medals within part of any great work they undertake, to perpetuate the memory even when their works come to be destroyed. On the face of the medal is the name of the Emperor HADRIANUS AUGUSTUS, and a little under it on the stone itself was this inscription HADRIANI AVG. COS II-N̄ CLXXII. (See his *Piombi Antichi*, Pl. 1, Fig. 2.) FICORONI *1741*

Spence refers to Ficoroni's book on lead medals, *I Piombi Antichi* (1740), pp. 8–9, where this information appears. Ficoroni also mentions it in *Vestigia*, i. 189.

1402. Knapton, the English painter then at Rome, spoke of the ancient paintings as excellent for design in the basso relievo way, but as deficient in colouring. Their want of knowledge in lights and shades, and of varieties in their colours, made them inferior in those respects. Their design is juster, but often too stiff. He observed that as Raphael made his drapery too stiff too, by imitating so perpetually the ancient sculpture, so Bernini latterly made the drapery of his statues too large and unbecoming by endeavouring to imitate the modern painters, particularly Rubens, in stone.

KNAPTON *14 March–30 June 1732*

George Knapton (1698–1778), son of the well-to-do bookseller James, after studying with Jonathan Richardson went to Italy in 1725, where English travellers regarded him as a sound judge of old masters. He returned to England in August 1732 shortly after this conversation with Spence, and became a pillar of the Dilettanti Society and a successful portrait painter, first in crayons (then a novelty) and later in oils.

1403. This Leda (at the Palazzo Colonna) is said to be Correggio's, but there is not any one undoubted picture of that great master in all Rome.

KNAPTON *14 March–30 June 1732*

This painting hung in the Palazzo Colonna until 1818, when it was acquired by the Rospigliosi family. It is now considered a copy of some details in Correggio's *Leda* which before World War II was in the Kaiser Friedrich Museum in Berlin. Spence was uncertain whether this information derived from Knapton or Ficoroni: because the painting is not mentioned in the full account of those in the Palazzo Colonna in *Vestigia*, ii. 55–56, and because it conforms with Knapton's critical viewpoint, it has been assigned to him.

1404. The front pillars of the Temple of Concord, those of Antonine and Faustina, and those of the Rotunda are the most perfect of any in Rome, and in each of them the opening between the two middle pillars is larger than the openings between the side ones. The difference is not enough to be observed by a common eye, and in some of them not enough to be sure of it till you measure them. By this means the entrance has a freer and nobler air, without breaking the regularity and harmony of the building. PHILIPS *1732*

The identity of the speaker is uncertain; Spence first attributed this anecdote to Ficoroni, and then replaced the name with 'Mr Philips'. The list of possibilities under this name is too long to enumerate; but it should be noted that Spence's list of Englishmen met abroad includes one Philips at Venice before Spence left for Rome (where they may have met again) in the early months of 1731/2. On the Rotunda, see also § 1389.

1405. At Assisi (between Perugia and Foligno—one post only from the latter) is the *entire front of an ancient temple to Minerva*. 'Tis now a church, and is called la Santa Maria di Minerva. [It has] six Corinthian pillars in front, steps up, and pediment over the pillars. SPENCE *1734 ?*

Eighteenth-century travellers were intrigued by evidence that the Roman Catholic Church had taken over pagan customs and structures. Santa Maria sopra Minerva is built on the remains of a Roman forum.

The position of this anecdote among others recorded from conversations with Pope in 1735 suggests that it is the result of contact with some traveller in that year. In any case the church was well known to travellers of the mid-eighteenth century, and is described in detail in Thomas Nugent's *Grand Tour Containing an Exact Description of . . . Europe*, (1749), iii. 283–4, where it is called 'La Madonna della piazza di Minerva'.

¶ *Among the characters Spence met in Rome in 1732 was the French Jesuit, Jean-François Foucquet (1663–1740), titular Bishop of Eleutheropolis, who had returned to Europe in 1723 from twenty-three years spent as a missionary in China. While there he concocted a bizarre theory concerning the origins of Christianity, based on parallels in early Chinese writings. Spence's introduction to Foucquet came through the Chevalier Ramsay (§ 736); many letters from Ramsay to Foucquet are preserved in the Vatican Library, but none of them mention Spence.*

These conversations tell more about the eighteenth-century attitude towards China than about China itself. For an account of Foucquet see V. Pinot, La Chine et la formation de l'esprit philosophique en France, *(Paris), 1932, pp. 251–6.*

1406. I intend to publish all these most select and sacred books of the Chinese in one volume, which will not be so much as the Pentateuch: A Latin translation of their *Family Ritual* (*Ritualis Domestici Sinensium*, *Traductio Latina* are the words of the title), with a dissertation on their funerals prefixed to it, [and] a treatise to prove that the character *Tao* signifies the Great God. In this I shall show, (1) that their *Tao* is One and Three, (2) that he created the material world, (3) that he created all intelligent beings, (4) that he was incarnated, and (5) that though he has the attributes of whatever is excellent, yet he is but one. (They call him *Ching Gin*, or the Holy One.)

[In addition, I shall publish] *The Temple of the Most Ancient Wisdom* (*Templum Veteris Sapientiæ*), in which I shall show: (1) that Adam was informed of the doctrine of the Trinity and that of the future redemption, (2) that this knowledge was delivered down to Moses and revived by him, (3) that it was preserved in other mystic books, and (4) that several of these books are still preserved in China.

I intend, too, to republish my Chronological Table, with an account how to manage it. In that table Confucius is set down as born 551 years before our Saviour, but the time is disputed. FOUCQUET *14 March–30 June 1732*

I got this list of what the good Bishop designed to publish, by the desire of his great friend, Chev. Ramsay, and when I sent it to the latter, said in my letter, that 'his Lordship was working on so many designs together that I feared he would never finish any one of them', which, I believe, proved to be the case. SPENCE

Spence's fears that the venerable Father Foucquet would not publish any of his projected writings proved to be correct. His orthodoxy was open to question, so publication was not encouraged. Masses of Foucquet's papers are preserved in the Vatican Library and elsewhere (see R. Streit, *Bibliotheca Missionum*, vol. viii, Aachen, 1931). Thus the only one of Foucquet's writings published was his *Tabula chronologica historiae Sinicae* (1729), a translation of a Chinese chronology, consisting of three lists of names and dates.

1407. Chi Hoang Ti, Emperor of China, began his reign 246 years before the birth of our Saviour. It was he who burned all their books, except such as treated of physic or judicial astrology, in the thirty-fourth year of his reign. Their philosophers had written against the tyrant, and argued against him and his vices from their sacred books. He was by their laws the grand interpreter of those books, and on that pretext sent out an order to them to bring in all their books to his palace by a time named. They suspected his design, and several of them concealed the copies in their hands. There were four hundred and seventy philosophers who were buried alive by his order on that account. They talk of this prince to this day in China, as we Europeans do of Nero.

MONSIGNOR FOUCQUET, *Bishop of Eleutheropolis, then residing at the College de Propaganda Fide, at Rome. He had lived in China as a missionary for twenty years, chiefly at Peking and Nanking 14 March–30 June 1732*

Shi Hwang-ti (246–210 B.C.) ended the old feudal system in China, and became the first 'universal' emperor. Because he completely remodelled the political and economic organization of the State (and also constructed roads, handsome public buildings, and the Great Wall) the upper class voiced their resentment by praise for the heroes and literature of feudal days. Hence Shi Hwang-ti in 225 B.C. decided to break once and for all with the past and ordered the destruction of all books except those concerning medicine, agriculture, and a few other subjects. Four hundred and sixty scholars were condemned for disobedience and put to death.

Pope alluded to the incident in the 1728 *Dunciad*, iii. 67–70:

> One man immortal all that pride confounds,
> He, whose long Wall the wand'ring Tartar bounds.
> Heav'ns! what a pyle! whole ages perish there:
> And one bright blaze turns Learning into air.

1408. Several of the books that had been hid in the time of this persecution were afterwards discovered, and there was one very excellent one which was spared by the Emperor himself, on his mistaking it for a book of judiciary astrology, relating to the future events in the Chinese Empire. Their most select and most ancient sacred writers put all together will make but one volume not so big as the Pentateuch, and their authentic accounts reach so high as within fifty years of the deluge.

When I first read these books, I thought (as the Chinese themselves do) that they related to some very powerful prince that was to rise among that people, and what made me discover my mistake was the nature of the Kingdom promised in them. It was plainly described as universal, and without end.

This led me to see that what was said in them could not be meant of an earthly prince, and when I had once found out that clue, I could easily perceive that everything else spoken of him agreed with an heavenly one. The Chinese in general mistake the nature of this Kingdom, as the Jews did, and perhaps the Romans. All the description of the Kingdom promised to them, and all the laws of it, are heavenly, and by following those laws through this mistake, their constitution has some of the finest rules in it that can be imagined. It has breathed a spirit of goodness throughout their government.

FOUCQUET *14 March–30 June 1732*

Foucquet's reading of these books as religious allegories parallels his readings of Chinese pictograms; both substantiated his hypothesis that Chinese religion was in agreement with the essential doctrines of Christianity.

1409. In these their sacred books are preserved some inscriptions of the greatest antiquity, their history, an account of the great hero and the promised Kingdom, etc. Their original characters in writing, too, are preserved by them. In process of time, the Chinese have continually varied from these original characters, though they still retain a good deal of resemblance to many of them. These old characters were hieroglyphical, or significant in themselves. As, for instance, the word that stood for a ship was composed of one character in the form of a bark, and of another which signified eight men—alluding to the first ship and the history of the deluge. The characters for the word 'man' include the doctrine of the Incarnation, and those for the word 'virtue' signify that 'Christianity is the most perfect system of morality'. The characters for the latter are as in the two following columns:

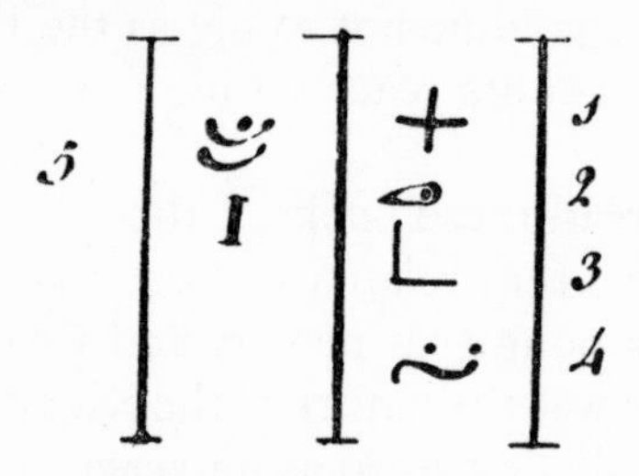

The first of these characters signifies a cross, the second an eye, the third a square or rule, the fourth a heart, and the fifth man, and all put together in their natural order compose the following sentence, 'La Croix devant les yeux règle le cœur des hommes', or, 'The observation of the Christian doctrines is the best regulation for the mind of man'. Even the learned among the Chinese now do not understand these implicated meanings. They know that there were such included in the old characters, but they don't know how to interpret them. Though the characters have been so much changed, they know too that the first is a cross, the second for an eye, and so on, but they don't know how to put them together into a sentence.

FOUCQUET *14 March–30 June 1732*

When I signified my surprise at their characters for the name of man including the doctrine of the Incarnation, the Bishop said that my surprise would be much greater if I could read their sacred books, and that he was very much surprised himself to find how exactly they agreed with ours, even in the highest mysteries.

I have since seen the copy of a letter which was sent to the good Bishop from a brother missionary of his that had lived two and thirty years in China, which turned wholly on this subject. It says that the Y KING is the oldest of these sacred writings, that in it are contained most of the great truths and mysteries of the Christian religion, and that the Y KING and the rest of them teach, in particular, 'the doctrine of the fallen angels, the creation of the world, the state in paradise, the fall from thence, the incarnation of the great hero, his birth, by a virgin, his low estate, his teaching for three years, his suffering for the sins of the whole world, his resurrection, ascent into heaven, and coming in judgment, the eternal happiness of the good and eternal misery of the wicked'.

He supposes all this knowledge to have come by tradition from Adam to the antediluvian patriarchs, and by Noah to his children, in whose time some of these books were written. SPENCE

Chinese writing is derived from pictograms, but Foucquet's ingenuity in reading their symbols exceeds that of even some modern critics. At the end of this anecdote Spence copied out the letter from the French missionary: for this see Appendix, pp. 653–5.

1410. The Chinese have a vast number of characters—about forty thousand. They write in columns, from the top of the page to the bottom, and begin on the right hand of the page as we do on the left.—Printing is extremely ancient among them, and possibly the hint for our printing might be brought from thence by Paulus Venetus [Marco Polo]. The fineness of the print in any book depends chiefly upon the author or his amanuensis: for they don't print by detached letters, but by one solid plate for each page. The engraver lays the copy as sent in upon one of these plates, and follows the traces of the letters as he finds them.

FOUCQUET *14 March–30 June 1732*

The estimate of the number of characters is fair enough. Of these about four thousand Chinese words are in common use and another five thousand are in literary use. The remainder are obsolete, found only in ancient writers. For Dean Lockier's remarks upon Chinese printing, perhaps derived from Foucquet, see § 737.

1411. I brought away near four thousand of their books with me out of China into Europe, though I lost almost half of the collection I had made in the hurry of our coming away. FOUCQUET *14 March–30 June 1732*

When Foucquet arrived in France in 1723 a struggle ensued between the French Crown, the Vatican, and the Jesuits for possession of the rare volumes he had brought from China. Since the French had sent Foucquet on the mission, they confiscated the books by an order of Versailles, dated 15 April 1723; unfortunately they have since been dispersed. Three manuscript catalogues have been preserved which record a total of 3,980 books, almost exactly the figure reported by Spence (see H. Omont, *Missions archéologiques françaises en Orient au XVIIe et XVIIIe siècle*, Paris, 1902, ii. 1155–78).

Foucquet then left his religious order and went to Rome, where he was created Bishop of Eleutheropolis in March 1725, and lived for many years in the College de Propaganda Fide (whose librarian reports that they have none of Foucquet's Chinese books). The Vatican contains two lists of the books Foucquet left in China, and an order dated 12 October 1724 from the Papal Secretary of State to the Father General of the Jesuits instructing him to deliver the Chinese books and a sum of money that Foucquet had also left behind (MS. Borgia lat. 565, ff. 16, 593, 595).

1412. There are three sorts of idolatry among the Chinese. They worship the heavens as chief governor of all things, Confucius as their great teacher, and their ancestors in each particular family, as the Romans did their Lares and Manes.

FOUCQUET *14 March–30 June 1732*

1413. There is no soldiery of the Chinese themselves. The Tartars who have been their masters about ninety years forbid any Chinese having a gun in his house or keeping a horse fit for military service.

FOUCQUET *14 March–30 June 1732*

Edward Holdsworth and other friends of the artist, James Russel
(Russel at the far left, then Messrs. Drake, Holdsworth, Townson, and Moxwell)
Collection of Captain Tyrwhitt-Drake

The conquest of China by the Tartars began in 1644 and was completed in 1662. See § 737.

1414. The Chinese architecture is bad now: it was very solid when their famous wall was built. If there was any place into which you could drive a nail of a certain size with a hammer, it was ordered by Chi Hoang Ti that the overseer of that part of the work should be put to death. This great work was finished two hundred and fourteen years before the beginning of our era.

FOUCQUET *14 March–30 June 1732*

1415. I have seen a bridge in China of a league long, built all of vast rough stone, and some pieces of it of an extraordinary size. These vast bridges are generally carried from one hill to another, to avoid the heavy swampy roads or waters in the valley between.

FOUCQUET *14 March–30 June 1732*

The bridge in question has not been identified.

1415a. Cardinal Polignac had an intaglio of Hercules delivering a soul from Hell, and carried a statue of him into France, destroying the serpent in his cradle. He asked the Bishop at his table what he thought of them. The Bishop immediately thought they might be mysterious, and the Cardinal approved what he said. (Query: whether in earnest or in jest?) The Bishop in speaking of him, called him *Homme universel.*

FOUCQUET *14 March–30 June 1732*

For Cardinal Polignac's collection see § 280. A fuller version occurs in *Polymetis*, pp. 124–5.

¶ *The following series record the remarks of the Virgilian scholar Edward Holdsworth (1684–1746). After a promising career at Magdalen College, Oxford, Holdsworth's Jacobite sympathies caused him to leave the University in 1715 to spend most of the rest of his life as travelling tutor to Jacobite families. One of his ancillary functions was to carry letters between the Pretender's court and sympathizers in France and England (S.P. 98/50, f. 66).*

Holdsworth was an early practitioner of the geographical approach to literary history. He traversed Italy with an interleaved Virgil in hand, recording data to illustrate various passages, especially in the Georgics. Spence met him first at Rome early in 1732 (letter of 1 May) though he mistakenly stated it was in Florence in the laborious publication of his old age entitled Remarks and Dissertations on Virgil, with some other Classical Observations, by the late Mr. Holdsworth. Published with Several Notes and Additional Remarks, by Mr. Spence (*1768*). *Because Spence utilized many of the Holdsworth conversations in the 1768 volume, they have not been reprinted here. Similarly, others which appear in Spence's manuscripts but which he incorporated in* Polymetis *are also omitted.*

1416. The amphitheatre of Vespasian is raised four stories high, and is adorned all round on the outside with four different degrees of pillars: Doric, Ionic, Corinthian, and composite. It is an oblong of 820 Roman palms, by 700, and the height of it is 222. There were places in it for 87,000 persons. They formerly ascended by three steps to it, but they are now hid by the raising of the ground. There was no cement used in the whole building, but the stones are cramped with lead and pieces of iron.

HOLDSWORTH *May 1732*

The Colosseum, as it is now called, was only two stories high when Vespasian dedicated it in A.D. 79; these arcades are Doric and simplified Ionic in style. Titus added a third Corinthian story, and a fourth tier of wood which after a fire in 217 was replaced with stone. Although the ancients speak of 80,000 or upwards as its capacity, the modern estimate is about 50,000.

1417. They found a vast piece of marble last summer at Rome, near the Forum Antonini, which had been part of the architrave of that building. It was the only piece of antiquity I ever met with that might serve to illustrate a passage in Vitruvius, where he is speaking of a particular manner of disposing the roses on architraves. On going to see it I found the workmen very busy in sawing it out, like common marble, to repair Constantine's arch, and after all the remonstrances that I could make to ⌜Sir T. Dereham,⌝ Galileo the architect, and others, there was only a rose or two saved at last, and sent into the Capitol.

HOLDSWORTH *May 1732*

Holdsworth refers to Vitruvius, Book iv, Chapters 1 and 2. The name of Sir Thomas Dereham, Bart. (d. 1739), occurs in the earliest manuscript. Alessandro Galilei (1691–1736) of Florence had been summoned to Rome in 1730 by Pope Clement XII to work on the basilica of St. John Lateran.

1418. The Italian noblemen have been so fond of getting the old Roman milestones to set before the entrance into their houses, and the collectors of antiquities so wrong-headed, that between them they have not left any two standing together in their old places all over Italy, to determine exactly how much the Roman mile was. The taking the first milestone from its proper spot to place it in the Capitol has something of the same gothicism, or ignorance, in it too. HOLDSWORTH *May 1732*

The Roman mile (*mille passuum*) was 142 yards less than the English mile. By 'the first milestone' Holdsworth means the central milestone placed in the Forum by Augustus to mark the centre of the Roman world; distances, however, were marked outward from the gates of Rome.

1419. The three most celebrated triumphal arches in Italy are all either Trajan's, or ornamented from Trajan's.
HOLDSWORTH *May 1732*

He had been speaking of those at Ancona and Benevento, and that of Constantine at Rome. SPENCE

The arch at Ancona was erected in A.D. 115 on the mole that Trajan had constructed to improve the harbour. That at Benevento across the Via Appia was built A.D. 114–16. The arch in Trajan's Forum, erected in 116, is known only from coins, so little can be determined about which parts of it may have been used in building Constantine's arch in A.D. 312. Ficoroni propagated the idea that its principal ornaments came from Trajan's arch (*Vestigia*, i. 34–35, and § 1393; Wright's *Observations*, p. 349).

1420. The arch of the bridge built by Augustus at Narni is a semi-circle (as all the old Roman arches are), and measures 110 feet on the surface of the water. HOLDSWORTH *May 1732*

This bridge carried the ancient Via Flaminia over the River Nera. Originally it consisted of three arches about sixty feet high of which only one remains. Spence passed through Narni on his way to Rome in April 1732, for he mentions both the town and Holdsworth in his letter of 1 May 1732 from Rome. The ruined bridge was pictured by Wright in his *Observations*, p. 131.

Because the next series of conversations are dated 1738 when Spence was back in England, it would appear that Holdsworth also was in England where the friends enjoyed a reunion.

1421. Hannibal, according to Livy, did not go over Mount Cenis, but passed a little on the right of it. Others will have it that he passed so much on the left as Mount Bernard, but then he would not have come into the country of the Taurini so soon as, by all accounts, he did.

HOLDSWORTH *1738*

The route that Hannibal followed when he crossed the Alps in 218 B.C. has been a perennial problem that classical historians do not consider possible to solve definitely. Livy suggested Mt. Genèvre and Polybius the Little St. Bernard; it may have been somewhere between the two.

The Huntington manuscript adds Holdsworth's own opinion. 'He himself thought 'twas to the left, but not so far to the left.'

1422. Polybius is much more to be trusted in his account of Hannibal's passage of the Alps than any other historian. He lived but a little after Hannibal's time, and went himself to trace all his marches over those mountains. He makes him pass a little on the left of Mount Cenis, and descend into the Milanese. That road had been often used before, and Hannibal was invited over by a Regulus of the Boii, a people that lived in the Milanese and were in enmity with the Taurini.

HOLDSWORTH *1738*

[He] spoke as slightingly of Livy in general, for his beautifying, making fine speeches rather than true ones, and being more of a romance-writer than an historian, as he did strongly of Polybius for a good and solid writer, and one that might be safely confided in. SPENCE

Polybius was born 202 B.C., only sixteen years after Hannibal had crossed the Alps; Livy was born in 59 B.C. Holdsworth's opinion of the two historians is that generally held.

1423. The French officer that wrote dissertations and notes on the French translation of Polybius has a whole chapter on Hannibal's passage over the Alps. HOLDSWORTH *1738*

The Chevalier Jean-Charles Folard (1669–1752) wrote much on military matters, but published six quarto volumes entitled *Le Commentaire sur Polybe*, Paris, 1727–30, which was long considered a classic work.

1424. The Arar and Rhodanus in Livy (*Lib.* 21) should be the Isara and Rhodanus. That historian, in mentioning those two rivers, says that they both come from the Alps, which is true of the Isara and not of the Arar. Most of the manuscripts have Isara. This is the river which we pass and repass so often in going from Lyons to Mount Cenis. It falls into the Rhône near Valence. HOLDSWORTH *1738*

Holdsworth is correct, most of the manuscripts of Livy do read 'Isara'. The Arar is now known as the Saône.

1425. One of Martial's friends had a delightful villa on the Monte Mario near Rome, which he celebrates and points out very distinctly in one of his epigrams. 'Twas on that delicious little hill where the Villa Madama now stands—where the garden theatre is still shown, in which they acted Guarini's *Pastor Fido*, and where Barclay wrote his *Argenis*.
HOLDSWORTH *1738*

This friend, as the Huntington manuscript records, was 'one of his own name', i.e. Julius Martialis, who had a rural seat on Monte Mario, about two miles from Rome. Martial celebrated the estate with a long description in Book iv. 64 (quoted with an English translation by John Russell, *Letters from a Young Painter Abroad*, 1750, ii. 364–8).

The Villa Madama is now used by the Italian Foreign Office as a residence for distinguished guests. The theatre still exists; a charming description of its appearance in 1741 occurs in Lady Pomfret's letters (Hertford *Correspondence*, iii. 149–50).

Pastor Fido was first performed at Crema in Northern Italy in 1595. The Latin prose romance *Argenis*, the masterpiece of John Barclay (1582–1621), was written after he settled in Rome in 1616.

1426. What they now show for a *temple* of Janus in the Forum Boarium was only an open place there ⌜which they called Janus', and⌝ of which they had one in all their forums (like the openings under part of our market-houses), for the convenience of people to deal and converse in when it rained. It was probably the name of Janus, which the Romans used for an open arch, that led people at first into this mistake. HOLDSWORTH *1738*

The Janus Quadriforis is a double-arched thoroughfare; built in the third or fourth century, it served as an entry between the Forum Boarium and Velabrum.

1427. The Lacus Fucinus could not have been drained all at once. Claudius began upon it, and Suetonius says the work was 'invidia successoris *intermissum*'. People have puzzled themselves so much, and accused Suetonius of contradicting himself in his account of this affair, purely from their own ignorance and their having got it into their heads that all the water must have been let out at the same time. Claudius actually sunk it twice, and then probably quitted his design on finding the sides of it so rocky that the ground would have been good for nothing. HOLDSWORTH *1738*

The lake is thirty miles round, so that if the ground had proved good it would have been a considerable acquisition. The drain remains through which Claudius carried off part of the water, and Mr. Holdsworth's curiosity carried him so far into it, and the place was so damp and wet, that it gave him a rheumatism which often returned, and hung about him as long as he lived. How much do I wish that Claudius had either never begun, or had quite finished that work, and stopped up his drain! For it seems to have much contributed toward shortening the days of one of the most knowing of men and one of the most sincere friends that ever lived. SPENCE

Lake Fucino was finally drained in 1874–5, providing 42,000 acres for cultivation, mostly as vineyards. The modern name is Celano. The fullest reference in Suetonius to Claudius' attempt, which tells how he employed 30,000 men for eleven years in building a ditch and tunnel three miles long, occurs in Chapter xxii. It does not, however, contain the phrase Holdsworth quoted to Spence, nor is it found elsewhere in Suetonius. The phrase, however, may be drawn from Pliny's remark about the Lacus Fucinus, '*quamvis destitutum successoris odio*' (*Nat. Hist.*, xxxvi. 124).

1428. The Greeks were of as romantic a turn as the Spaniards in more modern times, and possibly might deal as much in romances. The 'Εφεσιακά, or works of Xenophon the Ephesian, is a remainder of this kind, and might have been as unknown as the rest, had not our friend Dr. Cocchi found it out in the Lorenzo Library, and published it.

HOLDSWORTH *1738*

Holdsworth was speaking of the 'Greek Romances' of the Hellenistic period; Xenophon wrote in the third century A.D. When in London in 1726 Dr. Cocchi, the learned Florentine physician, published his edition of the 'Εφεσιακά based on a transcript made by Salvini (§ 711) in 1700 from the unique manuscript in the Laurentian Library. Two years later Cocchi collated the original and entered corrections in a copy of his book, now in the Bodleian.

1429. 'Imperatorem decet stantem mori' seems such odd sense to us partly from our having shifted the sense of the word *imperator*. It then signified a commander or general, not an emperor. 'A general should die ⌜in the field or⌝ in action', is much the same sentiment with that of Marshal Villars when he was told of the death of the Duke of Berwick.

DE PR *or* HOLDSWORTH *28 July–4 August 1738*

The Latin phrase comes from Suetonius' account of the death of Vespasian, Chapter xxiv. The emperor had been ill for some time, and when he felt himself dying he struggled to his feet while uttering these words.

The Duke of Berwick (an illegitimate son of James II) was inspecting the field of battle at the siege of Phillipsburg on 12 June 1734 when a cannon ball carried off his head. The Duc de Villars, when he learned of the death of his comrade-in-arms, is said to have exclaimed: 'Cet homme a toujours été heureux.'

The identity of the speaker is uncertain: see the textual note.

1430. We often stare at the customs of other countries and condemn them, only from our ignorance of the original design of them. What seems more ridiculous to us than that the blacks should cut and slash their faces by way of ornament? And yet if we consider their perpetual wars, and that this might be designed to make them less afraid of wounds in the face, it would not be ridiculous at all.

DE PR *or* HOLDSWORTH *28 July–4 August 1738*

⌜Many of our young officers, and perhaps some of our old ones, would have more courage (or if you will have it so, less fear), had they been bred up to the same notions of beauty from their youth. This [was] plainly the sentiment of so great a general as Julius Caesar, before the battle of Pharsalia. SPENCE⌉

Spence misinterpreted Caesar's meaning. The source of the story is Plutarch's Life of Pompey, Chapter lxix, where Caesar is said to have told his troops before the battle to strike upwards with their javelins at the faces and eyes of the enemy, who would retreat rather than risk having their youthful beauty marred.

Spence echoed Holdsworth's thought in *Crito; or, A Dialogue on Beauty* where he speaks of 'the most military nations of Africa' in which the faces of the warriors are decorated with scars, a custom that altered their idea of masculine beauty. The source of the anecdote is in dispute: see textual note.

¶ *The following short series of anecdotes consists of conversations with other learned personages in Rome in 1741, or on Roman subjects.*

1431. There are no paintings so good for prints as those of Guido, from his disposition of the lights and shades.

GIACOMO FREY *February–June 1741*

Giacomo Frey (1681–1752) was recognized as the finest engraver in Italy. During his third tour Spence seems to have purchased some engravings from Frey (B.M. Egerton MS. 2235, f. 124).

1432. 'Why have you not done more of Raphael's?' [asked Spence].

Because many of his are done already, and others are ill-placed. I wanted to have done the Transfiguration, but when I took a view of it with that design, I found I could not see it enough to do it. GIACOMO FREY *February–June 1741*

1433. 'Why are the fine arts so much fallen in Italy?' [asked Spence]. ⌈We had been speaking of painting in particular.⌉

Because vice is so much increased. ⌈The reigning things now are the love of gaming, of music, of conversation and of the ladies. He who loves music or a woman never elevates his head—it is always so.⌉

CAMILLO PADERNI *February–June 1741*

Camillo Paderni (*fl.* 1738–69) was the Neapolitan painter who became supervisor of the excavations at Herculaneum. Spence recorded the conversation in Italian, here translated, but truncated it to two English lines in the Folio manuscript. The inserted sentences are from the Huntington manuscript, in which the original reads: 'Perchè è tanto cascata la virtù?' (We had been speaking of painting in particular:)—Perchè crescono i Vizi.—The reigning things now are, L'amore del Giuoco, della Musica, delle Conversationi, e delle Donne.—Qui [*sic*] ama la Musica, o una Donna, non alza mai la testa; va sempre così—.'

1434. In the school of the Jesuits at the Nazarene College in Rome, the boys are divided into five classes: each class has its distinct master, and we reckon ten boys a great many for a class.

The first class is called the grammar class. In it they learn Emanuel Alvari's *Grammar*, the *Colloquies* of Ludovicus Vives, and *Phædrus*.

In the second, or that of humanities, they learn Martial's *Epigrams*, some select stories out of Ovid's *Metamorphoses*, the *Familiar Epistles* of Cicero, and some of his chosen orations.

In the third or rhetoric class, other chosen orations of Cicero, the rest of his epistles; Virgil, Horace, and Juvenal; Livy's *History*, and an *Art of Rhetoric.*

The fourth class is for the study of philosophy. In this they are taught logic, physics, and metaphysics; arithmetic, geometry, and geography.

The fifth and last is for divinity. In this they also study the civil law.

The three first of these classes are called the *parva*. ⌜Has our parvise any reference to this?⌝ There are two years allowed for each of them, the same for the fourth class, and double the time for the fifth. So that a boy who does not begin till he is twelve years old, may go through the whole course of his studies by four and twenty.

ABBÉ GRANT ⌜*who was bred up at that college*⌝ *February–June 1741*

James Grant (1706–78), a Scottish Catholic prelate, was popular among the English colony in Rome. He became the active but unofficial leader of the Jacobite party centred about the Pretender and his family.

De Institutione Grammatica, by Manuel Alvarez, first published in 1572, became a standard textbook in Jesuit schools. The *Linguae Latinae Exercitatio* (1538) of Giovanni Ludovico Vives, written in dialogue form, was popularly known as *Colloquia*. The two inserted passages come from the Huntington manuscript; Spence's conjecture is unfounded. Abbé Grant also supplied a list of the books and subjects taught in the Collegio Romano in Rome (see Appendix, pp. 656–9).

Spence confused the Collegio Nazareno (which belongs to the order of the Scolopi, and has no connexion with the Jesuits) and the Collegio Romano, founded by St. Ignatius Loyola in 1551.

1435. A nobleman of Naples built a very pretty house, to retire to and enjoy himself in his latter days, at Portici. It was just finished, and the gardens coming to perfection, when the King happened to pass by and like it. The next morning a courtier was sent to the nobleman to let him know that his majesty had taken a fancy to his house. The nobleman was extremely struck with the message and only said, 'If the King likes my house, to be sure he must have it.'

MR. ALLEN *at Naples March 1741*

This is the house where the King now keeps all the best of the statues and paintings that are found in the subterraneous city of Herculaneum, near Portici. SPENCE

Don Carlos de Bourbon (1716–88), son of Philip V of Spain, became King of Naples in 1734. The nobleman of Portici (a suburb of Naples) was probably one D. G. Falletta, who in July of 1716 purchased the house from Emmanuel-Maurice de Lorraine, Duc d'Elbœuf (1677–1763), whose workmen had discovered the remains of Herculaneum. His villa, the Casino d'Elbœuf, was purchased by Don Carlos for 5,250 ducats and maintained as a repository for antiquities found in the new excavations begun in 1738.

Spence and Lord Lincoln visited Herculaneum in March 1741. Edward Allen served as British Consul at Naples *c.* 1737–53; apparently it was he whom Spence mentions three times on the 1739–41 tour, in Turin, Rome, and Naples (B.M. Egerton MS. 2235, f. 94^{v}).

1436. Mrs. Allen's story of his [the nobleman's] fingers. He was drinking his chocolate when they came to tell him that the King liked his house. He held out his hand in surprise, and could never contract his fingers again. The Neapolitans [are] of so strong passions that 'tis not uncommon for them to die on sudden very ill news.

MRS. ALLEN *March 1741*

The speaker, Catherine, daughter of Sir John Shadwell, was the wife of the British Consul at Naples. Spence contributed this story to the second edition in 1750 of John Russell's *Letters from a Young Painter Abroad*, i. 205–6 (where it appears almost verbatim and is signed 'S'). Undoubtedly he was the 'Mr Russel' whom Spence recorded meeting in Rome in 1740 and 1741 (B.M. Egerton MS. 2235, f. 94^{v}).

1437. I am very apt to believe that there must be a future life, that tyrants may be punished and that those who have suffered under them unjustly may have it made up to them—but I don't know how to persuade myself that either will be without end or without measure. MONSIEUR W *June 1741*

Because this conversation occurred while Spence and Lord Lincoln were travelling with Horace Walpole it is tempting to ascribe this sentiment to him. The use of 'Monsieur', however, precludes this possibility.

¶ *Another of the colourful characters Spence met in Rome was Antonio Niccolini (1701–69). Called 'Abbé' though he had never taken orders, Niccolini was in fact a Florentine marquis who dressed in ecclesiastical fashion in order to enjoy the many benefices belonging to his family and to have full leisure for study. In his youth he had travelled extensively and formed friendships with many eminent men, including Montesquieu in France and George II (then Prince of Wales) in England. Niccolini was especially cordial to travelling English nobility; Lady Pomfret's letters speak of him frequently.*

In May 1741, when Pope Benedict XIV made his ceremonious entry into St. John Lateran, Niccolini was in Rome and helped his English friends, including Spence and Lord Lincoln, to obtain good places to observe the ceremony. Doubtless the following conversations occurred at about this time. A number of them concern Spanish religious customs; Spanish subjects were topical because war between England and Spain had recently darkened the horizon for English tourists in Italy.

1438. In Spain the people are so over-run with devotion that they have not a grain of religion left among them. (His words were 'En Espagne il n'y a point de religion, et beaucoup de dévotion'.)

On the hearing of the Ave Maria bell the Spaniards who happen to be in the theatre, and even the actors on the stage, fall down on their knees, and then rise again and carry on their diversion as before. A French gentleman who happened to be present on one of these occasions and [who] had never seen anything of the kind before, seemed at first extremely surprised at it, and then burst out a laughing, and cried out, 'bis, bis!' with a great deal of vehemence. ⌜The common women *stop* on the same occasion, let it happen *when it will*, and then go on with *their business*.⌝

ABBÉ NICCOLINI *February–June 1741*

1439. The courtezans there do something of the same nature that is yet more extraordinary. Indeed they are very great worshippers of the Virgin, and among other things, pray to her for good trade.

ABBÉ NICCOLINI *February–June 1741*

1440. The nuns in Spain take very great freedoms, and one of their prayers at the foot of the crucifix is 'to beg pardon of their sweetest spouse, represented on it, if they should happen to add a pair of horns to his head.' (Perdona, O Dolcissimo Sposo, si te voi aponer guernos.)

ABBÉ NICCOLINI *February–June 1741*

1441. Their very bull-feasts are a sort of religious act, as stage-plays were among the old Romans. They are generally to celebrate their rejoicings on some Saint's day, or other great holiday of the church.

They seem almost as fond too of the sanguinary effects of those feasts as the Romans were of those in their amphitheatres. When a bull that has got a character in some of the former feasts has been passing by, I have heard some of the ladies cry, 'O the dear creature!' and others, 'Blessed be the soul of the mother who bore thee, thou hast killed thy six men!' (Benedetta sia l'alma della madre che lo pariò! Mattò sei ombre.) ABBÉ NICCOLINI *February–June 1741*

1442. The Spanish ladies are of a constitution particularly apt to take fire. As they are more confined they are fuller of passion than other women are, ⌜they consent with a turn of the eye⌝ and sometimes actually faint away from a look at a window. ABBÉ NICCOLINI *February–June 1741*

1443. Santa Teresa, in one of her exclamations, makes the chief misery of the damned consist in their being incapable of love. 'Sono infelicissimi i dannati: non possono amare!' was what he quoted as her words.

ABBÉ NICCOLINI *February–June 1741*

This is the saint who is so generally represented as fainting away, upon an Angel's touching her with a dart tipped with fire. SPENCE

An Italian poem on the subject of St. Teresa and the angel who thrust a fiery dart into her heart (the verses being considered proper for a girl entering a nunnery) was printed by John Russell in *Letters from a Young Painter Abroad*, 1750, i. 72–73. The quotation from St. Teresa has not been found in her printed works, though it occurs in Diderot's essay 'Sur les femmes' published in 1772 (*Œuvres*, ed. André Billy, Paris, 1951, p. 983).

1444. There is a French author who has writ a very pretty piece in three or four volumes to show that the warmest flights of some of our greatest saints are nothing but lust in disguise. This is most evident in our nuns and female saints. ABBÉ NICCOLINI *February–June 1741*

Mr. Coventry has treated it in the same light in his *Philemon to Hydaspes*. SPENCE

The French author has not been identified. Spence refers to Henry Coventry (d. 1752), author of *Philemon to Hydaspes, relating a conversation with Hortensius upon the subject of False Religion*. This work in five parts was then incomplete, volumes having appeared in 1736, 1737, and 1739. The others were published in 1742 and 1744. Spence may have had the first volume in mind, the title of which adds: 'With a more particular Application to the Case of an Extravagant Devotion'.

1445. The Pope complains of being quite tired of being Pope already. ABBÉ NICCOLINI *February–June 1741*

This was a very little after his first Holy Week. SPENCE

Niccolini was well informed about the papal court, his brother being married to a niece of the late Pope Clement XII. Spence also reported that the new pope, Benedict XIV, appeared 'quite tired & apprehensive of the fatigue he was to go through' at the ceremony of his entry into St. John Lateran (letter dated 6 May 1741, B.M. Egerton MS. 2234, f. 262^{v}). He was then sixty-five years of age, but reigned for another seventeen years.

1446. If you observe his Holiness at any long religious ceremony, especially if he is to officiate himself, you will see that he has a faint look and a tired eye: but see him in a conclave on business—you will find his look more enlivened and his eyes quick and piercing. He has always loved business, and has no relish for formal devotions.

ABBÉ NICCOLINI *February–June 1741*

Spence had an opportunity to confirm these observations at first hand. His letter of 22 December 1740 reports that he had 'at last, had a very full opportunity of seeing the Pope. A few mornings ago there was a Consistory, which is a Council of the Pope & Cardinals', the purpose of which was to settle 'the long Dispute that has been between this Court & the King of Portugal . . . I took notice that the Pope, in these private audiences [with the cardinals], look'd like a man that was a Master of business' (B.M. Egerton MS. 2234, ff. 231).

Spence's next letter, written on 31 December, adds: 'We have since seen the Pope at mass; he performs his part very well: but of the two, his religious look is not so good as his look of business' (ibid., f. 233).

1447. 'What, Sir, is your opinion of Lord M?' [asked Spence].

He is an *Alcibiade*. (Great sense and great vices, as he explained it.) ABBÉ NICCOLINI *February–June 1741*

The nobleman who received this doubtful compliment has eluded identification.

¶ *The identity of the 'Mr. T' to whom Spence credited the following series of remarks is a riddle that has resisted all efforts towards a satisfactory solution. When Singer faced the problem he suggested 'Most probably Mr. Townley' (p. 222), but offered no evidence. The Spence Papers show nothing to support this ascription, nor indeed to support any other candidate. Spence's list of Englishmen met on his tours includes a Mr. Tripland, otherwise totally unknown. For a discussion of the enigma and a substantial body of 'Mr. T''s comments on Horace, see Appendix, pp.* 660–79.

1448. Some of the Greek artists seem not to have liked the terminal sort of figure used by the Egyptians. There is one in the Montalto gardens at Rome, which is as broad at bottom as it is at top, and I have seen several others of the same kind. [The one at Montalto] appears to be a Greek terminus by the inscription, which is '*ΘΕΜΙΣΤΟΚΛΗϹ Ο ΝΑΥΜΑΧΟϹ.*' MR. T. *1741*

The Villa Montalto, once the largest and most beautiful estate in Rome, occupied the area between Santa Maria Maggiore and the Baths of Diocletian; it was demolished and built over in the second half of the nineteenth century. The headless statue of Themistocles is recorded in several eighteenth-century catalogues. Sometime after 1786 a head was added and the statue (a Roman copy of a Greek original) is now in the Berlin State Museum.

1449. The old figure of a gardener, in the Montalto gardens has only a loose vest or shirt on, and over that, what some call a *toga viminalis*, or coat of twigs. I don't know how they came to mistake it for such, for 'tis evidently meant to imitate straps of leather. MR. T *1741*

This statue is now in the Vatican. Because it has a knife with a bent blade it was believed to represent a gardener, or the god of orchards. However, Winckelmann recognized the statue as one of Auriga Circensis; the knife was the same as that carried by the warrior in a quadriga-race, as depicted in a bas-relief in the Villa Albani (*Geschichte der Kunst des Altertums*, Book xii, Chapter 2).

1450. The famous forge of Vulcan there is on what seems to have served for a tombstone, and is perhaps only a common blacksmith's shop, for you have a cutler's shop on the opposite side. They are both very neat work, and much better than the poulterer's shop on a marble in one of the gardens just out of the Porta del Popolo. MR. T *1741*

These two bas-reliefs are on opposite sides of one marble, which is now in the Vatican. The depiction of the poulterer's shop, formerly in the Gardens of the Giustiniani family, is now in the Museo Torlonia in Trastevere.

1451. The three altars in one of the rooms in the Capitoline Gallery were all found in the port of Nettuno. That with a Neptune standing in relievo on it is inscribed *Ara Neptuni*, that with a wind deity, flying, *Ara Ventorum*, and that with a ship sailing gently along, *Ara Tranquillitatis*. They are all three just alike: small, round, and with a rostrum coming out in the front. They are portable enough, and are supposed to have been carried to sea in their voyages for the devotions of the ship's crew. MR. T *1741*

These three pieces of statuary, now in the Capitoline Museum, were found during dredging operations undertaken by Pope Innocent XII in the harbour at Antium.

1452. One of the centaurs in black marble at the Monte Citorio, has a tiger's skin over his left shoulder, and his hands are tied together with the tail of it. He looks back with pain and dejection on his face. There was probably a cupid behind him originally, and there is the hole in his back in which it might have been fixed. Centaurs are thus represented by the ancients in other monuments to show that love conquers the roughest monsters.

The other centaur there has bacchanalian attributes about him too, but looks with a much gayer air. The former is elderly, and this, young. As they are of black marble and were found in Hadrian's Villa, 'tis possible that they were part of the furniture in the first apartment of Hades, which historians tell us was represented there, and they might have their bacchanalian attributes because the secrets of that place were laid open to those who were initiated in mysteries of Bacchus.

If this conjecture should happen to be true, it might be very well worth while to carry on their searches about the spot where these figures were found, because there is no sort of statues more scarce than those relating to the infernal beings in general. MR. T *1741*

Both of these statues were found in December 1736 by the excavators employed by Alessandro Furietti (later Cardinal) at Hadrian's Villa near Tivoli. They were later purchased by Pope Clement XIII for the Capitoline Museum.

1453. The fine old mosaic picture (now placed near them [the curtains]) of four pigeons drinking out of a basin of giallo antique, is much the finest mosaic work that ever I saw of the ancients, and is almost as good as what they do at present at Rome. 'Tis an absolute painting, and the basin is so admirably rounded and hollowed at the bottom that you see quite under the sides of it. MR. T *1741*

Like the statues of the centaurs, the mosaic of the doves was a recent discovery during the excavations of Furietti. They were brought to light in April 1737 and are now in the Capitoline Museum (Sala delle Colombe).

1454. The persons who fixed the fine figures relating to the history of Niobe and her children at the Villa Medici did not either understand them or place them so well as they ought to have done. They seem to have mistaken Amphion for one of his sons, so that there are but six sons at present and seven daughters, and the faces of all the figures in general, except two of the sons, are disposed so as to regard the spectators in front of the group, rather than to follow their proper business in the story—just as one sees in bad actors who speak rather to the pit than to one another, or in injudicious painters who make the persons in their history pieces regard you rather than those with whom they should be wholly concerned. MR. T *1741*

Spence utilized this information in *Polymetis*, pp. 98–99, where he described the arrangement of statues in much greater detail. The statues were taken to Florence in 1775 and are now in the Niobe Room at the Uffizi.

1455. The whole rise of the Monte Testacio, from the vigna of the Cavalier Corradini quite up to the cross or the highest point of it, is upward of eight hundred feet and consists of broken pieces of earthenware quite up to the top. About that cross, 'tis a sort of plain, of a considerable breadth, all consisting of these fragments, sometimes bare and sometimes covered only for two or three inches deep with earth. At the bottom there are excellent vaults almost all round it, in which wine is kept extremely well and cool. The vaults are plastered on the top and on the sides, except that side next the mountain which consists wholly of potsherds without mortar, and with twenty or more round holes in each to attract the air from the mountain. This convenience was found out about a hundred years ago by the Jews who spin silk in the valley. MR. T *1741*

Monte Testaccio is the mound, only 170 feet high, on the west side of the present-day Protestant Cemetery. It was formerly called Doliolum, both names being taken from the fragments of earthenware jars and casks found there, refuse from Spanish and African imports of wine and oil. Edward Wright described it in some detail, especially the chilly air in the vaults (*Observations*, p. 359). The Corradini who owned the vineyard was probably Antonio (1668–1752), a celebrated sculptor.

1456. The convent that is said not to take up so much ground as the base of one of [the] supporters of the Dome of St. Peter's, is near the Quatre Fontane. The court is forty-two feet by thirty, and the building twenty-one feet. I think 'tis dedicated to St. Silvester. The diameter of the base of the column opposed to it is said to be ninety feet, and the whole circuit of it should be about two hundred and fifty four feet by my paces, but the outline of it is too irregular to be taken exactly by paces. MR. T *1741*

This convent of St. Silvester has now disappeared, but records show that it was much larger than the dimensions given here. 'Mr. T' apparently confused it with the nearby church of San Carlino alle Quattro Fontane, whose dimensions are the same as one of the pillars supporting the cupola at St. Peter's. Since Ramsay (§ 1285) had in 1729 told Spence about St. Silvester's the comparison appears to have been a stock topic of English travellers.

1457. The genius of the Danube, in the first round of figures on the Trajan pillar, holds the beginning of the bridge of boats in his right hand.

In the fourth is a battle, and a deity like Jupiter fighting for the Romans.

In the fifth are several boats, and two biremi in particular. The larger of the two has but ten oars, which may serve to show the minuteness of the Roman vessels, for a galley of ten oars on a side, all in one line, would be but a very pitiful galley.

In the sixth, there is one soldier supporting another that is wounded, and a third person holding his hand or feeling his pulse. All their faces are very fine and pathetic, and have a much stronger expression of the several passions than appears in the prints from Bartoli.

In the seventh is a person embracing the Emperor's knee, and my eye could not reach well any higher.

It might be worthwhile to carry the prints and compare them and the original, as far as the eye will reach. The very first article I have mentioned, though a very significant one, is dropped in the prints. MR. T *1741*

An engraving of Trajan's column in a hundred and nineteen plates, from the hand of Pietro Santo Bartoli (1635–1700), had been published at the end of the previous century.

1458. Might it not be worthwhile for anyone who is to stay long at Rome to make a collection of all the religious inscriptions in the churches and other parts of that city, and to publish them, as Gruter has his *Old Inscriptions*? This would show how vast a share of their religion in that holy city is turned to the Virgin, how little has remained, for so many centuries back, to our Saviour, and that God himself is almost wholly forgot among them. MR. T *1741*

Evidence of Mariolatry was a common topic among English travellers. Jan Gruter's *Inscriptiones Antiquae totius orbis Romani* was published at Heidelberg in 1602–3. Among the Spence Papers is a loose sheet showing that Spence had begun to make a similar collection when he wintered at Blois in 1738, but did not carry it further.

1459. If Coypel has represented Charon with a switch in his hand in his history of Achilles, there are as ridiculous things to be met with in some of the works of the ancient artists, and among these very gems there is one with a centaur upon it, holding a whip to lash himself upon occasion.

MR. T *1740*

The reference is to Coypel's design for a series of Gobelin tapestries depicting scenes from the *Iliad*.

1460. The finest remains I ever saw of the deluge are at Pianoro, the first post from Bologna, in the way to Fiorenzuola. There are several pieces of rock full of shells lie scattered behind the post-house there, in the channel that the torrents make as they fall down the Appenine, and in particular one square slab large enough to make a pretty table, which I have often wished that I had brought away with me in my chaise. MR. T *1740*

Spence later incorporated this anecdote in his travel papers. Unaware that scientists had disproved the popular theory, he still believed that conchitic stone was formed in the few weeks of the Biblical flood. He had an opportunity to inspect the stone as he passed from Bologna to Florence in October 1740.

1461. The country by the road from Ferrara to Padua grows more and more cultivated and pleasing, in proportion as you get farther and farther from the ecclesiastical state, and in some of the best parts of it the cultivation of the fields has a good deal of the air of a garden. They leave a level border of eight or ten foot on each side of the corn fields, which is sown with grass, and after mowing makes a handsome grass-walk all round each field. In some of these the fosses were made like canals, and the grass-walks formed in easy slopes down to them. MR. T *1741*

The papal state extended about one-fifth of the distance between the two cities. English travellers frequently contrasted the state of cultivation within the Pope's dominions with that outside.

1462. There are no less than three of those odd fires which constantly appear by night, by the road from Bologna to Florence. When we were got a mile beyond Pietra Mala we saw the largest of them. 'Twas an even yellow light, like the body of the sun, and seemed to be about three foot long and one broad. At the place itself they say 'tis about ten feet long. There is no cavity; the earth on the spot is of a reddish colour, and so is the soil for a good way round about it. It will burn a piece of paper, if put into it, and may be lighted with a candle when it does not appear of itself. The people of the country say it has been there, time out of mind, and indeed it is mentioned so long ago as by Pliny. 'Tis occasioned by what the Italians call 'oleo de' sassi', the physicians 'petrolium', and we 'petrol', or 'oil of rocks'. MR. T *1740*

Spence's Travel Notes report this incident in greater detail, and were written after he stopped there on 19 October 1740. From them we learn that the postillion called the oil 'oleo de' sassi' but Dr. Cocchi called it 'petrolium', and that Holdsworth supplied the reference to Pliny. This source of methane at Pietramale is now called 'Fuoco del legno'.

1463. In the *Camera Madama* there are two antiques of the story of Laocoon. The less is of a different design from the famous Laocoon in the Belvedere, but the larger is just like it. It has the arm that is wanting to the famous one, and might direct a good artist how to supply it. MR. T *1740*

Bandinelli has actually done this, in his copy of the famous Laocoon at the end of the gallery. BIANCHI

The copy by Bandinelli was made for Pope Clement VII, who presented it in 1531 to the Medici family. It is now in the west corridor of the Uffizi. For Ficoroni's account of the missing arm in the original group at the Vatican see § 1384. The comment was presumably made by Francesco Bianchi, for whom see § 1569.

1464. The bust of Julius Caesar in the long open gallery has a very weakly look, and is as like Mr. Pope as any bust [that] has been made on purpose for him. MR. T *1740*

This bust stands near the entrance in the main corridor of the Uffizi.

1465. The sea-born Venus, most commonly known by the name of the Venus de' Medici, is placed in the Tribuna, or chief room in the great Duke's gallery, between two other Venuses: the celestial and the victorious. If you observe them well, you will find as much difference between her air and that of the celestial Venus, as there is in Titian's wife, where she is in a tempting posture, and where she sits as a Madonna in the same room. MR. T *1740*

The Chevalier Ramsay had earlier described the Venus de' Medici to Spence in glowing terms (§ 1289). The two other statues are the Venus Victrix and the Venus Urania, both made familiar to travellers by Richardson's *Statues and Pictures in Italy*, pp. 56–57. Evidently two of Titian's paintings then hung in the same room; the Venus and Cupid is a late work of about 1550, or twenty years after the death of the artist's wife.

The Tribuna is an octagonal room specially built in 1610 to display the antique statuary.

1465a. The Pan in the same gallery who has a face fit to frighten people has the eyes painted with red, but that is not of any authority, because it has been done by somebody probably since it was set up there. Bianchi tried it, and the red came off upon his fingers. MR. T *1740*

Spence described the statue in a letter (*c.* 1734) to his friend Henry Rolle, as follows: 'This head between ye two Pillars, that has an Air horrid enough to frighten one, is a Pan. . . . His eyes you may see have been painted with red or minium; whether antiently or latterly I cannot say, but that too was an antient custom (Virgil: *Ecl*: x, 27).' The letter is humorously signed 'Sebastiano Bianchi' (B.M. Egerton MS. 2234, f. 294^v).

1466. The little figure in the Tribuna with a musical instrument like a violin is left rough and unfinished by the artist, and particularly the violin and stick to play upon it are so. 'Tis held as we hold our violins.

There are buskins on the legs of the person who holds it, a fawn's skin over his back and breast, and he is crowned with ivy. The face is handsome and there is a bacchanalian air in the head. Sebastian Bianchi used to say that it was Orpheus who brought the bacchanalian ceremonies into Bœotia. MR. T *1740*

I have met with but two figures besides this with the modern violin. One of them is in a relievo, on the death of Orpheus in the University at Turin, and the other is a statue, either of Orpheus or Apollo in the Montalto gardens at Rome. 'Tis unlucky that all three have something to be said against them. That at Florence is an unfinished piece and perhaps not quite indisputable, that at Turin of a very bad taste or low age, and in that at Rome the fiddle, at least, is evidently modern. SPENCE

The Dancing Faun is probably a Hellenistic original of the late fourth century. Spence described the Orpheus in the University at Turin in his travel notebook: 'very bad work; Orpheus's face much better than the rest' (B.M. Egerton MS. 2235, f. 78^v).

1467. There are two history pieces in the *Camera dei Cabinetti* in the Great Duke's gallery at Florence by the famous Mantegna. Some of the faces are very well, but the manner in general is still stiff and dry. The ground of both is all gold, and there is a good deal of gold in several other parts of the pictures. Mantegna was much the best painter of all in Europe, till Leonardo da Vinci so greatly advanced that art. It seems from hence that the tawdry taste brought into Italy by the Greeks continued quite down to the improvements of the latter, and the banishing of it ought most probably to be reckoned among the many very high merits of that extraordinary man. MR. T *1740*

Mantegna died in the year 1517, Vinci the year after, so that the tawdry or bad taste must have continued above 450 years in Italy. SPENCE

Spence probably had in mind Mantegna's 'Ascension' and 'Circumcision', which together with his 'Adoration of the Magi' form a triptych in the Uffizi. However, in the seventeenth and eighteenth centuries the triptych was broken up and the 'Adoration' (the middle panel) attributed to Botticelli. One of the most striking characteristics of the triptych is the frequent use of gold.
He was misinformed about the dates: Mantegna died in 1506 and Leonardo in 1519. The Byzantine style of painting brought in by the Greeks was held in low esteem until the late nineteenth century.

1468. There's a loadstone in the *Camera Matematica*, which holds up a piece of iron of forty pound weight fast to it. Two of double or treble that force might have kept up an iron tomb, perhaps with Mahomet in it, suspended in the air. MR. T *1740*

This loadstone, supposedly found on Elba, is now in the Museo di Storia delle Scienze in Florence. Edward Wright also reported seeing it in 'the Mathematical Chamber' (*Observations*, p. 405).

Perhaps the most remarkable man that Spence knew in Italy was his 'particular friend', the learned Florentine, Dr. Antonio Cocchi (1665–1758). Besides his medical skill and knowledge of other sciences, Dr. Cocchi possessed a gift of tongues; in addition to Greek and Latin he read and wrote in five modern European languages. His knowledge of painting and sculpture led to his appointment as antiquary to the Grand Duke in charge of the galleries in Florence. Cocchi was also the first to organize the Biblioteca Magliabecchiana, now the National Library. Among his many publications is the first printing of the autobiography of Benvenuto Cellini (1730).

Having lived in England for three years (1723–6) Dr. Cocchi counted many English friends and was sought out by visitors to Florence, especially by Freemasons, for he was a leading member of the Florentine Lodge. The following conversations occurred when Spence and Lord Middlesex settled in Florence from July 1732 until April 1733.

1469. Dante wrote before we began at all to be refined, and of course his celebrated poem is a sort of gothic work ⌜a vast imagination⌝. He is very singular and very beautiful in his similes, and more like Homer than any of our poets since. He was prodigiously learned, for the times he lived in, and knew all that a man could then know. Homer, in his time, was unknown in Italy, and Petrarch boasts of being the first poet that had heard him explained. Indeed, in Dante's time there was not above three or four people of all our country that could read Greek (one in particular at Viterbo and two or three in other parts). But though he had never seen Homer, he had conversed with the works of Virgil much.

COCCHI *July 1732–April 1733*

The inserted phrase is from the earliest manuscript; it also speaks of 'The beauty & particularity of his Similies', which is probably nearer to Cocchi's meaning than Spence's word 'singular'.

Petrarch knew enough Greek to be enthusiastic about Homer, and engaged Leontius Pilatus, one of the few Greek scholars of that day, to translate parts of Homer from manuscripts recently become available. Petrarch wrote an 'Epistle to Homer' in which he names the men of his time in Italy who understood Greek, but does not mention one at Viterbo.

It was Boccaccio, however, who made the explicit claim to be the first Italian to understand Homer properly, for Pilatus lived with him for two years, during which time he gave Boccaccio a complete explication of Homer, in contrast to the fragmentary passages known to Petrarch (P. de Nolhac, *Pétrarque et l'humanisme*, Paris, 1907, ii. 156–88).

1470. Dante's address in bringing the Pope then living, and a villain of Genoa into his Hell.

COCCHI *July 1732–April 1733*

This refers to Dante's portrayal of Pope Boniface VIII and Guido, Count of Montelfetro, in the *Inferno*, c. xxvii. A recent critic has commented, 'It is in the line of Dante's most characteristic irony that he should find the shrewdest man of his age, the Fox, tricked by the Pope to his damnation, cheated and caught like any fool by his own guile. [Guido] was after all only "a half-baked knave, who did not understand the sacrilegious trickery of the expert in knavery" (V. Rossi). Here again as in the nineteenth canto by the evidence of the damned themselves, Boniface . . . is the blackest villain of the piece. The spiritual head of Christendom is "the Prince of the new Pharisees" ' (*Divine Comedy*, tr. J. D. Sinclair, New York, 1948, i. 343).

1471. His poem got the name of *Commedia* after his death. He in that piece had called Virgil's works 'tragedies' (or sublime poetry), and in deference to him, called his own 'comedy' (or low), and hence was that word used afterwards by mistake for the title of his poem.

COCCHI *July 1732–April 1733*

Dr. Cocchi was mistaken, for the earliest manuscript is entitled, 'Incipit Comedia Dantis Alagherii florentini natione non moribus'. The epithet 'Divina' was added as part of the title in Giolito's edition, Venice (1555). In the poem Dante has Virgil speak of the *Aeneid* as 'l'alta mia tragedia' (*Inferno*, xx. 113) in contrast to which at the beginning of the next canto (xxi. 2) he calls his own poem 'la mia comedia'.

1472. Petrarch is the best of all our lyric poets, though there are several now that are very warm for preferring Chiabrera to him. It has divided the wits into two parties, and they are called Petrarchists or Chiabrerists according to which of these two poets is their favourite. The dispute turns wholly on their lyric pieces.

Chiabrera is not so equal a writer as Petrarch. Some of his odes are extremely good, and others full of false thoughts. Those that are his best are warm and lofty, and much after the manner of the Greeks.

Petrarch's language is excellent and reads extremely well, even though you fling it into prose. His poetry is often fine, soft, and moving, but he is not without his false thoughts too sometimes.

COCCHI *July 1732–April 1733*

The dispute was between two factions in the Academy of the Arcadi. The eighteenth-century revival of Italians' interest in Petrarch was similar to the English revival of interest in Spenser. Gabriello Chiabrera (1552–1638), once considered 'the new Pindar', was a sort of Italian Cowley, and his reputation has suffered a similar decline.

1473. Among all our poets we have not any one good love poet. They all follow Petrarch, and his is not a good love for poetry ⌜too romantic—unnatural—Platonic, from the Provençal ?⌝. Some of Ariosto's rhymes are the best this way, he having formed himself on the ancients, and on Tibullus in particular. COCCHI *July 1732–April 1733*

Ariosto's elegiac poetry (not his amatory verse) is considered to have been inspired by Tibullus.

1474. Dante, Galileo, and Machiavelli are the three greatest geniuses that Florence has ever produced.
COCCHI *July 1732–April 1733*

1475. Machiavelli has been generally called so wicked from people's mistaking the design of his writings. In his *Prince* his design at bottom was to make a despotic government odious. 'A despotic prince', he says, 'to secure himself must kill such and such people.' He must so, and therefore no wise people would suffer such a prince. This is the natural consequence, and not that Machiavelli seriously advises princes to be wicked. COCCHI *July 1732–April 1733*

Here Dr. Cocchi may have been replying to Spence, and defending Machiavelli's character as a moralist (as he has since come to be regarded) against the narrower viewpoint held by most foreigners that he was an unscrupulous materialist.

Spence probably had seen *Machiavel's Vindication of Himself and his Writings* (1691), the third part of which is devoted to the same attempt to clear Machiavelli of the charge of '*teaching Monarchs . . . all the execrable Villanies that can be invented*', etc. This spurious work (reprinted in the *Harleian Miscellany*, i. 55–64) has been attributed to Spence's distant relative, Col. Henry Neville (1620–94), who, in 1675, had published an edition of Machiavelli's *Works*. Spence referred to the reprint of Neville's work in a marginal jotting (see textual note).

1476. The best traditions concerning Machiavelli are that he was a good honest man himself in his way of living, and rather weak and ignorant in his private affairs than otherwise. His familiar letters are now in the hands of Abate del Riccio at Florence, and there are several things in them that show him to have been a good sort of man. He kept the best of company, and consorted with good men.
COCCHI *July 1732–April 1733*

The Abate Corso de' Ricci was a descendant of Machiavelli's grandson, Giuliano de' Ricci, custodian of Machiavelli's manuscripts, who transcribed his familiar letters. An edition of his letters at Florence in 1767 contained only formal and official correspondence; in 1883 E. Alvisi published the first scholarly edition, *Lettere familiari di N. Machiavelli*, also at Florence, and in the preface he lists the locations of the original letters. This edition has been superseded by *The Private Correspondence of Niccolò Machiavelli*, ed. Orestes Ferrara (Baltimore, 1929).

1477. We have several societies of men in Florence, who (though they are of no religious order) profess a greater strictness and a higher love of religion than ordinary. They are a sort of voluntary religious societies. Machiavelli was of one of these confraternite demi-religiose. They used to meet once a week for devotion in a church of theirs, and among other good things, one of the society made a moral discourse, or sermon, to the rest. There are several of these discourses of Machiavelli's composing in the same Abbé's hands, and one in the Great Duke's, on repentance (in lode della Penitenza), which were spoken by Machiavelli in the confraternity he belonged to. COCCHI *July 1732–April 1733*

Signor Sbarra, at Lucca, did not carry this point so far. He only said 'that Machiavelli advised politicians to be good—that was their best and easiest way—but if they must be bad, he laid down rules how they should be so most wisely and politically.' SPENCE

For an account of the religious confraternities see Oreste Tommasini, *La vita e gli scritti di Niccolò Machiavelli* (Roma, 1911), ii. 733–5. A manuscript of his *Discorso morale*, begun in 1513, is preserved in the National Library at Florence.

1478. Tasso followed Ariosto too much in his particular faults, so that they are a good deal alike so far, but he [Tasso] was more classically read, and especially in the old critics. He endeavoured also to write on a more correct plan. Sperone Speroni brags of finding out and disposing the subject for him. COCCHI *July 1732–April 1733*

When writing *Gerusalemme Liberata* Tasso continually asked his friends for advice so that a large number of them boasted, rightly or wrongly, that they had a hand in the epic. One historian lists eighteen persons whom Tasso consulted (G. Fontanini, *Biblioteca dell'eloquenza italiana*, Parma, 1803, i. 360). Among them is Sperone Speroni (1500–88) who in one of his letters describes the part he contributed (A. Solerti, *Vita di Tasso*, Turin, 1895, i. 205); Cocchi may have known of this letter.

1479. Ariosto loved the classics too, and in particular understood Horace better than any man in his time. When he first came to Rome, Bembo and several of the greatest wits there were endeavouring to get to understand Horace. Ariosto joined them, and they all allowed him to have a greater insight into that author than any of them.

'I believe he did not understand Greek?' [asked Spence].

No, Sir, and he owns it, in a letter to Bembo.

COCCHI *July 1732–April 1733*

In Satire vii, addressed to Bembo in 1525, Ariosto complains about his own lack of opportunity to learn Greek, and asks Bembo to find a Greek master for his son Virginio, whom he had sent to study in Padua.

1480. Ariosto was a vast master of poetical language; his imagination is strong, and his description often extremely lively and natural. He wrote his *Orlando* to divert himself, and did not care whether he was correct or no. The great Galileo used to compare that poem to a melon-field: 'You may meet with a very good thing here and there in it,' says he, 'but the whole is but of little value.'

COCCHI *July 1732–April 1733*

Ariosto's descriptions are remarkably concrete; his stylistic ornaments are usually similes rather than metaphors. As Singer pointed out, Ariosto was actually a restless corrector and reviser of his poetical works.

The remark about the 'melon-field' attributed to Galileo seems to be apocryphal; it cannot be found among the many references to Ariosto in the twenty volumes of the *Opere di Galilei*, 1938, and is inconsistent with the high admiration Galileo always expressed towards Ariosto. Cocchi may have allowed his own attitude to intrude (see below).

1481. In all the disputes between the Tuscan literati, whether Tasso or Ariosto be the better poet, the debate always runs on the outside. Those numerous pieces are entirely taken up in speaking of the style and colours of poetry, and the writers of them seem never to have thought anything of the plan or composition.

Ariosto's poem is like the fine habit of a harlequin, made up of pieces of the very best silks, and of the liveliest colours. The parts of it are many of them more beautiful than those in Tasso's poem, but the whole in Tasso is without comparison more of a piece and better made.

COCCHI *July 1732–April 1733*

The earliest manuscript shows that when Spence read this passage back to Dr. Cocchi the simile of the harlequin's habit was considered 'too low', so the phrase was altered to 'richer harlequin's habit'. Spence also wrote in the margin Cocchi's observation 'Spencer [*sic*] has taken much from him'.

1482. Tasso's madness some think was only a pretended madness. He was caught making too free with a princess of the Duke of Ferrara's family in which he lived. To save her honour and himself, he from that time, say they, began to play his melancholy tricks. There is a passage in his *Aminta* which may allude to this. 'Tis in the end of the first act and is spoken by Tirsi, under which character Tasso meant himself. COCCHI *July 1732–April 1733*

This romantic incident connecting Tasso's mental difficulties with Leonora d'Este is unfounded. Tasso's mind began to deteriorate about his thirty-third year, and during the remaining eighteen years of his life he had frequent outbursts which made confinement necessary. Cocchi probably picked up the story about Tirsi's speech (*Aminta*, I. ii. 553–652) from Gilles Ménage's *Osservazioni sopra l'Aminta del Tasso*, reprinted in Venice in 1730, which suggests that Tasso there predicts his later insanity. Modern scholarship has shown this passage to be a later insertion, not found in the early manuscripts.

1483. Ariosto, Boiardo, and Berni have written all on the same subject, the siege of Paris, and took it from a romance called *I Reali di Francia*—as the ancients used to write in droves on the siege of Thebes or the siege of Troy.

COCCHI *July 1732–April 1733*

Boiardo's *Orlando Inamorato*, though unfinished at the time of his death in 1494, was written under the patronage of the d'Este family in Ferrara. Ariosto was also attached to the d'Estes, and carried on the story (and the development of the Italian romantic epic) in *Orlando Furioso*, published in 1516. Francesco Berni, a generation younger than Ariosto, took Boiardo's poem and rewrote it in the new style of the sixteenth century, publishing it in 1541. Boiardo's original text then lay forgotten until it was finally published in the nineteenth century. *I Reali di Francia* is a compilation in prose of stories from the Carolingian epics, made about 1400 by Andrea da Barberino (*c.* 1370–*c.* 1432).

1484. Berni's way of writing is genteel, and his introductions, in particular, are very beautiful.

COCCHI *July 1732–April 1733*

'⌜Nel[l'] Orlando di Berni⌝ i preamboli sono superbi,' were his words. SPENCE

The inserted words come from the earliest manuscript. Cocchi was referring to the poetical dedications and introductions which Berni added to Boiardo's cantos.

1485. In speaking of their Latin poets, he mentioned Vida, Sannazzaro and Fracastorio, and [went] no further.

COCCHI *July 1732–April 1733*

Spence had discussed these neo-Latin poets with Pope and Bolingbroke (§ 552a) and with Lockier (§ 705).

1486. Folingius's poem is written in mixed language; Latin, with several of the words italianized, as the *Fidenzian* is Italian latinized. Macaronic poetry is the general name for both of them, or any such confused ridiculous stuff.

COCCHI *July 1732–April 1733*

Teofilo Folengo (1496?–1544) burlesqued the romantic epics in his *Orlandino* (1525–6) and in the *Macaronea* (1552), written in Latin macaronics. 'Fidenzian' took its name from Fidenzio, pseudonym of Camillo Scrofa (1526–65), inventor of this manner of writing, intended to ridicule pedantry.

1487. Lippi's *Malmantile* is very good. Though 'tis a mock epic, his style is that of Tasso, Petrarch, and the best Tuscan writers. For the common people in Florence talk the language of the nobility and gentry—'tis not there, as it is in the other cities of Italy. COCCHI *July 1732–April 1733*

Il Malmantile Racquistato (i.e. 'The Towel Regained') was published in 1676, under the pseudonym Perlone Zipoli, by the Florentine painter and poet Lorenzo Lippi (1606–64). The colloquial language employed makes it a valuable linguistic document, aside from its lively style and allegorical portrayal of Florentine personalities and scenes.

1488. If you look for a *right good* poet among us, 'tis a thing that you must look for in vain. ⌜He spoke contemptibly of Lorenzo Crasso's elegies.⌝ COCCHI *July 1732–April 1733*

The inserted sentence is from the earliest manuscript. Lorenzo Crasso flourished in the early seventeenth century, but wrote works unworthy of comment.

1489. Menzini is generally considered as our best satirist, and Ariosto as the next. I don't speak of my own taste, for I like Ariosto better than the other. Menzini is more like Juvenal, and Ariosto more like Horace.

COCCHI *July 1732–April 1733*

Benedetto Menzini (1646–1704), a frustrated poet, achieved posthumous fame when his satires, long circulated in manuscript, reached print in 1718 in Florence under a fictitious Amsterdam imprint. In style they are more libellous than Juvenalian, for he accuses the entire populace of hypocrisy and other vices, giving special attention to his personal enemies. Because of their liveliness and topical interest, they were still highly regarded when Spence first visited Florence. See § 1532.

1490. Mauro has written on low subjects in the common genteel style, but Crudeli is the first among us that ever attempted to treat of low things in the high epic manner. I gave him the hint from Mr. Pope's *Rape of the Lock*, and what is handed about of his in that style has pleased extremely. ⌜Crudeli has published nothing.⌝

COCCHI *July 1732–April 1733*

Giovanni Mauro (*c.* 1490–1536), burlesque writer, was a friend of Berni, but far below him in poetical powers. For about three centuries after them the two friends influenced writers of burlesque. For Tommaso Crudeli see the series of conversations recorded below, beginning with § 1535. His poems were not published until 1746, the year after his death.

Another jotting on a different page of the manuscript adds the detail that Crudeli imitated John 'Cyder' Philips's 'manner of low things (Breeches &c) in a grand style'.

1491. I have just received a letter from Vienna; Metastasio's operas have made him the favourite of all the world there. They say he'll certainly make his fortune by them.

COCCHI *July 1732–April 1733*

Cocchi's information was well founded. In 1729, after an early success in his native Rome, Metastasio (his real name was Pietro Trapassi, 1698–1782) received an offer of 3,000 florins a year to become court poet in Vienna. In the ten years after his arrival he produced his nine finest libretti for operas that made him perhaps the most popular writer of his age.

1492. 'Oh, ella sa che ci sono altre strade, la sodamia,' [said Cocchi].

'Gravina, his master, I think was infame per questo,' [added Spence].

'Non, signor,' [replied Cocchi]. 'Era famosa per questo, si piace.'

'D'ye speak seriously?' [asked Spence.]

To prove it he told the story of Marchetti, the famous translator of Lucretius, as he had it from himself—

' "E ainsi questo va dishonorar la sua famiglia."

"Crede che puo ingravidarlo?"

"Oh, si burla di me."

"E bene, dunque Signor Abbate, non puo dishonorar la mia famiglia." '

COCCHI *July 1732–April 1733*

There has been no attempt to correct the mixture of English, Italian, and French which Spence used in recording this anecdote. However, the punctuation has been normalized and the speeches divided between speakers. The conversation can be translated as follows: 'Oh, there are other ways for doing that, you know—sodomy.' 'Gravina, his master, I think was infamous for that.' 'No, signor, if you please, he was famous for that.' . . . ' "And so this will dishonour his family." "Do you believe that he could make him big with child?" "Oh, you are teasing me." "Well, then, my dear abbé, he could not dishonour my family." '

The attitude towards homosexuality in Italy was much more tolerant than in eighteenth-century England, where stories such as this rarely reached print. Metastasio's first patron was Gian Vincenzo Gravina (1664–1718), poet and critic (often accused of homosexuality), who picked him up off the street at the age of twelve, adopted him, and on his death nine years later left the twenty-year-old Metastasio a fortune.

Alessandro Marchetti (1633–1714) translated Lucretius, his admirable version being published posthumously in 1717. The story has the sound of a stock smoking-room joke, antedating Gravina and Metastasio.

DR. ANTONIO COCCHI
By an unknown artist
Uffizi Gallery, Florence

1493. 'Why are the Italians, that are a solid and grave people, the most fond of drolleries on their stage, and greater dealers in burlesque than any other nation?' [asked Spence].

Salvini used to think it was because when people have a mind to divert themselves they generally choose what is most different from their ordinary temper and practice, as most likely to divert them. That may be the reason, but I should not be apt to acquiesce in it.

COCCHI *July 1732–April 1733*

Perhaps he thought that their gravity was a cheat and ridicule their natural bent. ⌜LORD MIDDLESEX⌝

On the other side, 'tis evident that most of their drolleries are very low and violent. There is the same difference between fine drollery and theirs as there is between true and false wit. This would rather incline one to think that they are really grave, and only affect gaiety, because they pursue it so boisterously and so injudiciously. SPENCE

Spence was in Florence at Carnival time in February 1733, and the conduct of the participants may have prompted this conversation. That Lord Middlesex participated we learn from the earliest manuscript; doubtless Spence suppressed his name in deference to his rank. For 'Old Salvini', Professor of Greek at Florence, see § 711.

1494. Our not having any settled stage for tragedies in Italy is a great blow to our dramatic poetry. The actors indeed that stroll about from city to city do now and then act a tragedy, but even when that happens, and the king of the play is seated in his throne, 'tis ten to one but in a few minutes you shall see a harlequin come in upon the stage and place himself just by him. COCCHI *July 1732–April 1733*

The low state of tragedy on the Italian stage is the subject of a chapter entitled 'The Design proposed by the first Writers of Greek Tragedy. The Rise, Progress and Ruin of Italian Tragedy . . .' in L. Riccoboni's *Historical and Critical Account of the Theatres in Europe* (English translation, 1741; first published 1736). Spence had seen an example of how the Italian players 'mix buffoonery with everything' in a performance of *Don John* at

Turin, just a few weeks before this conversation with Dr. Cocchi. In a letter to his mother, dated 23 August 1732, he described the 'Harlequin who blunders about everything', distracting attention from Don John, even in the Hell scene.

1495. Lord Burlington was so much for Palladio that he used to run down Michelangelo. 'Tis true the latter did not follow the rules so much as the former, but then he had a most correct eye, and is universally reckoned the best architect of the moderns by the best judges at Rome as well as at Florence. COCCHI *July 1732–April 1733*

It is possible that the paths of Lord Burlington (Richard Boyle, 1695–1753, third Earl) and Dr. Cocchi crossed when Burlington was studying the beauties of Palladio in northern Italy for several years before 1716. More likely, however, they met in England during Cocchi's residence there in 1723–6. Burlington may have objected to the gigantic scale of St. Peter's.

1496. I must own that to my taste Correggio is the best of all our painters. His pieces are less pictures than those of Raphael himself. COCCHI *July 1732–April 1733*

The virtuosi of the eighteenth century chose Correggio and Raphael as a favourite comparison. Jonathan Richardson the younger discussed the subject intermittently in his *Statues and Pictures in Italy* (1722) summarizing the differences in a long passage, pp. 173–4: '*Raffaele* is vastly Great, and Sublime, and withal has a Grace like that of the Best of the Ancients: But no Master, that ever was, Surprizes like *Correggio*; and yet without an Equal Measure of Greatness, and with a Grace not Antique, nor like any other Master. . . . The Chief Beauties of *Raffaele* we see often, and almost as often Out-done in the Best Antique: And all his Other Qualities are formed in a higher degree than he possess'd them in the Works of *Correggio*, and other Masters. Besides He frequently wanted One of vast Consequence to a Painter, and that is Harmony; whereas *Correggio* had That, which set his Fine Pencil, Lovely Colouring, and enchanting Grace in full View. 'Tis That Grace, that Angelick Grace of his which is purely Original, and no where else to be seen: 'Tis This that surprizes us; and the more because all is accompany'd with Faults like those of the most Inferior Painters.'

1497. It was objected to Copernicus in his own days that if his scheme was true, Venus must appear to us with different phases just as the moon does. 'So she would, I believe,' replied he, 'if we could see her aright.' This was a noble guess for the time, and what has proved to be actually the case since Galileo has found out new eyes for us.

COCCHI *July 1732–April 1733*

This anecdote has been repeated in successive books on Copernicus without any indication of who made the objection to Copernicus, or the nature of the occasion. Galileo described his discovery of the phases of Venus, confirming Copernicus's theory, in a letter about sunspots to Marco Velseri, 4 May 1612 (*Opere di Galilei*, v, 1932, 98–99).

1498. Cardinal Barberini had made some of the same objections to Galileo's scheme that are put into the mouth of Simplicius (the foolish character that personates the Aristotelians) in Galileo's dialogues. This was one of the chief motives made use of for the persecution of so great a man, under that Cardinal when promoted to the papacy.

COCCHI *July 1732–April 1733*

The character Simplicius appears in Galileo's *Dialogo . . . sopra i due Massimi Sistemi del mondo Tolemaico e Copernicano* (1632). The editors of the *Edizione Nazionale* (vii, 1932, 9) consider that Galileo had no particular person in mind, and specifically not Pope Urban VIII, as Cardinal Barberini had become in 1623. Galileo was examined and condemned by the Inquisition in 1633 for adhering to the heresy (so defined in 1616) that the earth moves around the sun.

1499. Kepler, a German, carried things rather further than Galileo. It was he that found out the gravitation of the planets, but not the proportions of it.

COCCHI *July 1732–April 1733*

Johann Kepler (1571–1630) observed in his *Astronomia Nova* (1609) that the movement of the planets in their orbits was determined by some force or influence exerted by the sun, but he was not able to develop a precise theory of the nature of the force. The law of gravitation was first clearly formulated by Sir Isaac Newton.

1500. The pursuit of the greatest trifles may sometimes have a very good effect: the search after the philosopher's stone has preserved chemistry, and the following astrology so much in former ages has been the cause of astronomy's being so much advanced in ours.

Sir Isaac Newton himself has owned that he began with studying judiciary astrology, and that it was his pursuits of that idle and vain study which led him into the beauties and love of astronomy. COCCHI *July 1732–April 1733*

Dr. Cocchi knew Sir Isaac during his residence in England, 1723–6. For Newton's interest in judicial astrology and alchemy see § 684.

1501. When I asked Sir Isaac how the study of the mathematics flourished then in England, he said, 'Not so much as it has done here, but more than it does in any other country.'

COCCHI *July 1732–April 1733*

When this conversation took place cannot now be determined; it may have been on 14 January 1724, when Dr. Cocchi met Sir Isaac for the first time at the Royal Society (Andrea Corsini, *Antonio Cocchi*, Milan, 1928, p. 29).

1502. Mr. Locke spent a good part of his first years at the university in reading romances, from his aversion to the disputative way then in fashion there. He told Coste so, and gave that reason for it to him.

COCCHI *July 1732–April 1733*

[Cocchi] had it from Coste, who gave him Mr. Locke's physical commonplace book, which seemed by what I could see of it [more] valuable for being written in Mr. Locke's hand than for the matter contained in it. ⌜The only recipe I saw there, of his own, was a cure for the c[ra]bs.⌝ SPENCE

Locke was admitted to Christ Church, Oxford, in 1652 and graduated B.A. in 1656. Like his predecessor Hobbes and other fertile minds, Locke reacted against the Aristotelian philosophy that then dominated the University, and sought instead the company of congenial and witty fellow students.

Pierre Coste (1668–1747) knew Locke intimately from 1697, when he joined the household of Sir Francis Masham in Essex, where Locke also lived. Coste translated several of Locke's works, most notably the *Essay Concerning Human Understanding* under Locke's supervision.

Spence's comment is marked for omission in the Folio manuscript. The inserted sentence comes from the earliest manuscript.

1503. My wife is inquiring so much into questions of religion that I fear she'll soon lose the little she has. For my part, I don't trouble my head about those affairs; all I can say is, that Christ when he was upon earth kept very bad company. COCCHI *July 1732–April 1733*

Dr. Cocchi married twice, and the date shows that he was speaking of his first wife, Gaetana Debi. Cocchi's liberal views towards orthodox religion caused him to be persecuted by the Inquisition in 1737.

1504. 'Pray, Sir Isaac, may I ask you what is your opinion of the immortality of the soul?' [asked Cocchi's wife].

Madam, I'm an experimental philosopher.

COCCHI *July 1732–April 1733*

This and the following anecdote precede § 1503 in the manuscript. 'Madam' and the sequence of anecdotes give the questioner's identity. Both exchanges probably took place while Cocchi was living in England from 1723 to 1726.

1504a. 'What do you think of the nature of Christ's soul?'

I don't know the nature of my own, and how should I know that of another person?

COCCHI *July 1732–April 1733*

The manuscript shows that this question also was asked by Dr. Cocchi's wife. The reply is that of a 'Dr. Clarke', but it is not clear whether Dr. Alured or Samuel Clarke was the man involved.

1505. If a lady applies to learning among us, and comes to excel eminently in it, she is admitted to her degrees as well as the men. Antonia Maria Bassi was lately made a doctoress at Bologna, and a famous Venetian lady was doctored a good while ago at Padua. COCCHI *July 1732–April 1733*

Laura Maria Catarina Bassi (1711–78; after her marriage her name became Bassi Verati) was widely celebrated for her knowledge of literature, philosophy, and science. In 1732 she was appointed to the professorship of Philosophy at Bologna, an event that became a topic for discussion in learned circles. It was even reported in the *Gentleman's Magazine* (ii (1732), 777). When Dr. Charles Burney visited Bologna in 1770 he called on her as one of the sights of the city, and she showed him her electrical machine and discussed Benjamin Franklin's experiments. Burney reported her to be 'though learned, and a genius, not at all masculine or assuming' (*Dr. Burney's Musical Tours in Europe*, ed. P. A. Scholes, 1959, i. 159–60).

The Venetian lady was Lucrezia Elena Cornaro-Piscopia (1646–84), who received the doctorate from the University of Padua in June 1678, and was the first woman to earn the honour.

1505a. The first four hundred years of the Roman history are supposed to have been fabulous by Senator Buonarotti, and he gives several reasons for his opinion. He suspects that Rome, in particular, was built by the Greeks, as Tarentum, Naples, and several other cities in Italy were.

COCCHI *July 1732–April 1733*

Filippo Buonarroti (1661–1733) published two works on the history of Rome. In contrast to the coastal cities, the Greek influence in Rome during the early centuries was slight. Questions concerning the early history of Rome were widely discussed in the early eighteenth century (§§ 884–5).

1506. Galen's book, *De Consuetudine*, has never been published, except in a barbarous Latin translation, drawn off from an old Arabic one, and that so bad that it was suspected of never having come from any piece that really was Galen's. The Greek original, or at least a great part of it, is in the Lorenzo Library, where there are also the unprinted works of five or six other Greek physicians which I have transcribed and since published.

COCCHI *July 1732–April 1733*

The last three words are pencilled in the margin of the Folio manuscript by Spence, and refer to Cocchi's *Graecorum Chirurgici Libri*, published in Florence in 1754. In the preface Cocchi says that his translations had long been in manuscript, as this conversation of 1732 confirms. Cocchi also says that Dr. Mead had urged their publication.

1507. There is a manuscript in the Lorenzo Library at Florence of a Greek physician of the tenth century, in which the elephantiasis is described just like the pox, and he is the only one of all the ancients who speaks of that distemper as infectious. The instance he gives too is particular. He speaks of a woman who caught the elephantiasis, infected another, and by that means cured herself. In the margin is an epigram of the same age, which turns on the wisdom and goodness of

God in punishing a sinner and providing for the physicians at the same time. COCCHI *July 1732–April 1733*

Dr. Cocchi had a professional interest in elephantiasis and wrote three essays on the disease (*Opere*, Milan, 1824, iii. 30–32, 35–37, 37–39). He does not, however, identify the manuscript referred to here.

1508. All the greatest physicians in Italy a little after America was discovered agree in speaking of the pox as a new distemper in Europe. The only dispute among them was what old distemper it might be a species of.

Nicolaus Leonicenus is one of the first that mentions it, and Antonius Musa Brasavolus some time after. ⌜Fallopius speaks of having observed the clap as a symptom of it, some twelve years before the date of his book, which was about 1542.⌝ COCCHI *July 1732–April 1733*

The outbreak of syphilis following the return of Columbus from his first voyage is one of the most remarkable events in medical history. There is ample documentation to show that soldiers and sailors who returned to Barcelona in 1493 were infected with the new disease, acquired from Indian women in the New World. Early reports indicate that the disease was first observed in Haiti. Charles VIII of France was then recruiting an army of mercenaries to invade Italy to enforce his claim to the throne of Naples. This army, gathered from various parts of Europe, cut through Italy in the autumn of 1494 in what has been described as more a triumphal march of debauchery than a serious military campaign. Among them were Spanish troops, infected with the new disease.

Naples fell in 1495, but the army was so decimated by what was known as the plague that the soldiers beat an undisciplined retreat to their homes in various countries. Contemporary records agree in describing the symptoms of the disease and in attributing it to the scattering of Charles VIII's troops. By 1497 the pox had reached England and Scotland, and by 1499 Hungary and Russia. It was spread to India, China, and Japan by explorers. Like other cases of new diseases it was particularly virulent, though after fifty years it settled down to the symptoms known ever since.

Efforts have been made to equate syphilis with diseases known to the ancients, but with scanty success, and no proof, literary or otherwise. The evidence is heavily in favour of Columbus's introduction of the disease to Europe and from there to the Asian world (E. Jeansalme, *Histoire de la syphilis*, Paris, 1931, i. 54–96).

Cocchi's references are to Niccolò Leoniceno, *Libellus de epidemica quam vulgo morbum Gallicum vocant* (Venice, 1497), Gabrielle Fallopia, *De morbo Gallico* (Padua, 1564), and Antonio Musa Brasavola, *De morbo Gallico* (in L. Luisini, *De morbo Gallico*, Venice, 1566–7). Cocchi was wrong about the date of Fallopia's book.

1509. The paraphrases written in the margin of Theodore Gaza's *Homer* in the Lorenzo Library have been often of particular service to me when I have been at a loss to fix the meaning of any passage in that poet.

COCCHI *July 1732–April 1733*

Theodorus Gaza (*c.* 1400–75) was one of the Greek scholars who gave impetus to the Renaissance of classical studies in Italy by his numerous translations from Greek into Latin. The volume is still in the Laurentian Library (Plutarch 32, Codex 1).

1510. There are three thousand manuscript books in the Lorenzo Library (including a *few* printed books, equivalent to manuscripts), and in many of them the works of several different authors are bound up together, which they call 'catenas'. If you take them singly there are about ten thousand.

There is no other library so well stocked in three of the best sorts—physical, mathematical, and poetical manuscripts. COCCHI *July 1732–April 1733*

The Laurentian Library in Florence, formed on the Medici collections, was opened to the public in 1571. It contains only about 11,000 books, most of them of the greatest rarity, and 9,693 manuscripts, many of supreme importance as well as beauty.

1511. Several pieces of authors, not anywhere published, are preserved in the catenas (collections from different authors who have written on the same subject). [There are] such in the Lorenzo Library.

COCCHI *July 1732–April 1733*

1512. The Spaniards were at the top of their poetry under the reigns of Charles V and Philip II. They imitated the Italian poets and would fain set up Garcilasso de la Vega for their Petrarch. Their poetry is generally bad, and even Lope de Vega's is wretched stuff. Gonzalo Perez's translation of the *Odyssey* is very good. COCCHI *July 1732–April 1733*

The Spanish dominions in Italy opened a door for Italian models to influence Spanish writers greatly. For example, Garcilasso de la Vega (1503–

36), the 'Prince of Castilian poets', learned new methods when on military duty at Naples. Dr. Cocchi underestimated Lope de Vega's lyrical gifts, and over-praised Perez's *Ulyssea* (1550), which suggests that his reading in Spanish poetry was not very extensive.

1513. By a reckoning made from the best dictionary for each of the following languages, there are about twenty thousand words in the Spanish, twenty-two in the English, twenty-five in the Latin, thirty in the French, forty-five in the Italian, fifty in the Greek, and eighty in the German.

COCCHI *July 1732–April 1733*

Such estimates are of doubtful accuracy, for they were limited by the extent of the labour of the individual compiler. Judging from the English example, Cocchi may refer to Edward Phillip's *New World of Words* (1658) which lists about 23,000 words. However, John Kersey's *Dictionarium* (1708) contained over 50,000, and Bailey's *Dictionary* (1721) added many more.

Languages held a fascination for Dr. Cocchi; his unpublished diaries and notebooks are written in Italian, English, Latin, and Greek, with extensive use also of French, Spanish, and German.

1514. Of the twenty-two thousand words in the English language, there are about fifteen thousand that a man understands who is before master of Latin, French, and Italian, and three thousand more if he be master of German. The other four thousand are probably the old British.

COCCHI *July 1732–April 1733*

Seventeen hundred radical words in the Hebrew, according to Buxtorf, three hundred and sixty Chaldaic words in the Bible, according to Bythner. (2,060 in all.) MR. HILL

The comment apparently quotes Robert Hill (1699–1777), 'the learned tailor of Buckingham', one of the natural prodigies sponsored by Spence. Hill refers to the *Lexicon Hebraicum*, published in 1607 by Johannes Buxtorf, and the *Lingua Eruditorum* (1638) and *Lyra Prophetae* (1650) of Victorinus Bythner.

1515. 'As cunning as old Nick', and 'as wicked as old Nick' were originally meant of our (Nicholas) Machiavelli, and came afterwards to be perverted to the devil.

COCCHI *July 1732–April 1733*

Dr. Cocchi had a special interest in etymology. In the earliest manuscript this and the following anecdote are headed 'Derivations of some English phrases'.

The *OED* can offer no explanation of the phrase (first example, 1643) and it is possible that Dr. Cocchi's ingenious interpretation may be right. Ben Jonson alludes to Machiavelli as St. Nicholas (*Discoveries*, l. 1178, *Works*, ed. Herford and Simpson, 1925–52, viii. 599), but the term seems to have had a Nordic tradition (R. Nares's *Glossary*, 1847 ed., p. 602).

1516. When the English were good Catholics, they usually drank the Pope's health in a full glass every day after dinner: *au bon père*, whence your word *bumper*.

COCCHI *July 1732–April 1733*

A writer in the *Gentleman's Magazine* for June 1759 (pp. 270–2), who signed his name as Paul Gemsage, discussed this derivation at some length. He pointed out that this Roman Catholic story is contradicted by the fact that the Pope would never be spoke of as 'le bon Père' but as 'le saint Père'. The *OED* suggests the word derives from the practice of bumping glasses together.

1517. Those Arabians had the name Saracens from a Scripture name: Sarah. COCCHI *July 1732–April 1733*

[Rather] from Sahara Deserts, in the Arabic. They are the same as the followers of Mahomet; they came out of their deserts and conquered Africa, etc. SHAW *1732*

According to the *OED* the etymology of 'Saracen' is uncertain; St. Jerome identified the Saracens with the descendants of Hagar, 'who are now called Saracens, taking to themselves the name of Sarah'.

Thomas Shaw (1697–1751) had reached Florence in the autumn of 1732 on his return from travelling in Africa; 'Sahara' is simply the Arabic word for desert.

1517a. 'Why don't the N[orthern] nations flow down to conquer Europe now, as they did formerly?' [asked Spence].

Because they are in possession of it.

COCCHI *July 1732–April 1733*

1518. Perfetti was crowned about four years ago for his talent at improvisoing, or making extempore verses, but Manfredi is the best poet we have now in Italy.

'I thought the impromptu way had prevailed all over Italy, and was regarded as the highest excellence of poetry at present?' [suggested Spence].

No, 'tis only admired so much by the little and great vulgar. COCCHI *July 1732–April 1733*

Bernardino Perfetti (1681–1747) of Siena, probably the best known of the *improvvisatori* in his time, was crowned on 13 May 1725 by order of Benedict XIII (for Vanneschi's account see § 1522). Perfetti's improvised verses were written down and eventually published in two volumes in 1747 and 1748.

Eustachio Manfredi (1674–1739), Professor of Mathematics at Bologna, was leader of a group of poets who reacted against the excesses of baroque poetry and attempted to return to the simplicity and lightness of Petrarch. See also §§ 1525 and 1527.

1519. The first time I heard them [the *improvvisatori*], I thought it impossible for them to go on so readily as they did without having agreed things together beforehand. It was at Florence at our resident's, Mr. Colman's, and when that gentleman asked me what I thought of it, I told him that I could not conceive how they could go on so readily, and so evenly, without some collusion between them. He said that it amazed everybody at first, that he had no doubt of its being all fair, and desired me, to be satisfied of it, to give them some subject myself, as much out of the way as I could think of. As he insisted upon my doing so, I offered a subject which must be new to them and on which they could not well be prepared. It was but a day or two before that a band of musicians and actors set out from Florence to introduce operas for the first time in the Empress of Russia's court. This advance of music and that sort of dramatic poetry (which the Italians at present look upon as the most capital parts of what they call *virtù*) so much farther north than ever they had been, under the auspices of the then Great Duke, was the subject I offered for them.

They shook their heads a little and said it was a very difficult one. However, in two or three minutes' time one of them began with his octave upon it, another answered him immediately, and they went on for five or six stanzas alternately, without any pause, except that very short one which is always allowed them by the going off of the tune on the guitar at the end of each stanza. They always improviso to music (at least all that I ever heard), and the tune is somewhat slow—but when they are thoroughly warmed they will sometimes call out for quicker time.

If two of these guitarers meet in the summer nights in the very streets of Florence, they will challenge one another and improviso sometimes as rapidly as those in set companies. Their most common subjects are the commendation of their several mistresses, or two shepherds contending for the same, or a debate which is the best poet—and they often put one in mind of Virgil's third, fifth, and seventh eclogues, or what he calls the 'contentions' of his shepherds in alternate verse—and, by the way, Virgil's shepherds seem sometimes to be tied down by the *thought* in the preceding stanza, as these extempore poets are by the preceding *rhyme*.

SPENCE *August 1732–March 1733*

Francis Colman (1690?–1733) became British envoy at the court of the Grand Duke in 1724. He was a keen opera fan, and wrote the libretto for Handel's *Ariadne in Crete*, performed the year after Colman's death. His love of the theatre was inherited by his son, George Colman the elder. The band of musicians and actors who had set out for Russia was not, in fact, the first such expedition. A troupe, directed by Tommaso Ristori, had reached Russia two years earlier, their first performance being on 9 March 1731.

Spence's choice of subject contrasts with that offered by Lady Pomfret some years later, *Why women are generally more constant in love than men* (Hertford *Correspondence*, ii. 59–60). Charles de Brosses chose a more difficult subject, the aurora borealis (*Lettres historiques et critiques sur l'Italie*, Paris, 1799, ii. 95).

¶ *Francesco Vanneschi (died* c. *1756) is one of the shadowy characters who comes briefly to life in Spence's manuscripts, but whose chequered existence is otherwise traced with difficulty. When Spence and Lord Middlesex met him in Florence in 1733, Vanneschi was an abbot, though his specific religious connexions have not been identified. Besides his interest in poetry, and his early qualification as an* improvvisatore, *Vanneschi's principal concern was with the opera. His abilities so impressed Lord Middlesex that he carried Vanneschi back to England with him in 1741, where he became an impresario under Lord Middlesex's 'regency' (Dr. Charles*

Burney, General History of Music, *iv, 1789, 446). During the next fifteen years he wrote the librettos for half a dozen operas, and served as 'manager from the time that serious operas were renewed, in 1753, till . . . frequent contentions with Mingotti, which shook his throne, had prejudiced the public against both' (ibid., p. 467). Like Dr. Burney, Horace Walpole had little use for Vanneschi, saying 'what a coxcomb!' when they met at Calais on the return to England in 1741 (Walpole* Corresp., *xvii. 141) and subsequent references take the same tone. Considering his operatic activities over a span of fifteen years it is remarkable how little record of Vanneschi's work and life remains.*

1520. The improviso, or extempore poets in Italy are actually what they are called. They do it with great emulation and warmth, generally in octaves, in which the answerer is obliged to form his octave to the concluding rhyme of the challenger, so that all the octaves after the first must be extempore, unless they act in concert together.

Our method is to create our thought at the enemy's seventh verse. Then we have the idea, the rhymes, the words, and the verse to think of, only whilst our opponent is repeating his last line, which we take no manner of notice of at all. We almost always do better the second half hour than first, because one grows warmer and warmer, to such a degree at last that when I have improviso-ed a whole evening, I can never get a wink of sleep all the night after.

VANNESCHI *an Abbé of Florence, and very ready in that sort of poetry July 1732–April 1733*

The earliest manuscript adds the detail, '& most of 'em love to Improviso ye glass in hand'. Among the Spence Papers there is a specimen of improvised Italian poetry; see Appendix, pp. 680–1.

1521. Tuscany is almost the only place for extempore poetry, particularly at Florence and Siena; and in the country for five or six miles round them. There are a few indeed at Rome, but even those are chiefly Tuscans.

VANNESCHI *July 1732–April 1733*

1522. The Cavalier Perfetti is of Siena, and is the best *improvvisatore* at present in Italy. He was crowned in the Capitol about five years ago by order of the Pope, at the desire of the Princess Violante, widow to Ferdinand, Prince of Tuscany. He had laid in a heap of different sorts of learning (una grande infarinatura di tutte le scienze), and has an extraordinary fluency of language, but is rather a versifier then a poet. He is so impetuous in improviso-ing that sometimes he will not give way for the guitar ⌜for three or four stanzas together⌝. VANNESCHI *July 1732–April 1733*

For an account of Perfetti's crowning see § 1518. The honour may be judged by the fact that only two earlier poets, Petrarch and Tasso, had been so recognized. Violante Beatrice of Bavaria (1673–1731) survived her husband for eighteen years. The inserted phrase comes from the earliest manuscript, which begins 'They always improviso to music, which hides the breaks, and gives them time'. The French traveller, Charles de Brosses, saw 'le spectacle le plus singulier' of Perfetti improvising at Siena in 1740, and described the poetical performance in great detail (*Lettres historiques et critiques sur l'Italie*, Paris, 1799, ii. 95–97).

1523. There are two tunes chiefly used for improviso-ing: the *Passo Gallo* ⌜like the beginning of 'All joy to Great Caesar'?⌝, and the *Foglia di Siena*. The latter is so called because it is generally made use of in that city, as the other is at Florence. The *Passo Gallo* is more like recitative than the *Foglia*. ⌜'Tis this [the *Passo Gallo*] that they generally sing Tasso to, in the streets, and at Venice, etc. The air to the pastorals [has] something pretty in it.⌝

VANNESCHI *July 1732–April 1733*

The term 'Passo Gallo' is derived from the Spanish 'Passacalle', a formula for singing poetry with instrumental improvisation. The ballad 'All joy to Great Caesar' used as its base that of the well-known tune 'Folia di Spagna'.

1524. The first time I met with the famous Scarpellino, or Stonecutter, of Settignano, he got the better of me in improviso-ing. He has no learning, but is a great reader, and remembers a vast deal of Petrarch and some other of our best poets. When we are hard put to it, we sometimes fling in some of the most difficult rhymes we can think of at the close of a stanza, to get the better of our rival—and the Scarpellino is very notable at that, in particular.

VANNESCHI *July 1732–April 1733*

Settignano is a village about four miles east of Florence, famous for its school of sculptors. The earliest manuscript shows that Spence employed a nickname for it reads 'ye Scarpellino (Stonecutter)'; the modern spelling is 'scalpellino', meaning 'little chisel'.

The man so designated was Domenico Ciottoli, who died in Florence in 1750 at more than seventy years of age. Though he lacked learning he could read and write, was considered a gifted poet, and regarded as an excellent improviser. The fullest account of him is in the obituary written by Giovanni Lami (who had improvised against him) in *Novelle letterarie di Firenze*, xii (1751), cols. 33–35.

1525. Let a man excel as much as he please in anything else, he is not esteemed in Tuscany unless he can write verses. This is the reason of Redi, ⌜Manfredi,⌝ and several others being poets as well as philosophers.

VANNESCHI *July 1732–April 1733*

Manfredi (for whom see §§ 1518 and 1527) is mentioned only in the earliest manuscript. Francesco Redi (1626–98) applied his talents with equal success to medicine, biological research, poetry, and philological studies.

One of the reasons Spence received such a warm welcome from the literary luminaries of Italy is that in addition to being Professor of Poetry at Oxford, he was considered to be a poet. In one of his letters he reported, 'they take me for a poet here'; similarly, in a Latin panegyric written in Spence's praise by some Italian admirer (among the Spence Papers) his poetical achievement is praised in hyperbolic terms.

1526. Redi's dithyrambic of *Bacco in Toscana* is as lively and excellent as his sonnets are low and tasteless.

VANNESCHI *July 1732–April 1733*

The fame of Redi's dithyramb (1685) far exceeded that of his other achievements. It recounts a visit of Bacchus to Tuscany to sample its wines; the god's praises increase in extravagance as his sobriety declines. For Lady Walpole's opinion of Redi see § 1565.

1527. Manfredi of Bologna is a great mathematician and the very best of all our poets.

VANNESCHI *July 1732–April 1733*

For Eustachio Manfredi see §§ 1518 and 1525. The first manuscript has the additional word 'Sonnets', showing that Vanneschi referred to Manfredi's sonnets, which were written in the Petrarchan style, as examples of his excellence.

1528. Muratori, an ecclesiastic of Modena, is one of the most learned men at present in Italy: ⸢Notes to Petrarch, etc.⸣ VANNESCHI *July 1732–April 1733*

Lodovico Antonio Muratori (1672–1750), librarian of the Bibliotheca Ambrosiana at Milan after 1695, became archivist of the Estense Court at Modena in 1700. Now recognized as the founder of modern Italian historiography, Muratori published over fifty volumes of scholarly works, including *Osservazioni* on Petrarch's poems.

1529. Salvini was an odd sort of man, subject to gross absences, and a very great sloven.

VANNESCHI *July 1732–April 1733*

His behaviour in his last hours was as odd as any of his behaviour in all of his lifetime before could have been. Just as he was departing, he cried out in a great passion, 'I will *not* die! I will *not* die, that's flat.' ('Je ne veux pas mourir; absolument!') ⸢CRUDELI⸣

Antonio Mario Salvini, Greek Professor at Florence, died in 1729 only a few years before this conversation occurred. According to his biographer, Camelo Cordero, the last year of Salvini's life found him weak physically and mentally, though this incident is not recorded (*A.M. Salvini*, Piacenza, 1906). For Tommaso Crudeli see headnote before § 1535.

1530. The Count Torquato Montauto of Arezzo, has translated about forty-eight of Ariosto's cantos into Latin verse, and has but two or three more to finish the whole. It is an excellent translation, but 'tis doubted whether he will ever publish it. He is one of the most modest men in the world. VANNESCHI *July 1732–April 1733*

The Marquis Torquato Barbolani (d. 1756) stemmed from the Montauto family; Spence erred in calling him 'Count'. His translation of Ariosto was published at Arezzo the year of his death.

1531. La Fontaine's *Joconde* is all taken from Ariosto, and the part it is taken from is particularly well translated by Count Montauto. VANNESCHI *July 1732–April 1733*

The fable is taken from *Orlando Furioso*, xxviii. 4–74.

1532. Menzini's *Poetic* is very good, and so are his sonnets. In the latter he is a constant imitator of Chiabrera, with more grace but with less of spirit and majesty.

VANNESCHI *July 1732–April 1733*

For Cocchi's opinion of Benedetto Menzini (1646–1704) see § 1489. His pastoral sonnets were published posthumously in his collected works (1730–4) while Spence was in Italy; recent critics consider the sonnets to be Menzini's best work. For the rival schools of Petrarchan simplicity and the Pindaric 'sublimity' of Gabriello Chiabrera (1552–1638) see § 1489.

1533. Menzini in his *Poetics* gives the truest idea of Ariosto's and Tasso's rival pieces of any of our writers.

'The poem of the former,' says he, 'is like a vast palace very richly furnished, but built without the rules of architecture, whereas that of Tasso is like a neat palace, very regular and beautiful.' VANNESCHI *July 1732–April 1733*

⌜[He added that] Ariosto had the greater imagination: 'più creatore' (so they use *creare*, too, for finding the matter for the stanza in improvis[o-]ing).⌝ SPENCE

The passage occurs at the beginning of Book ii of Menzini's *Dell'arte poetica* (Florence, 1688), ll. 13–24. Spence's remarks are in the earliest manuscript only.

1534. Filicaia in his sonnets makes use of many expressions borrowed from the Psalms, and consequently not generally understood among us. A gentleman of Florence, on reading some of the passages in him (which were taken literally from David), cried out, 'Oh, are you there again with your barbarisms!' and flung away the book as not worth his reading. VANNESCHI *July 1732–April 1733*

Vincenzo da Filicaia (1642–1707) is now remembered chiefly for patriotic verses that foreshadowed the unity of Italy. His attempts to elevate his style to match the loftiness of his subjects resulted in sonorous but empty lines.

In place of 'barbarisms' Spence first wrote, 'Oh these are some of your Lombardisms, are they!', with the original French version in the margin, 'Oh ho! ces [*sic*] sont des Lombardismes'.

¶ *Tommaso Crudeli (1703–45), the poet, played an active part in the literary life of Florence. Popular with the English colony, he was in demand to give Italian lessons to English visitors. When a Lodge of Freemasons was established in Florence he apparently served as secretary; action was taken to suppress the Lodge in 1739, and Crudeli was imprisoned by the Inquisition. This situation prompted the Grand Lodge in London to send a gift of money for his benefit. Crudeli was later banished to the village of his birth; his poems were not published until 1746, the year after his death (F. Sbigoli,* Tommaso Crudeli, e i primi Framassoni in Firenze, *Milan, 1884).*

1535. Camillo Querno was sometimes a dealer in monkish verse. When he was at Leo X's table one day, some time after dinner, that Pope said to him, 'How comes it about, Querno, that Bacchus, who was the old inspirer of poets, cannot inspire you?' Querno immediately answered him in the following couplet:

In cratere meo Thetis est conjuncta Lyæo:
Est Dea juncta Deo; sed Dea major eo.

CRUDELI *July 1732–April 1733*

Camillo Querno (1470–*c.*1528) displayed prodigious ability in turning out Latin verse, as well as having a personality that caused him to be accepted as a sort of buffoon laureate to Pope Leo X. Spence possibly knew about him from one of Alexander Pope's papers in the *Grub Street Journal* that appeared 19 November 1730, about a month before Spence and Lord Middlesex left England. This paper described the mock ceremony in some detail, and how Querno was crowned with ivy, bay, and cabbage leaves, an event that Pope had earlier mentioned in the *Dunciad* (1728), ii. 11–12,

Rome in her Capitol saw Querno sit,
Thron'd on sev'n hills, the Antichrist of Wit!

The incident related here by Crudeli involves Leo X's ruling that Querno should supply verses extemporaneously on any subject proposed at table, and if the lines were judged unsatisfactory, water was to be poured into Querno's wine cup. The couplet made on this occasion may be translated as follows,

'In my cup Thetis [a water goddess] is joined with Bacchus;
A goddess joined with a god, true;
But she more esteemed as a goddess than he as a god.'

1536. The octave [ottava rima] was first well used by Politian. All the eight verses are equal—of eleven syllables each; the same alternate rhyme in the six first verses, and an immediate rhyme in the two last.

Tasso's are sung much all over Lombardy, and particularly at Venice. The common tune to which they sing them is called *il passo gallo*, and sounds something like church music.

CRUDELI *July 1732–April 1733*

When we were at Venice, there was a common gondolier that could repeat all Tasso's *Gerusalemme Liberata* in this manner. Dip where you pleased, and show him the top of the page, and he'd sing three or four stanzas on immediately. SPENCE

Politian (Angelo Poliziano, 1454–94) employed the octave form in his incomplete 'Stanze per la giostra', written between 1475 and 1478, but not published until the year of his death. For the 'Passo Gallo' see § 1523. Spence visited Venice in January and February 1732, with Lord Middlesex, and again in 1741 when he and Lord Lincoln were joined by Horace Walpole.

1537. The last syllable but one in the octave verses is always long, except in the verses which they call *sdruccioli* (or verses that slide on). These end with a dactyl instead of a spondee, and are of twelve syllables, as the others are of eleven. This affects the whole stanza, for if there's one verse of this kind in it, they must be all so. These were used by Politian sometimes, but are now quite out of fashion.

CRUDELI *July 1732–April 1733*

1538. Ariosto's story of Orlando begins just where Boiardo's leaves off. CRUDELI *July 1732–April 1733*

Ariosto's poem begins approximately where Boiardo's ends, at the point when Orlando comes to join King Charles's forces near the Pyrenees to fight the Moors. See § 1483.

1539. Il pover uomo, che non se n'era accorto,
Andava combattendo, ed era morto . . .

is a couplet of Berni's in his burlesque of Boiardo's poem. He laid that poem before him, generally used his very lines, and only changed some of them to make the ridicule appear the stronger. CRUDELI *July 1732–April 1733*

This couplet is analysed at length as an example of Berni's attitude by Andrea Sorrentino in his *Francesco Berni*, Florence, 1933, pp. 189–90. It had earlier been picked out for criticism by Dominique Bouhours (1628–1702) who, however, falsely attributed it to Ariosto in *La maniere de bien penser dans les ouvrages d'esprit* (1687; 1709 ed., p. 10).

1540. The gentlemen of the Academy della Crusca study words more than things, and therefore the definitions in their dictionary are often extremely absurd.

CRUDELI *July 1732–April 1733*

The Accademia della Crusca, founded in the mid-sixteenth century, published its important *Vocabolario* in 1612. In 1729 a new six-volume edition (the fourth) began to appear; the second volume reached the public in 1731 and the third in 1733. Undoubtedly this new edition prompted Crudeli's comment.

1541. Operas were at first set on foot by a set of gentlemen who acted not for money, but for their own diversion. There were about thirty of them.

When they first came to be acted for money, there was one of the actresses who had a hundred and twenty crowns for acting one season. This was then looked upon as such a vast reward for a singer that she got the name of *La Cento-Venti* by it. CRUDELI *July 1732–April 1733*

This group of Florentines assembled at the house of Count di Vernio in Florence late in the sixteenth century, and histories of opera refer them as 'the Vernio group'. Public performances followed in the early seventeenth century; the opera theatre in Venice, for example, was founded in the early 1640's.

The singer called 'La Cento-Venti' (at the height of her popularity about 1674) seems to have paid for her large fee by losing her real name. She is mentioned by Algarotti in his *Essay on the Opera* (1767, p. 15), and in modern works, but not identified.

1542. Metastasio [is] the best for operas.

VANNESCHI *July 1732–April 1733*

I have heard him disapprove that way of writing, but ⸢shrugs up his shoulders and says⸣ 'one must get money'.

CRUDELI (who says he is the best, too)

Metastasio had recently become court poet at Vienna, and his financial success there caused much comment in Italy (see Cocchi's remarks § 1491).

1543. Gravina wore the *petit collet*, and was as great a free-thinker as any of them. When he died all his papers were secured by the Emperor's ambassador at Rome. Among other things, there were notes of his upon the Bible which, considering his character, would be curious enough to see.

He was no poet, and his five tragedies are very indifferent things. The criticisms in his *Ragion Poetica* are often false.

CRUDELI *July 1732–April 1733*

Gian Vincenzo Gravina (1664–1718) published five tragedies in 1712, which show a frigid classicism. His literary fame rises chiefly from his critical work, *Della ragion poetica* (2 vols., 1708), in which he endeavoured to free poetry from fixed rules. In 1691 he had become involved in quarrels between the Jesuits and the Jansenists but his printed works do not show him a 'free-thinker'. Joseph Warton somewhere picked up the story that Gravina 'missed a cardinal's hat because of his satyrical and severe turn of mind. When he was at Rome, he used to bow to coach horses, because, said he, was it not for these poor beasts, these great people would have men, and even philosophers, to draw their coaches' (*Essay*, i. 387–8).

1544. What the monk said of Virgil['s *Aeneid*] 'that it would make an excellent poem if it were only put into rhyme', is just as if a Frenchman should say of a beauty, 'Oh, what a fine woman that would be, if she was but painted!'

CRUDELI *July 1732–April 1733*

The monk is probably a fictional device. Spence, like most other Englishmen, found the heavy cosmetics applied by French ladies of fashion distasteful. He reported, they 'lay on the Red so unmercifully; that . . . they look like a bed of old overblown Piony's' (B.M. Egerton MS. 2234, f. 85).

1545. Marchetti's translation of Lucretius in blank verse is the best translation in our language. *Le Sette Giornate*, or Creation, of Tasso is in blank verse too, and is much esteemed by the best judges—but not generally read, because without rhyme.

CRUDELI *July 1732–April 1733*

Alessandro Marchetti (1633–1714) taught mathematics and philosophy at Pisa. His original poetry is undistinguished, but he produced a good translation of Anacreon (1707) and a very fine translation of Lucretius (1717). Tasso's *Le sette giornate del mondo creato*, composed 1592–4, reveals the decline of his poetical powers in old age.

1546. The author of the *Circulus Pisanus* is very strong for the modern system of the earth's moving round the sun, and says in that work that the world would certainly come into it hereafter, and all unanimously cry out, 'V.G.'—by which he meant, 'Vicisti, Galilæe!'

The inquisitors did not understand the passage, took it for 'Verbi gratia', and so let it pass.

CRUDELI *July 1732–April 1733*

Claude Guillermet, Seigneur de Beauregard (1591–1664), French physician, became a teacher at the University of Pisa. The name *Circulus Pisanus* refers to a discussion group held at the University; from which Beauregard derived a book with this title published in 1643.

'Vicisti Galilæe' is the type of Latin pun relished in the eighteenth century: the phrase echoed the legendary last words of Julian the Apostate, referring to Christ (the Galilean).

1547. Read books of D[ivinity] till fifteen. Then Euclid set him to reasoning. Began to ask questions, so his c[onfesso]r forbid him to read the N[ew] T[estament]. Some say the latter was stolen chiefly from the works of Pl[ato] by some of the learned (such as Philo) at Alexandria, but it hardly seems w[orthy] of such an origin. There are a great many good things in it, but it's too much clogged with improb[abilities]. [CRUDELI] *July 1732–April 1733*

This seems to be an autobiographical revelation by Crudeli who cast a sceptical eye at dogma, was an active Freemason and was later persecuted by the Inquisition.

¶ *The following group of anecdotes preserves the conversation of one of the most notorious personalities of the age of* Connoisseurs and Secret Agents, *described by Leslie Lewis in a book of that title published in 1961. Baron Philip von Stosch (1691–1757) established himself in Rome about 1722 as an art expert and collector of gems, virtù, rare books, and manuscripts. The British Foreign Office hired him to spy on the Pretender and his court, which produced a series of weekly reports, signed 'John Walton'; they fill sixteen folio volumes in the Public Record Office. However, a threat against the Baron's life in January 1731 drove him out of the papal dominions, and he spent the rest of his life in Florence. Horace Walpole detested him, calling Stosch 'a man of a most infamous character in every respect'* (Corresp., *xvii. 164*), *and Dr. Cocchi recorded in his* Effemeridi *on 21 September 1739, 'Stosch is a really vicious man'. To avoid his company the Florentine Lodge of Freemasons shifted their sessions from Thursday to Saturday, when Stosch found it inconvenient to be present (J. H. Lepper,* The Earl of Middlesex and the English Lodge in Florence, *privately printed, London, 1945, p. 12). There was no denying, however, his expert knowledge of virtù, especially engraved gems, which is demonstrated by Winckelmann's report,* Descriptions des pierres gravées du feu baron de Stosch, *Florence, 1760.*

1548. Signor Recanati, a nobleman of Venice, has the best collection of the Provençal poets of anyone. When the Duke of Mantua's library was sold, Maffei got all the Greek books, and Stosch and Recanati bought all the rest. Recanati had all the Provençal manuscripts, and Stosch all the antiquity and historic. STOSCH *July 1732–April 1733*

The sale occurred in Venice after the death in 1708 of Ferdinand Charles IV, Duke of Mantua. Giovan Battista Recanati (1687–1734) left at his death a rich collection of books and 200 codices, willing them to the Republic of Venice. The rulers of the state promptly sold them in 1735, but a large number were reassembled by the Abbé Canonici (d. 1806) and were purchased, along with the rest of his collection, by the Bodleian in 1817. A list of the Provençal manuscripts may be found in an article on the French manuscripts in the library of the Duke of Mantua, written by M. Braghirolli, P. Meyer, and G. Paris in *Romania*, ix (1880), 497–514.

Stosch's library totalled over six thousand printed books and two thousand manuscripts in Greek and Latin. After his death they were sold at auction; the catalogue, *Bibliotheca Stoschiana* . . . (1758), lists most of the rarities.

1549. Crescimbeni was continually inquiring for twenty-eight years together into the subject he has written upon (his history of the Italian poetry), and was much the chief man in Italy for that sort of knowledge. His being a member of the Arcadi, and being acquainted with all the poets in Italy of his time, must have given him great lights for all the latter part of it. He had at first a very huddled method, but that is in a great measure remedied by the edition at Venice in 1730. STOSCH *July 1732–April 1733*

Giovanni Mario Crescimbeni (1663–1728) was one of the founders at Rome in 1690 of the Accademia dell'Arcadia, whose purpose was to restore Italian poetry to its earlier purity by ridding it of the affectations of the Baroque style. He served as secretary to the organization until his death.

Crescimbeni's *Istoria della volgar poesia* first appeared in 1698, but a much revised edition was published in 1730, shortly before this conversation.

1550. There is a book of immense erudition which is almost unknown. It is called *La Crusca Provenzale e Catalana*, in two volumes, in folio. It was written by a Spanish Abbé at Rome, and he proves in it that the Tuscan is absolutely derived from the old Catalan language. He left Rome soon after his publishing it, and carried almost all the copies with him into Catalonia. STOSCH *July 1732–April 1733*

This 'Etymological Dictionary', as the first manuscript calls it, carries the title *La Crusca provenzale ovvero voci, frasi, forme e maniere di dire, che la gentilissima e celebre lingua toscana he preso dalla provenzale*... (Roma), 1724. The author was Antonio de Bastero y Lledó (*c.* 1675–1737), who had lived in Rome since 1709. He intended to publish other volumes, but this folio is the only one to reach print. The book is rare, but copies are preserved in the British Museum, the Bibliothèque Nationale, the Vatican Library, and elsewhere.

Bastero returned to Barcelona in 1724 carrying with him twenty-four volumes in manuscript, which were preserved into the nineteenth century, when some of them disappeared.

1551. I wonder how they came not to find out printing sooner. STOSCH *July 1732–April 1733*

We had been just speaking of the old emperors of Rome impressing their whole names at once on their grants and letters, and this was so common that the very shepherds impressed theirs on their sheep and cattle. This was a sort of printing, and it was as easy to impress a whole line as two words, and a page as a whole line. Had they gone but these two easy steps farther, it would have been just what the Chinese printing is now. SPENCE

In the Folio manuscript Spence originally attributed the whole conversation to Stosch, but later inserted the name after the first sentence. Then, when preparing Holdsworth's *Remarks on Virgil* (1768) for the press, Spence inserted the passage among his own contributions to the volume (p. 70). As illustrative quotations Spence also placed in the margin Virgil's *Georgics*, i. 263, and Calphurnius's *Eclogues*, v. 82–85.

1552. ⌜Alexander's [was] the great age for Greek statues.⌝ The Greek statues are nine faces [tall] and the Roman eight. STOSCH *July 1732–April 1733*

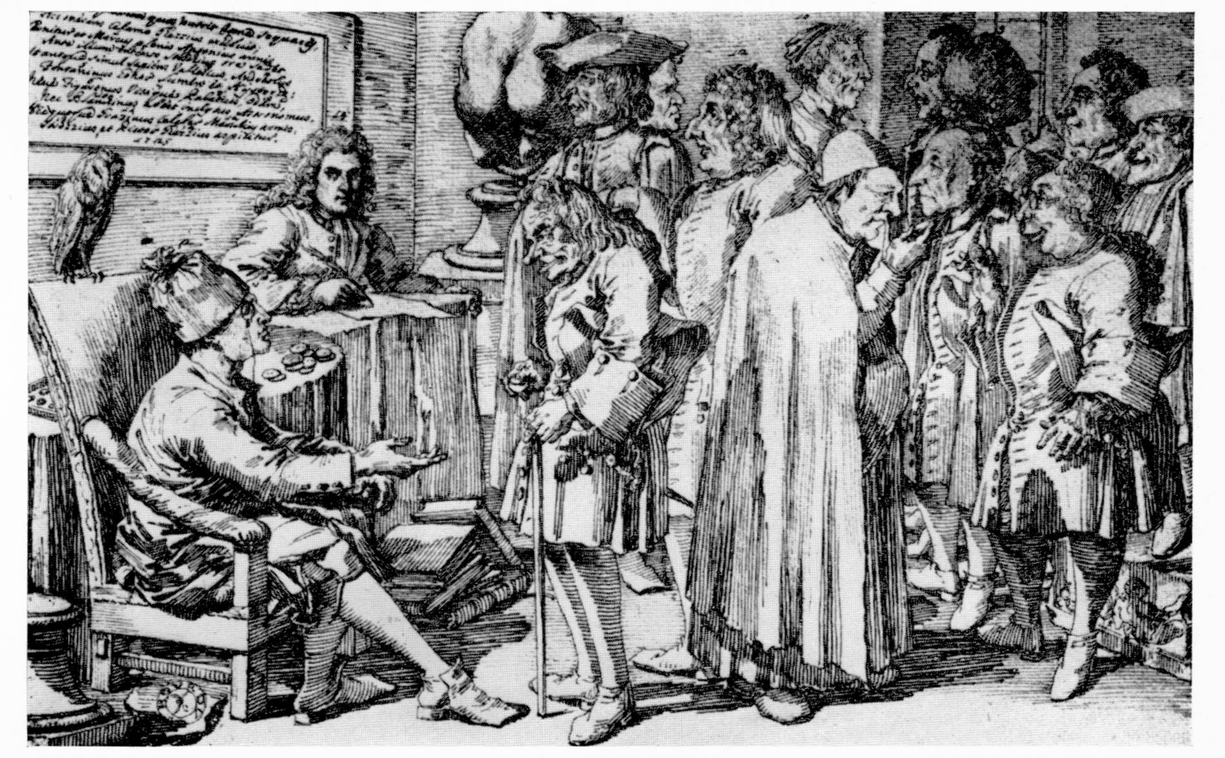

Baron Philip von Stosch receiving the antiquaries of Rome, including the Abbé Ficoroni
Drawing by the Chevalier P. L. Ghezzi
The Albertina, Vienna

At this time knowledge of Greek statues derived from the detached pieces found in Italy. Later in the century travellers to Greece brought word of the Periclean style; once the Elgin Marbles reached London the shift in taste became complete.

1553. The famous Arrotino (or Whetter) is in just the same attitude as the attendant at the feet of Apollo, in a gem which represents that god punishing Marsyas.

STOSCH *1740*

It might be well worthwhile to inquire where that fine statue was found, and to search for the rest of the figures: for if this will hold, 'tis probable that it was not alone.

SPENCE

This statue is, and was in Spence's time, in the Tribuna at the Uffizi Gallery in Florence (cf. J. Richardson, *Statues and Pictures in Italy*, p. 57, where it is called the 'Grinder'). Like the near-by Venus de' Medici it was found in Hadrian's Villa in 1680, acquired by Cardinal Ferdinand de' Medici, and brought to Florence in 1717. The figure was originally part of a group, but the Apollo has not been found. The gem showing Apollo punishing Marsyas is reproduced in Spence's *Polymetis*, plate xiii, fig. 3.

1554. The good taste for medals continued from Augustus's time to Hadrian's; that for building to Septimius Severus.

STOSCH (*the author of the* Gemma Liberata, *residing at Florence*) *and* FICORONI *July 1732–April 1733*

The first manuscript shows that Stosch was quoted on medals, on which subject he was an acknowledged authority, and that Ficoroni was the source for the remark on architecture. For Bianchi's similar opinion on medals see §1574.

1555. [Good taste] in sculpture [went] farther: a great many very good of Hadrian's time: busts of Caracalla and Plautilla, one so soft and the other so strong, and both so good. Nothing in any degree approaching them after?

?STOSCH *July 1732–April 1733*

The identity of the author of these remarks is uncertain, but it may have been Baron Stosch.

These statues stood in 'a yard of the house by the Dome' in Florence, according to Jonathan Richardson, who commented on the Caracalla—'this Bust is the same as that of [the Villa] *Farnese* . . . but the Nose in this is longer'

(*Statues and Pictures in Italy*, pp. 50–51). The bust of Plautilla Richardson described as being 'very young, and a natural pretty Air: This is not common in the Antique' (ibid., p. 52). Spence repeated this contrast between the strength of the Caracalla and the softness of his empress, Plautilla, in a letter to Henry Rolle (B.M. Egerton MS. 2234, ff. 292–3).

¶ *The final series of Florentine conversations record the talk of the notorious Margaret Rolle (1709–81), Lady Walpole. In 1724, at the age of fifteen, she had married Robert, Baron Walpole (elder brother of Horace), but ten years later she scandalized society by running away to the Continent with Samuel Sturgis (1701–43), Fellow of King's College, Cambridge. They were living in Florence when Spence and Lord Lincoln arrived there in October 1740. The accounts of Lady Mary Wortley Montagu and others agree that she was attractive and interesting company, yet her house was avoided by ladies of reputation, not because of her amorous intrigues but because Lady Walpole surrounded herself with free-thinkers.*

Spence reported in a letter to his mother, dated 29 October 1740, 'I was this morning with Lady Walpole (with whom I am a sort of favourite, as being a very great philosopher)' (B.M. Egerton MS. 2234, f. 222). Thus her conversations show that she aspired to pass as a 'blue stocking'.

1556. The chief aim of any young nobleman on his travels should be to make a man of sense his friend, as his great care should be not to be pleased with agreeable fools.

LADY WALPOLE *October–November 1740*

Clearly Lady Walpole knew how to flatter Spence. Since the Folio manuscript was transcribed after 1745 when Lady Walpole had become the Countess of Orford, Spence so designated her in the Folio version of these conversations. Singer erred in crediting them to 'Lady Oxford'.

1557. I should rather think that the wise are happier than the fools, but indeed, that must be all according to the circumstances each fall under. A man of sense feels things stronger than the fool, and consequently in the same good circumstances must be happier, and in the same bad circumstances more unhappy.

LADY WALPOLE *October–November 1740*

1558. One of the chief things I wonder at is that a person who has courage enough to do an out-of-the-way thing, should be coward enough to be ashamed of it after 'tis done. LADY WALPOLE *October–November 1740*

This observation would appear to have autobiographical implications.

1559. I wonder how anybody can find any pleasure in reading the books which are ⌜Lady Mary's⌝ chief favourites! (romances and novels). There's no imitation of nature in the characters, and without that how is it possible for anything to please?

Even the Princess of Cleves is monstrous and unnatural in loving another while she loves her husband, and not taking that other after her husband is dead. Her friendship for her husband (if one must call it by that strange name) need not have interfered at all with her making herself happy after he was gone. LADY WALPOLE *October–November 1740*

Lady Mary Wortley Montagu had left Florence for Rome on 16 October 1740, a week before Spence and Lord Lincoln arrived there. Hence she was a subject of curiosity to Spence who did not meet her until he and Lord Lincoln reached Rome at the turn of the year. *La Princesse de Clèves* is, of course, Mme Lafayette's famous romance, first published in 1678.

The phrase 'friendship for her husband' has personal overtones in the case of Lady Walpole. According to her brother-in-law, she 'made it a point after her son was born, not to let her husband lie with her; and at last stipulated for only twice a week' (Walpole *Corresp.*, xix. 203).

1560. 'Has your Ladyship Lady Mary's copy of verses on her lover?' [asked Spence].

Oh, I have not got that! for 'tis so different in every article from the lover I should choose that I don't care even to read it. LADY WALPOLE *October–November 1740*

These verses entitled 'The Lover: a Ballad' were addressed to Richard Chandler (d. 1769), son of the 'rich' Bishop of Durham. They began,

At length by so much importunity press'd,
Take (Chandler) at once the inside of my breast.

For other details see Walpole *Corresp.*, xiv. 245.

1561. That happiness you mention of England as an island does not so much consist in the difficulty of an invasion from a foreign power, as in the difficulty which our own people have of flinging themselves into other hands.

LADY WALPOLE *October–November 1740*

1562. The court of Rome has more or less power in all the states of Italy. 'Tis their interest that the people should be kept in ignorance. Knowledge is therefore more or less discouraged in all the states of Italy, and if any person shows a particular eagerness for it, they either drive him away, or at least oblige him to hold his tongue. ⌜There's no impunity for sense in this country.⌝ When one considers how far this is carried in most parts of Italy, one would rather wonder that there should be so much knowledge left than that it should be so much fallen among them.

LADY WALPOLE *October–November 1740*

The power of the Court of Rome varied greatly from place to place. The weight of the Inquisition fell heavily upon both the native independent thinkers, such as Crudeli (headnote before §1535) and visitors from northern Europe. Because Lady Walpole made her household a centre for free-thinkers she was particularly aware of the contrary climate of mind in the papal dominions.

1563. Yes, they do well enough hitherto. They are but young kings and scarce know that they are kings yet, but let them alone a little and I'm afraid you will find them as bad as the rest in some time.

LADY WALPOLE *October–November 1740*

We had been speaking of the King of Prussia and the present Pope, Benedict XIV. SPENCE

Frederick had succeeded to the Prussian throne on 31 May 1740; he soon became known as a liberal thinker and Freemason, and, as the ultimate in enlightenment, a monarch who repudiated Christianity. Benedict XIV was elected on 17 August 1740, after a conclave which lasted for several months. Lady Walpole was right in predicting a difference of degree rather than kind.

1564. Yes, he has some warmth at first, but he grows dull and falls asleep too soon.

LADY WALPOLE (*speaking of Petrarch's sonnets to Laura*)
October–November 1740

1565. Redi is the very best Italian writer that they have had of late. LADY WALPOLE *October–November 1740*

For Redi see § 1526.

1566. The three first books in Giannone's history were not writ by himself, and the rest, that were, are but indifferent.
LADY WALPOLE *October–November 1740*

The book in question is *L'Istoria civile del regno di Napoli* (4 vols., 1723) written (definitely) by Pietro Giannone (1676–1748). Because the book described the history of the Roman Church at its lowest state of corruption, a papal bull was issued, denouncing it and prohibiting people from reading it. In 1736 Giannone was seized and put in prison, where he died twelve years later.

1566a. *Don Quixote* is good because 'tis natural, though 'tis such odd nature.
LADY WALPOLE *October–November 1740*

1567. The best talkers among the ladies at Naples pique themselves on talking in Boccaccio's 'novelle' style.
LADY WALPOLE *October–November 1740*

The new freedom for women allowed them to be slightly risquée, provided they were so within a literary frame of reference.

1568. As you are to go through Germany, I should think 'tis very happy that you don't understand the German language, for by what I have seen of that people 'tis much better not to know what they say than to know it.
LADY WALPOLE *October–November 1740*

English travellers were alarmed by reports that the Spanish, with whom they had been at war since October 1739, planned to invade Italy. Many of them, therefore, chose to return through Germany rather than risk the route through France. In the Folio manuscript this anecdote has been inked out with heavy strokes of the pen; possibly Spence feared that it might be misinterpreted as a slur on the Hanoverian royal family.

¶ *Grouped together below are conversations with various people, English and Italian, whom Spence met in Florence between 1732 and 1733. Apart from those of Sebastian Bianchi (§§1571–9), the anecdotes consist of scattered observations.*

569. Our painter Aikman, after he had been in Greece and returned to the Florentine gallery, told Bianchi that 'the Venus of Medici had the true Grecian face'.

F. BIANCHI *July 1732–April 1733*

Mr. Shaw and his friend of a very different opinion.

SPENCE

William Aikman (1682–1731), an able Scottish portrait painter, spent three years in Rome before travelling to Turkey, visiting Constantinople and Smyrna. There is no evidence that he visited Athens or the Greek mainland. For Thomas Shaw, African traveller and, later, Principal of St. Edmund Hall and Regius Professor of Greek at Oxford, see §§ 947 and 1582; apparently he penetrated no nearer to Greece than the Holy Land.

The speaker seems to have been Francesco Bianchi (1670–1752), brother of Sebastian, who served as guide to Spence on his visits to the Grand Duke's Gallery.

1570. Caligula used to powder his hair with gold dust; we have Suetonius' authority for it. L. Verus used the same both for his head of hair and beard. Hadrian is the first bearded emperor, and he brought up the fashion to hide the wound he had received in his face.

F. BIANCHI *July 1732–April 1733*

Caligula, who was almost bald, powdered his beard with gold dust, not his hair (Suetonius, *G. Caligula*, ch. lii). Lucius Verus dyed his hair and sprinkled it with gold dust (Aeli Lampridii, 'Commodus Antoninus', *Scriptores Historiae Augustae*, xvii, 3). According to his recent biographer, Hadrian 'first set the example of wearing a beard, which he kept always carefully trimmed' (B. W. Henderson, *Life and Principate of Emperor Hadrian*, 1923, p. 265).

¶ *The next nine anecdotes pose a problem in dating. They are taken from conversations with Sebastian Bianchi (1662–1738), Keeper of the Grand Duke's collection of gems and medals, who served as cicerone to Spence and Lord Lincoln on their visits to the Grand Duke's Gallery during their long stay in Florence from July 1732 to April 1733. However, in the Folio manuscript (the earliest to have them) they occur in Century VII among other conversations late in 1740, two years after Sebastian's death.*

It seems clear that Spence made a mistake, and that the proper date is 1732–3. The most likely explanation is that Spence had a 'loose paper' containing these conversations. Years later, when he compiled the Folio manuscript, he had forgotten the date and so inserted them in the 1740 section from Florence. The fact that they occur at the end of the Florentine section and just before the account of Lady Mary in Rome, supports this conjecture. Accordingly, the dates have been changed to 1732–3.

1571. The heads of Romans are without beards all the time between the elder Brutus and Hadrian, unless a head of Nero and of two or three before him, who had let them grow on some melancholy occasion or other.

SEBASTIAN BIANCHI *July 1732–April 1733*

Presumably Bianchi made this observation while showing Spence the busts of Roman emperors in the Uffizi Gallery. They now stand in the foyer corridor.

1572. Pescennius is the first emperor's head that is wanting in the gallery. There are several wanting after him, and that which they call by the name of Albinus (his successor) is misnamed.

SEBASTIAN BIANCHI *and* STOSCH *July 1732–April 1733*

A mark in the Folio text shows that Stosch was responsible for the suggestion (a note which Spence apparently added after his 1740 visit to Florence) that the bust called Albinus was erroneously designated. The 1790 *Description de la Galerie royale* named it as a bust of Albinus (p. 66); today it is labelled 'Unknown Roman. Formerly called Claudius Albinus' (Cat. No. 215).

At the end of the eighteenth century one of the busts was considered to represent Pescennius. It was listed as '*Pescennius* niger' in the *Description de la Galerie royale* (1790, p. 66).

1573. There are a very fine Caracalla, and a very fine Plautilla in the Great Duke's collection of gems, and three or four very wretched ones before them. After their time, the art fell in general, though you have now and then a tolerable head after them.

SEBASTIAN BIANCHI *July 1732–April 1733*

Bianchi spoke with the authority of the curator of the Medici collection of gems. The collection is now in the Pitti Palace, though Bianchi's manuscript catalogue remains at the Uffizi.

1574. In the gold medals here, the taste ends with Pertinax, though there are some pretty good of Caracalla, and particularly one with Severus's arch for the reverse.

SEBASTIAN BIANCHI *July 1732–April 1733*

Since Pertinax was assassinated a few months after he was chosen emperor against his will in A.D. 193, Bianchi's date is adequately specific. Baron Stosch placed the termination of 'good taste in medals' about fifty years earlier (§ 1554).

1575. In the Great Duke's collection of medals there are twelve of Antoninus Pius, each with a sign of the zodiac for the reverse, and eight with as many different labours of Hercules. SEBASTIAN BIANCHI *July 1732–April 1733*

In Spence's *Polymetis* two of the illustrations of the labours of Hercules are taken from gems in the Great Duke's collection at Florence (plate xviii, figs. 1 and 2). He discussed the Zodiac at length in Dialogue xi, illustrated by plates xxiv–xxv.

In the Folio manuscript Spence added a marginal note listing the eight labours of Hercules: 'That of the Lyon; Diomedes's horses; the Centaur; Antaeus; Cerberus; the Bull; Augeas's Stables; and the Hesperides.'

1576. The Bacchus that holds a mask in his right hand, and leans on a boy that is going to steal some of his grapes, with something both of drunkenness and lust in his face, has its head joined on, and is disputable enough.

SEBASTIAN BIANCHI *July 1732–April 1733*

This statue now carries the description: 'Bacchus—replica of a Pompeian bronze, of Hellenistic origin, restored by G. Ceccini (1562–1612).'

1577. 'Is not the pleasure in the face of that very pretty Bacchus, who holds up a cantharus in his left hand and regards it so fondly, too violently expressed for the ancient manner?' [asked Spence].

'Tis modern, and was made by Sansovino.

SEBASTIAN BIANCHI *July 1732–April 1733*

This statue is now in the Bargello in Florence. It is one of the earliest and most famous works of Jacopo d'Antonio Tatti, called Sansovino (1486–1570).

1578. The lyre, in the hand of that Apollo so much adorned with tortoise-shell, and resting on a column of fine marble of different colours, is modern, and so is the odd plectrum which Apollo holds in his other hand.

SEBASTIAN BIANCHI *July 1732–April 1733*

Spence mentioned this statue in *Polymetis* (p. 107, n. 134), saying it stood 'in the open part of the Great Duke's gallery'.

1579. In the chamber of painters' heads drawn by themselves, out of 240 there are but five from England, and not any one of these properly an Englishman. Kneller's is of a larger size, set up above all the rest, and is full of his usual vanity: he has inserted his gold chain, diamond ring, and his house at Twickenham. We don't much like it, and I believe it will soon be removed quite out of the room. We have no head of Correggio's, out of his modesty, nor of Carlo Maratta's, for the reason just contrary.

SEBASTIAN BIANCHI *July 1732–April 1733*

Besides the self portrait of Sir Godfrey Kneller (a German) the others were Sir Peter Lely, a Hollander, and two Scots, Thomas Murray and William Aikman. The fifth from England has not been identified.

No authentic picture of Correggio is known. The Uffizi subsequently acquired a self-portrait of Maratta, for it is listed in the *Description de la Galerie royale* (1790, p. 266); its present number is 1686. Spence added a marginal note: 'He call'd him [Correggio] Uomo buono (modest he explain'd by Modesto) & added, non aveva il malo Francese (by wch he meant Forwardness.)' The last phrase raises a question whether Spence's knowledge of Italian was not fairly literal; most eighteenth-century Italians would have considered it a reference to syphilis.

1580. Etruria anciently had two kings: the seat of one of them was at Caere, or Cerveteri, and of the other at Coritum, or Cortona.

There were twelve chief cities in Etruria, the deputies from each of which met to elect these kings. Their establishment had an air of freedom.

CAVALIER VENUTI (*a nobleman of Cortona*) *1733*

Although there were three Venuti brothers, all eminent antiquaries (Niccolò, 1700–55; Rodolfino, 1705–63; Filippo, 1709–69), it is likely that

Spence knew Niccolò. As the eldest son, later to become a marquis, Niccolò from childhood was styled 'Cavaliere'. Moreover, the only reference to Spence in Dr. Cocchi's unpublished 'Effemeridi' (that for Tuesday, 16 September 1732) couples him with 'Cav^r Venuti'. He is frequently designated by his second name, Marcello.

The three Venuti brothers were active in founding the Etruscan Academy of Cortona in December 1726. The pre-Roman history of this area is shrouded in legend, with such traditions as the twelve-city confederation probably being connected with the Panhellenic precedent (R. Bloch, *Les Étrusques*, Paris, 1954, p. 67).

1581. In Aeneas's time, Mezentius was the king at Caere, and Tarchon at Cortona. Hence, Silius Italicus, under the names of these two cities, seems to comprehend all Etruria:

> Lectos Caere viros; lectos Cortona superbi
> Tarchontis domus . . .

where, by the way, 'superbus' seems to be used in a good sense (as it often is in the Latin and several of the languages derived from it) because Tarchon assisted in helping Aeneas to the throne, and consequently toward the establishment of the Caesars. This alliance of Aeneas and Tarchon is pointed out by Virgil so early as in the third book of the *Aeneid*, where his *great gods* tell him, that Crete is not the place he is to fix at—no, he is to go on for Italy, and Cortona.

?CAVALIER VENUTI *1733*

The manuscripts do not identify the speaker, but subject-matter and propinquity suggest that Spence is quoting the Cavalier Venuti. Here again the subject deals with legendary matters. The quotation is from Silius Italicus's *Punica*, Book viii, ll. 472–3. As examples of 'superbus', Spence's marginal notes cite the *Aeneid* (i. 21) and *Punica* (x. 573). For the last sentence Spence quotes the *Aeneid* (iii. 171).

1582. The attitude in which Virgil describes Iarbas[1] (the then king of Mauritania) praying, is used in the same country and other parts of Africa to this day.

DR. SHAW *1733*

This seems to have been the general attitude of the ancients when they prayed. Virgil in another place[2] mentions it of his hero, who was an Asiatic, and Horace speaks of it in general, as the Roman or European mode.[3] SPENCE

[1] *Aeneid*, iv. 204–5 [Spence's note]
[2] *Aeneid*, i. 93 [Spence's note]
[3] *Odes*, III. xxiii. 1 [Spence's note]

For Shaw, whom Spence saw in Florence in November 1732 and January 1733, see §§ 947 and 1517. Spence used the substance of this conversation in *Polymetis*, p. 188, n. 49, about the Genius of the city of Rome: 'She holds the palm of her hand open, towards heaven. This was an attitude used by the Romans of old, when they prayed; and is used among the Africans, to this day. There are several passages, in the old Roman writers, relating to this; but it may be sufficient to quote two or three only, from Virgil' (he refers to *Aeneid*, i. 93; ii. 688, 406).

1583. Beasts machines because so extremely subjected to man.

BOWMAN (*the only reason why a friend of his believes so*)
spring 1732–April 1733

Walter Bowman (d. 1782), the Scottish traveller and antiquary, made these remarks in Florence, where he, like Spence, was travelling as tutor to a young nobleman, the eldest son of the first Marquis of Hertford. For the controversy on bêtes-machines, arising from Descartes, see § 269.

1584. Society for Belles Lettres: [it should have] none but effective members. BOWMAN *spring 1732–April 1733*

Literary academies flowered profusely in Italy, where this conversation occurred, but did not take root in England until several generations later.

1585. Fr[ench] Pol[ity became a] gr[ea]t Mon[archy under] Louis XI, and established by Louis XIV.

BOWMAN *spring 1732–April 1733*

These jottings are so abbreviated that this expansion is rank guesswork: see textual note.

¶ *The scene now shifts to Turin, where Spence and Lord Lincoln spent almost a year while the young man attended the military academy to learn to ride, to fence, and to dance. The first group of conversations convey the comments of Dom Villa, described as archivist of the Royal Academy in Turin. Records at Turin do not identify him; possibly he was a Benedictine or Carthusian since the appellation 'Dom' is in common use among them. Spence and Lora Lincoln lived in the Academy buildings so that contact with Dom Villa was a daily affair.*

1586. Turin of old had been very large: it was destroyed in the beginning of the fifth century, and was soon after rebuilt, but upon a very little scale. Its form was square, and one may still trace the walls.

It has been much increased of late. 'Twas let out toward the Porta Nuova by Charles Emanuel I, toward the Porta del Po by Emanuel II, and toward the Porta Susina by Victor.

'Tis on the scheme of the last that it is (or at least will be) one of the prettiest and most regular cities in Europe. Most of the streets are laid out in direct lines, and they are all designed to be brought to the same—which will yet cost above a million sterling before 'tis completed. They are now carrying on this scheme very briskly in the Strada della Dora Grossa, and anyone who builds in any other of the irregular streets is obliged to build according to the line that is to be, not to break in upon the universal regularity which is designed hereafter. DOM VILLA *1740*

Turin was famous in the eighteenth century as a city planned on a rational design. Thus, after the Lisbon earthquake, the city was rebuilt using Turin as a model. A footnote explains where the ancient walls formerly ran:

'One angle was very near the subtendent of the Bastion Verde, and run on in a line with the king's palace and through the college of the nobles to the farther side of the Strada Teresa. The second wall went straight along with the farther side of the street and a little way into the citadel. The third, from thence to the Madonna della Consolà, and the fourth from the Consolà to the angle by the Bastion Verde. D V.'

This information also occurs in Spence's Travel Notes with a few unimportant verbal variants, and the following additional details: 'Turin is, at present, scarce three mile round. . . . The Strada del Po is the best built street in the town; all Uniform, & [. . .]: the Strada Nuova the most striking from the Houses being all stucco'd; from its falling in so with the Place of St Charles, & its being terminated with the Porta Nuova at one end of the Kgs Pallace at the other. The general fault of the Town is that you have some Houses covered with Stucco, & some not; & as in the latter they always leave the Scaffold-Holes open (in order to Stucco whenever they may have a mind to it) this has an extream ill effect almost all over the Town; & as much in the Kings Pallace as any where. The City is at present of an Oval Figure: the longest line of it, from the Porta del Po to the P: Susina. Half of it is defended by the River Po, & the River Dora; the other half, by the Citadel; very advanc'd out-works; & perpetual Minery.'

1587. The dilatoriness of the French and the art of Victor was what saved Turin in the last siege of 1706. The French took a view of the town in order for a siege the year before, but as they imagined they could take it whenever they pleased, and as the season was far advanced, they deferred it for the next summer. In that interval Victor added all the works which took up the French all the first part of the siege, as his decoying La Feuillade and so many of the troops into a wild goose chase after him, toward the latter part of it, drew the siege into so great a length that Prince Eugene had time to come up and join him—and then, you know, they were above a match for the French when they were at last got all together again. DOM VILLA *1740*

Besides the information derived from Dom Villa's conversation, Spence had read the *Journal historique du siège de . . . Turin* (Amsterdam, 1708; attributed to Giuseppe Mario Solaro della Margarita) as some of Spence's notes show.

1588. The late reign, which was so long and so military an one, has made the Piedmontese a nation of soldiers. And as they are the only military people in Italy, what might they not do there if the Greater Powers were to let them alone? Or what may they not do in time if they should have a run of political and warlike princes, able to carry on this spirit among the people and to make the best use of all the quarrels that may arise between those Greater Powers?

DOM VILLA *1740*

Victor Amadeus II (1666–1732) succeeded to the throne in 1675. He assumed direction of the government at the age of sixteen, and abdicated in 1730 (§§ 594, 1595). Spence described the 'nation of soldiers' in a letter to his mother, dated 16 December 1739: 'The temper of this nation at present seems to be warlike: they have a military air, & there's scarce a gentleman in the country that does not know how to manage his arms & ride a war-horse. The situation of Piedmont (on the frontiers of Italy, & between the chief contending powers) makes this necessary, & the king does everything in his power to encourage this humour in them' (B.M. Egerton MS. 2234, f. 141).

1589. Emanuel I and his son, Cardinal Maurice, were pretty warm in making a collection of statues, busts, medals, and pictures. His grandson, Emanuel II, began a gallery for them which might have been one of the most considerable in Italy. It was to have been almost 1,000 feet long. The design of it is in the Théâtre de Piedmont. The late king was so perpetually engaged in affairs of so much greater consequence to his family and his country that the taste which began to arise was quite chilled and continues so to this day. Most of the antiques that had been got together were flung as rubbish into a ground room of the palace ⌜this [Dom Villa] called 'Le Cimetière des Statues'⌝, and that part of the gallery which was built for them is turned into archives and offices for the Secretaries of State.

DOM VILLA *1740*

Charles Emanuel I of Savoy (1562–1630) was the grandfather of Charles Emanuel II (1634–75). His son, Cardinal Maurizio di Savoia (1593–1657), was a generous patron of literature and the arts. While in Rome he enriched the Palazzo Orsini at Montegiordano with paintings and frescoes. Equally splendid was his villa, 'La Vigna', near Turin.

When Spence came to repeat this account in his Travel Book he prefaced it with the following: 'The Beaux Arts are in a very low state at Turin at present; unless the Art of War, the Art of Love, & the Art of Chit-Chat, The Art of Gaming, may be reckon'd among the Beaux Arts. These indeed are all very well studied, & in a very flourishing condition. The other Arts are very little regarded, & less understood there; & there is scarce any Prince (ev'n on our wrong side of the Alps) who has a worse Painter, a worse Statuary, or a worse Architect, than his Majesty of Sardinia is furnisht with at present. In former times, 'tis said, they had some taste for the Virtù here' (B.M. Egerton MS. 2235, f. 76).

1590. It was Cardinal Maurice who bought the Tabula Isiaca after the taking of Mantua, and sent it to Turin, where it is now kept in the archives of the Royal Academy. 'Tis one of the finest Egyptian antiquities in the world, and had run a great many risks about that time. At the sacking of Rome, five years before [Cardinal Bembo acquired it], 'twas sold to a locksmith. Bembo bought it of him and gave it to the Duke of Mantua. At Mantua it fell into soldiers' hands again, and was saved the second time by the Cardinal of Savoy.

'Tis a sort of table of a particular metal or composition: 4 feet 2 inches long, and 2 feet and a half wide. The ledges are 2 inches and a quarter, and figured. The figures on the table are, or were, all inlaid. They are neater and of a better taste than those on the obelisks, but not so high as some Egyptian statues and relievos at Rome. They are disposed in three long compartments or ranges, and in the midst of the second range Isis sits enthroned, whence 'tis called the 'Tabula Isiaca'. The things inlaid are of a different colour from the ground, or table itself. There's a great deal of mighty pretty silver work among it, and you see the places where there was more, before the soldiers picked it out to sell it. They found it so thin that it was scarce worthwhile, or [else they] met with a purchaser for the table before they had time to do more damage to it.

DOM VILLA (*and the table itself*) *1740*

This famous Egyptian relic, considered to date from the first century B.C., is now in the Museo di Antichità at Turin. The risks it survived and hands through which it passed are detailed in a monograph by Ernesto Scamuzzi, *La 'Mensa Isiaca' del Regio Museo di Antichità di Torino* (Roma), 1939.

1591. Qui dit peu, dit presque rien.
Molte cose piccole fanno una grande. DOM VILLA *1740*

¶ *The following series concerns Doctor Carlo Richa (modern spelling, Ricca), the chief physician to the King of Sardinia, and his son, called Count Richa. The doctor treated Lord Lincoln when the young man had a riding accident in 1740. The first three remarks belong to him, and the others to his son. Count Richa came to a sad end in 1749, as Spence was to learn in a letter from his friend Robert (later, Bishop) Lowth, then travelling in Turin. Shortly before his death Richa's mind began to weaken and he was apprehended pilfering china from the house of a friend (Singer, pp. 431–2). When Spence knew him, however, Richa took a keen interest in state affairs.*

1592. Il n'y a que deux religions dans le monde: des gens qui croient, et des gens qui ne croient rien. DR. RICHA *1740*

1593. Da che me fido, me ne guardi Dio!
Da che non mi fido, me ne guarderò io.

DR. RICHA *1740*

This is similar to the English saying: 'God save me from my friends; I can protect myself from my enemies.'

1594. Che più carrezze ti fa che non suole;
O ingannato ti [h]a, o ingannarti vuole.

DR. RICHA *1740*

Here again this appears to be proverbial:

'He who flatters you more than usual
Either has deceived you, or wishes to do so.'

1595. The true cause of King Victor's resigning his crown was his passion for glory ('La véritable cause que le Roi Victor quitta la couronne, fut la Gloire', were his words). He had thoughts of it for ten years before he did it, and his friends had a great deal of difficulty to dissuade him from doing it sooner. COUNT RICHA *at Turin 1740*

[Count Richa was the] son of that King's physician. His father was one of the very few that were confined when Victor was making some motions to recover the crown again. SPENCE

Victor Amadeus II set many people guessing when he abdicated the throne in 1730. For the explanation offered by the Sardinian Ambassador to St. James's see § 594.

1596. When Victor first came to the throne, his home dominions consisted only of the ten provinces of Piedmont, the six provinces of Savoy, and a part (not one third) of Montserrat.

COUNT RICHA, MR. V. *and* MR. D. V. *1740*

'Mr. V.' is Arthur Villette (1702–76) British Secretary at the Court in Turin, raised to the rank of Resident in 1741. 'D.V.' is Dom Villa; Spence evidently asked them questions, answered jointly by the three friends.

1597. The King of Sardinia's home dominions at present consist of the same sixteen provinces, all Montserrat, and six new provinces gained from the Emperor (the Valle de

Sesia, Novarese, Lumellina, Alessandrino, Tortonese, and Terra delle Langhe).

What is added is about one fourth of the whole at present.

COUNT RICHA *1740*

1598. Victor was not only a very politic and warlike prince, but ought to be looked upon as a great legislator and benefactor to his country. The latter appears from the advancement of his kingdom in extent, riches, and strength, and the former from the laws and regulations which he printed—some for public use, and others only for presents to some of his more particular friends. COUNT RICHA *1740*

[Count Richa] was so extremely good as to make me a present of five of these books, which I apprehend to be all that were published by his Majesty:

The first [of these books] is entitled *La Mendicità sbandita*, and relates to the institution of hospitals and the rules to be observed in them all over Piedmont and Savoy.

2. The regulation of fees and demands of all the officers of state.

3. Constitutions and rules for the university.

4 and 5. The other laws and constitutions of that Prince.

The first of these was printed in 1717, and the four other in 1729. SPENCE

The titles of these works are as follows (using Spence's numbers):

1. Andrea Guevarre, *La Mendicità sbandita col sovvenimento dei poveri tanto nelle città che nei borghi, luoghi e terre de' Stati . . . di S. M. Vittorio Amedeo* . . . (Torino, 1717); it had a sequel, apparently unknown to Spence, *Nuova aggiunta al libro della mendicità sbandita* . . . (Torino, 1738).
2. *Nuovo regolamento delle provincie, quale contiene il dipartimento di ogni prefettura de' Stati di S. M* . . . (Torino, 1729).
3. *Costituzioni di Sua Maestà per l'Università di Torino* (Torino, 1729).
4. *Leggi e costituzioni di S. M. da osservarri nelle materie civili e criminali* . . . (Torino, 1723). Spence was mistaken both in the date and in thinking that these were two books; instead they were the two parts of one book.

1599. When Victor came to the throne the commerce was very low. He made several good edicts in relation to it, raised it very much, and introduced some new manufactures. The silk trade alone now brings in between six and seven millions of livres a year. The most considerable, after the silk, are corn and cattle.

At Victor's coming to the throne, the revenues of the state were not above six millions of livres (about £300,000 sterling), and are now about eighteen (about £900,000 sterling). COUNT RICHA *and others 1740*

1600. When Victor came to the throne, their forces were not above 6,000, and are now, in all, 36,000.

Of their troops at present, 26,000 are on the usual footing, and 10,000 are what they call 'nationals'. These live and work in their provinces, are called together and exercised for eight or ten days twice every year, and have but one third of the usual pay, and their regimental clothing like the others.

The usual pay is but three Piedmontese sous a day, under three farthings of our money, so that the pay for the nationals in particular must be very easy to the state. The clothing (even for the others) is the burdensome expense.

The regiment of each province is exercised in the chief town of the province they belong to. COUNT RICHA *1740*

1601. We may from all these particulars very well assert that Victor was not a little bustling, cunning prince, but an enterprising, wise, and great one. He had perhaps as cunning and penetrating a head as any man of his time, but that does not give a true or complete idea of him. To do him justice, he ought to be considered as a great politician and the father of his country.

By the augmentation of its territories and commerce, and consequently of its revenues and forces, he raised his house much more than when he changed their ducal into a regal crown.

As to church affairs, it was he who brought about the concordat with the court of Rome. As to civil affairs, he raised the commerce, opened and enlarged the fountains for wealth, and made admirable orders for the poor. His ideas for regulating of them by founding hospitals or societies in every town in his dominions, were they always as effectual as they are well calculated, would alone be sufficient to make his memory blessed by all posterity.

He reduced the laws of the land (which were before his time very numerous, perplexed, and inconvenient) into one body which might be very well contained in a single quarto.[1]

He had all the lands in his dominions reviewed and their extent and conditions entered in a book, which is kept in writing, and there is a book of agenda (on things fit to be done for the good of the nation) printed, but not published.

As to military affairs, it was he who brought the spirit of war (which is so necessary for us from our situation) to be so general a thing among us. He left our country much less exposed than he found it, and made the people much more able to defend it. And it was he who instituted the national regiments and was the first that put so fine an idea in practice.

COUNT RICHA *1740*

[1] They are published in two volumes in quarto, but printed in a large letter and with large margin. SPENCE?

1602. All the passages over the Alps into Piedmont are very well defended. That into the Val [d']Aoste from the little St. Bernard, by the difficulty of the passes and by the Barde and Ivrée—that from Mount Cenis by the Brunetta—that of Mount Geneva by Exilles and Fenestrelle—and that of Barcellonette by Coni and Demont.

All these passes might be defended against all the force of France by 20,000 men.

If an enemy was to come from the coast of Nice, they must still pass by Coni and Demont, and no good general would leave such strong places unconquered behind him.

COUNT RICHA *1740*

Victor Amadeus II made special and effective efforts to fortify the Alpine passes.

1603. When you come near Poverino (two posts from Turin, in the way to Alessandria), the sand looks just like the sea shore. I have tried it in several places and always found a stratum of shells five or six feet under the surface.

COUNT RICHA *1740*

This village is now called Poirino. The remark is given to Richa because the manuscript assigns the ones before and after to him. Between the lines in pencil Spence wrote 'A great Legislator & Adm[r] of King' and 'These Queries flung out of that from C[ount] R[icha] Mr V[illette] Mr D[om] V[illa]'.

1604. A patriot is an angry man that wants to be a courtier, and a courtier is a quiet man that is too much at his ease to be a patriot. COUNT RICHA? *1740*

1605. Corsica was made over as a security from the Spaniard to the Genoese for the great debts they owed them. The principal and long run of interest [is] now more than the island is worth. The Genoese use them hard. The particular tax which caused their mutinying was about $3\frac{1}{2}^{d}$ on each house.

The old senator (Minorusa) who had been so good a governor there so long, and [who had been] so kind to any of the Corsicans that came over to Genoa, was sent to appease them. He and the four chiefs agreed on articles in about twelve days. He sends them to the Senate, who approved of what he had done, but when they came to sign them, the party of young senators proposed to have it signed with a *durante beneplacito serenissimus Senatus*.

The Corsicans could not like the clause, and their old friend stayed there endeavouring for a better answer from the Senate for five months. When he found it in vain, he desired leave to return, and when he was gone, the Corsicans immediately took to arms.

On the new one proposed in the Senate to [let] go out every fifth man (by lot) with their servants and dependents, nobody seconded him, and they at last agreed to beg help of the Emperor. They were to pay the imperial troops and to allow the Emperor 200 German florins for every horse, and 100 for every German soldier that should be killed. The Emperor's were ten thousand, and they sent over 6,000 of their own troops.

The Corsicans got the better of the Genoese on all encounters, and put all to the sword. They even killed several of the Germans from their holes, and at last had surprised the prince of Wirtemberg with a body of his troops, among the rocks, in such a manner that they could have cut him off and every soul of them.

They all along wanted to agree with the Germans; they thought this a good opportunity. The chiefs showed the Prince their advantage, said they wanted only peace and some degree of liberty, and on his parole of honour lost their advantage and went with him amicably into the city to agree at leisure on the articles.

The Prince, after some days, said that 'twas not safe for them to walk about the city, which was in the hands of the Genoese, advised them to keep (till things were agreed on) in such lodgings, which was a fortress and was really a prison for them. The Genoese sent to their leader to get the chiefs into their hands and send them immediately to Genoa. The Prince got so many leave to go and talk with them, and suffered them to seize them and carry them away through the only gate which was guarded by the Genoese.

On their arrival at Genoa, 'twas proposed to behead them immediately. The Doge hindered it by saying 'twas necessary to know the Emperor's mind first. They are now at liberty; the articles the Corsicans have got at last are better for them than the first they proposed before the war, and by the first article the Emperor makes himself guarantee to see them kept on both sides, which sits the most heavy of all of them on the Genoese stomachs.

In the time of the war, the Corsicans wanted any master but the Genoese. They offered to crown their old friend the senator with any powers he pleased to accept, and actually sent two envoys (Grimaldi and ——) with a message to Rome to the Pretender to beg he would come and be King over them. They say the Pr[ince] of W[irtemberg] has done himself a disservice with the Emperor by his behaviour in this affair. *spring 1732–April 1733*

The Corsican revolt broke out in October 1729 and lasted until May 1732, when a peace treaty relatively favourable to the Corsicans was signed. Spence passed through Genoa shortly afterwards and may have written this account at that time, the paper being dated '1733?', indicating that he guessed at the time some years later.

Spence's informant is not named, the only possible clue being '(Neg^{r}?)' at the beginning. Judging from some of his remarks (viz. 'the Corsicans got the better in all encounters') he was a Corsican, or at least sympathized with that side. There are other minor discrepancies (thus the senator's name was Gerdamo Veneroso, not 'Minorusa'), but Spence's account preserves a generally accurate contemporary viewpoint.

1606. Czas plynie,—Jak woda na mlynie. Le temps coule comme l'eau sur le moulin. LANSKARONSKI *1740*

Lanskaronski (Lanckoroński) was a young Polish nobleman whom Spence knew at the Military Academy in Turin. Ten years later Spence learned that after being an officer in the Sardinian Army, Lanskaronski had joined the Saxon service (Singer, p. 433). This conversation shows him trying to teach Spence a sentence in Polish.

1607. Under the bust of the builder of a convent in Placentia [are the words]: 'Vir fuit ista domus quod conditur indicat eius.' LOWTH *1756*

These words were engraved above the main entrance to the convent of S. Agostino in the Stradone Farnese. Above this, with a larger inscription, was a bust of the builder, Marco Antonio Bagarotti. The convent is now a barracks and the bust has disappeared.

1608. [An] inscription on a church in Vicenza dedicated to the Virgin Mary [reads], 'Salve, Mater Pietatis, et totius Trinitatis nobile Triclinium.' MASSINGBERD *1756*

('The Noble Couch for all the Trinity to recline upon', [as Dr. Lowth translated the second part]).

DR. LOWTH *1756*

This conversation shows Spence and two of his closest friends looking back on amusing memories of travel, fifteen years after Spence's last tour. When William Burrell Massingberd (see § 1061) visited Italy is not certain, though it was probably in 1739. Robert Lowth, later Bishop of Oxford and of London, returned in 1750. Vicenza has two churches dedicated to the Virgin Mary; this inscription is on the portal of Santa Maria dei Servi, built in 1531.

¶ *The final group of conversations are those between Spence and the famous pastel portraitist of Venice, Rosalba Carriera (1675–1757). Spence and Lord Lincoln arrived in Venice in June 1741 on their return journey to England. Horace Walpole had travelled with them following Spence's action in saving his life at Reggio a few weeks earlier. One of the things travellers 'did' in Venice was to be painted by Rosalba, an arrangement possibly facilitated by the fact that Sir Robert Walpole already had four of her portraits* (Vertue Note Books, *v. 126*).

Probably most of the talk occurred while Spence's portrait was being made. Readers who have experienced the atmosphere of Austin Dobson's Rosalba's Journal *(1915) may feel themselves in the studio with the gentle old lady and the spry Mr. Spence.*

1609. I have been so long used to study features, and the expressions of the mind by them, that I know people's tempers by their faces.

⌜'For God's sake, what is my temper?' [asked Spence].
Ni allegro, ni malinconico, ma un buonissimo misto. She said her turn was to melancholy.⌝

SIGNORA ROSALBA *June 1741*

She added as a proof of this, the characters of two of my friends whom she had seen but twice or thrice, and my own, as justly—and the last perhaps rather more justly—than I could have done myself. SPENCE

Spence's two friends were undoubtedly Lord Lincoln and Horace Walpole, both of whom Rosalba had painted, as she had done Spence. The inserted portion comes from the Huntington manuscript.

1610. The eyes are everything. When a person was once saying to me, 'that picture is like in everything but the eyes', my answer was, 'then 'tis not like at all'.

SIGNORA ROSALBA *June 1741*

1611. Everything I do seems good to me just after I have done it, and perhaps for seven or eight hours after.

SIGNORA ROSALBA *June 1741*

Though one of the most modest painters of the age—so that the difference between the modest and sensible artists, and those that are ignorant and impudent, seems to be that the former can find out their own faults soon, and the latter never. SPENCE

The Huntington manuscript begins, 'How near she was to take a leap out of her life when about six year old—How extremely modest!' The childhood incident is not recorded elsewhere.

Lady Pomfret also testified to the evenness of Rosalba's temperament, '. . . we went to see the paintress Rosalba, who is now old [she was then sixty six], but certainly the best (if not the only) artist in her way. This her excellence does not, however, make her the least impertinent, her behaviour being as good as her work' (Hertford *Corresp.*, iii. 225–6).

1612. She is extremely good-natured, and yet in speaking of a woman who had used her very ill, when I said, 'Non volesse far male a nessuna', she answered with surprise, 'Non poteva!'

'And did this heart-burning stay long with you?' [asked Spence].

'Un pezzo.' (Till her journey to Paris, some years after.)

SIGNORA ROSALBA *June 1741*

This grievance occurred sometime before October 1720, when Rosalba visited Paris at the invitation of the eminent patron of art, Pierre Crozat. There she was a great success, painting many portraits including Watteau and the boy King, Louis XV. She was singled out for the honour of being elected to the Académie de la Peinture. Rosalba returned to Venice in 1722.

1613. The German painters are not so genteel (*si valent-uomini*), nor so good painters as the French.

SIGNORA ROSALBA *June 1741*

An unidentified Man by Rosalba
(Probably *not* the lost portrait of Spence)
National Gallery, London

1614. That Magdalene is a very fine one! If you observe it, 'tis not only her eyes that cry; she cries all over. ('Elle pleure jusqu'aux bouts des doigts', were her words.)

SIGNORA ROSALBA *June 1741*

Spence introduced this story as a footnote to his *Crito: or, A Dialogue on Beauty* (1752), from whence we learn that Rosalba was speaking about a Magdalene by Titian that hung in the Barberigo Palace in Venice.

1615. I have seen but very little of Sir Godfrey's. There's a Moncenigo done by him here at Venice that is a very good piece.

SIGNORA ROSALBA *June 1741*

After a period of studying in Rome and Naples, Sir Godfrey Kneller set up a studio in Venice, *c.* 1673. He received commissions from several leading families, including the Basadonna, Garstoni, Donati, and Mocenigo. Writers on Kneller do not, however, mention any paintings of the Mocenigo family.

Whatever picture it may have been that Rosalba chose to praise, Spence's marginal note shows that her word was 'bravo'.

1616. In speaking of Sir Godfrey on a particular occasion, she said, 'No, I concluded he could not be religious because he was not modest.'

SIGNORA ROSALBA *June 1741*

Evidently Spence had reported to Rosalba some of the stories about Kneller's loose attitude towards formal religion. See §114.

1617. I was always imitative in everything, as far back as I can remember. As to painting in particular, I began with miniature, and it was a good while before I drew any portrait as big as the life.

SIGNORA ROSALBA *June 1741*

Actually, she began with painting the lids of snuff boxes, from which she graduated to miniatures. She studied under a succession of masters, and became so successful that her miniatures were in steady demand. When her eyesight began to suffer she turned to pastel work (Austin Dobson, *Rosalba's Journal*, 1915).

The earliest manuscript also has the jotting, 'first Opera; Concerto'; this may be connected with her performing on the violin.

1618. I pray in English because that language is so short and so expressive.

SIGNORA ROSALBA *June 1741*

Spence specified English in the first two manuscript texts of this anecdote, but in the Huntington MS. wrote '(or German? Q. See Paper)'. Thus, when he wrote the Folio manuscript he substituted 'German', though that language is not renowned for its brevity.

The 'Paper' in question was that containing the original notes of the conversation. It reads, 'Prays in Eng: because expressive & so short'. Above the line is the interlinear addition, 'Germ: book. Germ^{n}', and then, '(whole Bible by Taylor, for D. of Gloster).' Whatever the meaning of this cryptic jotting, Rosalba evidently preferred English to German for her worship, though other evidence that she spoke English is slight.

1619. If spies are bad people, the great part of the people of Venice must be bad. There are no less than 33,000 pensioned by the state ⌜*salariati*⌝, among which are all the gondoliers, and a great number of priests and abbés.

SIGNORA ROSALBA *June 1741*

This situation was general in large cities in Italy (L. Lewis, *Connoisseurs and Secret Agents in Eighteenth Century Rome*, 1961). In Venice the practice was dramatized by the necessary dependence on gondoliers for transportation. During his first visit to Venice in 1731 Spence had written in his Travel Notes: 'There's a strange spirit of inquisitiveness reigns among ye Venetians; they know every little triffle: perhaps in hearing a thousand frivolous things, they meet with one that may be of some concern to them. The great channel y^{t} Secrets are disperst by is ye Gondoliers; & this may be one reason why ye Nobles walk so much. A Foreigner's Gondoliers there tell every thing he does. I believe y^{e} servants you have to attend you there too often understand more Languages than they pretend to' (B.M. Egerton MS. 2235, f. 10).

The inserted word appears in the two earliest manuscripts.

APPENDIXES

APPENDIX TO § 18

Pope at Bromley's School

INFORMATION about Pope's supposed attendance at a school kept by John Bromley comes from two sources, the second possibly derived from the first. The earlier is a letter published by Curll in 1735 from a correspondent named 'E.P.':

The last school he was put to, before the twelfth year of his age, was in Devonshire Street, near Bloomsbury; there I also was, and the late Duke of Norfolk, at the same time. It was kept by one Bromley, a Popish renegado, who had been a parson, and was one of King James's converts in Oxford, some years after that prince's abdication. He kept a little seminary till, upon an advantageous offer made him, he went a travelling tutor to the present Lord Gage. Mr. Alexander Pope, before he had been four months at this school, or was able to construe Tully's Offices, employed his muse in satirising his master. It was a libel of at least one hundred verses, which a fellow student having given information of, was found in his pocket, and the young satirist was soundly whipped, and kept prisoner to his room for seven days; whereupon his father fetched him away, and I have been told he never went to school more. How much past correction has wrought upon him, the world is judge; and how much present correction might, may be collected from this sample. I thought it a curious fact, and therefore it is at your service, as one of the ornaments of this excellent person's life. Yours, &c., E.P. (EC, vi. 440–1.)

The second source is the *Church History of England . . . Chiefly With Regard to Catholics* (Brussels, 1742), iii. 459, by Charles Dodd (pseudonym for Hugh Tootel), who wrote that Bromley 'was well skilled in the classicks; and, as I am informed, mr *Pope*, the celebrated poet, was one of his pupils'. It would be difficult to show that Tootel's information was independent of Curll.

George Sherburn considers that Pope may have written the 'E.P.' letter himself in a deliberate attempt to mislead Curll into inserting mistaken details into his publications. The following details seem to invalidate E.P.'s report:

1. The eighth Duke of Norfolk (1683–1732), being five years older than Pope, would have been seventeen when Pope was twelve, an improbable age for his Grace (who succeeded to the title in April 1701) to have been attending 'a little seminary'.

2. In the 1730's when Pope attempted to obtain a position for one of his Rackett nephews with the ninth Duke of Norfolk (brother to the eighth Duke) he sought the aid of John Caryll and other friends, pleading that he had no connexion with the Duke. If Pope had been a schoolmate of the eighth Duke, he could have utilized the fact.

3. Thomas Gage, first Viscount Gage was a Protestant, though many members of his family, including his brother, the notorious 'Count Gage', were Roman Catholics. Under these circumstances it is unlikely that Lord Gage would have had 'a Popish renegado' as his travelling tutor.

4. Though the incidents of Pope's expulsion and his memory of Cicero are described in vivid details, they echo events at Twyford school as told to Spence by Pope (§§ 14, 15, 18), Mrs. Rackett (§ 20), and the Rev. Mannock (§ 19).

APPENDIX TO §57

When did Pope see Dryden?

POPE told Spence that when he was about twelve he saw Dryden and remembered his face. In 1730 Jonathan Richardson recorded, after a conversation with Pope, 'He has told us himself, that he only Saw Mr *Dryden*, which was at Wills Coffee House, where Dryden frequented, but had no Acquaintance with him, He Dying Soon After' ('New Anecdotes', p. 347). The anecdote is no doubt related to the Wycherley letter of 26 December 1704, intended to appear in *The Posthumous Worksof William Wycherley*, vol. ii (1729), but suppressed and kept in sheets until issued as part of Pope's *Letters* in 1735.

Warburton gave an additional detail in his note on the Wycherley letter: 'When a very young Boy, he prevailed with a friend to carry him to a Coffee-house which Dryden frequented; where he had the satisfaction he speaks of' (Pope's *Works*, 1751, vii. 4). This raises the question, who was the friend? It is tempting to identify him with Sir Charles Wogan (d. 1752) who wrote to Swift in 1733 that 'Mr Pope and I lived in perfect union and familiarity for two or three summers before he entered the stage of the world' (Williams, iv. 113). He says further, 'I had the honour to bring [Pope] up to London, from our retreat in the forest of Windsor, to dress à la mode, and introduce at Will's coffee-house' (*Works of Jonathan Swift*, ed. Sir Walter Scott, 1814, xviii. 21). This may be true enough, but Wogan says nothing about seeing Dryden.

The chronology of the event argues against Wogan being the friend involved in Warburton's account. Dryden died on 1 May 1700, about three weeks before Pope's twelfth birthday, and for five months or so earlier he had been confined by erysipelas and other illnesses. During most of August and September of 1699 he had been away on his annual summer visit to Northamptonshire. If the incident occurred before 21 May 1699, Pope would have been only ten years old. The young Chevalier Wogan was 'about as old as Pope' according to Sherburn in correcting the *DNB*, which gives Wogan's birthdate as 1698? (a mere two years before Dryden's death). But whoever the friend may have been, for once Pope did not exaggerate the tenderness of his years when recounting an event of his childhood.

Another story is recorded by Joseph Warton in 1797 (Pope's *Works*, 1797, i, p. xiii): 'Mr. Harte informed me that Dryden gave Pope a shilling for translating, when a boy, the story of *Pyramus and Thisbe*.' No other evidence has been found to support this anecdote or the translation. Malone accepted it, and speculated further, 'Probably he carried this early specimen of his abilities in his pocket when he went to Will's Coffee [house]'... (James M. Osborn, *John Dryden: Some Biographical Facts and Problems*, Gainesville, 1965, p. 156).

APPENDIX TO § 61

Dryden's *Virgil*

DRYDEN spent four years in the translation of Virgil (C. E. Ward, *Life of John Dryden*, Durham, N.C., 1961, pp. 271–87). He began late in 1693 (see his letter to Walsh, written 13 December) but the formal agreement with Tonson was not signed until 15 June 1694. The volume was in the press in February 1696/7, and reached the hands of subscribers early in August 1697. In the agreement Dryden pledged himself 'to do nothing in ye meantime except the Translation of Fresnoy, or any Poem, or Book in Prose, not above 1 s price, when printed', except to assist in the production and printing of his son John's comedy *The Husband his own Cuckold* (1696). His translation of Du Fresnoy's *De Arte Graphica* appeared at the end of June 1695, with Dryden's statement in the preface (p. iv) that he 'borrow'd only two months' for it from the *Virgil*. His 'Ode on the Death of Mr. Henry Purcell' though dated 1696, was probably written soon after that untimely event which occurred 21 November 1695.

APPENDIX TO §66

Royal Hints to the Poet Laureate

THREE other instances occur of hints by Charles adopted by Dryden; the first was *Aureng-Zebe* (1675) 'the most considerable event of it was modelled by his royal pleasure'; next came *Limberham, or the Kind Keeper* (produced in March 1677/8), concerning which Dryden wrote that the King was 'parcell poet with me in the plott; one of the designes being a story he was pleased formerly to tell me' (*Letters of John Dryden*, ed. C. E. Ward, Durham, N.C., 1942, pp. 11–12). The third was the *History of the League*, 1684, written 'According to His Majesty's Command', as Dryden stated on the title-page of the Epistle Dedicatory to the King. (See also Ward, op. cit., p. 21).

Concerning the Oxford speech, Pope had in mind not the King's speech opening the Parliament at Oxford on 20 March 1681, but *His Majesties Declaration To All His Loving Subjects, Touching the Causes & Reasons That moved Him to Dissolve The Two last Parliaments*, dated 8 April 1681. This prompted Dryden's tract, *His Majesties Declaration Defended*, issued in June 1681, which contains most of the points that Dryden versified several months later in the concluding passage to *Absalom and Achitophel.* Godfrey Davies has examined this subject in detail, and has demonstrated that the passage is not a flaw in the design of the poem. See his article 'The Conclusion of Dryden's *Absalom and Achitophel*', *Huntington Library Quarterly*, x (1946), 69–82, and also his introduction to *His Majesties Declaration Defended* (Augustan Reprint Society, 1950).

APPENDIX TO § 70

Abbé Southcote's Abbey

THE abbey was that of St. André, situated under the walls of the great fortress of Philip the Fair at Villeneuve-lès-Avignon, across the famous 'pont d'Avignon' from the papal city. The circumstances behind Southcote's appointment involve machinations far beyond Spence's simple story of personal gratitude. Thomas Southcote had emerged as one of the foremost leaders in the Jacobite cause, especially active in collecting and transmitting money (G. H. Jones, *Mainstream of Jacobitism*, 1954, pp. 107, 126–7). By 1721 he settled in Northern France as president of the English congregation. The following year he performed distinguished service in fighting a threatened capital levy that the Walpole government proposed to inflict on Catholics in England. His letters to James at Rome were largely responsible for obtaining an official protest from the French government to London against the action. One of his henchmen was the transplanted Scot, the Chevalier Ramsay (see § 1245).

Then and later, the problem of finding an income for Ramsay concerned the group, and the best solution seemed to be to obtain the abbey at Avignon for Southcote (a Benedictine, and thus eligible) as absentee, who agreed to pass on the pension to Ramsay. Pope's part in the incident involved persuading the Walpole government to accept the appointment of a known Jacobite, instead of protesting to the French government. Thus Pope's motives were much stronger than mere recollection of Southcote's friendly act of more than twenty years earlier. See Henderson, pp. 62–64, 89–91.

APPENDIX TO § 74

Who read Pope's *Pastorals*?

BESIDES this statement, Pope left four other lists of eminent men of literary taste who early encouraged him to write and publish. The first occurs on the fly-leaf of the original manuscript of his *Pastorals*, now owned by Mr. Arthur A. Houghton, where Pope stated, 'This copy is that wch past thro ye hands of Mr Walsh, Mr Congreve, Mr Mainwaring, Dr. Garth, Mr Granville, Mr Southern, Sr H. Sheers, Sr W. Trumbull, Ld Halifax, Ld Wharton, Marq. of Dorchest^{r}. D. of Bucks. &c.' (*Early Career*, pp. 52–53).

In a note printed in 1709 with the *Pastorals*, Pope gave a similar list, but with eight changes. Lord Somers and Wycherley were added, but Congreve, Southerne, Sheers, Wharton, Dorchester, and Buckingham were omitted (though covered by the phrase 'and others').

On 5 August 1730 Pope 'dictated' various biographical details to Jonathan Richardson, Senior, a transcript of which by his grandson was preserved by Bishop Percy (Bodleian, English Letters, MSS. d. 59, ff. 80–81, printed in 'New Anecdotes', pp. 346–7). The relevant portion reads:

> [His *Pastorals*] Occasion'd his being known to Dr Garth, Mr Walsh, Mr Grenville, with whom he both Convers'd & Corresponded, & Sir Wm Trumbal, with whom on his having then resign'd the Office of Secretary of State, he lived Familiarly being his near Neighbour. By some or other of These he was soon Introduc'd into the Acquaintance of the Duke of Shrewsbury Lord Somers Mr St John & L[or]d Halifax. He has told us himself, that he only Saw Mr *Dryden*, which was at Wills Coffee House, where Dryden frequented, but had no Acquaintance with him, He Dying Soon After. But as he fell into the Society of all the Friends of that great Poet, he Succeeded to all their Intimacies Particularly Mr *Congreve*, & thereby into a very large Acquaintance of most of the Distinguished Persons at that Time. The First Works of His that were publish'd were his Pastorals & some pieces of *Homer* & *Chaucer* in 1709. His Windsor Forrest in 1710 [published 1713 in fact] & the Essay on Criticism in 1711 (1707 & 9) tho written some time before.... About the same time [1712] his Friendship began with Dr Arbuthnot & Dr Swift, who brought him into the Familiar Acquaintance of the Lord Oxford, then Lord Treasurer.

It should be noted that Pope's acquaintance with the Scriblerus group dates from about 1712, or several years after the Kit Kat members.

A few years later, in the *Epistle to Dr. Arbuthnot* (1734), Pope inserted an autobiographical passage describing the cordial sponsorship given him by the friends of Dryden:

> But why then publish? *Granville* the polite,
> And knowing *Walsh*, would tell me I could write;
> Well-natur'd *Garth* inflam'd with early praise,
> And *Congreve* lov'd, and *Swift* endur'd my Lays;
> The Courtly *Talbot*, *Somers*, *Sheffield* read,
> Ev'n mitred *Rochester* would nod the head,
> And *St. John*'s self (great *Dryden*'s friends before)
> With open arms receiv'd one Poet more.
>
> (ll. 135–42)

One name appears here for the first time, that of Atterbury. The box score thus stands as follows:

	MS. *Pastorals*	printed *Pastorals*	Richardson	*Ep. to Arbuthnot*
Walsh	×	×	×	×
Garth	×	×	×	×
Granville	×	×	×	×
Mainwaring	×	×	—	—
Trumbull	×	×	×	—
Halifax	×	×	×	—
Congreve	×	—	×	×
Sheffield	×	—	—	×
Southerne	×	—	—	—
Sheers	×	—	—	—
Wharton	×	—	—	—
Dorchester	×	—	—	—
Somers	—	×	×	×
Wycherley	—	×	—	—
Swift	—	—	×	×
Shrewsbury	—	—	×	×
Atterbury	—	—	—	×
Bolingbroke	—	—	×	×

Since the series of names in the *Epistle to Arbuthnot* has a different reason for existence, as has Richardson's account of Pope's friends, from the two *Pastorals* lists, we should not expect greater concurrence.

Within the few lines that Pope thought proper for the subject in the *Epistle*, only a few names could be listed. Probably all the persons named, with the possible exception of Lord Dorchester (father of Lady Mary Wortley Montagu), knew Dryden, though some were acquaintances rather than friends.

APPENDIX TO § 102

A Rejected Couplet

The motto is from Virgil (Eclogue *VI*, lines 10-12), translated by Dryden thus:

'... while every pen prepares
To write thy praises, Varus, and thy wars,
My past'ral Muse her humble tribute brings,
And yet not wholly uninspir'd she sings.'

Among the Boswell Papers at Yale is a slip of paper bearing a couplet said to have once been part of *Windsor Forest*,

'Hears his own feet, and thinks they sound like more
And fears the hind feet will oer take the fore'.

The paper explains it as follows, 'Dr Ridley told Mr Steevens that Mr Spence told him these lines were originally in Windsor Forest as Mr Pope had acknowledged to him'[.] Dr. Gloster Ridley (1702-1774) was one of Spence's most intimate friends and an executor of his estate. George Steevens (1736-1800) succeeded Dr. Johnson as editor of Shakespeare.

The handwriting has not been identified, but jottings in the hand of Dr. Johnson, unconnected with this anecdote, are on the other side of the paper. It appears to be an item submitted for use in Johnson's 'Life of Pope', but not utilized for some undisclosed reason. Probably Johnson learned that the couplet appears in chapter vii of *Peri Bathos* where it illustrates 'a frightened Stage in full Chace.' Since Pope utilized other rejected verses of his own in this satire it is not unlikely that these lines suffered the same fate. See Twickenham vi, 413-14.

The place where the couplet might have fitted in *Windsor Forest* is not readily apparent, but possibly following line 158 of the earliest manuscript text, now in the Bixby Collection at Washington University, St. Louis, Missouri. See the edition by R. M. Schmitz, 1952, p. 64. (Quoted by permission) of the Yale Boswell Committee and the McGraw Hill Company.)

APPENDIX TO §109

Pope and Tillemans

WHERE did the 'stealing' of Tillemans's strokes by Pope occur? The original record of this conversation (see textual note) reads: 'at Mr. Roberts' (Lord Radnor's uncle?)' This apparently refers to Francis Robartes (1650?–1718), uncle of the third Earl of Radnor (d. 1741) who held the title at the time of this conversation in 1730. Chronology poses a problem, however, for Pope did not move to his villa at Twickenham, bordering the grounds of Radnor House, until 1719, the year after Robartes's death. The next occupant was probably John Robartes (1686–1757), son and heir of Francis. Thus he was a cousin of the third Earl whom he succeeded to become fourth Earl in 1741. Spence's wording in the Folio transcript (written many years after the conversation in 1730) reads 'at Ld Radnor's', meaning at the Twickenham estate occupied by the fourth Earl. Since Tillemans lived for many years nearby at Richmond, the incident was something of a neighbourhood affair.

Radnor House contained a large collection of paintings; their present location is unknown, though possibly they were dispersed in 1791 (F. C. Hodgson, *Thames-side in the Past*, 1913, p. 227). Pope may have owned the Tillemans himself, for the inventory of his estate lists 'a Landskip by Titeman [*sic*]' (*N & Q*, 13 May 1882, pp. 363–5). Since there is no other painter whose name comes close to this misspelling, it seems reasonable that Tillemans was intended.

APPENDIX TO §114

Enigmatic Spence Jottings

A HINT for this anecdote appears among some jottings in Spence's hand, sold among a collection of his papers, mostly verses, at Sotheby's on 24 May 1960, lot 542, now reunited with the Spence Papers at Yale. Evidently Spence scribbled them down as reminders after a conversation with Pope in 1735. They read:

Sr Godfry Kneller, & Mr Pope; what is that they cry, Carps?—Dit: O they canot do without you there!—By God, & so he wou'd—then please to take wch seat you will

B^{p} T. kept down by the Queen: broke, very honourably, with ye D of S, who got him the B^{k} of Oxford: usd to send his Chaplains to bring him an acc^{t} of each New play.—Marg. & William supposd universally by ye Town to be made on ye D^{s} of—& L^{d} S: Mallet says, that ye Stanza in one of Fletcher's Plays gave him the Hint.—

Of the four items concerning Kneller, only the last two occur in expanded form (§§113–14).

'B^{p} T.' may be William Talbot (1659–1730) who served as Bishop of Oxford from 1699 until translated to Salisbury in 1715. Talbot is the only incumbent whose name begins with this initial; nothing is known of his reported passion for the theatre. It is tempting to suggest that Archbishop Tillotson was meant (§ 793), but the details disqualify him.

David Mallet's ballad of 'William and Margaret' was written before he left Edinburgh in 1723. It is substantially an older ballad rewritten, a circumstance which Mallet seems to have conveniently forgotten. One stanza of the ballad had been quoted by Fletcher in *The Knight of the Burning Pestle* (1607), II. viii.

These jottings were once part of the Loose Papers among the Spence Papers, and appear to have formed part of lot 205 of Sotheby's sale of Singer's manuscripts on 3 August 1858. When Spence was preparing the abstract for Warburton (B.M. Egerton MS. 1960) from his notes, he gave an alphabetical sequence to those papers he used. This sequence is almost intact, so that it is possible to say that this manuscript was probably 'D' (see p. lxix). Because Paper 'C' (i.e. L13) is dated August 1735 and Paper 'E' is headed 'Oxf: Sept^{r}, 1; 1735', the conversations recorded in these jottings probably took place at some time in August. However, of the two anecdotes (§§ 113–14) recorded here as very brief notes, § 113 is dated 1736 by the Folio. Whether this represents an error by Spence or a second telling of the tale by Pope is not clear. The date in F, which represents Spence's final thoughts on the matter have been retained in this case, though both should perhaps be dated, along with the paper, 'August 1735'.

APPENDIX TO § 125

Pope's Portrait of Swift

COULD Pope and Spence have been looking at one of Pope's own portraits of Swift when this conversation occurred? Probably not, since Spence scarcely would have omitted the information. A better possibility is the picture of Swift, supposedly by a professional artist in Pope's villa at Twickenham, 'in gold frame' in a 'room fronting the Thames', as it is described in the inventory of Pope's estate (*N & Q*, 13 May 1882, p. 364). Pope's remarks, however, apply equally to other portraits of Swift, especially the one by Jervas in the Bodleian Library, presented in 1739 by Swift's printer and friend, Alderman Barber. Other portraits by Jervas include two in the National Portrait Gallery, one bequeathed by Swift's eminent editor, Sir Harold Williams, and another at Knole. Earlier information is summarized in 'The Portraits of Swift', by Sir F. R. Falkiner, in the Temple-Scott edition of *Swift's Works*, 1908, vol. xii.

APPENDIX TO § 162

A Pope–Addison Crux

POPE's account of Addison's breaking the news about the rival translation of the first book of the *Iliad* raises several problems. The first is how to reconcile it with the letter to Addison dated 10 October 1714 that Pope printed in the early summer of 1735, a few weeks before this conversation occurred. There Pope mentions 'late malevolencies' and hints at two-faced conduct on Addison's part. He then asks a favour of Addison: 'It is, that you would look over the first two books of my translation of *Homer*, which are now in the hands of my Lord *Halifax*' (*Corresp.* i. 263; for Halifax see § 204).

Thus the dinner would appear to have been after the letter. But, was this letter ever sent to Addison? Sherburn suggests the possibility that it was written about 1730, adding: 'All the other letters printed as sent to Addison are demonstrably fabricated from letters to Caryll; for this letter there is no "source".' Furthermore, chronology offers some difficulties: on 6 October Pope was at Bath, whence he wrote to Martha Blount that he planned to 'take a trip to Long-leat (which is twelve miles hence) to visit my Lord Lansdowne, and return to London' (*Corresp.* i. 261). Bath is 105 miles and Longleat 99 miles from London, a two-day journey at the least. If the letter is genuine we must presume that Pope returned promptly to London, probably without visiting Longleat; and on his arrival heard reports of Addison's conduct that moved him to write Addison with minimum delay.

Another slight difficulty concerns the date of the dinner (after the letter of 10 October) and the date of Budgell's departure for Ireland. On 8 October Addison wrote a letter of introduction for Budgell to present to Archbishop King in Dublin. The difficulty is surmounted, however, if Budgell's departure was delayed for a week or so after Addison wrote the letter.

In any case the dinner occurred well after 31 May 1714, when Tickell signed an agreement with Tonson to translate all twenty-four books of the *Iliad*, an undertaking to which Addison undoubtedly was privy by October. Smithers assumes that Addison invited 'Pope to dine privately so that he might explain the transaction' (p. 322). But this assumption will scarcely stand up under examination. News of the Tonson–Tickell project would have been a shock to Pope, whose financial future was deeply involved in the subscriptions for his translation, entered into with Lintot on 23 March 1714. All of Pope's references to Tickell's translation speak of the first book of the *Iliad* only. There is no evidence that either Pope or Spence ever learned of the existence of the Tonson–Tickell contract. To the modern reader, Addison's conduct on this occasion seems very close to double dealing.

William Ayre in his *Memoirs of the Life and Writings of Alexander Pope* (1745) gives a long account of the quarrel behind the Atticus lines (i. 98–102). It brings in Sir Richard Steele and John Gay as bystanders and relates some circumstances not easily accounted for, though others could have been taken from Pope's published correspondence. Smithers and other writers on the subject have chosen to ignore it, but in any fresh study of the problem it deserves attention. Even though it is a second-hand story circulating after all the principals were in their graves, it was published when many men who knew Pope, Addison, Steele, and Gay were still living and in a position to confute it, had they cared to so dignify Ayre and Curll, his publisher.

APPENDIX TO § 165

Gildon's 'thing about Wycherley'

THIS anecdote has received a good deal of attention because the Folio text (here followed, as by Singer, who, however, did not notice the query in the margin) indicates that Gildon's attack on Pope was his 'thing about Wycherley', namely his *Memoirs of . . . Wycherley*, published in 1718. But this date is two years too late for the events.

In 1935 Arthur E. Case showed in an ingenious paper (*MP*, xxxiii, 1935, 187–93), based on a study of the manuscript notes that Spence sent to Warburton (BM. Egerton 1960), that the query mark obviated the interpretation that the attack must be in some 'thing on Wycherley'. Instead, Case argued that the trouble should be traced to the anonymous *True Character of Mr Pope and his Writings* (1716), once considered to be from Gildon's 'venal Quill', but now attributed to Dennis.

Ault (*New Light*, pp. 112–17) in turn objected on chronological grounds. Since Addison had publicly paid passing compliment to Pope's *Iliad* in the Freeholder of 7 May 1716, he was unable to believe that Addison would have encouraged the personal attack on him in the anonymous *True Character of Mr Pope*, also dated 7 May, but probably in the hands of the public some days later (advertised in the *Flying Post*, 31 May). In reply to his own objections, Ault suggested that Gildon's caricature of Pope as the little poet 'Sawney Dapper' in *A New Rehearsal, on Bays the Younger* (published 6 April 1714) was the original cause of Pope's animosity against Gildon. It is possible, of course, that Gildon wrote another attack on Pope, not now known or attributed to him.

Regardless of these earlier attacks, it is clear that Pope was deeply wounded by Gildon's *Memoirs of . . . Wycherley*, where the youthful poet was described as looking like the son of a rustic tenant farmer 'in his own cropt Hair, and Dress agreeable to the Forest he came from' (p. 16).

APPENDIX TO § 180

Addison in Parliament

THERE are numerous contemporary echoes of the charges of Addison's inadequacy in Commons and in official business. Dr. King recorded that Addison 'could not speak a word in the house of parliament; and, which is more surprising, he could not dictate the common letters of business which were necessary to be sent from his office' (*Anecdotes*, 1818, pp. 111–12). See also *Quin's Anecdotes* (1765), p. 67.

According to the *Egmont Diary* (i. 105): 'Lord Sunderland made him [Addison] Secretary of State to keep others out who would not be his tool, and when that end was served, he was discarded again for he knew nothing of business; but this was no reflection on him, his fine parts and genius lying another way, viz. to polite studies.' Still another story occurs in *Addisoniana* (ii. 10) of Addison's 'embarrassment' at being unable to write an official letter 'to Hanover that Queen Anne was dead: he found it so difficult to express himself . . . that the lords of the regency were obliged to employ . . . one of the clerks'. Thomas Tyers reports the same incident in less detail in his *Historical Essay on Mr. Addison*, 1783. Macaulay (*Works*, 1871, vi. 105–6) and Bohn (*Works*, vi. 728) argue that the point of these stories, despite Addison's years of official employment, is only that he was ignorant of official forms.

Budgell wrote of Addison's 'silly sheepishness . . . that makes thee [Addison] sit in the House, and hear a fellow prate for half an hour together, who has not a tenth part of thy good sense' (*A Letter to Cleomenes*, 1731, pp. 209–10). Smithers gives other examples of his being abashed on rising to speak and sitting down without saying a word (p. 377). But, as Smithers points out, the *Journals* of the House of Commons record that Addison did rise from time to time to declare the policy of the government on matters under discussion.

APPENDIX TO § 233

Atterbury's Speech

THE speech, as first printed in folio soon after it was made, 11 May 1723, contains about 10,000 words. The *True Briton*, 24 June, warned the public that this version 'is surreptitiously printed, without the knowledge or consent of the Bishop, or any of his friends . . . it is spurious, it is very imperfect; several entire paragraphs being omitted, and many others vilely mangled, as any person that heard his Lordship speak will readily observe'. At the end of the century two other texts were printed by John Nichols, both about 16,000 words, but differing in many passages. In volume iv of his edition of Atterbury's *Epistolary Correspondence* (1790, pp. 383–439) Nichols printed it from 'an authentic MS in the possession of Dr. [William] Morice', son of the second wife of Atterbury's son-in-law. But in vol. v of the second edition, retitled the *Miscellaneous Works* (1798 on the title, 1799 on the half-title, but actually completed 1800 or later), Nichols used a different text 'transcribed *verbatim* from a MS . . . in the Bishop's own writing . . . it evidently . . . received the Bishop's LAST CORRECTIONS' (pp. 365–94).

Singer (pp. 156–7) prints the following note, part ascribed to John Peele (d. 1772) the printer, and part to Spence (it is not among the known Spence MSS.): 'A copy of the bishop's speech was taken in shorthand (by order of the ministry) for the use of Mr. [Clement] Wearg [1686–1726], one of the king's council, soon after made solicitor general, for his exertions on this occasion. It was printed by Woodward and Peele, from a copy sold them by Wearg's clerk!—Francklin had another short-hand copy, taken by a different person, which they were forced to buy off, and burnt the sheets. The two copies agreed verbatim.—*Peele.* Hoadly answered this speech of Atterbury's distinctly and fully, in several letters published in the London Journal, under the name of Britannicus. In the whole course of this dispute, the printed speech was always considered the right one; and was never denied to be so by the bishop or his friends.—All the letters in the London Journal about that time, signed Britannicus, were Hoadly's—1758.—*Spence.*'

The title-page of the 1723 speech reads 'printed for A. Moore'. The thirteen 'Britannicus' letters by Benjamin Hoadly (1676–1761), then Bishop of Hereford, were reprinted in the folio edition of his *Works*, 1773.

APPENDIX TO § 265

How many Bounces?

ALTHOUGH readers of Pope's poetry or of books about him have been familiar with the fact that he had a dog named Bounce, until Norman Ault wrote his sympathetic chapter on 'Pope and his Dogs' no one had realized that there must have been at least two with this name. The first is the Bounce of 1728 described by Mrs. Rackett, which on meagre evidence Ault decided was a male. The second Bounce was a bitch whose puppies Pope distributed among his friends in 1736, one of the recipients being the Prince of Wales.

We now know, however, that Pope had a dog named Bounce before he left Binfield early in 1716. A letter from Gay to Parnell written in March of that year reports, '... when I took my leave of Pope I recommended Bounce to his care as he was a f[riend of mine?] and yours' (*RES*, x, 1959, 380). Whether this dog was a Great Dane we cannot be certain, though the name suggests a creature 'big rather than elegant or graceful', thumping vigorously with ungainly movement (*OED*). If this Bounce was two years old when Gay wrote about him or her, we have a span of thirty years until the last Bounce expired in April 1744 at the Somersetshire seat of the Earl of Orrery, only a few weeks before Pope's own death. In fact, the epitaph Pope wrote may be the last verses he penned:

> Ah Bounce! ah gentle Beast! why wouldst thou dye,
> When thou hadst Meat enough, and Orrery?
>
> (*Corresp.* iv. 517.)

In pondering the question of how many dogs of this name Pope may have had it is necessary to consider the life expectancy of the Danish breed. True to the rule that 'the larger the dog, the shorter the life span', Great Danes live to an average of only eight or nine years, with eleven or twelve being quite exceptional. However, this estimate holds true only under the conditions of modern veterinary science and proper feeding procedures, which have lengthened animals' lives just as medical and dietary science have altered human life expectancy. Specialists consider that any of the Bounces in Pope's day would have been lucky to reach a seventh birthday.

In July 1742 Pope gave up keeping a dog and sent his last Bounce to Lord Orrery at Marston in Somersetshire. A letter from Lady Orrery written the following spring reveals that this Bounce was a male (*Corresp.* iv. 508). Although she reported that Bounce had been bitten by a mad dog, he survived for another year.

Thus we can be certain that Pope had at least four dogs named Bounce from the evidence of 1716, 1728, 1736, and 1742–4. Because Pope had grown up in a dog-loving family and evidently found solace in their company it is likely that he was never without one for long. They may even have been descendants of one line, though not of pedigree stock ('whatever their Father's Race', *Bounce to Fop*, l. 53).

A portrait of an early Bounce has been preserved, for Jonathan Richardson included him in the picture now owned by Lord Cobham. It is reproduced as the frontispiece of Ault's *New Light*. Another occurs in the sketch of Pope in his garden by Richardson, but beyond the dog's size little can be seen which might determine the breed.

APPENDIX A TO § 310

Which Gardening Poem?

POPE's bibliographer, R. H. Griffith, has established that the 1728 reprint of Gardiner's translation of Rapin's *Of Gardens* was revised by Pope and Walter Harte ('Pope on the Art of Gardening', Univ. of Texas *Studies in English*, xxxi, 1952, 52–56; see also § 338). Hence, he contends that Pope's reference to 'the gardening poem' means this translation of Rapin, and not the *Epistle to Burlington*, as Bateson suggested in his discussion. Further examination of the subject upholds Bateson's contention:

1. There is nothing in Rapin's poem that fits the requirements of the context ('the happiness of contentment. Prodigality flings away all in wrong tastes'). The *Epistle to Burlington* opens with this idea.

2. Chronology supports Bateson: the edition of Rapin had appeared in 1728, but in 1730 Pope said 'the gardening poem will be of service', the *Epistle to Burlington* not yet having been completed.

APPENDIX B TO § 310

Bolingbroke and the *Essay on Man*

THAT Lord Bolingbroke took an active interest in Pope's ambitious plans to versify philosophy is clear. The nature of his help, however, is more difficult to determine. This much we know: in May 1730 Savage told Spence (§ 310) that Bolingbroke had sent Pope a 'long letter', a remark which Spence first recorded only as 'L^{d} B: very much assisting in the materials'. Eighteen months later on 1 December 1731, in a letter to Swift, Pope used a cryptic phrase. Urging Swift to come to England, Pope says: 'You will see a word of Lord B—'s and one of mine; which, with a just neglect of the present age, consult only posterity; and with a noble scorn of politicks, aspire to philosophy' (*Corresp.* iii. 249). Editors have interpreted this passage in various ways; Elwin considered it a reference to Bolingbroke's 'Essays on Human Knowledge' (EC, vii. 258) and Ball to his 'Essays on Philosophy' (iv. 277). Sherburn, however, said: 'The "words" were Pope's *Essay on Man* and Bolingbroke's parallel prose writing' (*Corresp.* iii. 249).

The story of the parallel prose writing cannot be traced before 1763, nearly twenty years after Pope's death and a dozen after Bolingbroke's. In that year the aged Lord Bathurst told Hugh Blair that the *Essay on Man* 'was originally composed by Lord Bolingbroke in prose, and that Mr. Pope did no more than put it into verse: that he had read Lord Bolingbroke's manuscript in his own hand-writing; and remembered well, that he was at a loss whether most to admire the elegance of Lord Bolingbroke's prose, or the beauty of Mr. Pope's verse' (Hill-Powell, iii. 402). Mallet was present, and seemed anxious that the story be perpetuated. In 1769 Lord Bathurst testified further that Lord Bolingbroke turned the prose version over to Pope 'and I believe gave him leave to burn it. It has never appeared since, and perhaps I am the only man now alive who has read it' (quoted by Sherburn, *PQ*, xii, 1933, 402). That Bathurst in his old age was fond of relating this story appears further from Joseph Warton's testimony in 1780: 'Lord Bathurst repeatedly assured me, that he had read the whole scheme of the Essay on Man, in the hand-writing of Bolingbroke, and drawn up in a series of propositions, which POPE was to versify and illustrate' (*Essay*, ii. 62).

The evidence of Pope's own 'very large prose collections', to which Bolingbroke may have contributed a considerable part of the 'material', would seem to suggest that Bathurst's testimony had probably grown in the telling, and should be taken with reserve. On Pope's death, Bolingbroke—and through him, Mallet—received Pope's papers, so Mallet could have printed it, had it still existed. Bolingbroke's influence, both in conversation and letters (such as Savage mentions) did, of course, contribute much to Pope's thinking (see § 311 and Twickenham, III. i, pp. xxix–xxxi). Whether Bolingbroke composed a prose version of the *Essay on Man*, is, however, quite another matter.

APPENDIX TO § 323

Who Rejected Murray?

POPE's 'Epistle to Murray' (*Imitations*, I. vi) is addressed to William Murray, then at the outset of a brilliant parliamentary and legal career that led to his becoming Lord Chief Justice. 'High born wife' refers to lines 38–43:

> But wherefore all this labour, all this strife?
> For Fame, for Riches, for a noble Wife?
> Shall One whom Nature, Learning, Birth, conspir'd
> To form, not to admire, but be admir'd,
> Sigh, while his Chloë, blind to Wit and Worth,
> Weds the rich Dulness of some Son of Earth?

The young lady who refused Murray, to marry 'some Son of Earth', has never been identified. Horace Walpole wrote 'Miss Foley' in the margin next to this passage, leading John Butt to suggest that she may have been the sister of Thomas Foley (1703–66), second Baron Foley, who financed Murray's legal studies (Twickenham, iv. 238–9). Or, she may have been the 'Miss Foley' who married George Carpenter, 2 October 1736 (*GM*, vi, 1736, 620). Perhaps the bridegroom was the 'squire of broad acres in a midland county', reported as the husband by John, Lord Campbell, in *Lives of the Chief Justices*, 1849, ii. 340.

Another possibility hitherto unmentioned is Lady Oxford, who in July 1734 married William Bentinck, second Duke of Portland. To her Murray left in his will a picture 'to put her in mind of one she knew from her infancy'. For her son Murray also wrote a guide book in the form of a series of letters.

Whatever Murray's 'then views' may have been when Pope wrote the poem, they soon changed, for in September 1738 he married a 'noble wife', Lady Elizabeth Finch, daughter of the Earl of Nottingham and Winchester.

APPENDIX TO § 330

A Passage in the *Dunciad*

WHY did Spence in April 1742, three weeks after the publication of Book iv of the *Dunciad*, mistakenly cite Pope's attack on politically active clergymen as being in this new book? The lines did not reach the public until October 1743 when the revised version of all four books of the 'Cibber' *Dunciad* appeared. There the satirical passage on 'Heaven's Swiss' appears as ll. 355–64 in Book ii:

> Around him wide a sable Army stand,
> A low-born, cell-bred, selfish, servile band,
> Prompt or to guard or stab, to saint or damn,
> Heav'n's Swiss, who fight for any God, or Man.
> Thro' Lud's fam'd gates, along the well-known Fleet
> Rolls the black troop, and overshades the street,
> 'Till show'rs of Sermons, Characters, Essays,
> In circling fleeces whiten all the ways:
> So clouds replenish'd from some bog below,
> Mount in dark volumes, and descend in snow.

I suggest the following explanation. Spence had heard Pope speak of this controversial passage, perhaps sometime before April, for he seems to be jotting down notes from memory. At any rate, Spence had the definite impression that the anticlerical passage was to be part of Book iv. He obviously was not familiar with the printed version of Book iv that had reached the public in March.

Why did Pope then change his plans and place the passage in Book ii instead? The simplest interpretation is that Pope realized that Book iv, being entirely a *new Dunciad*, would be read by his enemies with gimlet eyes, seeking to fasten on any passages that might seem vulnerable. Hence he slipped the passage into Book ii, which was not seen by the public until it appeared in the complete *Dunciad* in October 1743, in which interval his new victims' wrath had had time to cool. Moreover, public attention was now focused on a new subject, the enthronement of Cibber as chief dunce in place of Theobald.

That Pope was apprehensive about the way the clergy would accept the passage is indicated by the long note he got Warburton to append to the lines, explaining that Pope was lashing out at corrupt churchmen only (Twickenham, v. 314). Despite this precaution a number of Anglican clergymen felt themselves affronted, as Pope reveals in a letter to Warburton written in the following January: 'I am much more concerned to hear, that some of your clergy are offended at a Verse or two of mine, because I have a respect for your Clergy (tho the Verses are harder upon ours) But if they do not blame *You* for defending those verses, I will wrap myself up in the Layman's Cloak, & sleep under Your Shield' (*Corresp.* iv. 492).

APPENDIX TO § 395

Pope on Milton's Style

POPE's attitude towards Milton's style echoes Addison's opinion expressed in *Spectator*, No. 285: 'I think [Milton's] style, though admirable in general, is in some places too much stiffened and obscured by the frequent use of . . . several ways of speech which Aristotle calls foreign language, and with which Milton has so very much enriched and in some places darkened the language of his poem, [this method being] the more proper for his use because the poem is written in blank verse.'

There are several anecdotes by Pope's contemporaries prompted by this attitude towards Milton and blank verse. Warton called attention to Voltaire's statement about a conversation with Pope on this subject: 'Je me souviendrai toujours que je demandai au célèbre POPE, pourquoi Milton n'avait pas rimé son Paradis perdu; & qu'il me répondit, *Because he could not*; parce qu'il ne le pouvait pas' (*Essay*, ii. 155 n.).

So, too, Percival Stockdale reported a conversation with Lord Lyttelton: 'My translation of the AMINTA, gave occasion to his lordship [Lyttelton] of saying something on blank verse. He told me, that on a visit to Mr. POPE at TWICKENHAM, while he was translating the iliad, he took the liberty to express to that great poet, his surprise that he had not determined to translate HOMER's poem into blank verse; as it was an epick poem;—and as he had before him the illustrious example of MILTON, in the paradise lost.—Mr. POPE's answer to lord LYTTLETON was, that "he could translate it more easily into rhyme."—I communicated this anecdote to Dr. JOHNSON; his remark on it to me, was very erroneous, in criticism; and it was very irreverent, and rude, to a memory which deserved more respectful treatment. "Sir,—when POPE said *that*, he knew that he lied"' (*Memoirs of Percival Stockdale*, 1809, ii. 44.).

Since Lord Lyttelton was born in 1709 and apparently did not know Pope until about ten years after he had translated the *Odyssey*. the story as it stands is an anachronism.

APPENDIX TO § 678

Whom did Etherege Portray?

DRYDEN's epilogue to the *Man of Mode* stressed the point that the character for whom the play was named did not represent any individual member of London society, but 'represents ye all . . . a people in a man' and that 'no one fool is hunted from the herd'. Nevertheless, the audience considered that Etherege had drawn the characters from well-known figures in the Court. A letter has recently come to light from Peter Killigrew to his sister, written three days after the first performance. Because their brother, Thomas Killigrew, owned a quarter interest in the rival company at the Theatre Royal, Peter was well placed to hear the gossip:[1]

> On Satturday I went to ye new play, & was very well all the time. This Sr Fopling Flutter makes at present all the discourse, to discover the persones meant by it. I find the generall opinion will have Sr Fopling to be Mr. Villers, Ld Grandisons eldest son. Mr. Batterton under the name of Dorimant meanes the Duke of Monmouth & his intrigue with Moll Kirke, Mrs. Needham, & Lady Harriott Wentworth, though Sr Fopling, speaking in the Epilogue protests he is Knight of ye Sheere & represents them all, & concludes that nothing was there of what was feared, for noe one fop was hunted from the heard.

'Mr. Villers' was Edward, son and heir apparent of the fourth Viscount Grandison of Limerick. Born about 1652, he married in 1677 (a year after the *Man of Mode*) Catherine Fitzgerald, an heiress who brought a huge estate on condition that he change his name to Fitzgerald.[2] Unhappily, information about his career before marriage is scanty and confirmation of his gallic mannerisms—or even of a sojourn in France—is lacking. John Bowman (1651–1739), who acted in the play with the Duke's Company, told William Oldys that Sir Fopling represented Sir George Hewett, known as 'Beau' Hewett (*Biographica Britannica*, 1750, iii. 1843).

[1] 14 March 1675/6; quotation from Maggs Brothers' Catalogue, 882 (1962), p. 17, now in the collection of John R. B. Brett-Smith, Esq.

[2] After his death in 1693 the widow obtained by Royal warrant the title Viscountess Grandison, the last such warrant ever issued. Their son John, born 1684, became fifth Viscount and in 1721 was created Earl Grandison.

The amatory prowess of the handsome royal bastard, the Duke of Monmouth, has been well established by his biographers, but there is no evidence to support Peter Killigrew's suggestion that Dorimant is intended to caricature him aside from the similarity between the names of Harriet Woodvil in the play, and his faithful mistress, Lady Harriet Wentworth. That anyone ever considered Monmouth a wit or discerned in him a fondness for quoting poetry is unrecorded; on the contrary his intellect was inherited along with his fair face, from his mother. Furthermore, a satirical portrayal of the Duke would have cut dangerously near the throne.

The tradition that Dorimant represented John Wilmot, Earl of Rochester, received its strongest statement from John Dennis, who was a nineteen-year-old member of the audience when the play was performed in 1676. Years later, in 1722, Dennis wrote (Hooker, ii. 248):

Now I remember very well, that upon the first acting this Comedy, it was generally believed to be an agreeable Representation of the Persons of Condition of both Sexes, both in Court and Town; and that all the World was charm'd with *Dorimont*; and that it was unanimously agreed, that he had in him several of the Qualities of *Wilmot* Earl of *Rochester*, as, his Wit, his Spirit, his amorous Temper, the Charms that he had for the fair Sex, his Falshood, and his Inconstancy; the agreeable Manner of his chiding his Servants, which the late Bishop of *Salisbury* takes Notice of in his Life; and lastly, his repeating, on every Occasion, the Verses of *Waller*, for whom that noble Lord had a very particular Esteem; witness his Imitation of the Tenth Satire of the First Book of *Horace*:

> Waller, *by Nature for the Bays design'd,*
> *With Spirit, Force, and Fancy unconfin'd,*
> *In Panegyrick is above Mankind.*

Bowman also told Oldys that the character represented Rochester. That the identification with Rochester was not unanimous we know from Peter Killigrew's letter. Descendants of Charles Sackville, the witty Earl of Dorset, considered that Dorimant was a composite portrait of Dorset and Rochester (T. Davies, *Dramatic Miscellanies*, 1784, iii. 169–70). The testimony falsely ascribed to St. Évremond in the 1707 (and following) editions of Rochester (for whatever it is worth) corroborates Dennis: 'Sir *George Etherege* wrote *Dorimant* in Sir *Fopling*, in Compliment to him, as drawing his Lordship's Character, and burnishing all the Foibles of it, to make them shine like Perfections.' Biographers of Rochester have been so convinced that Dorimant portrays the witty Earl that they have incorporated whole pages of conversation from the *Man of Mode* in their lives of the poet.

If Etherege inserted himself in the play, the chances are that he did so as Medley, the 'rhetorically drunk' confidant of Dorimant. So William Oldys reported in his account of Etherege in the *Biographica Britannica* (1750, iii. 1843), his information coming from John Bowman. H. F. B. Brett-Smith (*Dramatic Works*, 1927, i, p. xxv), tempted by the similarity of the name to Sedley's, suggested that Etherege may have been portraying his friend Sir Charles. More likely Etherege utilized the connotations of the word as an aid to characterization, as he did in using the 'type' names for other characters in this and his other plays.

APPENDIX TO § 680

Duke or Duchess?

If the Duke of Modena had come to England to visit his sister, the Queen, in February 1688 as Luttrell reported (i. 430), the incident of Sir Fleetwood Shepherd's witticism could be easily placed. But as far as we know, the Duke never came to England and Fleetwood Shepherd never travelled further than France, where he visited Henry Saville in 1681, probably returning in February 1681/2 (A. Wood, *Life and Times*, ed. A. Clark, 1891–1900, ii. 559; Luttrell, i. 165).

It seems more likely, therefore, that 'D. of Modena's' means 'Duchess of Modena's'. The Queen's mother, the dowager duchess, did visit England several times to attend her daughter's lying in, the last time apparently being in August 1682. But the point of the joke seems to require a year near 1688, or at least after James was King. Perhaps Lockier once more garbled the details of his story.

APPENDIX TO § 765

Lady Mary's Septennial Bill

IN Spence's letter to his mother from Rome, 11 March 1741, he described Lady Mary Wortley Montagu's ideas for a septennial bill:

'I have seen a paper written by her Ladyship on a very odd subject; "That it is possible, for two people to be happy in the State of Matrimony." She does not pretend to say, that this has ever happen'd; but she thinks 'tis not quite impossible that this may happen, one time or another, before the world is at an end. In spite of this she holds two Maxims, which she learn'd in the East; & which she wishes were put in practice among us.

The First is, that Husbands shou'd not have any portion with their Wives. This wou'd certainly have several good Consequences attending it. Men wou'd not then marry for money, but for the real Merit of the Woman; and women wou'd endeavour to deserve as much as they cou'd, when Merit was to be their only Fortune. If Husbands did not receive Portions, they wou'd not be [oblig'd] to pay them neither for their Daughters; nor Elder Brothers for their Sisters; nor wou'd Estates be clog'd, as they are at present, wth Jointures. This is what she says for it; and perhaps there may be a great deal to be said against it: but the Second Maxim, I think, all the World must be for. 'Tis as follows.

She wou'd have an Act of Parliament made in England, That at the end of every Parliament, when that is dissolv'd, it shou'd be at the choice of every married Couple in England, to dissolve their marriage too; & to chuse anew, if they did not like their old Choice. Any Couple that had a mind to continue together, might do so without any farther Ceremony; & every Couple that thought they cou'd better themselves, shou'd be at Liberty to part, without any ceremony likewise. The effect of this wou'd be, that a multitude of Slaves wou'd be set free with us, every seventh year; & possibly, after this Act was pass'd, all the world wou'd be for another, for Annual Parliaments; to the end that this General Release of Prisoners, might return too every year. This wou'd make Great Britain truly free; & we might then Boast, with all our other Liberties, of what is as great as any of them; "That with us only, of all Nations in Europe, a few words spoke by a Man in a black Coat, did not oblige two People to live together all the days of their life, who may wish themselves apart perhaps in two or three days after they came together." '

APPENDIX TO § 855

Young's Epigram on Voltaire

IN a defence of Milton in the *Gentleman's Magazine* (xxxv, 1765, 598 n.), the writer, who signed himself 'W.D.', describes the occasion and gives the epigram as follows:

As Mr *Voltaire* was talking one day very wittily and very profanely on this subject [the allegory of Sin and Death], at Mr *Pope*'s table, the late Dr *Young*, (who was one of the company) wrote down, and handed to him the following *extempore* Epigram:

Thou art so witty, proffligate [*sic*], *and thin,*
Thou'rt Milton'*s* Devil, *and his* Death, *and* Sin.

This version also occurs in the *Gentleman's Magazine*, xlix (1779), 363 n. However, a correspondent, calling himself 'Scrutator', writing in vol. l (1780), 64, says the epigram 'should stand thus:

Thou'rt so ingenious, profligate, and thin,
At once thou'rt Milton, and his Death, and Sin.'

Another version is given by Herbert Croft in his *Life of Young*, which he wrote for Dr. Johnson (*Lives*, iii. 376):

You are so witty, profligate and thin,
At once we think thee Milton, Death, and Sin.

Finally, Mrs. Delany in a letter to Mrs. Anne Granville, dated 29 February 1728 (*The Autobiography and Correspondence of Mary Granville*, ed. Lady Llanover, 1861, i. 160), attributes the following couplet to Lord Hervey:

So much confusion, so wicked and so thin,
He seems at once a Chaos, Death, and Sin.

APPENDIX TO § 1059

Spence's Letter to the Reverend Mr. Wheeler (1751)

SPENCE probably knew the Rev. Robert Wheeler at New College, Oxford, where Wheeler matriculated on 10 December 1722. He was given his B.A. on 1 March 1726/7, and received his M.A. before making his career in the Church. In 1737 he became prebendary of Wedmore, and of Haselbere in 1738/9. He was prebendary of Wells from 1737 until his death, and became rector of Dulverton, Somerset, in 1757. His name appears in the list of subscribers to Blacklock's *Poems* (1756), and he is probably the 'Mr. Wheeler' who wrote to Spence on 25 February 1748 about the 'Man of Ross', who, Wheeler notes, had a 'singular taste for Prospects' (Singer, pp. 423–6).

It is possible that Spence's letter to Wheeler, as Wright suggests (p. 230, n. 14), was intended for publication. The four manuscript versions in the Spence Papers (Box 1321) certainly support this hypothesis.

The earliest version is written on 2 quarto leaves, and is headed: '1st Copy. To Mr Wheeler on Gard^{g} Sep: 19, 1751. add: Surprizes conceal^{g} ye B^{d}s.' This version is much briefer than the final one. The rules are arranged in a different order, some are omitted altogether, and part of the description of Spence's garden is missed out. (Since this is the earliest manuscript, it is hereafter referred to as A.)

The next version to be written is headed 'Copy of part of a Letter to M^{r}. W. in Somersetshire; Sep^{t} 19th 1751 (in part:) wth Mr Southcote's Remarks'. It is superscribed in error, '3d Copy? wth Mr Southcotes Remarks'. Only the first part of the letter covering the rules is given, and the text follows that of A. It is written on 2 leaves of folio paper, torn in half vertically, forming 4 leaves. Spence's letter is written on one side of each, and Southcote's notes are added on the verso. (Referred to as A^{1}.)

Part of the notes recorded in L51 refer to this letter, and belong with the comments made by Southcote, which were incorporated in the B version. On the top right of L51 the following jottings are written in Southcote's hand: 'Cascades, Fountains, Statues, buildings, [see note k below] "I will weep for nothing; like Diana in the Fountain." Rosalind; in Shakespear's As you like it: Act: 4, (p. 54) 12mo not too thick shade: danc^g in the checquerd shade!—to more luminous &c.' Following this are notes for the final draft of the letter (see note i below).

After A[1] Spence expanded the text of the letter. He rearranged the order of the first part and added several rules and additional material in the marginal notes. He also added to the passages describing his own garden. The resulting text is essentially that given below, but with a few additional notes by Spence. (This version is referred to as B.)

Finally a fair copy was made by a hand other than Spence's. It is described as the '(4th Copy,)', and is the text followed below since it clearly represents the final version of the letter. The manuscript consists of 6 leaves of folio paper, vertically folded, the letter being written on the recto of each of the two leaves so formed. (This version is referred to as C.)

In transcribing C, capitalization, punctuation, and spelling have been modernized. No attempt has been made to give the textual variants in full since the differences between C and A, A[1] and B, are due to rearrangement and to the addition of new material. In a few instances, however, details are present in the early manuscripts not in C. These, together with Southcote's comments on A[1] and Spence's additional notes in B, are printed in alphabetical sequence. Explanatory notes are given in numerical sequence.

Copy of a Letter to the Reverend Mr. W[heeler], September 19,[a] 1751

Dear Sir,

When you set me to write about gardening, you set me upon a thing that I love extremely; but as to any large tract of ground, there is no saying anything in particular without being upon the spot; and having considered it well and often. Some general rules one might mention, but, after all, nine parts in ten depend upon the application. Yet I will just mention some that I followed myself.

The first and most material is to consult the Genius of the place. What is, is the great guide as to what ought to be. The making a fine plan for any place unknown is like Bays's saying 'that he had made an excellent simile, if he did but know how to apply it.'[1] To study

[a] 19] *emended from* 9 (C)*: both* A *and* A[1] *give* 19. B *gives no date. After the heading* B *adds:* (Add: ^ns Non fumum ex folgore &c to go from worse to better. Not to let all the design appear at once.

[1] *Rehearsal*, I. ii (which actually reads, 'one of the most delicate dainty Similes').

the ground thoroughly, one should not only take a view of the whole and all its parts, and consider the laying of it in general, and all its beauties and advantages or inconveniences and impediments, in particular, but also walk all round it in the line without your own bounds; to see what beauties may be added by breaking through your outline.

2dly To fix the principal point of view for the whole plan, and any secondary points of view that may be of consequence in the disposition of the parts.[b]

3dly To follow Nature. Gardening is an imitation of 'Beautiful Nature',[2] and therefore should not be like works of art. Wherever art appears, the gardener has failed in his execution.[c] Our old gardens were formed by the rule and square,[3] with a perpetual uniformity and in a manner more fit for architecture than for pleasure-grounds. Nature never plants by the line, or in angles. I have lately seen thirty-six prints of a vast garden belonging to the present emperor of China:[d4] there is not one regular walk of trees in the whole ground, they seem to exceed our late best designers in the natural taste almost as far as those do the Dutch taste, brought over into England in King William's time. As to angles, I have such a mortal aversion to them, that was I to choose a motto for myself as a pretender to gardening, it should be, 'Mutat quadrata rotundis.'[5] I should almost ever prefer serpentizing walks to straight ones, and round off the corners of groves instead of pointing them.[e]

[b] parts] B *adds:*—A Month may be too little for these two together, if the Ground is large, perplext, & difficult: & ½ an hour may be too much, if it lyes all under the Eye at once, & is naturally disposd in a happy manner [*Spence*].

[c] Wherever . . . execution] *this does not appear in* A *nor in the text of* A^1*: Southcote's note in* A^1 *reads:* notably: that where ever art is easily discerned by ye eye, ye gardener has failed in his execution. *In* B *Spence incorporated this as:* Wherever Art is easily discernable to the Eye the Designer has either committed a Fault in his Plan or faild in the Execution.

[d] China] *add* in Pequin (A, B).

[e] *Southcote noted in* A^1*:* there are some few instances where Regularity may be practised; 'tis in Forests, where Stars & different Cutts are made for ye Conveniency of Hunting.—also in ye approach to Houses I have seen regularity of planting very ornamental.

---

[2] For Spence's views on 'beautiful Nature' see §§ 1069 and 1070.

[3] See Chase, pp. 9–13.

[4] This book has not been identified. Possibly he was referring to *Recueil de lettres édifiantes et curieuses* (Paris, 1749; no copy of this book is available to the editor), which contained Attiret's account, translated by Spence as *A Particular Account of the Emperor of China's Gardens near Pekin* (1752).

[5] Horace, *Epist.* I. i. 100.

4ly To assist or correct the general character of the ground, if deficient or displeasing. Thus if your ground be all dry, a winding stream should be brought into it, if possible; if not, pieces of water, with alders and weeping willows and other aquatics about them, dashed here and there, at proper distances from each other.[f] If the ground be all flat, one should make risings and inequalities in it: very small swellings will help it much if properly placed,[g] and natural irregular risings (or mounts) where any particular object or pleasing prospect is to be caught, etc.

5ly To correct or conceal any particular object that is disagreeable.

6ly To open a view to whatever is particularly agreeable.

7ly To manage your plantations in such a manner that you may be led to some striking object, or change, unexpectedly: in which case not only the change or object, but the surprise itself is pleasing.

8ly To conceal the bounds of your grounds everywhere, if possible. This is done by grove-works, sunk fences (the best of which is the *chevaux de frise*) and what they call invisible fences, as being but little discernible to the eye. If you have sheep to keep and enliven the lawn, movable fences are the best, if any necessary, and of all such fences I should prefer what they call the Palladian rail, or wattles, in the following form:

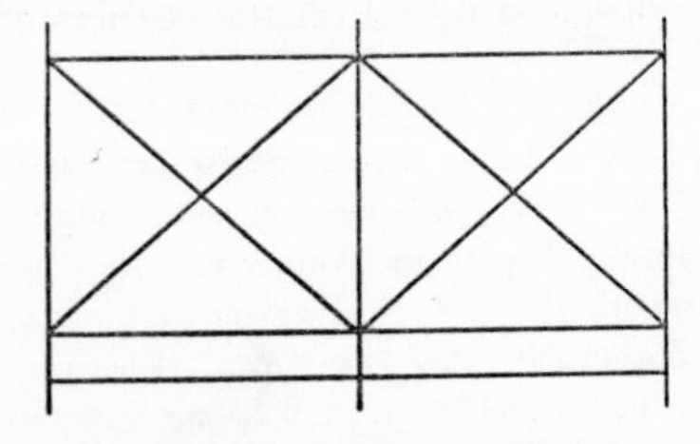

The fence most common in the Emperor of China's garden (of which eighteen prints are very soon to be published at London)[h6] is a good deal of this kind, and none of them are at all like those ridiculous things

[f] *Southcote noted in* A¹: always remembring, that a river, Brook Lake, or any other piece of water must be accompanied by trees properly placed—.

[g] *Southcote noted in* A¹: for planting; of trees, flowering shrubs, or to place any object for ornament on such rising or irregularity of ground.

[h] are very . . . published] *deleted, and* were publish't a few years ago *inserted in another hand* (C).

[6] Spence presumably was referring to the *Emperor of China's Palace at Pekin and his Principal Gardens* . . . (1753), which, however, contained twenty plates.

called Chinese rails, and which are got now so much in fashion in town as well as in the country.

9ly To unite the different parts of your garden gently together.

10 To contrive the outparts so, as to unite well with the country round about them.

11 To mix useful things even in the ornamental parts, and something of ornament even in the useful parts.

12 To make objects that are too near seem farther off: which is done by shewing more of the intermediate ground and narrowing your view to them more and more as it recedes from you.

13 To draw distant objects nearer to you and make them seem part of your work: which is done by hiding the intermediate length of ground and planting what may fall in and unite, to the eye, with such distant objects.

14 To study variety in all things, as nothing without it can be pleasing. Inequality of ground, mixture of land and water, opposition of lights and shades, or grove and open, breaking the lines of trees, interspersing different sorts of trees in each grovette, placing trees of different greens and flowers of different colours by one another, etc.—Mr. Kent always used to stake out his grovettes before they planted, and to view the stakes every way, to see that no three of them stand in a line: to which another, as necessary rule may be added: that in all smaller plantations one should never set above three or four trees of the same sort together.[i]

15 To observe the different friendships and enmities of different colours, and to place the most friendly ones next each other.

16 In the mixing of lights and shades, to let the former have the prevalence,[j] or, in other words, to give the whole a joyous air rather than a melancholy one. In this again the Chinese seem very much to exceed our pleasure-ground makers. They have scarce any such thing as close or thick groves in any of their near views: they fling them all on some of the hills at a distance.[k]

[i] Mr. Kent . . . together] *not in* A, A¹*: added in margin of* B. L51 *contains earlier notes towards this passage (apparently by Spence):* in ye Wild Grove Work no three trees s^d^ be in a strait line together An excell^t^ Rule of Kent's, for being Irregular.

Never above two or three trees of the same kind contiguous; wch will necessitate a Variety. If you have not sometimes two (at least) together, it will be less Various; & consequently, (acc^g^ to ye Logic of Gardening,) less Pleasing.

[j] prevalence] preference (A¹).

[k] A¹ *concludes here, and Southcote noted:* in all plantations made to cover ye pale, or fence of y^r^ Boundary where there is room for it, it is remarkably fine & agreeable

All that I have laid out here so particularly (and perhaps a great deal more) is included by Mr. Pope in two lines, where in speaking of gardens he says:

> He gains all Ends, who pleasingly confounds,
> Surprises, varies, and conceals the bounds:[7]

and in conversation, I have heard him include it in one single word, Variety.

* * *

These are all the general rules that I can recollect at present, but you ask me too what I have done to my own ground in particular.[8] This might be answered in four words: I found it all confined, gloomy, regular and flat, I have made it appear less flat, quite irregular, light and open.

If you desire a yet more particular account, take it as follows.

My whole domain is not above 16 or 17 acres. The acre next the house consists of a garden with a grove in the midst of it, a kitchen garden hid behind a fruit-wall, and a piece of nursery-ground concealed in the same manner. 'Tis fenced from the sheep that feed just beyond it by a winding brook,[1] instead of a wall which formerly stood there and used to say to the eye, 'Hitherto shall thou look and no farther.' The grass-field that spreads itself next to it, of about four acres, is dashed here and there with trees, with a dark clump towards the middle of it and two unequal openings or lawns (which with the scattered trees give it a parkish look) and a winding walk of sand runs all round it. Between this sand-walk and the hedge-rows I have scattered large flowers, flowering-shrubs, and evergreens in several places, so that this is a half-garden. The rest of my fields, which spread on wider all along

to see different plants rise one above another from ye shrub to ye tallest trees of various kinds; which is practised by planting upon hanging ground or slopes; from ye Pale; *After this rule* B *adds in pencil:* after y^{s} Article—*Buildings or seats where necessary for rest, or views, or to be viewed—*Statues,* Gardens, Pleasure-grounds: no unpleasing figures; (Lucretia stab^{g} herself, rape of ye Sabine, fighting Glad^{r} &c Instead of them, Fawns, Nymphs, Flora's, Seasons, &c.—[*cf.* § 1098] *Fountains,* the figures for them, if any, s^{d} be Aquatic (Cascades best) next Watergods, Nymphs, &c. The Fountains of the Antients, how reasonable; those at Versailles, &c. how unreasonable—*Buildings white, & accompanied wth Trees (Gr: & Wh:) Lively evergreens—not to look Townish, or Houselike [*Spence*].

[1] winding brook] A *adds:* of my own making.

---

[7] *Epistle to Burlington,* ll. 55–56. For Pope's remarks on this couplet see § 612.

[8] i.e. Byfleet, Surrey, where Spence had moved in 1748 or 1749.

beyond these, have the winding walk continued all round them, with here and there a rising, to take off the cornerings, and these risings are chiefly planted with lauristenas, laurels, and three or four different sorts of firs, which makes this farther part look like fields, only a little improved. By the help of these walks I can go all round my little territory in half an hour after a shower of rain, without being wet: for the sand dries soon and is much easier hoed and kept clean than gravel, besides its being much cheaper, especially to me: for, God help us, we live in the neighbourhood of one of the most dreary, sandy heaths in Europe.

In the midst of this abominable heath rises a large hill, on which Julius Caesar is said to have encamped[9] before he passed from this country through the Thames into Middlesex. The make of the camp is still very visible and spreads in its greatest length to the north-east of us. All the hither line of it I have planted here and there with clumps of firs, which in a few years will make it part of my garden: for the tops of the trees in my garden-grove[m] unite (to the eye) with the trees in my hedgerows, and both of them will hereafter unite with the trees on the hill: so that they will make as it were one continued wood, and at the same time hide all that barren side of the hill from me.

To the south and the south-west, we have a very beautiful run of hills at ten or twelve miles distance, and to the south-east four or five very pretty ones, about a mile off. You may be sure I was as ready to open a view to all these as I was to shut out the other, though I have not cut my hedges down all the way; but perhaps here for [a] hundred or hundred and fifty feet, and then left it uncut for fifty, and so of the rest. The nearer ones too, I have planted with clumps of firs and other trees.

The greatest misfortune of my ground was its being one flat. Toward the house I have helped it a little, by raising little knoles and terraces; so placed that whichever way you look, the eye will meet with some rising. But my greatest assistance was the opening the view to these hills, for as they lay semicircularly about me, when you take a view of the whole, my flat ground looks like half the arena of an amphitheatre, and in that light has rather a good look than a bad one.

I have said nothing of a walk that I have planted (not in regular

[m] garden-grove] A *adds:* from my study-windows.

---

[9] i.e. the 'Caesar's camp' on St. George's Hill.

lines, but scatteringly) for half a mile, from the bridge that leads into our village to the church, and another of about the same length half way to one of the best neighbours in the world.[10]

Won't you say that all these are great works for such a little man as I am in all respects, to engage in and finish before I was quite three years old in this place, and that I am a very fortunate man to have others join me in such odd undertakings? Yet this too has happened: the good neighbour I mentioned has planted his half mile to meet my plantation, and another gentleman has carried on the plantations on the hills round us in a much ampler and nobler manner than I ever intended. If one was to measure the farthest points that are already planted from east to west, I dare say it would be a line of near four miles, as these from north to south would, I believe, be three and a half; and supposing a circle drawn all round them, it would contain a much larger quantity of ground than the city of Geneva and all the contiguous land belonging to that state.[n]

But if you have a mind to get a true idea of all my great works here, I beg you would come and take a view of them: two or three days seeing would be more effectual than two or three years writing, and therefore if any business should call you to London, I conjure you to come to Byfleet. I must have quite tired you, as well as myself, and am, etc.[o]

n state.] B *adds:* When I was at Geneva a Mathematician of their University, at my desire was so good as to reduce a Map of their City, & y[e] ground about it belonging to them, into a regular figure; & it made a circle of but 3 Mile diameter [*Spence*]. *Spence visited Geneva in October 1731 (see* §§ 1313–17).

o I . . . etc.] where my Mother & I s[d] be extreamly glad of your good company; & much more so, if you c[d] bring M[rs] Wheeler with you (A). *This, clearly the original conclusion of the letter, also occurs in the text of* B, *where, however, the* C *version is given in the margin.*

---

10 Lord Lincoln, whose seat at Oatlands was near by. It was Lincoln who offered Spence the house at Byfleet (Wright, pp. 113–14).

APPENDIX TO § 1409

Foucquet's Letter

IN the Folio manuscript Spence originally continued this anecdote with the following sentence: 'But perhaps it may not be improper to annex my extract, from the letter itself; which contains the whole of it, except the compliments at the beginning, & at the conclusion.' The letter in French follows. Spence, however, crossed out the sentence just quoted, and made a marginal note, 'To App[x].' He then drew a vertical line alongside the French text, which lasts for almost three pages, and noted, 'Omit[d], now; as far as markt.'

The letter is not among the Loose Papers nor in the Newcastle manuscript. However, there is a version in the Vatican Library which is described as 'Lettre du Reverend Pere de Premare Jesuite Minimaire de la Chine a M. xxx. à Canton' (MS. Borgia lat. 565, ff. 629–37[v]). The manuscript is undated but follows other letters dating from late 1717. A comparison of Spence's version with this shows that he, or the copy which he transcribed, omitted considerably more than the opening and concluding compliments for words are altered and passages omitted or radically shortened. In the text of the letter given below, which is taken from F (pp. 92–95), '[. . . .]' indicates that Spence's text omits a phrase or substantial passage, and ⌜ ⌝ indicate that the passage so marked represents a résumé of the material in the original. There has been no attempt to note minor changes in the wording, and Spence's French is left as it was written.

'Il me paroit certain, qu'il y a un tems ou les Grans hommes tels qu'etoient les Patriarches Antidiluviens, sçavoient tres bien le sens de toutes les importantes Verités, que Dieu avoit revelées au premier homme. [. . . .] Ces Verités se reduisoient a trois points principaux: le 1, l'Etat heureux avant le Peché; le 2, la Misere dans laquelle l'homme etoit tombé par sa faute; le 3, tout ce qui regarde le Redempteur, [. . . .] dans les livres de Moise & des Prophetes. Presque tout se rapporte à ces trois points; surtout, au dernier. Les antiquitez de l'univers ne parlent d'autres choses; & les vieux monumens de la Chine tendent là uniquement.

Une Tradition, si necessaire, etant venue des enfans d'Adam jusqu'à Noe; c'est par le canal de Noe, qu'elle s'est repandue par tout:

plus ou moins claire, selon que les Fondateurs des premiers Empires en ont eu une connoissance plus ou moins nette. [. . . .]

Le plus ancien, & le plus admiré, de tous ces vieux monumens s'appelle Y KING; mais il y a long tems que les Chinois n'y entendent plus rien. [. . . .] Tous cependant ont taché de l'expliquer; tous disent, qu'il n'y a point de livre plus ancien: [. . . .] tous en ont une tres haute estime. [. . . .]

⌜Plusieurs des plus grandes verités & misteres de notre religion se trouvent, mais obscurement, dans ce Y KING: Pour exemple.⌝

Les Y KING disent en plusieurs endroits, que c'est le tres haut qui a produit le Ciel, la Terre, & toute choses. ⌜Ils font mention même de l'ordre dont ils etoient faits.⌝ Ils disent, que *Tchi yeou* a été le premier rebelle; & que sa rebellion s'est etendue jusque sur les hommes: ⌜On y trouve⌝ le Paradis terrestre admirablement bien designé. [. . . .] On y trouve aussi l'arbre de Vie; & la Fontaine, d'ou sortent quatre fleuves qui se repandent vers les quatre parties du monde.

Pour ce qui regarde [. . . .] la chute de l'homme; on dit, qu'il se perdit pour avoir voulu trop sçavoir. On attribue, dans le CHI KING, sa perte a la femme. [. . . .] On dit, comme il se couvrit des feuilles d'arbres; &, l'Y KING, qu'il s'attacha sur l'arbre nomme *Sang*.

⌜On dit aussi, qu'il falloit attendre un Sauveur: que ce Sauveur seroit ensemble Roi & Sujet, Terre & Ciel, Dieu & Homme.⌝ L'Y KING dit du Saint, en bien des endroits, qu'il est egal à son pere, & que son pere est plus grand que lui. Les interpretes Chinois ont assez d'orgueil & de folie, pour soutenir que cela doit s'entendre du premier Ministre de l'Empereur: ils disent, que bien qu'il soit inferieur au Roi, le Roi doit le traiter d'egal; le regarder même comme son maitre; & ne rien faire que par son avis. [. . . .] ⌜On trouve aussi dans l'Y KING, que⌝ le Sauveur est né d'une Vierge: [. . . .] qu'elle ne souffrit aucune rupture, aucune division: qu'elle n'eut aucun accident, aucun dommage. [. . . .] ⌜Que⌝ le Sauveur est notre Roi, & notre Maitre: [. . . .] le Ciel aime tendrement les hommes, dit le CHI KING; il leur donne un Roi, il leur donne un Maitre; & parce que ce Maitre & ce Roi est le ministre du tres-haut, le tres-haut lui donne toute la terre. [. . . .] On dit, d'apres LES KINGS, que quand le Sauveur viendra, il ne sera point connu. [. . . .] Le Sauveur a employé trois ans à detruire l'Empire de Satan: [. . . .] l'Y KING dit aussi, en deux endroits; que le fils [. . . .] detruira le Royaume de Demon, & qu'il en triomphera au bout de trois ans [. . . .] ⌜On y trouve en plusieurs endroits, son⌝ obeissance, son humilité, & sa douceur.

Nous sçavons les souffrances du Sauveur: mais on est surpris, quand on les voit si bien marquées dans le Symbole KOUEN. [. . . .] Entre autre choses on y dit, en termes expres; Qu'il donne sa vie, parce qu'il le veut bien. [. . . .] Le CHU KING dit du Sauveur, Que les pechés de tous les hommes sont sur luy. [. . . .] On appelle le Sauveur, L'Agneau de Dieu; [. . . .] le Sauveur est mort, & resuscité: [. . . .] le Sauveur est monté au Ciel, & viendra juger l'univers; [. . . .] & quand il paroitra, tous les hommes le verront: que ceux qui sont du Ciel, [. . . .] montreront [*sic*], en haut; & ceux qui sont attachés à la terre, descendront en bas.

Les Recompenses & les Chatimens se trouvent, [. . . .] à chaque pas, dans le CHU KING, CHI KING, & Y KING. Le chapitre *Isa Koue*, dit; Enfin le fort surmontera le faible: l'heureux sort des bons, sera eternal; & les pleurs des mechans, ne finiront jamais.)'

APPENDIX TO § 1434

A Jesuit School Reading List

SPENCE wrote the following note to introduce the list of books, and then crossed out the last part of the sentence, here indicated by half brackets:

'The same Gentleman was so good as to favour me with a List of the Books and Subjects, that were to be explained at the Roman College: publish'd in the latter end of the Year 1740 ⌜which as nothing of the kind has perhaps ever been printed in England, may not be improper to be annext under this Article⌝.[1]

Librorum Elenchus in Romano Societatis Jesu Collegio explicandorum; ex Nonis Novembris anni vertentis MDCCXL, in proximè sequentem: Moderatoris ejusdem Gymnasii auctoritate praepositus.

In Classe Theologiae.

Ex Sacris libris:

Quaestiones Selectae. Horâ 22½
De Beatitudine & de Actibus Humanis. Horâ 16.
De Incarnatione. Horâ 16½.

In Classe Theologiae Dogmaticae & Polemicae.

De Erroribus Jansenianis.

Ex Hebraicis:

Explicabitur Grammatica Hebraica P. Edwardi Slaughter, Soc: Jesu; et Liber Psalmorum. Horâ 21.

In Classe Theologiae Positivae.

De Beneficiis Ecclesiasticis. Horâ 17.

In Classe Theologiae Moralis.

De regulâ morum intrinsecâ, sive de Conscientia. Horâ 16.
De Sacramento Penitentiae. Horâ 21½.

[1] The first part of this sentence up to '1740' was meant to go with the anecdote, and the list itself was to go to the appendix.

In Classe Metaphysicae.

De Metaphysicis. Horâ 16, & Horâ 21½.

Ex Ethicis:

Philosophiae Moralis Libri tres. Horâ 22½.

In Classe Physicae.

Aristotelis, de Physico auditu. Horâ 16, & 21½.

Ex Mathematicis:

Elementa Geographicae Universalis. Horâ 20½.

In Classe Logicae.

Introductio ad Logicam. Horâ 16.
Logica Aristotelis. Horâ 21½.

Praeter haec, audita quotidianis repetitionibus recolentur; et privatis disputationibus acuentur ingenia. De propositis Philosophiae capitibus, octavo quoque die; & copiosiùs, menstruis concertationibus disputabitur. In anni exitu, de universâ Theologicâ & Philosophiâ Theses disputandae proponentur, ad celebrem Scholasticorum Exterorumque conventum.

In Classe Rhetoricae.

Tom: 2. Oration: M. Tullii Ciceronis. Horâ 15½.
Virg: Aeneid. Horatius Flaccus. Horâ 21.
Die Saturni. M. Val. Martialis.

Diebus Vacationis:

L: Flor: Hist. & Caesar: Comm: de Bello Civili. Horâ 15.

Ex Graecis:

Gretseri Lib: 1. Isocratis Orationes Selectae. Horâ 20½.

In Classe Humanitatis:

M. T. C. Orationes Selectae; Ars Rhetorica P. de Colonia: cum arte Poeticae P. Iuvencii. Horâ 15.
Ex Poetis; Virg: Aeneid: Lib: 9. Horâ 20½.
Ex Graecis; Gretseri Gram:

Diebus Vacationis:

Corn: Nepotis Vitae. Martialis Epigr. Horâ 15.
Die Saturni, Corn: Nep: Vitae; Martial: Epigr: & Ovid: Metam: Horâ 15, & 22½.

In Supremâ Grammaticae Classe.

Priore Semestri, M. T. C. de Off: Lib: 2; & Epistolae ad Familiares. Emman: Appendices, pro suprema. Figurata Constructio; Metricae artis praecepta: & Patronimica. Horâ 15.
Ex Poetis, Ovid: Nasonis de Ponto, Lib: 4. Horâ 20½.
Posteriore Semestri, Virg: Aeneid :Lib: 7. Epistolae ad Famil: Lib: 10.

Diebus Vacationis:

Q. Curtii Historiae. Horâ 15.
Die Saturni, Phaedri Fabulae. Horâ 15.

Ex Graecis:

Gretseri Instit: Grammat:

In Media Classe Grammaticae.

M. T. C. Epist: Lib: 6. Horâ 15.
Emman: Lib: 2, ad Figuratam usque Constructionem; & appendices, pro Mediâ.
Gretseri, Linguae Graecae Rudim. Horâ 20½.
Posteriore Semestri, Ovid: Trist: Lib: 3.

In Infimâ Classe Grammaticae.

M. T. C. Epist: Select: Lib: 3. Horâ 15.
Emman. Lib. 1. De Nomin. Declin: Praeteritis & Supinis. Introductio ad Syn.
Lib: 3. Ejusdem Emman: Rudimenta Linguae Graecae. Horâ 20½.

Praeterea praescriptum lege est, memoriam libris ad verbum ediscendis excolere; quotidie prosâ oratione, aut carmine, stylum exercere; praelecta recolere; decoris contentionibus, alere profectum & laudem. Ad moderandam verò pronuntiationem, frequentes ab Humanitatis Rhetoricaeque studiosis haberi declamationes; & in aulâ majore menstruo fere intervallo, Rhetores dicere ad confertam superiorum & inferiorum Classium coronam.

Ad haec, ut Divinae Gratiae serviatur (quod praecipuum omnibus esse debet) imbuendis utile sapientiâ mentibus, summa Doctrinae Christianae capita memoriter reddentur: piis sermonibus, ac religiosè obeundis Penitentiae atque Eucharistiae Sacramentis, juvenes ad studium virtutis excitabuntur.

Ad initia studiorum repetenda a Kalendis Novembris in aulâ maximâ Collegii, ad frequentiorem Auditorum conventum, de more perorabitur.

APPENDIX TO § 1448

The Identity of 'Mr. T'

AMONG the most quoted conversationalists in the Folio manuscript is a 'Mr. T' to whom Spence credited nearly seventy anecdotes. Nevertheless, Spence wrote out his name only once and this he later inked out so heavily that it is no longer decipherable. Furthermore, he proceeded to delete in pencil nearly all of the 'Mr. T' ascriptions, though the fair copy (the Newcastle manuscript) preserves three examples. In one case in the Folio (p. 274) Spence wrote in pencil next to a deleted 'Mr. T', 'always better omit', and later scribbled this out in pencil.

The first two, §§ 1460 and 1462, are written on pp. 267–8 of the Folio manuscript and concern roadside sights between Bologna and Florence. They are crossed out in pencil, with the explanation in the margin 'Omitted here; to Travelling Papers', referring to a projected book for travellers that apparently never was written (not to be confused with the Travel Letters written to his mother, of which an edited fair copy is among the Spence Papers).

These two anecdotes happen to appear in Spence's Travel Notes (B.M. Egerton MS. 2235, f. 80v) but no 'Mr. T' is mentioned there, though Spence quotes details from his postillion, Dr. Cocchi, and Edward Holdsworth, whom he met when he reached Florence on 21 October. Later conversations with 'Mr. T' occur in Florence and in Rome in the spring of 1741. The position of two others in the Folio manuscript suggests that 'Mr. T' was also in Venice on the return journey and in Paris on the eve of Spence's departure for England. It is possible, however, that when writing the Folio manuscript, Spence expanded items from his working notes without paying strict attention to chronology.

The long series of notes on Horace (see below) are marked 'Omitted'; the 'Mr. T' is deleted only sporadically. They cover pp. 310–27 of the Folio. Some of the later pages are heavily corrected, almost as if by an author; however, this is to be expected, since Spence here was expanding his notes for the first time, whereas most of the anecdotes, for example those concerning Pope, had already passed through an intermediate version (MS. B or H) before going into the Folio.

From the conversation of 'Mr. T' we learn a few things about him, viz. that he (1) travelled in a chaise, § 1460; (2) knew Pope or was familiar with his face, § 1464; (3) was an active student of antiquities, and (4) had a special interest in Horace.

There are only two candidates for 'Mr. T', both on meagre evidence. The first is the Mr. Tripland named among the Englishmen Spence met at Rome on this tour. Beyond this nothing is known of him, and indeed no person of this name appears in the index to the *Gentleman's Magazine*, in *Musgrave's Obituary*, or in any other eighteenth-century index. It sounds like a made-up name, except that Spence did not indulge in such devices in his anecdotes or travel letters.

The other candidate is some member of the Townley family, long prominent in Catholic affairs. Singer solved the problem by suggesting that 'Mr. T' was 'Most probably Mr. Townley' (p. 222), giving no evidence to support his conjecture. In 1732 Spence had recorded a story of Dr. Garth from 'Mr. Townley of Townley Hall' (§ 800), but there is nothing to connect him with the 'Mr. T' of 1740–1 except the initial letter of the name. The only other shred of evidence is the name deleted on p. 295 of the Folio manuscript, which seems to end in a 'y'; the remainder of the indecipherable word does not, however, seem to be Townley.

Of the Townley clan two brothers spent much of their lives on the Continent, active in the Stuart cause. The younger one, Francis Townley (1709–46), paid with his life for his prominence in the Jacobite invasion of 1745; his head mounted on Temple Bar was one of the grisly sights of London in 1746. More likely to have been Spence's friend was his older brother, John (1697–1782), who also saw military service in Scotland.

The 'Chevalier Townley', as he came to be known, earned a minor place in literary history because his French translation of *Hudibras* in 1757 refuted Voltaire's pronouncement that the poem was untranslatable. The Chevalier's whereabouts during the years 1738–41 are unknown, though he is reported to have been tutor to the Young Pretender for a time. If he was 'Mr. T', the motive for Spence's deletion of his name could be a prudent wish to suppress evidence of any association with a notorious Jacobite in the aftermath of 1745. Yet he quoted Ramsay and Holdsworth quite openly; perhaps they were not directly involved in conspiracy, as were the Townleys.

Because Spence chose to omit the remarks on Horace when the fair copy was made, Singer omitted them also. Thus they are here printed for the first time. They show once again the intimacy with which educated Augustans lived with the Roman poet. Spence's notes reveal his personal familiarity and interest in the works of Horace. The quotations and references in the footnotes appear in the margins of the Folio manuscript; they have been silently altered to conform to the text of the Loeb edition.

Mr. T's Notes on Horace

[1] The Julian star, according to Dr. Halley, was a comet, and the same that appeared (for the third time after) in 1680. He says that the tail of that comet in its nearest approach to the sun was sixty degrees long. So that it must have made a very considerable figure in the heavens, as Horace says the Julian star did:

> micat inter omnes
> Iulium sidus, velut inter ignes
> luna minores. *Od.* I. xii. 46–48.

[2] Horace in the beginning of one of his odes[1] speaks of his innocence in the middle of his obligations to heaven, and in the end, by way of gratitude, declares that 'he will love one of his mistresses ⌜Lalage⌝ as long as he lives.'

In another[2] addressed to Tyndaris, he talks of his piety and invites that minstrel to come down and play the Choice of Ulysses (a very moral subject) with him at his Sabine villa.

It appears hence that Lalage and Tyndaris were such women as the laws then allowed the use of, and that the character of common women was not then so abandoned as it is with us.

[1] *Od.* I. xxii.
[2] *Od.* I. xvii.

[3] Horace introduces good old Cato the Censor as commending a man for fornication[1] and his own father, whom he represents as a particular good man, advising him to whore legally.[2] 'Tis impossible to understand these and several other passages in that poet without first knowing which were the allowed, which the scandalous, and which the illegal amours among the Romans.

[1] *Sat.* I. ii. 32.
[2] *Sat.* I. iv. 113

[4] In one place Horace tells his friend that he ought not to be ashamed of debauching his maid[1] and in another he perfectly declaims against the debaucheries of the age.[2]—On several occasions he extols the chastity and regularity introduced in the state by Augustus[3] and on several others he boasts of his own debaucheries.[4] What can seem more inconsistent? And yet is he always very consistent with himself, for he never commends amours with married women, nor ever discommends them with those that were unmarried.

[1] *Od.* II. iv. 1.
[2] *Od.* III. vi. 17–32.
[3] *Od.* IV. v. 21; xv. 10.
[4] *Od.* III. xxvi. 1, *Epod.* xi. 4.

[5] What amours were legal and what illegal is laid down most fully by Ovid when the cause of his banishment was pretended to be his having published his *Art of Love*!

In his epistle to Augustus (the first he wrote after he got to the place of his banishment) he says:

> arguor obsceni doctor adulterii.
> . . .
> at si, quod mallem, vacuum tibi forte fuisset,
> nullum legisses crimen in Arte mea.
> illa quidem fateor frontis non esse severae
> scripta, nec a tanto principe digna legi:
> non tamen idcirco legum contraria iussis
> sunt ea Romanas erudiuntque nurus.
> neve, quibus scribam, possis dubitare, libellos,
> quattuor hos versus e tribus unus habet:
> 'este procul, vittae tenues, insigne pudoris,
> quaeque tegis medios instita longa pedes!
> nil nisi legitimum concessaque furta canemus,
> inque meo nullum carmine crimen erit.'
>
> *Trist.* II. 212, 239–50.

These four verses are quoted from the very beginning of his *Art of Love*, as he himself observes a little after:

> —procul ab scripta solis meretricibus Arte
> submovet ingenuas pagina prima manus.
>
> Ibid. 303–4.

According to his usual manner of writing, he repeats the very same defence over and over:

haec tibi me invisum lascivia fecit ob Artes
quas ratus es vetitos sollicitare toros;
sed neque me nuptae didicerunt furta magistro,
quoque parum novit, nemo docere potest.

Ibid. 345–8.

en iterum testor, nihil hic nisi lege remissum,
luditur; in nostris instita nulla iocis.

Art. Am. ii. 599–600.

nupta virum timeat; rata sit custodia nuptae:
hoc decet, hoc leges iusque pudorque iubent.

Ibid. iii. 613–14.

In other parts of his works he uses 'concubitus vestitus' for adultery[1] and gives the reason of the law as well as the law itself to keep people from it:

elige de vacuis quam non sibi vindicet alter,
si nescis, dominum res habet illa suum.

Her. Ep. xx. 149–150.

As he had told us here what amours were forbid by the laws in his time, he tells us elsewhere what amours were allowed them:

ludite, si sapitis, solas impune puellas. *Art. Am.* i. 643.

dum facit ingenium, petite hinc praecepta, puellae,
quas pudor et leges et sua iura sinunt.

Ibid. iii. 57–58.

[1] *Met.* ix. 124.

[6] The Julian law was the great law for chastity in the Augustan age, and that law was calculated only against adultery, whence Horace calls it 'the marriage law'.[1] It consisted of several privileges to encourage married men, and of several penalties against adulterers.

So Dr. Kennet *Rom. Antiq.*, pp. 175 and 181. If the bishop of Avranches intends amours with married women in the word 'l'amour', he carries the matter too far where he says: 'l'amour qui dans la morale de Rome payenne n'etoit pas un vice' (*Huetiana*, § 56), they being regarded with severer eye in ancient Rome than they are at Rome, or at least than they are in France, at present.

[1] 'lex marita', *Carm. Saec.* l. 20.

[7] The very best of the Roman poets copied so much after the Greeks that they sometimes give us ideas of things that would be proper enough for a Greek, but sound quite improper from a Roman. Virgil's and Horace's instancing Thessaly and Thrace as such very cold countries is a very strong proof of this.[1] Thrace was full north of Greece, and some of the Greeks therefore might talk of the coldness of that country as strongly perhaps as some among us talk of the coldness of Scotland. The Roman writers speak just in the same style of the coldness of Thrace, though a considerable part of Italy lay in as northern a latitude, and some of it even farther north than Thrace.

O qui me gelidis in vallibus Haemi
sistat, et ingenti ramorum protegat umbra. *Georg.* ii. 488–9.

[8] Horace's enthusiastic hymn to Bacchus[1] is very full of their old traditions and mythology, and 'tis no wonder that the circumstances mentioned in it should put so many of the critics in mind of Moses. The resemblances I have taken notice of are:

1. His being dreaded for his wand,[2] one of the distinguishing attributes in the figures of Moses.
2. Moses is sometimes represented with horns in his statues and with shining rays, like horns, in his pictures.[3]
3. Moses led his obstinate people to a land flowing with milk and honey.[4]
4. Moses caused a stream to flow out of a rock and divided the Red Sea.[5]
5. Moses rendered the serpents harmless to his people in the desert.[6]
6. Moses was as great warrior as he was a lawgiver.[7]

These are the likenesses that struck me at first, and of themselves; there might be more found out[8] if one was to consider it more thoroughly.

Each of these articles I only mention as hints, some of which I believe might be very much enlarged by additions from other of the ancient writers.

[1] *Od.* II. xix.
[2] 'gravi metuende thyrso', l. 8.
[3] 'aureo cornu decorum', l. 30.
[4] fas pervicaces est mihi Thyiadas
vinique fontem lactis et uberes
cantare rivos atque truncis
lapsa cavis iterare mella. (ll. 9–12).

[5] 'tu flectis amnes, tu mare barbarum' (l. 17).

[6] tu separatis —— in iugis
nodo coerces viperino
Bistonidum sine fraude crines. (ll. 18–20).

[7] idem
pacis eras mediusque belli. (ll. 27–28).

[8] as 'vidi docentem', l. 2, &c.

[9] Juvenal[1] instances this very ode of Horace as one of the noblest and most spirited productions of the Roman poets.

[1] *Sat.* vii. 53–68.

[10] Horace frequently acknowledges his obligations to the Greek lyric poets, and was, I doubt not, much more obliged to them than may be generally imagined. There are but two odes of Sappho left to us, and he has copied passages in each of them.

[11] The frequent grecisms in Horace's odes are another proof of what I was saying. We are apt to take them for beauties, whereas many of them were probably only escapes: as a writer now, who converses very much with the best French authors, will be but too apt to let gallicisms slip into his English.

[12] Horace in speaking of his own manner in writing odes[1] compares himself to 'a little industrious bee that flits from one flower to another and collects all the sweets he can.' This, I think, must be meant of his collecting here and there and copying from the Greek lyric poets, for the study of those days was confined to the Greek and Latin languages, and there was but very little of the lyric kind in his own language worth copying or even worth his reading. He never mentions even Catullus but once that I know of, and that is not to commend him,[2] and indeed he seems to speak of himself as the first lyric poet among the Romans.[3]

[1] *Od.* IV. ii. 25–32.

[2] neque simius iste
nil praeter Calvum et doctus cantare Catullum. *Sat.* I. x. 18–19.

[3] totum muneris hoc tui est,
quod monstror digito praetereuntium
Romanae fidicen lyrae. *Od.* IV. iii. 21–23.

[13] This will help to explain another passage in Horace, in his first ode to Maecenas.[1] He compliments that minister there for his taste in poetry, and says that if he should think him worth a place among

the Greek lyrics in his library he shall be very proud of it and think himself most highly honoured by him.[2]

[1] *Od.* I. i. 29–36.

[2]
me doctarum hederae praemia frontium
dis miscent superis, me gelidum nemus
nympharumque leves cum Satyris chori
secernunt populo,

. . .

quodsi me lyricis vatibus inseris,
sublimi feriam sidera vertice.

[14] Horace everywhere acknowledges his obligations to the Greek lyric poets, and 'tis remarkable that he does so in every one of the three odes which we have happened to be looking into just now. He hints his gratitude to Sappho in one of them,[1] to Alcaeus in another,[2] and the third[3] is expressly written in praise of Pindar.

[1]
si neque tibias
Euterpe cohibet nec Polyhymnia
Lesboum refugit tendere barbiton. *Od.* I. i. 32–34.

[2]
. . . quae Tibur aquae fertile praefluunt
et spissae nemorum comae
fingent Aeolio carmine nobilem. *Od.* IV. iii. 10–12.

[3] *Od.* IV. ii.

[15] That passage in Horace's jovial ode, the twenty-seventh of the first book[1]

vix inligatum te triformi
Pegasus expediet Chimaera

has puzzled me a good deal. I used to imagine that it might allude to some representation of the Chimera destroying a man in some of the old paintings, but I rather think now that it was meant to point out the very bad character with whom his friend was so deeply and unhappily engaged.

She seems to have been some common woman by Horace's calling her Charybdis before,[2] and the calling her Chimera here would then signify her lascivious, furious and villainous temper, or a mixture of the goat, lion and serpent—a monster at this day frequently to be met with in Drury Lane.

[1] ll. 23–24.

[2] l. 19.

[16] Where Horace seems to pay one of his greatest compliments to Cato,[1] he flings in an epithet that spoils all.[2] It may with that alloy

signify that 'everything in the world was conquered except Cato's obstinacy.' In another ode he speaks more handsomely of him,[3] and that in an ode where he incenses the Caesarean family as much as in any part of his works. Possibly, though they are otherwise placed in the present collection of his works,[4] this might be after the other and when Augustus was come to bear to hear Cato commended so highly.

[1] et cuncta terrarum subacta
praeter atrocem animum Catonis. *Od.* II. i. 23–24.

[2] 'Atrox' seems always to be used in a bad sense by Roman writers. 'Ante omnia invisum ipsum ingenium atrox, cognomenque imperiosi' says Livy of Manlius (vii. 4), and indeed I never remember to have seen it used in a good sense. Where our dictionary writers say that it signifies 'bold' or 'resolute' they don't bring anything except this passage to confirm that sense of it.

[3] Romulum post hos prius an quietum
Pompili regnum memorem an superbos
Tarquini fasces, dubito, an Catonis
nobile letum. *Od.* I. xii. 33–36.

[4] Sanadon's Horace.

[17] 'How comes Tarquin to be mentioned by Horace among the subjects of his commendation?'

'Tis Tarquin that is mentioned, but 'twas Brutus that would have been commended. This I think appears from the opposition used by Horace in that passage: 'Whom shall I celebrate next? The conquering Romulus or the peaceful Numa? The avenging Brutus or the dying Cato?'

[18] Horace, in his description of the Fortunate Islands, says a great many things which agree with England, and had not he mixed his Italian trees and some few other Italian ideas with it (as everybody forms their notions of countries they have not seen from countries that they have seen), the whole might have passed almost for a description of our island.

[19] Père Sanadon's thought about Horace's 'Carmen Saeculare' I should think a very good one, if he had not endeavoured to strain it farther than it will hold. He would make five parts of it, and has proved only three: the rest is purely conjecture. We might therefore allow the twenty-first ode of the first book, the 'Carmen Saeculare' as it is now called, and the sixth ode of the fourth book to be placed together as the three constituent parts of the 'Carmen Saeculare' in Augustus's time, and so have a different hymn for each of the three days; but I

can see no reason for breaking off a stanza from the first ode of the third book, nor a sufficient one for cutting the sixth ode of the fourth book in two.

[20] When the Roman writers use the word 'vetus' of Greek statues or relievos it signifies 'good'[1] (as 'alto greco' does among the Italians at present), when they use it of Roman works it signifies 'bad'.[2]

This shows that they did not look upon a thing as good because it was old, but that they valued a thing that was old because it was good: in which they may show somewhat more of discretion than is usual among modern virtuosos.

[1] 'Insanit veteres statuas Damasippus emendo. *Sat.* II. iii. 64.
—olim nam quaerere amabam,
quo vafer ille pedes lavisset Sisyphus aere,
quid sculptum infabre, quid fusum durius esset;
callidus huic signo ponebam milia centum. Ibid., ll. 20–23.
(The same Damasippus of himself)
—cum Pausiaca torpes, insane, tabella,
. . .
subtilis veterum iudex et callidus audis. *Sat.* II. vii. 95, 101.

[2] accipit ara preces votivaque tura piorum;
ara, per antiquas facta sine arte manus. Ovid, *Am.* III. xiii. 9–10.

And so 'catillus tritus Evandri manibus' in Horace (*Sat.* I. iii. 91) signifies a wretched old-fashioned dish, scarce worth anything.

[21] Horace in his 'Journey to Brundisium'[1] gives some obscene ideas in the coarsest expressions and in such a manner as one should think inconsistent with the politeness of the Augustan age. This might be done to ridicule Lucretius, who uses as coarse expressions on a like occasion,[2] but I should rather think that the piece we find it in was an epistle, though 'tis placed among his satires, and it might have been a private letter to one of his friends, not designed to be made public. Cicero in one of his epistles[3] lays down the measures of decency in speaking in his time, and Horace himself shows that the people of polite taste were against all such indecencies in the Augustan age.[4]

[1] *Sat.* I. v. 85.

[2] iv. 1030.

[3] IX. xxii.

[4] silvis deducti caveant me iudice Fauni,
ne velut innati triviis ac paene forenses
aut nimium teneris iuvenentur versibus umquam,
aut immunda crepent ignominiosaque dicta:
offenduntur enim, quibus est equus et pater et res. *Art. Poet.* 244–8.

[22] There is scarce any other passage in Horace that seems so trifling or so little to the purpose as where he mentions its being doubtful what province of Italy he was born in. I have sometimes thought that that digression might be an imitation of some like trifling passage in Lucilius that may be now lost to us with the greatest part of that poet's works. He mentions Lucilius just before his imitating of him.[1]

[1] me pedibus delectat claudere verba
Lucili ritu, nostrum melioris utroque.
ille velut fidis arcana sodalibus olim
credebat libris, neque si male cesserat, unquam
decurrens alio, neque si bene; quo fit, ut omnis
votiva pateat veluti descripta tabella
vita senis. Sequor hunc, Lucanus an Appulus, anceps:
nam Venusinus arat finem sub utrumque colonus,
missus ad hoc, pulsis, vetus est ut fama, Sabellis,
quo ne per vacuum Romano incurreret hostis,
sive quod Appula gens seu quod Lucania bellum
incuteret violenta. sed hic stilus petet ultro
quemquam animantem . . . etc. *Sat.* II. i. 28–40.

[23] When Horace speaks of the ancient writers as good[1] he means the Greek writers and not those of his own country; for the latter, 'tis plain, he thought at best but indifferent.[2]

[1] o rus, quando ego te aspiciam! quandoque licebit
nunc veterum libris, nunc somno et inertibus horis,
ducere sollicitae iucunda oblivia vitae! *Sat.* II. vi. 60–62.

[2] From several parts of his works, and from his epistle to Augustus in particular. *Ep.* II. i.

[24] If one was to judge of the company which Maecenas generally kept by the company one finds him in at Nasidienus's supper,[1] it would give one no very advantageous idea of that first minister's character. He is at a man's table that he comes to laugh at, a rich fellow that delights in eating and thinks he has a very good taste though he does everything with a very bad one.

Maecenas brings two scoundrels with him: one of them[2] a teaser, and the other[3] a jolly fellow, or rather one that puts on that character to help tease the master of the feast. These are on one side of the table. On the second are three poets, and on the third Nasidienus himself, with a buffoon[4] on one side of him and a flatterer[5] on the other.

This makes the opinion of those who imagine that Maecenas is meant by Petronius under the character of Trimalchio the more probable. Trimalchio's table is quite furnished with the lowest scoundrels that can be, and by the end of the feast all his own menial servants are got to the table among them. Trimalchio only says: 'They are all men born of women as well as the best of us,' and so they drink on all together very contentedly.

[1] *Sat.* II. viii.
[2] Balatro, ll. 40, 64, 83.
[3] Vibidius, ll. 33, 40, 80.
[4] Pocius, l. 23.
[5] Nomentanus, l. 25.

[25] 'Spectatus' was the word used by the Romans in the discharge of their slaves and gladiators, as appears jointly from Horace[1] and the discharges themselves. There are several of them in the Great Duke's collection at Florence. These are ivory tesseras, four-square and with an inscription on each side. On one side is the name of the slave, on another that of the master, on a third the day of the dismission, and on the fourth the names of the then consuls.

One of them runs thus: APOLLONTVS — PETICI — SP. I. APRIUS — L. AFR. Q. MET.

There is another of a slave of Maecenas's: ATHAMAS — MECENATIS — SP. I. IAN — C. SIL. L. MVN. COS.

The antiquarians read SP. here 'spectatus.'

[1] 'spectatum satis et donatum iam rude', *Ep.* I. i. 2.

[26] Horace seems to have had much the same idea of Homer's *Iliad* that Bossu revived so many ages since.[1] According to him 'tis (1) the delay of the success of the Grecian allies that is the subject of the poem, (2) the quarrel between Achilles and Agamemnon that was the occasion of that delay, and (3) the sufferings of the people from the foolish wrangles between their leaders that is the moral or principal doctrine to be learned from it. Whereas the greatest part of the mob of writers between Horace and Bossu seemed to have looked on that poem only as a tissue of wars and fighting, like our romance-works, purely to divert the reader.

[1] Fabula, qua Paridis propter narratur amorem
Graecia barbariae lento collisa duello, (1)
stultorum regum et populorum continet aestus. (2)
. . .
quidquid delirant reges, plectuntur Achivi. (3) *Ep.* I. ii. 6–14.

[27] Horace's 'quidlibet audendi'[1] is often quoted as giving poets a license without bounds, though what he says just before and just after shows the direct contrary. The poets have only the same liberty as the painters, and should really have no more than the ancient painters took, which was very different from the extravagances practised by the moderns.

1 'pictoribus atque poetis
quidlibet audendi semper fuit aequa potestas'. *Art. Poet.* 9–10.

[28] Though Horace was well turned for a court and was so great a favourite in that of Augustus Caesar, his chief delight seems to have been in retirement and in the ease and pleasures of a country-life; and by what he says himself, as well as from the descriptions of the ground about his Sabine villa, I am apt to think that he had that taste for wild natural gardening which has obtained so much among us of late.[1]

1 Urbis amatorem Fuscum salvere iubemus
ruris amatores. *Ep.* I. x. 1–2.
Villice silvarum et mihi me reddentis agelli. *Ep.* I. xiv. 1.
o rus, quando ego te adspiciam. *Sat.* II. vi. 60.
istuc mens animusque
fert. *Ep.* I. xiv. 8–9.
quae deserta et inhospita tesqua
credis, amoena vocat mecum qui sentit. Ibid., ll. 19–20.

[29] Horace was of so contented a temper that he did not make use of his most particular intimacy with Maecenas, or the easy access he properly had to Augustus, to get any large grants of land, as much as he loved country life.[1] He was of so uncommon a turn of mind that he knew when he had enough, and seems to have been as happy with his little Sabine villa as if he had as various and large possessions as the younger Pliny or poor Seneca.[2]

1 —nec potentem amicum
largiora flagito,
satis beatus unicis Sabinis. *Od.* II. xviii. 12–14.

2 cur valle permutem Sabina
divitias operosiores? *Od.* III. i. 47–48.

[30] The author of Horace's life (which goes under the name of Suetonius) says that he had two villas: that in the country of the Sabines and another near Tivoli, and that the latter was shown as a sight in

his time.[1] This may have given a handle to the priests at present to show what they call Horace's house opposite to the Cascatelli at Tivoli.

[1] 'Vixit plurimum in secessu ruris sui Sabini, aut Tiburtini: domus eius ostenditur circa Tiburni luculum.'

[31] 'Tis plain that Horace had only his Sabine villa when he wrote the eighteenth ode of his second book and the first of his third, and I do not know that he ever speaks of having one near Tivoli in any other part of his works.

[32] Indeed he was a great lover of Tivoli[1] and speaks of his being often there[2] and of his writing there:[3] but that might be either at the house which Maecenas had at Tivoli,[4] or Munatius Plancus's,[5] or Varus's,[6] or any other of his friends.

[1] mihi iam non regia Roma
sed vacuum Tibur placet aut imbelle Tarentum. *Ep.* I. vii. 44–45.

Tibur Argeo positum colono
sit mea sedes utinam senectae,
sit modus lasso maris et viarum
militiaeque.

unde si Parcae prohibent iniquae,
dulce pellitis ovibus Galaesi
flumen et regnata petam Laconi
rura Phalantho. *Od.* II. vi. 5–12.

[2] Romae Tibur amnem ventosus, Tibure Romam. *Ep.* I. viii. 12.

[3] . . . quae Tibur aquae fertile praefluunt
et spissae nemorum comae
fingent Aeolio carmine nobilem. *Od.* IV. iii. 10–12.

ego apis Matinae
more modoque

grata carpentis thyma per laborem
plurimum circa nemus uvidique
Tiburis ripas operosa parvus
carmina fingo. *Od.* IV. ii. 27–32.

[4] *Od.* III. xxix. 6.
[5] *Od.* I. vii. 21.
[6] *Od.* I. xviii. 2.

[33] There is one passage in Horace[1] which may incline his readers to think that he had a second villa at Frascati, but as that is in some of his last writings, if he ever had a villa there it was scarce given him till the latter end of his life; so that most of what he says of his country

seat must be understood of this Sabine villa, and perhaps all could not have been meant of anything else.

1 non ut iuvencis inligata pluribus
aratra nitantur mea,
pecusve Calabris ante sidus fervidum
Lucana mutet pascuis,
neque ut superni villa candens Tusculi
Circaea tangat moenia.
satis superque me benignitas tua
ditavit. *Epod.* i. 25–32.

[34] Horace's villa was in the hilly country of the Sabines,[1] not far from Vicovari.[2] Part of his ground was on the north side of Mount Lucretilis[3] and so run down between the spurs of the hills[4] into part of the valley.[5]

1 vester in arduos
tollor Sabinos. *Od.* III. iv. 21–22.

Ergo ubi me in montes et in arcem ex urbe removi. *Sat.* II. vi. 16.

2 habitatum quinque focis et
quinque bonos solitum Variam dimittere patres. *Ep.* I. xiv. 2–3.

3 Velox amoenum saepe Lucretilem
mutat Lycaeo Faunus et igneam
defendit aestatem capellis
usque meis pluviosque ventos. *Od.* I. xvii. 1–4.

Ustica was another of the hills near him, and perhaps made a beautiful slope in his prospect (ibid., l. 11). And it should seem that the village of Mandela and the river Digentia were in his neighbourhood:

quid pure tranquillet, honos an dulce lucellum,
an secretum iter et fallentis semita vitae.
Me quotiens reficit gelidus Digentia rivus,
quem Mandela bibit, rugosus frigore pagus,
quid sentire putas? quid credis, amice, precari?
sit mihi quod nunc est, etiam minus, et mihi vivam
quod superest aevi . . . . *Ep.* I. xviii. 102–8.

4 scribetur tibi forma loquaciter et situs agri.
Continui montes, ni dissocientur opaca
valle, sed ut veniens dextrum latus aspiciat sol,
laevum discedens curru fugiente vaporet. *Ep.* I. xvi. 4–7.

5 hic in reducta valle Caniculae
vitabis aestus. *Od.* I. xvii. 17–18.

[35] This situation afforded him a great deal of variety. There was wood and groves for himself to walk in,[1] rock for his goats and kids,[2]

hills for his vines and olives,[3] fields for his corn[4] and meadow-ground for his cattle.[5]

[1] . . . silva . . . in Sabina. *Od.* I. xxii. 9.

vilice silvarum. *Ep.* I. xiv. I.

Hoc erat in votis: modus agri non ita magnus,
hortus ubi et tecto vicinus iugis aquae fons
et paulum silvae super his foret. auctius atque
di melius fecere. *Sat.* II. vi. 1–4.

[2] *Od.* I. xvii. 3, 7.

[3] *Ep.* I. viii. 5.

[4] —segetis certa fides meae
fulgentem imperio fertilis Africae
fallit sorte beatior. *Od.* III. xvi. 30–32.

[5] ludit herboso pecus omne campo
. . .
festus in pratis vacat otioso
cum bove pagus. *Od.* III. xviii. 9–12.

tu frigus amabile
fessis vomere tauris
praebes et pecori vago. *Od.* III. xiii. 10–12.

[36] The air was temperate and like that of his favourite Tarentum.[1] It was warm in winter[2] and cool in summer,[3] so that it must have been, as he calls it, 'a pleasing retirement'.[4]

[1] temperiem laudes. quid si rubicunda benigni
corna vepres et pruna ferant? si quercus et ilex
multa fruge pecus, multa dominum iuvet umbra?
dicas adductum propius frondere Tarentum. *Ep.* I. xvi. 8–11.

[2] *Od.* II. vi. 10; *Ep.* I. vii. 45.

[3] est ubi plus tepeant hiemes, ubi gratior aura
leniat et rabiem Canis et momenta Leonis,
cum semel accepit Solem furibundus acutum? *Ep.* I. x. 15–17.

[4] hae latebrae dulces, etiam, si credis, amoenae. *Ep.* I. xvi. 15.

[37] He had a spring[1] in his estate, which (as I have been assured from very good hands) bursts out of the side of the hill and runs down till it joins the river in the lower grounds.[2] This spring I take to be his Bandusia,[3] as the river may be his Digentia.[4]

[1] fons etiam rivo dare nomen idoneus, ut nec
frigidior Thracam nec purior ambiat Hebrus,
infirmo capiti fluit aptus et utilis alvo. *Ep.* I. xvi. 12–14.

[2] addit opus pigro rivus, si decidit imber,
multa mole docendus aprico prato. *Ep.* I. xiv. 29–30.

[3] O fons Bandusiae, splendidior vitro,
. . .
gelidos inficiet tibi
rubro sanguine rivos
lascivi suboles gregis.

te flagrantis atrox hora Caniculae
nescit tangere, tu frigus amabile
fessis vomere tauris
praebes et pecori vago.

fies nobilium tu quoque fontium,
me dicente cavis impositam ilicem
saxis, unde loquaces
lymphae desiliunt tuae. *Od.* III. xiii.

[4] *Ep.* I. xviii. 104.

[38] His house was on the side of the hill near the source of this mountain rivulet:

[1] tecto vicinus aquae fons *Sat.* II. vi. 2.

[39] From Horace's taste[1] and his not saying anything descriptive of his garden in particular (though he is so minute in all other instances) I have sometimes been apt to imagine that his whole farm was a garden to him.

[1] Mentioned before.

[40] He seems to have had a grotto dedicated to Venus in one part of it[1] and a laurel seat or arbour in another.[2] An altar under a high spreading pine-tree sacred to Diana[3] and another to Faunus in the midst of the grove above his house or some other of his groves.

The place itself must have been very pleasing from variety and its frequent rises and falls, and must have been yet more varied by the different plantations and culture.

So that when his nightingales were singing[4] and the shepherds feeding their sheep and playing on their reeds all round him,[5] there could scarce have been a more delightful place.

[1] mecum Dionaeo sub antro
quaere modos leviore plectro. *Od.* II. i. 39–40.

[2] longa . . . fessum militia latus
depone sub lauru mea. *Od.* II. vii. 18–19.

[3] Montium custos nemorumque, Virgo,
quae laborantes utero puellas
ter vocata audis adimisque leto,
diva triformis,

imminens villae tua pinus esto,
quam per exactos ego laetus annos
verris obliquum meditantis ictum
sanguine donem. *Od.* III. xxii.

This ode might possibly have served for an inscription on an altar, either under or near that tree:

nunc decet aut viridi nitidum caput impedire myrto
aut flore, terrae quem ferunt solutae;
nunc et in umbrosis Fauno decet immolare lucis. *Od.* I. iv. 9–11.

He calls it 'vetus ara'. *Od.* III. xviii. 7.

[4] nidum ponit, Ityn flebiliter gemens,
infelix avis. *Od.* IV. xii. 5–6.

[5] dicunt in tenero gramine pinguium
custodes ovium carmina fistula. Ibid., ll. 9–10.

[41] Horace speaks of his house as plain[1] and of his estate as small, at least in comparison with some of the rich Romans of those days.[2] But it would not have been a small estate for a poet now, for there was as much ground as took up eight servants to manure and take care of it.[3]

Beside these he had a bailiff or woodward[4] who was not above putting his hand to any work himself[5] and another lad for the gardening and stables.[6]

[1] *Od.* II. xviii.

[2] te greges centum Siculaeque circum
mugiunt vaccae
. . . mihi parva rura. *Od.* II. xvi. 33–37.

[3] Ocius hinc te
ni rapis, accedes opera agro nona Sabino

says Horace to one of his town servants (*Sat.* II. vii. 118–19). By this we may guess at the size of his estate. Old Cato says that sixteen men are the proper number to take care of hundred acres of vineyard ground (of these 'operarii decem': that is one to ten acres, the best measure to go by) including the bailly (*De re rust.*, Chapter 11) and an old author quoted by Varro says in general that one man may manage eight acres (I. xviii), at which proportion Horace's estate would not be above fifty-six acres.

[4] *Ep.* I. xiv. 1.

[5] Ibid., ll. 4, 27.

[6] Ibid., l. 42.

[42] There was a good woman and her little family that lived in the house to take care of it in his absence. I have had some suspicions that she was a heathen Methodist, because Horace advises her to pray but seldom and assures her that virtue is the best sacrifice.[1]

[1] *Od.* III. xxiii. 2, 17.

[43] There seem to have been but five houses in the parish[1] in one of which perhaps Damasippus lived after he was ruined as an antiquarian and dealer in town[2] and in another old Cervius, the story-teller.[3]

[1] *Ep.* I. xiv. 2.
[2] *Sat.* II. iii. 10, &c.
[3] *Sat.* II. vi. 65–78.

[44] In this neighbourhood and at his villa Horace seems to have passed the greatest part of his time,[1] much in the same manner as we less significant people do in the country. He read, slept and sauntered,[2] lived pleasingly and forgot the bustle of the town. He composed much[3] and thought and talked much of moral subjects.[4]

[1] me constare mihi scis et discedere tristem
quandocumque trahunt invisa negotia Romam. *Ep.* I. xiv. 16–17.

[2] o rus, quando te adspiciam! quandoque licebit
nunc veterum libris, nunc somno et inertibus horis,
ducere sollicitae iucunda oblivia vitae! *Sat.* II. vi. 60–62.

[3] condo et compono quae mox depromere possim *Ep.* I. i. 12.

[4] quid verum atque decens curo et rogo et omnis in hoc sum. Ibid., l. 11.

nec male necne Lepos saltet; sed quod magis ad nos
pertinet et nescire malum est, agitamus: utrumne
divitiis homines an sint virtute beati;
quidve ad amicitias, usus rectumne, trahat nos;
et quae sit natura boni summumque quid eius. *Sat.* II. vi. 72–76.

[45] He sometimes had some of his neighbours with him,[1] and sometimes some of his great friends[2] or mistresses from Rome.[3] In his invitations to one of the former he seems to me to talk more jovially than perhaps he lived, but in those to the latter he speaks rather gaily than dissolutely.[3] With him everybody was at liberty and drank as much or as little as they pleased.[4] Latterly at least he did not drink much himself,[5] and as to his diet, he lived there very temperately and much more like a philosopher than a rake.[6]

[1] *Sat.* II. vi.
[2] Maecenas, Pollio, Virgil, Varus, &c.
[3] *Od.* I. xvii. 13–22.

[4] siccat inaequalis calices conviva, solutus
legibus insanis, *Sat.* II. vi. 68–69.

[5] quem tenues decuere togae nitidique capilli,
quem scis immunem Cinarae placuisse rapaci,
quem bibulum liquidi media de luce Falerni,
cena brevis iuvat et prope rivum somnus in herba.
Ep. I. xiv. 32–35.

6 o quando faba Pythagorae cognata simulque
uncta satis pingui ponentur holuscula lardo!
o noctes cenaeque deum! quibus ipse meique
ante Larem proprium vescor vernasque procaces
pasco libatis dapibus. *Sat.* II. vi. 63–67.

me pascunt olivae
me cichorea levesque malvae. *Od.* I. xxxi. 15–16.

[46] It is chiefly from his odes that people have got such a general notion that Horace was a very great débauché. This does not appear to me from them. All his odes amount but to 121, including the epodes and his 'Carmen Saeculare'. Of these there are twenty-one that are panegyrical[1] and satirical;[2] nineteen familiar or relating to his friends;[3] and nine personal or relating to himself;[4] eight political[5] or historical;[6] sixteen moral;[7] and eleven religious[8] or devotional;[9] seventeen gay[10] and jovial;[11] and twenty that are amorous.[12] So that above half of his odes are quite out of the question, and anyone who was to read over the rest (the familiar, the gay, and the amorous) will find that much the greater part of them turn on friendship, innocent mirth, and amours allowed by the laws of his country. Several of them are intermixed with morality and religion, and several others with religion, and I question whether there are so many as half a dozen in the whole number in which he ever speaks of excess or of his doing anything that was either illegal or irreputable in those days.

[1] *Od.* I. vi, xii; *Od.* III. iv, v, xiv; *Od.* IV. iv, v, ix, xiv, xv.

[2] *Od.* I. xxv, xxix; *Od.* III. xv; *Od.* IV. xiii; *Epod.* iv, v, vi, viii, x, xii, xvii.

[3] *Od.* I. xvii, xx, xxiv; *Od.* II. i, iv, vii, ix, xvii; *Od.* III. vii, viii, xvii, xx, xxvii, xxix; *Od.* IV. xi, xii; *Epod.* i, iii, xiv.

[4] *Od.* I. i, xxxii; *Od.* II. vi, xiii, xx; *Od.* III. xxx; *Od.* IV. ii, iii, viii.

[5] *Od.* I. ii, xiv, xxxvii; *Od.* III. iii; *Epod.* vii, xvi.

[6] *Od.* I. xv, xxii.

[7] *Od.* I. iii, xxviii; *Od.* II. ii, iii, x, xiv, xv, xvi, xvii; *Od.* III. i, ii, xvi, xxiii, xxiv; *Od.* IV. vi; *Epod.* ii.

[8] *Od.* I. xxxiv; *Od.* III. vi, xiii.

[9] *Od.* I. x, xxi, xxxi, xxxv; *Od.* III. xviii, xxii; *Od.* IV. vi; *Carm. Saec.*

[10] *Od.* I. iv, vii, ix, xi, xviii, xxvi, xxxviii; *Od.* II. xi; *Od.* III. xxviii; *Epod.* ix, xiii.

[11] *Od.* I. xxvii; *Od.* II. xix; *Od.* III. xix, xxi, xxv.

[12] *Od.* I, v, viii, xiii, xvi, xix, xxiii, xxx, xxxiii; *Od.* II. v, viii, xii; *Od.* III. ix, x, xi, xii, xxvi; *Od.* IV. i, x; *Epod.* xi, xv.

APPENDIX TO §1520

Examples of Improvised Verses

SPENCE brought back examples of the art of the *improvvisatori* from Italy. A manuscript among the Spence Papers, but not in Spence's hand, gives two improvised poems, a sonnet in Italian and a ten-line poem in Latin. They occur on the verso of a paper headed in Spence's hand, 'A Sonet: & An Improviso'; the recto contains a sonnet and another eight lines of verse, neither of which was apparently improvised. The two improvised poems are reproduced below (the Latin poem does not much resemble an improvised poem, but it may have been described as such to Spence):

One of their Impromptu's

Dove manca il potere, supplica ingegno
Scatoletta mia cara a dirle il vero
Risolvo confidar ti un mio pensiero
Ch'e dimandar ti tra Giudei in pegno
Poi che me ritrovo ad un certo segno
For' della patria & di denar legiero
Che recar non me posso a vitupero
Ponerti in man d'un Giudiccio indegno
  Vanne de vanne pur senza timore
Che spero in breve reaverti mia

E da tal schiavetu cavarti fore
Se tem star [illegible] quella gente via
Non paventar che averai forse ancitre
Il mio bravo spadino in compagnia.

Follows a latin impromptu:

  Extrema Verba Poetae Pyxidem, alloquentis.
Sit mea nota tibi, mea Pyxis amica, voluntas:
  Chara vale Pyxis :Pyxis amica, vale.
Iam procul à patriâ, nummorum podere influs,
  Nescio perpetuam quô relevare famem.
Non volui certè: sed fatum jubet. Ire necesse est
  Quo domina carem commiseranda pares.

Hebraicas mecum vicisti saepe tabernas:
Nunc ipsa Hebraeicis tu mihi pignus eris.
At metuis gentis mores vulteruque severum?
Nil metuas. Ensis te comitatur: abi.

[The spelling, &c., of the manuscript has been reproduced without comment]

Spence's Entry under 'Pope' in the Index to the Huntington MS. of the Anecdotes

POPE, Mr when Born, 416; & where, 340. — How early he began to make verses. 450 — Taught to read, by an Aunt. 458 — Learnt his accidence, & ye Gr: Alpabet, of Banister. 322, 432, 458 — His favourite books, about that time, 446, 450 — About a year, at Twiford. 322, 346, 418, 432: & two or three at (Dean's) Seminary, near London. 322, 418, 432. — Some months, under their Family Priest in Windsor Forest. 322. — — — — How very little he had learnt of them 432. — Set to reading, & getting the Languages by himself. 322, 418. — What the Books he read. 446, 452. — He translated, or imitated, what he lik'd particularly in reading. 324, 418, — Studied versification, from Dryden. 452 — Continu'd this sort of study till twenty. 432 — Had no taste all that time for anything but Poetry. 334 — How early he had formed his taste for that. 418 — Imitated not out of Vanity, but (as Painters copy) to learn 450. — — — — Wrote a satire on his master, at Twiford. 346, 418. — Made up a sort of a Play, out of the speeches in the Iliad; & got it acted by his school-fellows, while under Mr Deane. 450 — Wrote a Tragedy, from a story in the Legend of St Genevieve, in his first year in the Forest. 358 — wrote other Dramatic Pieces? about the same time. 330 — Began an Epic Poem; *Alcander*, *Prince of Rhodes*. 444: [t'was] two year in hand 452: & four Books of it, compleated 444. — It was a slavish imitation of the Antients, in several parts of the Story 452; — & an imitation of many very different poets, in the Stile: 444 & was to show away all the Learning he then had. 330 — Burnt, when & by whose advice. 330, 444. — Some Couplets that were in it. 444, 448. — Translated Tully de Senectute, 448: and wrote a Latin Treatise, on the Old Buildings in Rome. 344. — Early acquainted with Sr William Trumbull, & Walsh; 324: Ld Lansdown, Garth, Betterton, and Wycherley; 324. — Walsh's advice to him when about Fifteen. 452. — — — — —

Mr Pope's next work, after his Epic, was his *Pastorals*. 446. — The versification in them how much labour'd. 506. — wch, he himself lik'd the best of them. Ibid: — Ld Lansdown insisted on his publishing the *Windsor-Forest*. 336 — Wrote the *Essay on Criticism* two or three year before it was printed. 432. ([? what year] fro[m] 324.) — The reason of his writing the *Rape of the Lock*; & the good effect it had. 326. — His adding the Machinery to it. Ibid: — His translating Homer's *Iliad* how oppressive to him, at first. 364, 458. How long he was about that Translation. 458. — What parts of the *Odyssey*, he did himself; 434: & what he paid his assistants. 422. — How he manag'd, in translating both the Iliad & Odyssey. 432. — had the original Mss of both, bound; & how much corrected. 424. — The Use that might be made of them. Ibid: — The original Motto for his Dunciad. 482. — His first design for his great Moral Poem, much larger; & why contracted 462, 514. — Great part of what was design'd for an Epistle on Education in it, afterwards flung into the fourth Book of the Dunciad. 462. — his design in y[t] Essay, confin'd to the present state of man. 438 — Ethic Epistle, on Riches, much labour'd. 488 — Cotta, in his Epistle on Taste, who? 490. — His Satire on Addison (as 'tis call'd,) writ in that Gentleman's life time. 382. — Salust, in his second Satire from Horace, who. 502. — the First Satire of Horace, translated a good while before any of the rest. 482 — He has translated all, or good part, of the Fourth Satire of the Second Book. Ibid: — His part of the Seventh Epistle, of the First Book, did not please Dean Swift. 416 — The laying out a regular Edition of all his poetical Works 426. See, 480. — His Letter on his House, one of his favourite Letters? 382. — Part of what is his own in Swift's & Pope's Miscellanies, pointed out. 338.

M[r] Pope wrote part of, Duke & no Duke, 462; — & part of Mary Tofts, & one or two more Ballads, with L[d] Bath. Ibid: Several verses of his in (the last Edition of) Wycherley's Poems. 330. — His Idea for an Epic Poem, laterly: (Brutus) 460. — His Thoughts on Civil, & Ecclesiastical Government, would have been laid out there, at large. 462. — all plan'd, ibid: — even to some of the particular Speeches. 514. — Shou'd have wrote an Epic Poem much earlier, had not he translated Homer. 418 — & with what advantage s[d] have set about it. 458 — His intended Translations, from the Greek Poets; prevented by the same. 492.

His Escape at 3 Year old. 428 — How much acquainted with Wycherley, at first. 332. — When his acquaintance with Addison began. 326. — Apprehensive of danger, after publishing the Dunciad. 430.

Had all the Subscriptions for the Iliad, quite clear. 354. — What he got by the Iliad, & Odyssey. 478. — How he came to print, in

Twelves. 428. — His Income, what laterly. 354. — Why he never published anything of the Dramatic Kind. 330. — His last design, for the Slope before his House. 438. — Much encouraged by Ld Oxford. 494, Ld Halifax, & Crags 496; — but without any effect? Ibid: — How busied in his last Illness. 518 — How affected by it 518, 526 — Death 526.

His Stile, changd laterly. 420 — His memory 462; — Judgment; 488 — & extensive Knowledge. 344 — Love of Reading. 440. — His Sentiments; as to Marriage. 334 — as to his Critics. 442 — of a Future State. 434, 486, 524. — How slightly a Papist. 442, 524. —

How modest, 466, 518. — charitable 466 — generous, 500 — tender, 340 — & humane 474, 522, 524. — above flattering others, 498 what sort of character, he was most desirous of himself. 488 — A Verse of his, left as a Legacy. Ibid:

TEXTUAL NOTES

Explanation of Symbols used in referring to Textual Sources

THE top line of each textual note gives a list of the manuscript sources for every anecdote. Each symbol is followed by the relevant page or folio reference. The first symbol given designates the copy text. Other references to authoritative texts are arranged in descending chronological order; references thereafter to non-authoritative texts (normally N, S, and M) are put in ascending chronological order.

The symbols used for the texts are as follows:

B, MS.	The now missing 'MS. B' referred to by Singer
F	Folio manuscript
H	Huntington manuscript
L 1–54	Loose Papers
M	Murray's edition of Malone's transcript of the *Anecdotes* (1820)
MB 1755–8	Spence's Memorandum Books
N	Newcastle fair copy
S	Singer's edition of the *Anecdotes* (1820)
TN 1–4	Spence's Travel Notes
W	The notes Spence sent to Warburton

For a full description of these sources see the 'Description of the Sources Cited' (pp. xli–lxx).

Substantive variants are recorded in the textual notes; some of the most important, however, are discussed in the explanatory note to the relevant anecdote. For a discussion of the textual principles and policies in this edition see pp. xxxviii–xli.

Unless otherwise stated, the other texts support the manuscript source for the date, in all cases taken from the most fully dated text. Occasionally manuscripts were dated incorrectly; such instances are noted in the textual notes or recorded in the description of the Loose Papers (pp. xlvi–lxiv).

Textual Notes

1. F 339 H 415 N 490 S 259 M 33. *Date from* F.
H *adds:* about three weeks before the Chevalier [*Ramsay*]. *In* F *this phrase, following the word* born, *is deleted.*

The sentence quoted in the explanatory note is found in W 5, F 164, N 287, S 170, *and* M 15; *the date is deduced from the position of the anecdote in* F.

2. F 237 H 340 W 5 L 24 p. 1 N 390 S 203 M 24. *Date from* L (H *mistakenly gives* July 1739; F, 1739).

H *shows that Pope made the first statement, Hooke the parenthetical second.*

3. F 4 N 11 S 5. *Date from* F.

The inserted phrase is deleted in F.

4. F 343 H 428 L 30 p. 2 N 500 S 267 M 37. *Date from* L.

Insertion from L *and* H.

5. F 4 N 11 S 6. *Date from* F.

6. F 5 N 13 S 6. *Date from* F: *Martha Blount's remark dated from* §362.

took fright] F *and* N *read:* took a fright. *The inserted note is a comment by Martha Blount found in the Huntington MS.* (*p.* 429) *on Mrs. Rackett's description of the accident which reads as follows:* The other accident of his being so like to be kill'd, when he was overturn'd in the Coach and Six, was in the water just before you come to Twitenham. Mrs Rackett.—(rather somewhere ye Hounslow-Heath way, for he was coming home from Doily. M^rs^ B[lount]). *It is recorded in* F 343 H 430 L 30 p. 3 N 500 S 267 M 37.

7. L 3 p. 4 W 1. *Date from* L.

8. F 21 L 4 p. 15 N 89 S 26. *Date from* L.

a great deal of] *a pencil correction in* F *for* a particular. L *contains only the first clause.*

MANNOCK] Mannick (MSS.)

9. F 21 N 89 S 26. *Date is hypothetical, based on the preceding anecdote which is in* L 4 p. 14.

Spence is the author, though the last sentence is derived from Pope. Singer gave Mannock as the source, perhaps following the preceding anecdote.

drawn for him] *Spence inserted, then deleted,* by Jervas (F)

10. F 241 H 346 L 24 p. 2 N 400 S 206 M 25. *Date from* L (H *mistakenly dates* August 1739; F, 1739).

L *has only a note of Mrs. Rackett's remark,* H *only a part of Spence's expansion, i.e.* when . . . smile

11. F 7 L 3 p. 4 N 17 S 8. *Date from* L (F *omits query*).

Hollands] Holland's (MS.)

L *has only:* His Father no Poet. *The insertion is in Singer's hand in the margin of* F, *written over Spence's pencilled note, apparently taken from* MS. B. *Warburton paraphrased this anecdote as a footnote to the* Epistle to Dr. Arbuthnot, *l. 130*.

12. L 40 p. 1 S 357. *Date from* L.

the best of men] *Spence wrote and then deleted* a most honest *and* one of the honestest. *In the margin he added* (a Holland merchant)

13. S 357 (*from* MS. B). *The date is uncertain, depending on whether Martha Blount's remark was part of the text of* MS. B (*which would place it before 1739*) *or whether it was a marginal jotting in* MS. B, *such as those in* H *written* *when Spence showed her the* MS. *on 27 May 1749* (*see* §362). *The subject matter sounds* post mortem.

14. F 227 H 322 L 25 p. 1 N 372 S 192 M 18. *Date from* L (H *gives* April).
a priest . . . Banister] *Taverner*, a Priest; still living, somewhere in Hamshire (H, L)*; in* H *Spence lightly deleted all but* a Priest *and added a marginal note:* s^{d} be, Banister?
He . . . books] This was when he was about 8 year old. He began to teach him Latin & Greek together (H)*;* He taught him Latin & Greek together (L)
the seminary at] *omitted in* L, H.
my first] the former (F *originally*)*;* the first (L, H)
Corner] H *adds:* (How dangerous a place, & how negligent a master)*;* L *has the two phrases in reverse order.*
The last sentence omitted in L, H.
When transcribing F *from* H, *Spence consolidated the 'Aunt' story* (H 458) *with this anecdote. For a transcript of the story see explanatory note. See also the textual note to* §23.

15. F 339 H 416 N 490 S 259 M 33. *Date from* H.
He began . . . which he] He learn'd his Accidence at Twiford; where he satiriz'd his Master. ~~Then~~ began on Latin & Greek together, (which he (H)
priest who] priest, and who (MSS.)
H *is briefer and reverses the order of the second and third sentences.*

16. L 24 p. 2 H 346. *Date from* L (H *mistakenly gives* August 1739*; and* F, 1739).
H *omits the second sentence.*

17. F 358 H 458 N 528 S 283 M 52. *Date from* H.
family priest] Banister *in* F, *but deleted.* H *begins:* Banister? was the priest. . . .
figures] H *has a note on the opposite page* (457)*:* (the Greek Alphabet?)

18. F 346 H 432 L 31 p. 1 N 506 S 269 M 40. *Date from* L.
The insertion is from H. F *has a marginal note:* The alphabet only, as he explained it afterwards. *Both* F *and* N *have the note* Shd. it be recorded? *against this anecdote.*

19. F 21 L 4 p. 15 N 87 S 25. *Date from* L.
a satire] a just satire (L)
L *omits the first sentence.*

20. F 241 H 346 L 24 p. 2 N 400 S 206 M 25. *Date from* L (H *has mistakenly* August, 1739*;* F, 1739).
on that account] for his ill-usage there (L)

21. F 346 H 432 N 506 S 270 M 40. *Date from* H.
with an . . . years] to getting languages by himself (H)

22. F 339 H 418 L 31 p. 1 N 490 S 259 M 33. *Date from* L. (H *and* N *have* 1742).
a syntax] new rules to the syntax (H)
By that] and by that (MS.)
Spence questioned how to separate this from §15. *In* H *he pencilled opposite:* may be more divided.

23. F 358 H 458 N 528 S 283 M 53. *Date from* H.
it. I taught] it; & taught (MS.)
H *contains the sentence about Pope's fondness for reading given above in the explanatory note to* §14. *That Spence intended to consolidate the two anecdotes is shown by his pencil note on* H 458 *above the word* Aunt: (Enterd Cent. 6, 2). *By this he referred to the source of* §14.

24. F 228 H 322 L 25 p. 1 N 374 S 193 M 18. *Date from* L (H *gives* April).
Ampersands in F *before* in a few years *and* I still look *have been omitted. The inserted sentence is in* L *and* H.

25. F 358 N 530 S 283. *Date from* F.
and a nice regard] or a nice regard (N). *In* F *it is difficult to tell which word is superscribed.*

26. F 21 L 4 p. 15 N 87 S 25. *Date from* L.
a wildish sort of] a sort of maddish (L)

27. F 343 H 430 L 28 p. 3 N 500 S 267 M 38. *Date from* L.
L *and* H *read simply:* How hard he study'd in his youth.

28. F 21 (*transcribed by Singer from* first MS. copy [MS. B?]) L 3 p. 2 S 25 (*from* first MS. copy [MS. B?]). *Date from* L (*second paragraph only*).
Because L *contains the second paragraph only, the date of Mrs. Rackett's remark is uncertain.*
to you] with you (F *originally*)

29. F 356 H 448 N 522 S 279 M 51. *Date from* H.
some] several (F *originally*); many (H)
Spence's comment is from H.

30. F 353 H 444, 450 N 518 S 276 M 46. *Date from* H.
In H *the anecdote is split in two. The second half reads:* I was about 8, when Ogilby's Homer fell into my hands; that great Edition, with pictures.

31. F 354 H 446 N 520 S 278 M 49. *Date from* H.
Pencil note in the margin of H*:* Here Acis & Galatea

32. F 352 N 518 S 276 M 46. *Date:* 1743 *is from* F (*month is hypothetical, based on* H *date for* §30).

33. F 353 H 450 N 518 S 276 M 47. *Date from* H.
schoolfellows] several boys about my own age (H)
The detail cited in the explanatory note from the index to H *occurs on* H 537. *The complete entry reads:* Made up a sort of a Play, out of the speeches in the Iliad; & got it acted be [*sic*] his schoolfellows, while under (Mr Deane.) 450—.

34. F 232 H 330 L 25 p. 2 N 380 S 197 M 22. *Date from* L.
L *raises an interesting question, for it begins:* Mr P in his youth wrote a Comedy, & a Tragedy & a half. H *follows* L *in reading:* Mr Pope, when very young, wrote a Comedy; an Intire Tragedy & great part of another. *On the opposite page of* H *is the note concerning the otherwise unknown comedy, recording Martha Blount's response, undoubtedly when Spence showed her the* H *MS. in*

1749: Not probable: I never heard a word of it. Mrs B— (this the only place where anything is mention'd of it. Probably, a mistake; as great part of another Tragedy, may be; for his Homeric play [*Spence*]) *In pencil, before recording this note in ink, Spence had written a note of Martha Blount's remark:* Not probable never heard a word of it. *Walsh in fact urged Pope to write a pastoral comedy, but he declined* (*Corresp.* i. 18–19).

A similar note records Mrs. Blount's response to the Tragedy: he had burnt it; & I used to be griev'd that I had not seen it first. Mrs B. *Spence's original pencil note read:* destroyd y^t Tr[agedy].

For epic poem L *reads* Ducalion.

35. F 249 H 358 W 6 L 27 N 412 M 28. *Date from* L (H *mistakenly gives* Sept?).

36. F 20 L 4 p. 13 N 87 S 24. *Date from* L.
The insertion is from MS. B *via Singer. In* L *part of the couplet was in the text; so at first in* F, *but deleted and put into the notes. In* L *the order of the anecdote is different, but substantially it is the same.*

37. F 353 H 444 N 518 S 276 M 47. *Date from* H.
H *lacks the sentence about the underwater scene.*

38. F 355 H 452 N 522 S 279 M 50. *Date from* H.
The parenthesis in the first sentence is a marginal note of Spence.

39. F 232 L 25 p. 2 N 382 S 197 M 23. *Date from* L.
husband of Pyrrha] flood gentleman (L)
The Bishop . . . regret.] *In* L *this consists of a single sentence; for which see explanatory note to* §37.
The insertion is given by Singer as from MS. B; *he also copied it into* F *as a* note from 1st MS. Copy.

40. F 353 H 444 N 518 S 277 M 47. *Date from* H.
this or that story] single parts (H)

41. F 353 H 448, 444 N 518 S 277 M 48. *Date from* H.
A marginal note gives the sources of the quotations, each enough wrong that they may indicate the edition Spence was using: [*Essay Criticism l.*] 194; Dunciad. 3, 56 *and* Dunciad. 1, 182.

42. F 234 H 334 L 25 p. 3 N 384 S 199 M 23. *Date from* L.
H *has the note opposite the text:* (Those five or six years were wholy Poetical, or in the Belles Lettres.) L *has only slight variants.*

43. F 7 L 3 p. 4 N 17 S 8. *Date from* L (F *omits query*).
in . . . twelve] when about 12 Yrs old (L)

44. F 355 H 446, 445 N 522 S 278 M 49. *Date from* H.
The parenthesis is in the margin of F. H *reads:* Between that [the Pastorals] & twenty I read, *which would make the period somewhat later. Spence's note about the* Essay on Criticism, *printed in the explanatory note, appears in the text of* H, *but in brackets.*

Martha Blount's comment comes from H, *where it is placed on the opposite page* (445) *as a note to this anecdote.*

45. F 228 H 324 L 25 p. 1 N 374 S 193 M 19. *Date from* L.
Spence's comment in L *and* H *is simpler:* He read Rapin & Bossu then, & several of the best French books, to good service. *The remark on* Quintilian *appears to come from the same source as* §549, *i.e.* L 3 p. 1.

46. F 355 H 450 N 522 S 278 M 49. *Date from* H.

47. F 354 H 446 N 520 S 278 M 49. *Date from* H.
I did exactly . . . himself] I literally follow'd that passage in Virgil (H)

48. F 354 H 448 N 520 S 278 M 49. *Date from* H.

49. F 356 H 446 N 524 S 280 M 51. *Date from* H.
and against the methods used there] *not in* H. *In* F *an ampersand follows, which has been omitted.*
bred] educated (H, F *originally*)

49a. L 18.

50. F 7 L 3 p. 2 N 17 S 8. *Date from* L *which reads:* set down Aug. 1729; F *gives* 1728.
In F *the parenthetical phrase has been deleted, though some definite period of Pope's life is meant.* L *has:* at ab^t twenty? *Singer restored the deletion silently.*

51. F 7 L 3 p. 2 N 17 S 8. *Date from* F.
The anecdote concludes with an unrelated sentence: His first Education was at the Seminary at Twiford, near Winchester. *This has been omitted from the text here because it duplicates statements on preceding pages.*

52. F 21 L 4 p. 15 N 87 S 25 M 174. *Date from* L.

53. F 369 H 472 L 33 p. 1 N 541 S 293 M 174. *Date from* L *and* H. *In* F *this is the last anecdote for the year* 1743.
saw.] *the* MSS. *have a colon.*
in Betterton's days] in his time (L)

54. F 4 L 3 p. 3 N 11 S 5 M 81. *Date from* L (F *omits query*).
and is] *not in* L.
against one another] with each other (*later revision in* N)

55. F 357 H 452 N 524 S 281 M 52, 114. *Date from* H.

56. F 357 H 454 N 524 S 281 M 114. *Date from* H.

57. L 7 p. 6 S 332. *Date from* L. *Spence comments:* not written down till 1730, but certain.
I remember his face] *originally:* I remember something of his face. *Spence wished to make the remark stronger, as did Singer who altered the passage to read:* remember his face well.

58. F 340 H 420 L 30 p. 1 N 494 S 260 M 112. *Date from* L.
next] toward (H); to (L)

59. L 3 p. 3 S 261 (*from* 'Papers'). *Date from* L.
Only the two first sentences are in L, *the rest being given by Singer as* 'Addition from Papers'. *It is not in the known Spence papers, so it may have derived from* MS. B.

60. F 341 H 420 L 30 p. 1 N 494 S 261 M 112. *Date from* L.
One of them was a priest . . . guards] *In* L *this information follows* §63 (*same page* L 30 p. 1), *in* H *it occurs on p. 422.*
worth . . . him] worth him about (F, H, L); worth to him about (N)

60a. F 163 N 285 S 177. *Date from* F.
For a deleted note in F *see explanatory note. Against this anecdote, Singer wrote* see N° 94, *i.e.* § 61, *in the margin of* F. *For his consolidation of* §§60a *and* 61, *see* §61 *textual note.*

61. F 170 W 5 N 295 S 177 M 16. *Date from* F.
Singer glossed twenty-fifth year *in the margin of* F *as* in the year 1712; *in* S *he inserted* (1712) *in the text. Singer took this date from* §60a, *which he cross-referenced to this anecdote in* F (*see* §60a *textual note*).

62. F 341 H 420 L 30 p. 1 N 494 S 262 M 113. *Date from* L. H *has year only.*
chiefly] *from* H, F *reads:* a good deal.
up. The] up; & as the (MSS.)

63. F 341 H 420 L 30 p. 1 N 494 S 262 M 113. *Date from* L.
⌜a⌝ line] *from* H, L*;* each line (F)
sometime ⌜too⌝] *from* H*;* F *and* L *omit* too

64. F 164 N 287 S 170 M 111. *Date from* F.
Singer omitted Cleomenes *which Spence added in the margin of* F, *and which also appears in* N.

65. F 153 N 269 S 158 M 12. *Date from* F.

66. F 165 N 289 S 171 M 112. *Date from* F.

67. F 4 L 3 p. 3 N 11 S 5 M 81. *Date from* L (F *omits query*).
Pitt's comment is from L.

68. F 341 H 422 L 30 p. 1 N 494 S 263 M 113. *Date from* L.
Insertion from H. F *has a marginal note that does not mention* Tom's, *whereas* L *mentions* Tom's *but not* Russel Street.
After . . . Button's] as after his death Addison set up at Button's (L)

69. F 5 W 1 L 3 p. 4 N 15 S 7. *Date from* L (F *omits query*).
For a deleted passage in F *see explanatory note.* W *is in note form and begins:* Gave up all hopes in a feaver, Aet: 17. . . . L *reads only:* That obligation of his to M^{r} P, w^{n} ye latter was about 17. M^{r} P.

70. F 6 W 1 L 3 p. 4 N 15 S 7. *Date from* L (F *omits query*).
sent a letter] went (F *originally*)
L *reads only:* —that beautiful piece of gratitude to Fr Southcot, now an Abbé near Avignon: twas just after the French court had insisted upon our not pensioning Courayer. *The version in* W *is a brief note but retains the detail about the French court which occurs in L.*

71. F 229 H 324 L 25 p. 1 N 376 S 194 M 19. *Date from* L.

72. F 229 H 324 L 25 p. 1 N 376 S 194 M 20. *Date from* L.
in [Worcestershire]] *all MSS. leave a blank*

73. F 356 H 452 N 524 S 280 M 52. *Date from* H.
to the last] *here the anecdote ends in* H

74. F 229 H 324 L 25 p. 1 N 376 S 194 M 20. *Date from* L.

75. F 21 L 4 p. 15 N 87 S 25. *Date from* L.
L *reads:* Walsh his first . . ., then Wycherley, *In* F *Spence wrote them in this order but later corrected to place Wycherley first.*

76. F 13 L 15 p. 4 L 4 p. 3 N 71 S 17 M 117. *Date from* L 4.
a little after] 2 years after (L)
Insertions from L 4. *For the note in* L 15 *see textual note to* §79.

77. F 13 L 4 p. 5 N 71 S 17 M 117. *Date from* L.
L *omits* He . . . climacteric *and* and . . . emphasis

78. F 156 N 273 S 161 M 125. *Date from* F.

79. F 13 L 15 p. 4 (*brief*) L 4 p. 3 N 69 S 16 M 116. *Date from* L 4.
her Grace] her Ladyship (L 4)
L 15 *is a note for this anecdote and for* §76: Wycherley's first acquaintance with y[e] D[s] of Cl[d]. He was well with Madam de Rambouillet too: he was a very handsome man.

80. H 340 L 24 p. 1. *Date from* L (H *mistakenly gives* July 1739; F, 1739).

81. F 13 L 4 p. 3 N 71 S 17 M 116. *Date from* L.

82. L 4 p. 15 S 336. *Date from* L.
The opening sentence is the same as that of §11 *though the two anecdotes are quite different and are separated by two years. The differences between* S *and L are probably due to Singer's 'improvements'.*

83. F 148 W 4 L 13 N 259 S 150 M 123. *Date from* L (F *gives* 1734).
it . . . last] they bore it very well at last together (L)
some hundred] above 400? (L)
W *has only:* A great number of M[r] P's Lines in Wycherley's Poems.

84. F 232 H 330 L 25 p. 3 N 382 S 198 M 126. *Date from* L.
The insertion is from L *and* H, *which also read:* they are easily to be distinguisht *expressions to be found in* F *and* N *with anecdote* §83.

85. F 368 H 472 W 8 L 33 p. 1 N 541 S 292 M 128. *Date from* L.
Essay on Poetry] Essay (L, H); Essay on translated Verse (*originally in* F *and* N, *but deleted in favour of the present reading*). W *mentions only Buckingham's* Essay.

86. F 235 H 338 L 25 p. 4 N 386 S 200 M 126. *Date from* L.
He . . . general] He was not *Slow* (H); Wycherley not Slow (L)

87. F 233 H 332 L 25 p. 3 N 382 S 198 M 126. *Date from* L.
[He would]] *replaces an ampersand in* F *and* H, *preceded by semicolon*
obliged to them] H *and* L *name Seneca and Gratian*
all their thoughts] all his thoughts the same as theirs (L, H)
one of the strangest phenomenons] a most strange Phaenomenon (L, H)

88. H 480 L 33 p. 3. *Date from* L.
two or three golden pippins] a Gold[n] Pippin or two (L)

89. F 15 L 15 p. 4 (*brief*) L 4 p. 5 N 75 S 18 M 121. *Date from* L 4.
two or three years] a year or two (L 4)
a year or two] two year (L 4)
dispraise of liberality] Praise of Prodigality (L 4)
liberality. In] liberality; & in (MS.)
The sketchy L 15 *version reads:* He lost his Memory when ab^t 40 by a feaver. The same thoughts recurring on a like Paradox: (enc: on Avarice, & Praise of Prodigality 2 Year after.)

90. F 2 L 15 p. 4 L 3 p. 3 N 4 S 2 M 118. *Date from* L (F *omits query*).

91. F 155 N 273 S 160 M 124. *Date from* F.

92. F 14 L 4 p. 5 N 73 S 18 M 118. *Date from* L.
when he was so old] L *continues:* The person mention'd by Pack, was he who recomẽnded his Wife to him under ye Notion of a relation of his of a 1000 £ fortune. (*'Major Pack' wrote the* Life *of Wycherley prefixed to Theobald's 1728 edition.*)
money] L *adds:* (on compact?)

93. H 334 L 25 p. 3. *Date from* L.
L *omits* again.

94. F 2 L 3 p. 3 N 4 S 2 M 118. *Date from* L (F *omits query*).

95. L 4 p. 5
SAVAGE] Mr. Sav.

96. F 14 W 1 L 15 p. 4 (*brief*) L 4 p. 5 N 71 S 17 M 118. *Date from* L 4.
peevish] a little peevish (W)

97. L 4 p. 5 S 335. *Date from* L.

98. F 164 W 5 N 287 S 170 M 15. *Date from* F.

99. F 346 H 432 L 31 p. 1 N 508 S 270 M 41. *Date from* L.

100. F 351 H 442 L 31 p. 3 N 516 S 275 M 46. *Date from* L. *In* H *the anecdote appears under February.*

101. L 40 p. 1 S 356. *Date from* L.
of White Knights] *was written later in the margin with the query:* (in Oxfordshire?). *A query also occurs over* house. *Spence originally wrote* uncle *in both cases, but changed the first to* Grandfather, *and placed a query above the second. The meaning clearly requires* grandfather *in both places. Singer used* grandfather *in the first instance, and* uncle *in the second.*

102. F 236 H 336 L 25 p. 4 N 388 S 202 M 24. *Date from* L.
The motto, written in the margin of F, *was designated for Spence's notes.*

103. F 162 N 283 S 167 M 14. *Date from* F.

104. F 229 H 324 L 25 p. 1 N 376 S 194 M 20. *Date from* L.
a common acquaintance] *See textual note on* §106.
for so long a time] more than once (L, H)
Sir George] Sir Charles (*a change by later hand in* N)
Sir Plume] *See textual note on* §106.

105. F 229 H 326 L 25 p. 2 N 376 S 195 M 21. *Date from* L.

The tribute to Garth quoted in the explanatory note is from both L *and* H.

106. F 230 H 323, 325 N 378 S 195 M 21. *Date from* §362.

The first clause was added later by Spence in the margin of F, *when he noticed that the passage was incoherent as it stood.*

The information here is expanded from notes in H, *in which the intimate friend is identified as* M^rs^ B [*Martha Blount*]. *The notes read:*

The Peer in ye Rape of the Lock, Ld Petre. Mrs B.—old Mr Caryl of Sussex. Mrs B.—the Picture of the man. M^rs^ B.

107. F 140 W 2 L 21 p. 1 N 249 S 142 M 3. *Date from* L.

digested] F *continued:* & writ, *which was later deleted in pencil.* L *reads:* had laid in, *with* digested *written above;* W *reads* laid in

added afterwards] superadded (L, W)

published before] writ before (F *originally*)

on journeys] often on ye Road (L, W)

on a morning] on mornings (F *originally*)

W *omits* from . . . bed; L *omits* and . . . bed

108. F 19 L 15 p. 5 L 4 p. 7 N 83 S 23, 336. *Date from* L 4.

Jervas] Gervaise (MSS.)

Insertion from L 4, *where queries are placed after* Lucius Verus *and* from the life.

109. L 4 p. 7 F 19 N 83 S 23. *Date from* L.

The text here is taken from L *because it is much fuller than* F, *which reads:* With what pleasure he [Pope] stole some strokes, (in Tilleman's? absence,) in the lanskip he was drawing at Ld Radnor's. *The query after* Tilleman's *is in pencil.*

110. F 19 L 15 p. 5 L 4 p. 7 N 83 S 23. *Date from* L 4.

111. 1756 MB p. 9 S 368. *Date from* MB.

Singer expanded the anecdote from the notes.

112. F 173 N 299 S 180 M 178. *Date from* F.

113. F 173 N 299 S 180 M 178. *Date from* F (*however, see also Appendix to* § *114*).

que voilà] que vous avez depeinte ici (F *originally*)

As reported in the explanatory note, Spence recorded an earlier version of this story from 'Colonel' Hay (L 7 p. 7 *dated* 28 July–4 August 1730). *The differences between the two versions indicate that he heard it anew from Pope in 1736. The 1730 version reads:* S^r^ G: Kneller took ye grossest flattery very kindly. Mr Pope resolv'd to try how far it w^d^ go. That Picture (says he) of yours, is ye truest thing y^t^ ever was;—Surely, Was God to create a man again he'd do it by that Image, By God, & so he w^d^ says Sr Godfrey. *For what appears to be a further manuscript jotting for this anecdote, dating from 1735 (?), see Appendix to* § *114*.

114. F 160 N 279 S 165 M 175. *Date from* F (*however, see Appendix to* § *114*).

the company] the good company (F *originally*)

world.] world: & (MS.)

For what appears to be a further manuscript jotting for this anecdote see Appendix to § 114.

115. F 159 N 279 S 165 M 175. *Date from* F.
lie] lay (MS.)

116. L 21.

117. L 5 p. 1 S 337. *Date from* L.

118. F 36 L 5 p. 1 N 95 S 46 M 143. *Date from* L.
In L *the order of the names is* Congreve, Garth and Vanbrugh, *and they are numbered* 1, 2, 3.

119. L 5 p. 1 S 338. *Date from* L.
Steele *is numbered* 8, Pulteney 13, Lord Dorset 14, the Duke 15, *and* the Earl of Essex 17.
Singer printed the names of Congreve, Garth *and* Vanbrugh *after that of* Addison. *But they do not appear at this point in* L. *They had been mentioned above on the same page.* (*See* §118).—§120 *occurs in* L *before the name of* Lord Stanhope, *but has been treated separately in order to reveal the three speakers.*

120. L 5 p. 1 S 338. *Date from* L.

121. L 5 p. 1 S 337. *Date from* L.
Tonson *is numbered* 4, Lord Mohun 5, *and the* Earl of Berkeley 6.
The parenthetical sentence at the end is bracketed by Spence, and is presumably his own comment.

122. L 5 p. 1 S 338. *Date from* L.
Lord Halifax *is numbered* 7.
they broke up] *followed by a query*

123. L 5 p. 1 S 338. *Date from* L.
Kneller is numbered 18. *Singer altered the text in some details.*

124. F 156 N 273 S 161 M 131. *Date from* F.
In the margin of F *Spence wrote in pencil:* omit?

125. F 153 N 269 S 158 M 135. *Date from* F.

126. L 38 p. 2 S 350. *Date from* L.
JONES] *Singer added* of Welwyn

127. F 16 L 15 p. 5 L 4 p. 7 N 77 S 19 M 132. *Date from* L 4.
There are slight verbal changes in Warton's transcript of this anecdote (Essay, *ii.* 55).
L 15 *has only brief note:* Dr Swift's blunt way (supper).

128. F 338 H 414 N 488 S 256 M 134. *Date from* H. *In* F *the anecdote comes under the years* 1742 *and* 1743.

129. F 338 H 414 N 488 S 256 M 134. *Date from* H.
Singer supplied: I once said to him, *but there is nothing in* F *or* H *to indicate who the speaker was. It could have been Pope, or anyone who told the story to Pope.*

130. H 412.

131. L 4 p. 7 L 15 p. 5. *Date from* L 4.
L 15 *omits* very good *and has* to P *in its place.*

132. L 13.

133. F 140 L 21 p. 1 N 247 S 141 M 132. *Date from* L; F *gives* 1734 *mistakenly.*
of Rabelais] of some parts of Rablais (L)
I could never . . . with patience] I could hardly ever . . . with any patience (F *originally*)
L *has a shorter form concluding with:* M^{r} P seems to be quite angry wth y^{t} Writer. *Spence deleted* Rablais *and substituted* y^{t} Writer.

134. F 169 N 295 S 176 M 16. *Date from* F.

135. F 8 L 3 p. 2 N 19 S 10. *Date from* L (F *omits query*).
Addison . . . was not disinclined to come] *according to* L: Addison likd it extremely & w^{d} have come in.
Spence in a marginal note suggests the present order: at first the paragraph on Henley preceded that on Deipnosophy.—For Spence's remark on the *Memoirs* themselves *see explanatory note. Against the comment on Henley's life of Durfey, Spence pencilled marginally in* F: I suppose at first design'd to come in after ye Advent[ure] of ye Shield.

136. F 162 N 283 S 167 M 14. *Date from* F.
Opposite the last sentence Spence pencilled a Q *in the margin of* F.

137. F 143 W 3 L 13 N 253 S 145 M 5. *Date from* L (F *gives* 1734).
I . . . with the help of a lawyer] I & a Lawyer (L, W)
Fortescue] *A query follows in* W, *and the case is described as the* case (of the Grey horses).
W *contains the substance of the first sentence only.*

138. F 169 N 295 S 176 M 16. *Date from* F.

139. F 366 H 466 N 537 S 290 M 57. *Date from* H.

140. 1755 MB p. 17 S 366. *Date from* MB.

141. L 24 p. 1 F 235 H 338 W 5 *and* 1 N 386 S 201 M 24, 140. *Date from* L (H *mistakenly gives* June 1739; F, 1739).
For significant variants in MSS., *see the editor's article cited in explanatory note. See also textual note* § *142 for the brief version in* W, *which, together with the conclusion to the* L *text of* § *142, shows that Spence was always likely to confuse the two pieces.*

142. F 19 W 1 L 4 p. 11 N 83 S 23. *Date from* L.
L *begins:* Five or six pleasant Imitations in P^{s} & S^{s} Misc: W *text is almost identical.*
by Swift] *omitted in* L *and* W
a line or two] a very little (F *originally*); a little (L, W)
L *concludes:* That of *Chaucer*, by Mr *Pope:* Ditton & Whiston, id:—*Pryor*'s Imitation of Chaucer is quite wrong. W *concludes:* Ditton & Whiston, by P? Mr. P 28.

143. F 338 H 416 N 488 S 256 M 32. *Date from* H.
this Epistle] part of one of Horace's Epistles (H *with a* [*mistaken*] *note on p. 415:* Ep: 7. B: 1.)
begun by Swift] in Swift's (F *originally*)
familiar, low familiar (H)
A pencilled note on H 415 *reads:* the most candid heart—some of the Irish women. *I am unable to explain it.*

144. F 153 W 4 N 269 S 158 M 12. *Date from* F.
W *text is less polished, but has substantially the same content.—Spence pencilled a note in* F *at the end of the anecdote:* Q[ery] in ye Miscell^s^ themselves.

145. F 230 H 326 L 25 p. 2 N 378 S 195 M 21, 153. *Date from* L.
1712] 1713 (*in both* L *and* H*;* 13 *is underscored in* L) F *originally read* 1713, *but was later changed to* 1712, *following a pencilled inquiry in the margin by Spence, who had noticed in the letters* (?) *that the* Iliad *was begun in* 1712.
liked him] H *and* L *insert:* de bon coeur

146. F 230 H 326 L 25 p. 2 N 378 S 195 M 22, 153. *Date from* L.
nation] H *and* L *add* &c *indicating that Addison's remarks extended beyond this happy phrase.*
advised me] mention'd (L)

147. L 3 p. 3 F 7 (*transcribed by Singer from* MS. B) S 9. *Date from* L.
S *does not note the source in* MS. B. *Since* MS. B *is unavailable and Singer usually 'improved' his text,* L *is used; the* B *text can be judged from* S. *The anecdote occurs in the margin of a paper recording Spence's conversations, apparently in 1728, to which Spence added:* certain, though set down August 1729.
that of half] *over this is written:* or vice versa (L)

148. F 40 L 5 p. 4 N 103 S 50 M 150. *Date from* L.
Insertion from L, *which, however, omits* and . . . man
seemed to preserve] preserved (L)

149. F 144 L 13 N 253 S 145 M 6. *Date from* L (F *gives* 1734).
I think] *omitted in* L

150. F 144 L 13 N 253 S 145 M 6. *Date from* L (F *gives* 1734).
Both insertions occur in L*;* F *and* S *give the first insertion only as preserved by Singer.*
⌜Lord . . . acquaintances⌝] *transcribed by Singer in the margin of* F *as* note *but printed in* S *as from* MS. B. *The sentence occurs in* L *but in reported speech:* L^d^ B one of his older acquaintance

151. F 144 L 13 N 253 S 146 M 6. *Date from* L.
introduced . . . company] with L^d^ B (L)
his conversation] his company (L)
Bullingbroke *in* F *is a pronunciation spelling.*

152. L 2 S 339. *Date from* L.

153. F 231 H 326 L 24 p. 2 N 378 S 196 M 146. *Date from* L.
The insertions are in H, *thus expanded from* L. *When Spence omitted them in* F *he ended with the last sentence as found in* S.

Both H *and* L *begin:* In the same year, (1713,) Addison had finsht his Cato. He brought. . . .

reputation enough] H *omits* reputation.

154. F 36 L 5 p. 2 N 95 S 46 M 146. *Date from* L.

to comply with popular taste] to oblige the town (L)

In L *the two statements are transposed, so that the remark about the last act forms the conclusion to* §817.

155. F 37 L 5 p. 2 N 95 S 46 M 156. *Date from* L.

The inserted phrase is from L.

156. F 37 L 5 p. 2 N 95 S 46 M 157. *Date from* L.

a purse of guineas] eighty guineas (L)

157. F 338 H 414 N 488 S 257 M 156. *Date from* H.

The first sentence in H *is scored through with a single line; over* somebody *is written:* (Mr P?)

158. H 414.

159. F 156 N 273 S 161 M 156. *Date from* F.

160. L 5 p. 2 F 37 (*transcribed by Singer from* MS. B) S 47 (*from* MS. B). *Date from* L.

161. F 230 H 326 L 25 p. 2 N 378 S 196 M 22, 154. *Date from* L.

[1713]] *This date is taken from* §153 *because the versions of this anecdote, which immediately follow* §161 *in* L *and* H, *specify* the same year *of* §153 *as being* 1713 (*see textual note to* §153).

162. F 144 W 4 (*brief*) L 13 N 253 S 146 M 7. *Date from* L (F *gives* 1734).

time. We] time; & we (F)

He must] That he must (MSS.)

Insertions from L. *Singer printed the second insertion as from* MS. B *but did not copy it into* F*; his version differs in minor details from that in* L *but is substantially the same.*

163. F 145 W 4 (*brief*) L 13 N 255 S 147 M 8. *Date from* L (F *gives* 1734).

owned] tacitly owned (L)

Spence's comment is not in L.

164. F 37 L 5 p. 2 N 97 S 47 M 147. *Date from* L.

preface] *Spence pencilled in the margin of* F*:* To quote the passage in a note.

165. F 146 W 3 L 13 N 257 S 148 M 9. *Date from* L (F *gives* 1734).

L *contains a significant variant, reading:* (about Wycherley?) *The interrogation point also occurs in* W (*as Arthur E. Case acutely observed; see explanatory notes*) *and in* F *Spence pencilled* Q *in the margin.*

166. F 146 W 3 L 13 N 257 S 148 M 9. *Date from* L (F *gives* 1734).

The inserted phrase is given by Singer as from MS. B, *but he did not copy it into* F*;* L *has a parenthetical reading:* (a weak man).

us'. To] us; & to (MS.)

167. F 49 L 9 p. 2 N 103 S 57 M 150. *Date from* L.
prose writings!] *question mark for punctuation in* F *and* N. *No corresponding sentence in* L.
indifferent] bad (L, F *originally*)

168. L 2 S 339. *Date from* L.

169. F 39 L 5 p. 3 N 101 S 49 M 149. *Date from* L.

170. F 39 L 5 p. 3 N 101 S 49 M 149. *Date from* L.
L *reads:* He said himself 'twas a poor thing, & w^{d} not have publish'd it in his large Works himself had he livd to have giv'n ye Edition.
Singer copied a version of the sentence in L *on to the margin of* F *with only minor differences. He may have taken it from* MS. B *for the source is given in* F *as* (Addition from first MS.).

171. H 414 F 339 N 490 S 257 M 155. *Date from* H.
The text is from H, *since it is much fuller than* F, *as may be judged by comparing the text with* S 257.
Cato,] Cato, & (MS.)
[He]] & (MS.)
were what] was what (F)

172. F 39 L 5 p. 4 H 101 S 50 M 150. *Date from* L.

173. F 149 L 13 N 259 S 151 M 147. *Date from* L (F *gives* 1734).
The inserted phrase is from L.

174. F 149 L 13 N 261 S 151 M 147. *Date from* L (F *gives* 1734).

175. S 151 (*from* MS. B) L 13. *Date from* L.
Insertions from L *which is in note form:* (stiffens as he stands, Mrs Oldf^{d}: Cato: ye Alt^{n} Stiffens yet alive, sug^{d} by Mr P.) *underlined in pencil with Spence's query* (Where?) *written above it.*
The inserted quotations are from L.

176. L 35 p. 2 F 385 H 516 N 567 S 316 M 155. *Date from* L.
The text is taken from L. F *and* H *have only the first sentence which reads* most *for* best, *and* more *for* better.

177. L 35 p. 2.

178. S 151 (*from* MS. B) L 13. *Date from* L.
L *reads:* Tautology a great fault of Mr. A[ddison's] poetry[;] more of them than one w[ould] Imagine in ye Campaign.

179. F 161 N 281 S 167 M 13. *Date from* F.
My letter] *Spence pencilled in* F*:* See the letter.

180. F 169 N 293 S 175 M 152. *Date from* F.
The inserted section is printed by Singer (*but not transcribed into* F) *as from a 'pencil note in MS B.'*

181. F 361 H 460 N 534 S 286 M 55, 155. *Date from* H.
party] admirers (H *originally*), friends (*superscribed in* F)
five or six] seven or eight (H)

182. F 362 H 460 N 534 S 286 M 114, 155. *Date from* H.

183. F 231 H 328 L 25 p. 2 N 380 S 196 M 154. *Date from* L.
The inserted sentence appears in H *and* L.

184. F 37 L 5 p. 2 N 97 S 47 M 148. *Date from* L.
L *shows that the first sentence was Tonson's, the second from both Pope and Tonson.*

185. F 37 L 5 p. 2 N 97 S 47 M 149. *Date from* L.

186. H 328 L 25 p. 2 *Date from* L.

187. F 147 MS. B L 13 N 259 S 149 M 138. *Date from* L (F *gives* 1734).
The wording of the second paragraph in L *should be noted since it is more explicit:* The present Family had made great promises to Gay at Hanover, wch had no effect w^{n} they came over. twas not impos: y^{t} Mr A[ddison] had prevented 'em, on his prejudice ag'st Gay for being acq[ainte]d too much with some of ye late ministry. MS. B, *according to Singer, was also more explicit:* The present family had made strong promises to him (S 150; *not copied into* F)
prejudice] *deleted in* F, *and the sentence weakened by a shift of tenses.*

188. L 24 p. 1.
An exact transcript of the first sentence reads: A & S a couple of H^{s}. *From the context, Addison is clearly intended, and Steele inferentially so.*

189. F 231 H 328 L 25 p. 2 N 380 S 197 M 154. *Date from* L.

190. F 227 H 322 L 25 p. 1 L 24 p. 2 N 372 S 191 M 152. *Date from* L.
so encouraging a] y^{t} publick (L)
Spence's note is written in the margin of F. L 24 *contains only earlier notes for the last two sentences.*

191. F 235 H 334 L 25 p. 4 N 386 S 200 M 153. *Date from* L.
Old Jacob] *omitted in* H *and* L
after . . . secretaryship] toward the end of his life (H, L; F *originally*)
used . . . to say] H *and* L *continue:* toward the end of his life.

192. F 376 H 492 W 9 L 34 p. 2 N 555 S 304 M 64. *Date from* L.
and less suited to my inclination] *not in* H, W, L
want of money] *A note opposite* (H 493) *reads:* have often heard him speak of this. Mrs. B[lount]. *In pencil:* often.

193. F 359 H 458 W 6 N 530 S 283 M 53. *Date from* H.
six] 5 or 6 (W)
particularly the first part of it] *not in* H *or* W
and being . . . it] &c. (H, W)

194. H 433.
The anecdote is not found among the Loose Papers with the others that Young told Spence in 1759. In the margin Spence wrote sooner, *apparently a hint to reorganize the sentence.*

195. F 359 H 458 W 7 N 530 S 284 M 54. *Date from* H.
sat down] set down (F, H); N *has a pencilled* a *over the* e.
In 1742 Pope told Spence: I should certainly have written an Epic Poem, if I had not engaged in the translation of Homer. (F 340 H 418 *dated 1742* N 492 S 259 M 34.) *Because it is a duplication, it is omitted in the text.*

196. F 138 W 2 L 21 N 245 S 137 M 1. *Date from* L; F *gives* 1734 *mistakenly.*

Insertion and Spence's comment from L. W *begins at* I collected *and briefly sums up the rest.*

life of him] life for him (MSS.)

197. F 251 H 364 N 416 S 218 M 28. *Date from* H (*the last page for the year 1739*).

The inserted sentence is from H.

Spence's comment is in F *marked for the notes.* H *ends at* times.

198. F 251 H 364 N 416 S 218 M 28. *Date from* H.

thirty or forty verses] some of the verses (H)

199. F 246 H 354 L 26 N 408 S 211 M 26. *Date from* L (H *mistakenly gives* Sept?).

for the *Iliad*] for Homer (L) *The inserted part is from* L.

who is . . . publishing] *not in* H, *or* L *which, however, after* into his own pocket *reads:* if he runs all the risks himself

For instance . . . £100] L *reads:* (E.G., 1000 copies of 3^s each to ye comon buyer s^d be 2000^s for ye Author, if all sold, & but 1000 for Printing, Paper, Publish^g, Selling, & all Incidents.); H *follows* F *but adds the phrase* for . . . Incidents

200. L 26.

These jottings appear immediately after §199.

201. F 371 H 478 W 8 L 33 pp. 2–3 N 545 S 295 M 61. *Date from* L.

subscribers] ? *follows in* W

202. F 347 H 432 L 31 p. 1 N 508 S 270 M 41. *Date from* L.

203. F 342 H4 24 W 6 L 30 p. 1 N 496 S 265 M 35. *Date from* L.

most corrected] excessively blotted (L, W, H)

Inserted passage, from H, *appears in similar form in* L *and* W.

204. F 135 L 21 N 239 S 134. *Date from* L.

Also printed by Jos. Warton in his edn. of Pope (*Works, 1797, i. 180*). F *has a marginal note in Singer's hand:* This is lengthened from the short hints in the first memorandum paper. Such fillings up, and this in particular, shou'd be flung into notes; for one can't answer for the particular circumstances, at such a distance of time. For instance accord^g to my memory 'twas Garth he return'd home with; but in my paper, Congreve's name has a particular mark under it; & so it might be he, & not Garth, that let Mr P. into this part of Ld Hallifax's character. Must be hinted at above and enlarged in the notes. *Singer quotes this and adds:* Note in pencil *in the margin by Spence. The whereabouts of the note in Spence's hand is not known. It is not in* L, *where, however, we do find the* particular mark *under Congreve's name. The short hints of the first memorandum paper* [L] *follow:* Ld Halifaxs part^r behaviour to M^r P wⁿ he was first ab^t the Iliad: Mr Addⁿ, Mr *Congreve*, Dr Garth &c there at ye Reading.—I hope my L^d you'll find that your objections to those passages are quite removd. Ay now, &c.

The famous Lord Halifax] *followed originally by* (tho' so much talkt of) (F)

205. H 360 W 6 L 27. *Date from* L (H *mistakenly gives* Oct?).

206. F 347 H 432–4 W 6 L 31 p. 1 N 508 S 271 M 41. *Date from* L.
Aeaean bay] *Singer misread:* Ocean bay.

207. L 7 p. 5 S 330. *Date from* L.
Layng] Leng (MS.)
tenth book] 10? book (MS.)

207a. F 347 W 6 L 30 p. 1 N 508 M 42. *Date from* L.
L *reads only:* Broome 500^{L} Fenton 300. Mr P. W *has substantially the same.*

208. L 7 p. 3.

208a. L 7 p. 3.
Broome] Br? (L)

209. L 14.

210. F 343 H 428 L 30 p. 2 N 498 S 266 M 37. *Date from* L.
The insertion is from L; H *has the same information in a less complete sentence.*

211. F 38 L 5 p. 3 N 99 S 48 M 130. *Date from* L.

212. F 38 L 5 p. 3 N 99 S 48 M 130. *Date from* L.
in prose . . . good] *omitted in* L
Adrian the Sixth] *in* L *this is written above* an old Gramarian
a fourth] L *ends here*

213. F 168 N 293 S 175 M 129. *Date from* F.

214. F 2 L 3 p. 3 N 4 S 3 M 129. *Date from* L (F *omits query*).

215. F 168 N 293 S 175 M 129. *Date from* F.

216. F 2 L 3 p. 3 N 4 S 2 M 129. *Date from* L (F *omits query*).
mean creature] nasty creature (L)

217. F 39 L 5 p. 4 N 99 S 49 M 130. *Date from* L.
poor woman] nasty woman (L)
Spence's comment was originally written in the margin of F *in pencil; Singer rubbed it out and inked the note over in his own hand, printing it in* S *as a* Note by Mr. Spence.

218. F 236 H 336 L 25 p. 4 N 388 S 201. *Date from* L.
not a very capable minister] no good (L)
had . . . bargain] a very negligent one (H); a very negl^{t} Minister (L)
trifling verses] foolish verses (L)
The order of the Scriblerians in L *and* H: Swift, Arbuthnot, Parnel, Pope; & sometimes Gay. *In* L, Parnel *is written over* Gay, *but is deleted.*

219. F 236 H 338 L 25 p. 4 N 388 S 202. *Date from* L.

220. F 236 H 336 L 25 p. 4 N 388 S 201. *Date from* L.
began] begun (MSS.)

221. F 171 N 297 S 178 M 144. *Date from* F.
It was he] was *is underscored in* F

222. F 384 H 512 L 35 p. 1 S 313. *Date from* L.

H *and* L *differ from* F*;* H *reads* (*and* L *is similar*)*:* Ld Oxford was, laterly, in the Pretender's interest; but not Ld Bolingbroke, Bromley, &c. He betrayd them, in making his peace there without their knowledge. *The* F *text reading*, not latterly, *corrects the other two by supplying the negative necessary to give the proper meaning. Sherburn* (Early Career, *p.* 6 *note*) *and others have been puzzled by the apparent contradiction in Singer's text and note.*

223. H 338 L 25 p. 4. *Date from* L.

In H *the anecdote is crossed out in pencil.*

224. F 236 H 338 *and* 336 L 25 p. 4. N 388 S 202. *Date from* L.

In L *and* H *the anecdote begins with the third sentence, followed by a sentence not in* F (*i.e.* § 223) *followed by the first and second sentences.*

sat out] set out (MS.)

225. H 338 L 24 p. 5. *Date from* L.

In H *the anecdote is crossed out in pencil.*

226. F 376 H 494 W 9 L 34 p. 2 N 555 S 304 M 64. *Date from* L.

pain to my parents] concern to my mother & father (L, W)*:* pain to my Mother & Father (H)

227. F 377 H 494 W 9 L 34 p. 2 N 555 S 305 M 65. *Date from* L.

228. F 377 H 494 W 9 L 34 p. 2 N 555 S 305 M 65. *Date from* L.

For the original reading in L *see explanatory note.*

229. F 378 H 496 W 10 L 34 p. 2 N 557 S 307 M 66. *Date from* L.

Mr. Pope declined even this] H (p. 497) *has pencilled note by Spence:* confirm'd *and in ink:* confirm'd by M^rs B[lount]. *Both remarks and that below date from 27 May 1749* (*see* §362).

or even five hundred] or two hundred (L, W)

that he ever did go] H *has opposite in pencil:* nor Mrs B, *and in ink:* nor I neither Mrs B. *This means that Martha Blount told Spence that she agreed with the other friends that Pope never asked Craggs for money.*

230. F 379 H 498 W 10 L 34 p. 3 N 557 S 307 M 66. *Date from* L.

231. L 4 p. 7 S 335. *Date from* L.

Edw:] *a query over the word.*

232. F 152 N 266–7 S 155 M 169. *Date inferred from* L 23 *which gives* §234*;* F *has year only.*

F *read originally:* A bad, bold, blustering, bustling, busy, Booby. *This was deleted, and a pencilled note in the margin gave the version here printed.* N *deleted* Blundering *and substituted* Boisterous, *adding on the margin the lines quoted in the explanatory note.*

233. F 152 N 267 S 156 M 170. *Date inferred from* L 23 *which gives* §234*;* F *has year only.*

234. F 152 W 4 L 23 N 267 S 156 M 11. *Date from* L.

two or three blunders] 2 blunders (W, L)

235. L 37 p. 1 S 348. *Date from* L.

236. F 368 H 472 L 33 p. 1 N 541 S 292 M 140. *Date from* L.

237. H 472 L 33 p. 1. *Date from* L.

238. F 237 H 338 W 5 L 24 p. 1 N 390 S 202 M 137. *Date from* L (H *mistakenly gives* June 1739; F, 1739).
served his] served him (H, L, W)

239. F 248 H 358 L 27 N 410 S 214 M 139. *Date from* L (H *mistakenly gives* Sept?).

240. F 248 H 358 L 27 N 410 S 214 M 139. *Date from* L (H *mistakenly gives* Sept?).

241. F 248 H 358 L 27 N 410 S 214 M 139. *Date from* L (H *mistakenly gives* Sept?).

242. L 3 p. 1 S 13 (*from* MS. B). *Date from* L.

243. F 155 N 271 S 160 M 137. *Date from* F; *from relative position apparently autumn 1735.*
remarkable] always remarkable (F), *but* always *deleted.*

244. F 154 N 271 S 159 M 136. *Date from* F; *judging from its relative position, apparently early autumn 1735.*
a Newgate Pastoral] *is underlined, indicating emphasis on that point.*

245. F 155 N 271 S 159 M 136. *Date from* F, *apparently autumn 1735, judging from its relative position.*

246. F 248 H 358 L 27 N 410 S 214 M 139. *Date from* L (H *mistakenly gives* Sept?).
£1,100 or £1,200] 11 or 12 hundred (F, H, L)

247. F 248 H 358 L 27 N 410 S 214 M 139. *Date from* L (H *mistakenly gives* Sept?).

248. F 359 H 458 N 530 S 284 M 143. *Date from* H.
H (p. 457) *has a variant for the second line of the couplet:* (For he, alas! can nothing do, but Cinna.)
when . . . name] *not in* H

249. F 359 H 458 N 532 S 284 M 144. *Date from* H.

250. L 4 p. 9.
Spence's punctuation is preserved in the first sentence because of the fragmentary character of the anecdote. Savage's last five words are underlined, perhaps to indicate direct discourse. Pope's comment follows Mr. Sav. without a break.
Kew] Cew (MS.)

251. H 428 W 6 (*brief*) L 30 p. 2 S 338. *Date from* L.
published] told (L)
carried . . . coach] carried by him with Cibber & another (L)
forgot it] forgot so material a circumstance (L)
In H *the anecdote is crossed out in pencil and marked with a* Q *in the margin. Singer's text differs from any MSS. wording, suggesting that he 'improved' this anecdote.*

252. L 37 p. 1 S 339. *Date from* L.
Cibber's slanders] L *has a query after the name. The last sentence is connected with the preceding one by a semicolon followed by ampersand.*

253. L 38 p. 1 S 348. *Date from* L.
printer's] bookseller's (L *originally*)

254. 1755 MB p. 17 S 366. *Date from* MB.

255. F 370 H 476 L 33 p. 2 N 543 S 294 M 173. *Date from* L.
friend] friend at y[e] University (L)

256. F 370 H 476 L 33 p. 2 N 545 S 294 M 174. *Date from* L.

257. S 314.

258. F 150 N 265 S 154 M 172. *Date from* F.

259. F 150 N 265 S 154 M 172. *Date from* F.

260. F 149 N 263 S 151 M 171. *Date from* F.

261. F 149 L 23 N 263 S 152 M 171. *Date from* L.
Insertion and date are from L, *which shows that the conversation with Spence occurred in Oxford.*

262. F 150 N 263 S 153 M 172. *Date from* F.
longer. Yet] longer; & yet (MS.)

263. F 158 N 277 S 164 M 13. *Date from* F.

264. F 150 L 23 N 265 S 154 M 172. *Date from* L.
Since at the time when it was jotted down Peterborow had not yet left for Lisbon, L *reads:* has markt, & is to carry the 2 Vol[s] with him to Lisbon &c.

265. F 344 H 430 L 30 p. 3 N 500 S 267 M 38. *Date from* L.
to . . . Richmond] (to Fortescue's, as she said; rather to —) *a comment in* H 429 *by Martha Blount.*
to walk alone] to go without company (H)*;* to go without company as he used to (F, *but deleted*)
the least man in England . . . largest] a little man had as good a chance as a stout one (H, L)
The insertion is from margin of F.

266. F 344 N 502 S 268 M 38. *The date is inferential. See preceding anecdote. Being a comment by Spence, it may have been added later.*

267. F 345 H 426 L 30 p. 2 N 502 S 269 M 39. *Date from* L.
Danish] *from* H
he . . . garden] was buried in his Garden (H)

268. F 369 H 474 W 8 L 33 p. 2. N 543 S 293 M 60. *Date from* L.
so worthy and good] so good (L, H, W)

269. F 370 H 474 L 33 p. 2 N 543 S 293 M 60. *Date from* L.
And as our arguments . . .] *originally preceded in* H *by:* I was always inclined to do so, *later deleted.*
The insertion is from H. L *is less polished;* F *reads simply:* And what harm wou'd that be to us.

270. F 163 L 13 N 285 S 169 M 165. *Date from* L.
The inserted sentence is from L.

271. F 163 N 285 S 169 M 165. *Date from* F. *Possibly 9 August 1735 as in* §270.

272. F 163 N 285 S 169 M 164. *Date from* F.
writer as Lord Bolingbroke] *a query follows, as though Spence meant to say: This is my opinion, what is yours?*
the best old] some (F *originally*)

273. F 371 H 478 L 33 p. 2 N 545 S 295 M 166. *Date from* L.
sit down] set down (F, H *twice*)
it would appear under] flung into (L)
Insertion from H; L *has a similar addition.*

274. F 144 L 13 N 253 S 169 M 6. *Date from* L (F *gives* 1734).
quite] really (L, F *originally*)

275. F 385 H 514 W 11 L 35 p. 2 S 316. *Date from* L.
The anecdote does not appear in N *because crossed out in* F *with Spence's marginal comment:* Omitt. *Spence's revision from* H *to* F *sacrifices easy conversational quality to wordiness.*
looks as if] shows (H, W, L)
I had . . . carry him] I thought it was come to fetch him (H, W, L)

276. H 510 F 386 L 36 p. 2 S 317. *Date from* L.
The text has been taken from H *because the* F *text was carefully glossed over so as to exclude references to specific persons and places. Singer printed the version in* L *as a footnote 'from Papers'.*
Lord Bolingbroke] L^d B (F)
a great . . . Wyndham] much more money than those, who were principally concern'd, & cou'd better afford it (F)
about that time] *followed by query in* H, L
Pulteney and Sir William Wyndham] *reversed in* L *and in* S (*'from Papers'*)

277. H 484 L 34 p. 1 S 299. *Date from* L.
When . . . late King] He was several times wth ye K. He told him (L)

278. F 385 H 514 W 11 (*hint*) L 35 p. 2 N 565 S 315 M 167. *Date from* L.
a great way back] for about 200 Years back (L, H)

279. F 341 H 422 L 30 p. 1 N 496 S 263 M 165. *Date from* L.
Amicitiae et Libertati] *deleted and superscribed in* F: To Friendship & Liberty *with a marginal comment:* Amicitiae & Libertati S:—or Sacred, to Friendship & Liberty. L *and* H *give only the Latin, omitting* with an 'S' . . . it

280. F 245 H 354 L 26 N 406 S 210 M 164. *Date from* L (H *mistakenly gives* Sept?).
H *has in pencil at the end of the anecdote:* Martin? Fourbe's laughs at it much. L^d B approvd.

281. F 171 N 297 S 178 M 165. *Date from* F.

282. F 164 N 285 S 170. *Date from* F.
one or perhaps both] one or other of them (F *originally*)

283. F 374 H 484 L 34 p. 1 N 551 S 300 M 166. *Date from* L.
Feb. 21, to 24 *is written in* H *to agree with* L.

284. L 40 p. 2 S 358. *Date from* L.
The parenthesis reads simply: Y^{t} L^{d}, ye D^{s} of M, &c. *The Duchess of Marlborough probably never succeeded in deceiving Pope, but Martha might easily have thought so.*

285. 1756 MB p. 10 S 370. *Date from* MB.

286. 1756 MB p. 10 S 369. *Date from* MB.
fault in doing it] *followed by a deletion:* as ye world imagin'd

287. L 40 p. 5 S 360. *Date from* L.

288. F 142 L 22 N 251 S 143 M 4. *Date from* F.

289. F 142 L 22 N 251 S 143 M 4. *Date from* F.

290. 1756 MB p. 9 S 369. *Date from* MB.

291. H 502 L 34 p. 3. *Date from* L.
were he] was he (MS.); if he were (L)

292. H 412.
The anecdote is lightly crossed out in pencil, and hence not in F *and* N.

293. L 7 p. 7. *Date: though the beginning of* L 7 *is dated* 1729?, *the evidence points to early 1730 for this page.*

294. F 12 L 15 p. 4 L 4 p. 3 N 69 S 16. *Date from* L.
For the version in L 15 *see textual note to* §295 *and Sherburn's 'Pope at Work'*, Essays presented to David Nichol Smith, *1945, p. 51.*

295. L 15 p. 4. *Date inferred from* L 4.
The passage in which this sentence occurs is parallel with the material in L 4, *dated 1–7 May 1730, printed by Sherburn in 'Pope at Work', op. cit. pp. 50–51, but because of some differences and three additions, the whole passage is here transcribed:*

Mr P. 1730.
Montaigne's 1 Es: lib: 2? is ye best in ye whole book. M^{r} P^{s} present design wholly upon human actions, & to reform ye mind: A prevailing passion in ye mind brought into ye world with it & continues till death: [This in his Morals, w^{t} Humor in a Character.] We s^{d} not speak agst Avarice, w^{t} speaking agst Prodigality: & so of ye rest: The middle ye aimable point. L^{d} B: very much assisting in ye Materials. The first Ep: to ye Whole, w^{t} a Scale of Miles to a book of Maps. ye Man of Ross: Sr Balaam: fire, meat & drink: ye Dying Courtier &c.

The second sentence, the words in brackets (see §296), *and the concluding phrase (see* §318) *are all additions, not in* L 4. *The evidence of the whole paper suggests that both this version and that in* L 4 *were derived from a common source, probably notes jotted while talking to Pope, or soon after.*

296. L 4 p. 1 L 15 p. 5. *Date from* L 4.

297. L 4 p. 1 F 12 L 15 p. 4 S 15. *Date from* L 4.

F, *followed by Singer, breaks this into two anecdotes. The first is formed by the second sentence here. The first and last sentences form the second anecdote. Because the two sentences in* F *are taken from the larger context in* L *it seems best to give the whole passage from* L *as a continuation of* §296. *Spence himself took them from* L, *as his pencil note in* F *shows:* Addend: fro Pap. No. 4.

We should not] When we (F)
without speaking] we ought to speak too (F)
Avarice . . . hands] *omitted in* F *and* S
[is]] betwixt both is (F)

298. F 13 L 4 p. 9 N 69 S 16. *Date from* L.

Insertion from L, *which, however, lacks the parenthetical remark.*

299. F 37 W 2 L 5 p. 2 N 97 S 48. *Date from* L.

poem] Moral Poem (F *originally*); new Poem (L, W)
four or five] five or 6 (L)

300. F 136 N 241 S 136. *Date from* F.

afterwards called in again] *a pencilled marginal note by Spence reads* (*after a large* Q): Why? Frō his ments^{g} the heads of Ecc^{l} & Civil Polity, wch he aft^{ds} resolv'd not to touch upon in y^{t} Poem? *Spence then put a cross through the note. See* §302. *Among the Spence Papers the original paper with the contents of the* Index *is preserved. It is not in Spence's hand, and is headed:* a Page annex'd to the Quarto Edition (of 1734) of the Essay on Man. *Its readings have been followed in the text. At the bottom is a note in Spence's hand:* This was annext to about a dozen Books; that were sent as presents to particular friends. Most of them were call'd in again, by Mr P[ope]: but that to Mr Bethel was not; frō wch this is copy'd. *On the back of the leaf Spence wrote:* Mr Pope's Plan for his Ethic Epistles; in ye Y^{r} 1734.

300a. L 18. *Date inferred from* L.

canto, taste,] L *has no commas*

301. F 141 W3 L 22 N 249 S 142 M 4. *Date from* F *and* N; L *has* 1735, *but* 1734 *is confirmed by the opening sentence of Spence's comment on* §300.

The inserted sentence is in W *and* L, *which do not include* I don't know . . . Education. *This in* F *was meant to replace the inserted part.*

Epistle] Epistles (MS.)

Spence in F *gives a cross-reference under* coldly *to* §298.

302. F 384 H 512 W 11 L 35 p. 1 N 565 S 315 M 72. *Date from* L.

The text in H *is the closest to* F; W *has the information numbered in semi-outline form;* L *has only a brief hint.*

boiling water] hot water (W, L)

303. F 366 H 468 L 33 p. 1 N 537 S 290 M 58. *Date from* L.

school-metaphysics] L *has* vulgar *deleted, and* school *written above it.*
metaphysics. As] Metaphysics: & as (MS.)

303a. F 366 H 468 L 33 p. 1 N 537 S 290 M 58. *Date from* L.

304. F 367 H 478 L 33 p. 1 N 537 S 290 M 58. *Date from* L.

In L *Clarke's name was crossed out, and* schoolmen *substituted.*

305. F 141 W 3 L 22 N 249 S 142 M 3. *Date from* F.
W *has the substance of the first sentence only.*
subject] design (F *originally*)

306. F 348 H 438 L 31 p. 2 N 510 S 272 M 42. *Date from* L.
Some] H *and* L *both add:* Ramsay &c.

307. L 31 p. 1.

308. F 172 N 297 S 179 M 16. *Date from* F.

309. F 172 N 298 S 179 M 17. *Date from* F.
About this time] in ye Year 1736 (*marginal note in* F, *later crossed out since the anecdote falls under that year by its position in* F)

310. L 4 p. 1 L 15 p. 4. *Date from* L 4.
L 15 *has only the sentence:* L^d^ B: very much assisting in ye materials.

311. F 142 N 251 S 144 M 4. *Date from* F.
at several other times] often before (F *originally*)
supply the matter] direct the manag[ement] (F *originally*)

312. F 375 L 34 p. 1 S 304 M 64. *Date from* L.

313. F 375 H 488 W 9 L 34 p. 1 N 553 S 304. *Date from* L.
H *and* W *are somewhat shorter but have* Murray (Mr M. *in* F) *in full. Singer wrote in the margin of* F*:* Mr. Murray, afterward Ld Mansfield.

314. H 490 L 34 p. 1 S 300. *Date from* L.
The anecdote is crossed out in pencil in H, *and omitted in* F, *probably because of the confusion between Cotta and Sabinus.*

315. F 143 L 22 N 263 S 145 M 11 *Date from* F.
L *has in addition:* Promisd to send G^s^ and L^s^ Latin Act verses to him. *Chandos's letter* (*Twickenham, III. ii, pp. xxviii–xxix*) *contains nothing to explain this phrase: it is not even clear whether Pope was to be the sender or the receiver. Possibly the sentence is independent of the Chandos anecdote.*
In F, *where the anecdote appears under 1734, a pencilled note by Spence indicates that it was to be moved to the beginning of the next section—i.e.* F 149, *under the year 1735.*

316. L 4 p. 3 L 15 p. 4. *Date from* L 4.
In the MSS. *the parenthesis is unclosed.*
divides] gave out (L *originally*)
L 15 *reads only:* ye Man of Ross: Sr Balaam: fire, meat, & drink.

317. 1756 MB p. 11 S 371. *Date from* MB.
(Lady Mary and)] *the brackets are Spence's*
Skerret] Skirret (MS.)

318. L 4 p. 2 L 15 p. 4. *Date from* L 4.
The line appears opposite the detailed report on Pope's plans for his Moral Poem, *which Sherburn printed in his 'Pope at Work'*, Essays presented to David Nichol Smith, *1945, pp. 50–51.* L 15 *has merely:* ye Dying Courtier &c. *See textual note to* §295.

318a. L 4 p. 1 L 15 p. 4. *Date from* L 4.
L 15 *reads only:* Montaigne's 1 Es: lib: 2? is ye best in ye whole book.
Essay 1] 1 Essay (MSS.)
because] reason (L 4 *originally*)
In L 4 *the parenthesis in unclosed.*

319. 1755 MB p. 27.

320. 1755 MB p. 27.

321. L 18. *Date inferred from* L.
In pencil before the anecdote: W^r in? *The source* Ld Bol. *is pencilled in the brackets at the end.*

321a. F 372 H 482 N 547 S 297 M 62. *Date from* F.
Second Book] F *has a marginal note:*
Which begins thus:
Sunt quibus in Satyrâ videar nimis acer & ultra
Legem tendere opus.—
the most] some of the most (F *originally*)
H *has only a memo, written as a pencil note immediately above the first line of* §322*:* How he came to translate y^t between him & his Lawyer (*i.e.* Satire, *II. i*). *Although* H *gives the month* Jan: *the year only is given since the note was added after the body of the text.*

322. F 373 H 482 W 8 L 33 p. 3 N 549 S 297 M 63. *Date from* L *and* H.
L *has the material for the first and second paragraphs in the reverse order. It reads:* M^r P has translated ye first Satire of Horace; (a good while before any of the rest; & closer, than the rest.)—He has imitated too part, or all of Unde & quo, Cati? Non est mihi tempus (He repeated the 3 or 4 first lines; very well apply'd to—)H *contains the first four Latin words in the text, with the marginal note:* Lib: 2 Sat: 4. W *contains substantially what* L *has, with the exception of the final parenthesis.*

323. L 33 p. 1.

324. F 368 H 470 W 8 L 33 p. 1 N 541 S 292 M 59. *Date from* L.
In L *and* W *the compliment begins the anecdote, in* H *and other MSS. ends it.*
Lord Cornbury] *replaced by* Ld Hyde *in* F (*twice*)

325. F 368 H 470 L 33 p. 1 N 539 S 291. *Date from* L.
L *has only a reminder of the anecdote,* H *the inserted sentence.*
Lord Russell] Lord Edward Russell (F, N *margin, later crossed out in* F)
entreated . . . with] prest by him to relieve his (F *originally*)

326. L 37 p. 1.

326a. 1756 MB p. 12.

327. F 250 H 364 N 416 S 217 M 289. *Date from* H.

328. L 37 p. 1.

329. F 141 W 3 L 21 p. 2 N 249 S 142 M 3. *Date from* L*; F gives* 1734 *mistakenly.*

The anecdote was part of §107. *In* F *Spence crossed it out and wrote in pencil in the margin:* Q or transfer.

329a. F 245 H 354 L 26 N 406 M 26 S 211. *Date from* L (H *mistakenly gives* Sept?).
has already] has (L, H)
twice as much] *underlined in* L
L *and* H *lack the second part of the anecdote, but contain the interpolation, which in* L *reads:* (said twice follg)

330. H 420 L 30 p. 1. *Date from* L.
flattering] *followed by a query* (H, L)
God or man] L *has inserted after this:* Full in Sermons, Essays:
The anecdote is crossed out in pencil and hence not in F *and* N.

331. H 438 L 31 p. 2. *Date from* L.
Insertion from L.

332. L 31 p. 2.

333. L 31 p. 1.

334. 1757 MB p. 12 S 376. *Date from* MB.
Following this anecdote is a large hieroglyphic: AK *which presumably alludes to the two rhyme words in the* Dunciad: A *and* K.

335. F 342 H 424 L 30 p. 1 N 496 S 264 M 34. *Date from* L.
one of] *omitted in* L*; so at first in* H, *but added in pencil with a query.*
In the margin of F *Spence wrote the note:* The 4th Book. H *has these words in the text, with the marginal reference:* [lines] 282, to 334. *In* F *Spence added and later deleted the following comment:* This was said a little before the 4th Book of that Poem was publish'd. *Perhaps he deleted it because he later realized that he was mistaken;* The New Dunciad *was advertised on 20 March 1742* (*Griffith, No.* 546), *and Spence recorded the conversations with Pope as being* 6–10 April 1742.

336. F 342 H 424 L 30 p. 1 N 496 S 265 M 35. *Date from* L.
The two lines in F, H, *and* N *are quoted in a note.*
on Horace's old method] F *originally:* on the old principle (*without citing Horace*)
Ridenti Flaccus amico, Pers.] *included in the text* (H, L)

337. F 365 H 462 W 7 N 536 S 289 M 56. *Date from* H.
now inserted in] flung into (W, H)

338. 1755 MB p. 16 S 365. *Date from* MB.
This anecdote is followed by a parenthetical remark: (Very agreeable to what we saw of him last month). *Spence ostensibly refers to Warburton, but the meaning is not clear.*

339. F 139 L 21 N 247 S 140 M 2. *Date from* L*;* F *gives* 1734 *mistakenly.*
good genius that way] pastoral genius (F *originally*). L *has brief version of first sentence only.*

340. F 139 L 21 N 245 S 140 M 2. *Date from* L*;* F *gives* 1734 *mistakenly.*
description and imagination] L *has:* === above *written after, between the lines, and nothing to correspond to the last sentence.*

341. F 361 H 462 W 7 N 554 S 285. *Date from* H.
The Duke and No Duke] *appears in the margin of* F, *and in the text of* W *and* H.
Ballad on the rabbit-woman] H *has a note on the page opposite;* (to enquire, by Mr Hooper.)
Mr. Pulteney] Ld Bath (H, W)

342. H 472 L 33 p. 1. *Date from* L.

343. F 365 H 460 W 7 N 536 S 288 M 56. *Date from* H.
from Troy] *inserted interlineally in* F*; not in* W, H
and the doctrines of morality] *not in* W, H *which have simply:* &c.
more than half] greater part (W)*;* the greatest part (H, F *originally*)

344. F 317 S 252. *Date from* F.

345. F 159 N 279 S 165 M 13. *Date from* F.
Tagus] *a query over it in* F

346. L 48. *Date inferred from* L 3.
Spence's note to No. 3 *is the only clue to the date:* No. 3 *is dated* 1728, L 4 *is dated* May 1730. *It seems likely that the anecdote falls between 1728 and 1730.*

347. H 426 L 30 p. 2. *Date from* L.
a patient's case] *followed in* L *by:* in 4 verses
The insertion is from L*; in* H *two footnotes are used.*

348. L 13.

349. L 13.

350. L 2.
Mr. Temple] *may read* Mrs Temple.

351. L 7 p. 3.

352. 1755 MB p. 15 S 364. *Date from* MB.

353. F 352 H 442 L 31 p. 3 N 576 S 275 M 46. *Date from* L.

354. F 343 H 430 L 30 p. 3 S 267 M 37. *Date from* L.

355. F 246 H 353 S 212. *Date from* §362.
In F *source of the anecdote was originally given as* Mrs P—— (*for* '*Patty*'). *The* P—— *is deleted and* B *substituted* (*for* '*Blount*'). *The anecdote is crossed out in pencil and marked:* Omit. *Hence it does not appear in* N.
In H *the anecdote is opposite* §199. H *shows the first part* (*up to* gardening) *was Spence's; Martha Blount confirmed it:* Ay, those were his ways, *and added the remark about the cost of Pope's grotto.*

356. F 366 H 466 W 8 N 537 S 289 M 57. *Date from* H.
fifty pounds or so] 40 or 50L (W)
Inserted words from H *and W: in* H *they occur as a marginal note before Mrs. Blount's remark* (*see explanatory note*).

357. F 380 H 500 L 34 p. 3 N 559 S 309 M 68. *Date from* L.
Mr. Pope's nephew . . . sea] his Nephew the sailor (H, L)
The inserted passage is from H*;* L *reads substantially the same.*

358. L 40 p. 1 S 357. *Date from* L.
value of money] *in the margin Spence wrote:* conf[irme]d.

359. L 40 p. 1 S 357. *Date from* L.
a great deal more] *originally:* more

360. L 40 p. 2 S 357. *Date from* L.
Another version of this anecdote occurs two pages later in the same manuscript: Mr P one day at Ly —— told Mrs B of the Paragraph in his Will relating to Mr A. She beg'd him to drop it, but cd not prevail. Sent a letter of his, which proves this, to Mr H[ooke].

361. L 40 p. 3 S 358. *Date from* L.
oddly] *originally:* very oddly

362. L 40 p. 3 S 358. *Date from* L.

363. F 139 L 21 N 247 S 141 M 2. *Date from* L; F *gives* 1734 *mistakenly.*
flattered] praised (L *originally*)
nor ever received anything] L *originally continued:* in ye manner of the oth[er poets?]. *This was deleted, and the text became:* for my verses of any man.

364. F 379 H 498 L 34 p. 3 N 559 S 308 M 67. *Date from* L.
great inclination] vast desire (L, H)
four or five] 5 or 6 (L, H)
[Warburton]] who (MSS.)
Against this anecdote in H *Spence wrote* confd *in pencil and* Confirm'd by Mrs B *in ink. These notes date from 27 May 1749 (see* §362).

365. 1755 MB p. 15 S 364. *Date from* MB.

366. F 141 W 3 L 22 N 249 S 143 M 4. *Date from* F.
from without] else (W, L)
in his own heart] *not in* W, L
It seemed . . .] *The sentence was crossed out in pencil, but then marked* in*; it was consequently copied in* N.

367. 1755 MB p. 17 S 366. *Date from* MB.

368. F 157 N 275 S 162. *Date from* F.

369. F 157 N 275 S 162. *Date from* F.
After viewing] & after viewing (MS.)
these pieces] this money (F *originally*)
how strong] how constantly (F *originally*)
L *reads only:* D of M, & Deane Jones

370. F 383 H 512 L 35 p. 1 S 313. *Date from* L.
The anecdote is crossed out; a pencil note in the margin reads: Omitt See separate paper. *Only initials of the nobles appear in* F. Marlborough *is in* H*;* Sunderland *and* Godolphin *in* H *and* L. *The inserted parts are from* H*;* L *has substantially the same.*

371. L 36 p. 4 S 314. *Date from* L.
The insertion is from Singer; it is not in L, *and may derive from* MS. B.

372. F 158 N 277 S 164. *Date from* F.

373. F 383 H 512 L 35 p. 1 S 313. *Date from* L.
F *shows that the anecdote was to be omitted.*

374. F 384 H 512 L 35 p. 1 S 313. *Date from* L.
The anecdote is crossed out in pencil.
loved. That] *underscored in* H
Sunderland] *from* H, L; F *has:* L^{d} S.

375. L 37 p. 1 S 364. *Date from* L.
Orsini] *followed by a query*

376. 1755 MB p. 17 S 364. *Date from* MB.

377. F 371 H 480 L 33 p. 3 N 545 S 295. *Date from* L.

378. L 35 p. 2.

379. 1756 MB p. 12.
The source is given as (M^{r} P frō dit) Q, *referring to Warburton, the source of the previous jotting. The query may question the meaning, the source, or the authority.*

380. F 19 W 1 L 4 p. 13 N 85 S 23. *Date from* L.
The parenthetical sentence is marked: To Notes.
manner] ye Degree & Manner (L, W)
design] *a query follows in* L

381. F 367 H 468 N 539 S 291 M 58. *Date from* H.
In H §381 *follows the first sentence of* §387.

382. L 4 p. 13.

383. F 1 L 3 p. 2 N 3 S 1 M 193. *Date from* F *and* L (*which has a query after* 1728).
L *lacks Spence's parenthetical remark.*

384. F 139 L 21 N 245 S 139. *Date from* L; F *gives* 1734 *mistakenly.*
Spence got to the middle of Thomson's name in F, *and then deleted the sentence; Singer filled it out in the margin. This passage and the other insertion are from* L.

385. L 4 p. 3.

386. L 25 p. 4.

386a. F 367 H 468 N 539 S 291 M 58. *Date from* H.

387. S 291 (*printed as* Addition from MS. B). *Date inferred.*

387a. S 291 (*printed as* Addition from MS. B). *Date inferred.*

388. F 367 H 468 N 539 S 291 M 58. *Date from* H.
whether . . . proper] *omitted in* H
it.] H *adds:* If you doubt whether such a word is too vulgar
that . . . wrong] it is not too vulgar (H)

389. F 381 H 504 L 34 pp. 3–4 N 561 S 310 M 69. *Date from* L.
Sir William Temple] F *at first read* Richard *but was corrected to* William
L'Estrange] *followed in* H *and* L *by:* for familiar Style, not for Historical

L *has the note:* In ye Vacancy Mr Pope's own name s^d^ be inserted, & the List will perhaps be pretty near compleat.

390. F 381 H 504 L 34 p. 4 N 563 S 310 M 70. *Date from* L.

L and *H read:* As authorities for poetical language, he began with Milton, Shakespear, Dryden, Spenser; & then we were interrupted.

H *has the list of poets on the opposite page, with Milton's name after Fletcher's and Pope's just before Swift's, probably Spence's addition.—A footnote to Fletcher reads:* For familiar Dialogues, etc.—*A note to Butler and Swift reads:* For ye Comical, or Burlesque stile. *Another note states:* This begun upon twice, but left very imperfect.

391. F 19 W 1 L 4 p. 13 N 85 S 23. *Date from* L.

392. F 162 N 283 S 168 M 14. *Date from* F.

Mr. Addison did not discover] certainly *is deleted after* Addison *in* F
Guardian] Guardians (MSS.)
likenesses] imitations (F *originally*)
a painter] a good painter (F *originally*)
talent] knack (F *originally*)
easy to be distinguished] easily known (F *originally*)

393. L 3 p. 2 S 11. *Date from* L.

394. F 247 H 354 L 26 N 408 S 213 M 27. *Date from* L (H *mistakenly gives* Sept?).

What is your] Pray w^t^ is y^r^ (L)

The insertion is from H. *For the last part of the anecdote* L *is substantially the same as* H. *For the text in* H *see explanatory note.*

395. F 234 H 334 L 25 pp. 3–4 N 386 S 200 M 280. *Date from* L.

396. F 386 H 508 W 11 L 36 p. 1 N 567 S 316 M 73. *Date from* L.

397. F 386 H 508 W 11 L 36 p. 1 N 569 S 316 M 74. *Date from* L.

The text in H *is a continuation of* §396.

great rule] first rule (W)

This [, however,] is] This other is (MSS.)*; the emendation was made to clarify the meaning.*

The insertion is in W *and* L (*here given from* W).

so swift] so quick (W, L *originally*)
imperceptible] unaccountable (L, W, H *and* F *originally*)

398. F 383 H 506 W 11 L 34 p. 4 N 565 S 312 M 72. *Date from* L.

ear] ear for Musick (L)
best compositions] most celebrated compositions (W)

H *has a pencilled note in Spence's hand:* M^rs^ B not fond / talk of being so.

399. F 386 H 510 W 12 L 36 p. 1 N 569 S 317 M 74. *Date from* L.

The line is written in the margin of F.

400. F 383 H 506 W 10 L 34 p. 4 N 565 S 312. *Date from* L.

The Messiah] *written in the margin of* F
scarce any] no (F *originally*)
work . . . laboured] verses . . . that I took more pains about or that are more finisht (L, W*;* H *lacks last five words*)

401. F 383 H 506 W 10 L 34 p. 4 N 565 S 312 M 72. *Date from* L.
Though Virgil] Even Virgil (L, H, F *originally*)
so scrupulous as] *not in* L, H

402. F 383 H 506 W 10 L 34 p. 4 N 565 S 312 M 72. *Date from* L.

403. F 20 L 4 p. 13 N 85 S 24. *Date from* L.
Singer recorded in the margin of F *and printed in* S *the* note by Mr. Spence *given in the text after Pope's remark. Perhaps Singer found it in* MS. B. *It must have been added sometime in the 1750's.*

404. H 510 L 36 p. 1. *Date from* L.
The version in L *is briefer, omitting the reference to Martial.*

405. F 151 N 265 S 155. *Date from* F.

406. F 170 N 295 S 176 M 259. *Date from* F.
will not hold] *originally:* is a bad one
Spence's comment is pencilled in the margin of F *with a query.*

407. F 233 H 336 L 25 p. 4 N 384 S 199 M 277. *Date from* L.
forgotten] unknown (L, H *originally*)

408. F 351 H 440 L 31 p. 2 N 514 S 274 M 45. *Date from* L.
conversation] company (L *originally*)

409. F 340 H 419 N 494 S 260 M 34. *Date from* §362; F *mistakenly dates* 1742.
tender and melancholy] moving (H)

410. F 165 N 287 S 171 M 85. *Date from* F.

411. F 15 L 15 p. 4 L 4 p. 7 N 75 S 19 M 84. *Date from* L 4.
L 15 *also gives the year 1730, but the text is not so full.*
the . . . natural way] ye true Naïf way (L 4, L 15)

412. F 166 N 289 S 172 M 85. *Date from* F.
Provençal] Provincial (MS.)

413. F 17 L 15 p. 5 (*brief*) L 4 p. 9 N 79 S 20 M 85. *Date from* L 4.

414. F 167 N 291 S 173 M 87. *Date from* F.

415. F 17 L 4 p. 11 N 79 S 21 M 86. *Date from* L.
the first Earl of Dorset] Ld Middlesex, & Ld Treasurer (L)
purer style] cleaner stile (L)
and . . . bombast] It is free from the general Bombast way of those times (L)
our first] our oldest (F *originally*)
and very poetical] *not in* L

416. L 4 p. 11.

417. F 17 L 18 L 4 p. 11 N 79 S 21 M 87. *Date from* L 4.
L 18 *has the brief note given in the explanatory note.*
pretty good] very good (L 4)
The insertion is from L 4. F *directs* 'twas publisht in 1567 *to go in the Notes.*

418. L 5 p. 3.
Heath . . . Habington . . . France] *underlined*
another] *is in brackets*

Map] L *reads* de Maay *or* de Maas
before Richard II's [time]] before? Rich 2[ds]

419. F 372 H 486 L 34 p. 1 N 547 S 296 M 86. *Date from* L.
a canto . . . two or three days ago] two or three cantos . . . a day or two ago (H*; not in* L)
an old lady] my mother (H, *with a note on the opposite page:* Aet. 74)
about a year or two ago] not above two or three year ago (H, L)

420. F 371 H 482 W 8 L 33 p. 3 N 547 S 296 M 61. *Date from* L.
the *Dunciad*] W *continues:* but thought it too long. *Similarly in* L.

421. F 167 N 291 S 173 M 81. *Date from* F.
The insertion is crossed out in F, *with a note:* Omit[d] in Vellum copy. *It is, however, in* N.

422. F 7 L 3 p. 2 N 19 S 9 M 84. *Date from* L (F *omits query*).
in his *Essay on Dramatic Poetry*] *marked for the notes in* F. *This final sentence in* L *reads simply:* Dryden somewhere: & M[r] P = Betterton = S[r] William Davenant.

423. F 8 L 3 p. 2 N 19 S 9 M 84. *Date from* L (F *omits query*).
In the margin of F *Singer queried whether Pope had Jonson in mind, but* §858 *makes the reference certain: there Young is recorded saying of Shakespeare* What trash his works are, *and Spence noted* Mr Pope says the same of Ben Johnson.

424. L 3 p. 3 F 4 (*transcribed by Singer as* Addition from MS. B.) S 5 (*from* MS. B). *Date from* L.
Horace] Hor! (L)
Camden] Camden? (L)

425. F 19 L 4 p. 13 N 85 S 23 M 82. *Date from* L.

426. F 345 L 30 p. 2 H 426 N 504 S 269 M 82. *Date from* L.
a head . . . colleges] one of the Heads of Houses (F *originally*)*;* a Head of a House (H)
whither . . . Shakespeare.'] H *has direct speech:* 'Where are you running, my dear, says he in such a hurry?' *and continues:* O, I am sent for, reply'd he, to my *God-Father* Shakespear.'
says the old gentleman] H *adds:* archly

427. F 18 L 4 p. 9 N 81 S 21 M 88. *Date from* L.
tolerable writers] writers (L)
instanced in] mentioned (L, F *originally*)

428. L 36 p. 1.

429. F 36 L 5 p. 1 L 4 p. 6 N 95 M 93. *Date from* L 4.
L 4 *reads:* Beaumont assisted Fletcher only in five Plays. Mr P? (or Dennis?) I think it verily the former.
L 5 (*dated* 28–29 Nov. 1730) *reads:* they wrote not above 5 or 6 together, of Beaumont & Fletcher, *and implies Pope is the speaker.*

430. F 18 L 4 p. 9 N 81 S 22 M 88. *Date from* L.

431. F 164 N 285 S 169 M 158. *Date from* F.

432. F 356 H 448 N 524 S 280 M 51. *Date from* F.
Aldrich] Aldridge (MSS.)

433. F 18 L 15 p. 5 (*brief*) L 4 pp. 9 *and* 11 N 81 S 21. *Date from* L 4.
In L 4 *the two sentences are separated by several anecdotes.*
Fairfax] *followed by a query in* L 4.
others] other (MSS.)

434. F 136 L 22 N 241 S 136 M 89. *Date from* F.
This anecdote also appears in the margin of F 143, *transcribed by Singer, where the text is substantially that in* F. *Apparently Spence took it from* MS. B (*see* §436 *textual note*).

435. F 18 L 15 p. 5 L 4 p. 9 N 83 S 22 M 88. *Date from* L 4.
Beaumont higher] *followed by a query in* L 4.

436. F 143 L 22 N 251 S 144. *Date from* F.
Insertion from L *where it is followed by* §434. *The insertion also occurs in Singer's hand in the margin of* F 143, *together with* §434 (*which occurs in the body of* F 136). *Since the two anecdotes are in the same order in Singer's transcript as in* L *but his text for* §434 *is related to* F *not* L, *his copy text on* F 143 *must have been* MS. B. *That is, the re-ordering of these anecdotes took place when Spence was working up* F *from* MS. B.

437. F 143 L 22 N 251 S 144. *Date from* F.
L *reads:* Cleaveland & Cartwright, Randolph, Donne, Sr Wm Davenant mentioned expresly each as better y^{n} any of ye foregoing.

438. F 18 L 15 p. 5 L 4 p. 9 N 81 S 22 M 88. *Date from* L 4.
L 15 *lacks the part on Bagnal.*
this class] F *indicates this refers to poets like Crashaw* (*in* §445)
mediocre] *deleted in pencil in* F*; not in* N
Bagnal] L 4 *reads clearly:* Th: Bagnel. F *looks like* Baghel *and was so copied in* N*; Malone read it as* Rughel. *In* F *the name is underscored in red pencil, with a cross in the margin.*

439. F 166 N 289 S 173 M 95. *Date from* F.

440. F 164 N 287 S 170 M 83. *Date from* F.

441. F 164 N 287 S 170 M 84. *Date from* F.

442. F 2 L 3 p. 3 L 24 p. 1 N 7 S 3 M 89. *Date from* L (F *omits query*).
The version in L 24, *evidently a repetition of a favourite story, is without significant variants.*

443. F 2 L 3 p. 3 N 7 S 3 M 90. *Date from* L (F *omits query*).

444. F 3 L 3 p. 3 (*brief*) N 7 S 3 M 90. *Date from* L (F *omits query*).
great vivacity] much boldness (L)*;* much warmth (F *originally*)
⌜into France⌝] *deleted by Spence, after having been marked with a query* (F)
instantly. In] instantly; & in (MS.)
after. However] after: however (MS.)

445. F 18 L 15 p. 5 (*brief*) L 4 p. 9 N 81 S 22 M 88. *Date from* L 4.
Cowley. He] Cowley: he (MS.)
good copy] excellent copy (L, F *originally*)

L 15 *adds:* buried at Loretto. *Crashaw died in Italy and was buried at Loreto.*

446. F 361 H 466 N 534 S 285 M 96. *Date from* H.

447. F 361 H 466 N 534 S 286 M 96. *Date from* H.

448. F 361 H 466 N 534 S 286 M 96. *Date from* H.

449. F 10 L 3 p. 4 N 25 S 13 M 96. *Date from* L (F *omits query*).
whilst . . . off] Two or three meaddows from his house at Chersey (L)
The last sentence was deleted by Spence, then marked stet, *but not copied in* N.

450. F 167 N 291 S 173 M 116. *Date from* F.

451. F 245 H 352 L 26 N 406 S 210 M 285. *Date from* L (H *mistakenly gives* Sept?).
[He]] who (MSS.)

452. F 18 L 15 p. 5 L 4 p. 9 N 81 S 22 M 88. *Date from* L 4.
L 15 *has the figure* 20 *over* Sylvester*; in* L 4 *a cross-mark before* this pitch *refers to Crashaw in* §445.

453. F 233 H 332 L 25 p. 3 N 382 S 198 M 99. *Date from* L.
In H *and* L *the anecdote follows* §554, *and in* L *the mention of Scaliger's* Poetics *as being* extreamly well collected *is followed by:* So Stanley's Philosophers.

454. F 358 H 454 L 32 N 526 S 281 M 97. *Date from* L.
H *begins with Spence's*, L *with Pope's note.*
⌜edition 1709⌝] *from* H*; in* F *placed in the margin.*
In Spence's note on the alterations, F *has by mistake:* v. 24 to 26*;* L *and* H *have correctly:* v. 24 to 30.
41 . . . better] H *and* L *add:* (from Ch: 1, to Ch: 2?)

455. F 18 L 4 p. 11 N 81 S 21 M 88. *Date from* L 4.
The second half reads in L*:* The Author of (I'le tell thee Dick), S[r] John Mennes, Pryor, dit:

456. F 237 H 340 L 24 p. 1 N 390 S 203 M 95. *Date from* L (H *mistakenly gives* July 1739*;* F, 1739).

457. F 20 L 4 p. 9 N 87 S 24. *Date from* L.

458. L 21.

459. F 168 N 291 S 174 M 94. *Date from* F.

460. F 169 N 293 S 175 M 95. *Date from* F.
Andreini's] Andreino's (MS.)
Singer inserts '*Adamo*', *the title of Andreini's work.*

461. F 242 H 350 L 24 p. 3 N 242 S 208 M 100. *Date from* L (H *mistakenly gives* Sept?*;* F, 1739).
LYTTELTON] *from* H*;* M[r] L[n] (L), Mr. L. (F)*; Malone mistakenly identified the speaker as* Mr. Locke.

462. F 339 H 416 N 490 S 257 M 128. *Date from* H.
Buckingham] *in* H '(Sheffield?)' *follows*
forte] fort (MSS.)

463. F 159 N 277 S 164 M 104. *Date from* F.

464. F 136 L 21 N 241 S 136. *Date from* L.
Sedley] Sidley (MSS.)

465. F 357 H 454 N 524 S 281 M 105. *Date from* H.

466. L 24 p. 1 H 340. *Date from* L (H *mistakenly gives* July 1739).

467. L 3 p. 2.

468. F 40 N 103 S 50 M 105. *Date from* F.
The next anecdote in F *has a marginal note:* [Section 3. 1730 to ye End], *so that the present text may still belong to* 1729. *A further pencil note reads:* Addend: frō P^r^, N° 5; & N°, 9.

469. F 357 H 454 N 526 S 281 M 105. *Date from* H.
diverted themselves . . . with] delighted . . . in (H)

470. F 4 L 3 p. 3 N 11 S 5 M 104. *Date from* L (F *omits query*).
a very bad turn] an ill turn (L, F *originally*)

471. F 357 H 454 N 526 S 281 M 104. *Date from* H.

472. F 136 L 21 N 241 S 136 M 89. *Date from* L.
Insertion from L, *which, however, omits the first two sentences. It also occurs in a slightly fuller form in Singer's hand as a marginal note to* F *and in* S 136 (*Singer probably took it from* L).

473. L 15 p. 4 L 4 p. 7. *Date from* L 4.
The text is taken from L 15 *as that in* L 4 *is briefer.*
like] like a (L 4)
delicacy] delicatesse (L 4)

474. F 153 L 23 N 269 S 157 M 105. *Date from* L.
dipping about this volume] turning over this Book (L *originally*)

475. F 153 L 23 N 269 S 157 M 145. *Date from* L.
Parenthetical notes from the margin of F. *Insertion from* L.

476. L 18. *Date inferred from* L.

477. F 166 N 289 S 172. *Date from* F.

478. F 369 H 472 L 33 p. 1 N 541 S 293 M 300. *Date from* L.

479. F 167 N 291 S 173 M 106. *Date from* F.

480. F 166 N 289 S 172 M 85. *Date from* F.

481. F 10 L 3 p. 4 N 25 S 13 M 115. *Date from* L (F *omits query*).

482. F 249 H 358 L 27 N 412 S 215 M 100. *Date from* L (H *mistakenly gives* Sept?–Oct?).
Two plays out of six] Two plays out of — (H, L)
Barnwell] *followed by ampersand and a nearly illegible insertion in* L*:* Q w others (His *Mar*[*ius*?]

483. F 36 L 5 p. 1 N 93 S 46 M 142. *Date from* L.
all the best of them] them all (L, F *originally*)

484. L 4 p. 7 L 15 p. 5. *Date from* L 4.
balm] baume (MSS.)
In L 4 *the anecdote was later crossed out, and on the opposite page was written:* Enter'd in Receit-Book.

485. F 151 N 267 S 155. *Date from* F.

486. L 18. *Date inferred from* L.

487. F 55 N 115 S 67 M 143. *Date from* F.

488. F 36 L 5 p. 1 N 95 S 46 M 143. *Date from* L.

488a. L 3 p. 1.

489. F 1 L 3 p. 2 N 4 S 2 M 140. *Date from* L (F *omits query*).

490. F 1 L 3 p. 3 N 4 S 2 M 140. *Date from* L (F *omits query*).

491. L 3 p. 2.

492. F 138 H 450 L 21 N 245 S 139 M 135. *Date from* L. F *gives* 1734 *mistakenly. In* H *the date is given as* Mar: 1743, *but this is because Spence added* §492 *to* §493 *in this MS. Thus when he rejected* §493 *as unworthy of inclusion in* F *but kept* §492, *he dated the latter from* L (*though giving* '*1734*' *instead of* '*1735*').
H *reads:* His Pilgrim is taken from a Spanish writer. L *read at first:* Tis written on a Plan . . ., *then:* The Story is in some Spanish writer. *Inserted in brackets is:* [in Howel's Letters].—*Pope made the first remark, Sir Clement added the comment.*

493. H 450.
The anecdote is crossed out in pencil and so is not in F *or* N.

494. L 21 F 138 (*transcribed by Singer from* first note book [MS. B?]) S 139 (*from* first MS. memoranda [MS. B?]). *Date from* L; F *mistakenly gives* 1734.
drinker] follower of Drams (F, S, *from* MS. B?)
In F *and* S *this occurs as a note to* Parnell's *in* §492. *Singer's note of his source in* F *almost certainly refers to* MS. B (*it does not refer to* L).

495. L 48. *Date inferred from* L 3.
1714 or 15] *written at the end of the first line of Latin.*

496. F 375 H 490 L 34 p. 1 N 553 S 302 M 155. *Date from* L.
Hughes] Heughes (MSS.)
good, humble-spirited] low, humble-spirited (L, H). *Compare Pope's correction of* low-born Allen *to* humble Allen *in the* Epilogue to the Satires, *i. 135.*
First two insertions from both L *and* H. *The long note by Spence was printed by Singer as* Addition from Mr. Spence's Papers, *but it is not present among the manuscripts in the Spence Papers.*

497. H 340 L 24 p. 1. *Date from* L (H *mistakenly gives* July 1739; F, 1739).
purely] *not in* L
got him] gave him (L)
all the] what (L)

498. F 339 H 416 N 490 S 258 M 298. *Date from* F *and* H.
none excellent] *Singer added:* except this.

499. H 412.
Jacob] Jacobs

500. L 22. *Date inferred from* F.
Theobald's] T's *in both instances; but the latter part makes it clear that Theobald is meant.*

501. F 15 L 4 p. 7 N 75 S 19 M 135. *Date from* L.

502. F 171 N 297 S 177 M 165. *Date from* F.

503. N 392 F 238 H 342 L 24 p. 1 S 204 M 157. *Date from* L (H *mistakenly gives* July 1739; F, 1739).
The text is taken from N *because of Spence's addition from Dr. Armstrong* ('Mr. Thomson . . . distich in it'). *Thomson was clearly in Pope's mind from the beginning.*
L *reads:* The Imitations on Tob: very well done: Tho^{n} ought not to be angry: his fault in being too manner'd. He cant write so well with^{t} it: but then &c—' H *reads the same with slight variants.*

504. H 342 L 24 p. 1. *Date from* L (H *mistakenly gives* July 1739. L *does not mention the name of the poem.*

505. L 22. *Date inferred from* F.
couplet] couplet?

506. L 22. *Date inferred from* F.
Orrery] Ossory? (*The title had lapsed in 1680*)

507. L 43 p. 1 TN 4 f. 183^{v} S 356. *Date from* L.
The TN 4 *jottings read:* Mr Pope 5 G^{s} (by Dr. Young to Savage in Newgate; & told ye D^{r}, that if he was in want of neces^{s} he had 5 more at his [*service?*]

508. H 440 L 31 p. 2. *Date from* L.
I never did] I never have (L)
I can't tell] No (L)
the first time] *not in* L
have desires enough] add new desires (L)

509. H 430 L 30 p. 3 S 337. *Date from* L.
L *lacks the parenthetical remark.*

510. F 234 H 334 L 25 p. 3 N 384 S 199 M 279. *Date from* L.

511. F 242 H 348 L 24 p. 2 N 400 S 207 M 282. *Date from* L (H *mistakenly gives* August 1739; F, 1739).

512. F 242 H 348 L 24 p. 2 N 402 S 207 M 282. *Date from* L (H *mistakenly gives* August 1739; F, 1739).
Insertion from H.

513. F 242 H 348 L 24 p. 2 N 402 S 207 M 283. *Date from* L (H *mistakenly gives* August 1739; F, 1739).

514. F 8 L 15 p. 5 L 3 p. 2 N 19 S 9. *Date from* L 3 (L 15 *and* F *omit query*).
L 15 *reads simply:* Voiture & Sarazin of y^e^ same School; L 3 *ends:* Voiture = Sarazin.

515. F 19 L 15 p. 5 L 4 p. 11 N 83 S 22. *Date from* L 4.

516. F 19 L 15 p. 5 L 4 p. 11 N 83 S 22. *Date from* L 4.
Insertion from L 4, L 15.

517. F 9 L 3 p. 4 N 23 S 11 M 194. *Date from* L (F *omits query*).
more agreeable] prettier (L, F *originally*)
overturn] shock (L)

518. F 19 L 15 p. 5 L 4 p. 13 N 83 S 22 M 83. *Date from* L 3 (L 15 *and* F *omit query*).

519. L 3 p. 3 L 15 p. 5 F 8 (*transcribed by Singer from* MS. B) S 10. *Date from* L 3 (L 15 *omits query*).
The only difference between MS. B *as quoted by Singer and* L 3 *is the omission in* B *of the word* all, *which occurs in* L 15 *also.* S *does not note the source in* MS. B.

520. L 3 p. 3 L 15 p. 5 F 8 (*transcribed by Singer from* MS. B) S 10. *Date from* L 3 (L 15 *and* F *omit query*).
S *does not note the source in* MS. B.

521. F 171 N 297 S 178 M 184. *Date from* F.

522. H 450.

523. F 249 H 360 L 27 N 412 S 215 M 185. *Date from* L (H *mistakenly gives* Oct?).
L *begins:* (Bayle) Ay, . . . *&c.* S *reversed the order in* F.
judgement] care (L, H)

524. F 140 L 21 N 247 S 141 M 163. *Date from* L; F *gives* 1734 *mistakenly.*
did not quite] cou'd never (L, F *originally*)
approve] admire (L *originally*)

525. L 3 p. 2.
See explanatory note.

526. H 416.

527. L 2.

528. F 125 N 235 S 132. *Date from* F.
with one] *taken from* N, *illegible in* F; *Singer copied:* with me.
agreed] agree (MS.)

529. F 340 H 420 N 492 S 260 M 34. *Date from* H.
H *reads:* (He read the account of Priam, scolding his Sons, &c; & wept, as he read it.)

530. F 138 L 21 N 245 S 138 M 1. *Date from* L; F *gives* 1734 *mistakenly.*
L *begins:* The Passage out of Vel: Paterc?

531. F 360 H 464 N 532 S 285 M 55. *Date from* H.
orchards] orchats (F, H *originally*)
stern Achilles] bold Achilles (H)
Spence pencilled a note on the opposite page in H*:* The passage from the Odessey.
F *has a marginal note:* Q in Hrs Od: *V*, abt 400

532. F 360 H 462 W 7 N 532 S 285 M 54. *Date from* H.
Hades] Ades (MSS.)
Osiride] Osyride (MSS.)

533. F 171 N 297 S 178. *Date from* F.
tiresome. This] tiresome: & this (MS.)

534. F 250 H 362 L 27 N 414 S 216 M 288. *Date from* L (H *mistakenly gives* Oct?).
The parenthetical quote is in the margin of F*; in* H *and* L *it appears in the text.*

535. F 234 H 332 L 25 p. 3 N 384 S 199 M 23. *Date from* L.
very strange and inconclusive] very bad (H, L)
our Mr. Locke] our Locke (H, L), our *is deleted in* F.
⌜or even so well as Hobbes⌝] *from* H *and* L*; originally in* F *but deleted; not in* N.

536. F 348 H 436 L 31 pp. 1–2 N 510 S 272 M 42. *Date from* L.
H *and* L *begin:* A Grand Peut-etre. *Insertion from* H *and* L.

537. F 1 N 3 S 1 M 193. *Date from* F.

538. F 1 N 3 S 1 M 193. *Date from* F.

539. F 247 H 356 L 26 N 408 S 213 M 286. *Date from* L (H *mistakenly gives* Sept?).
True politeness] The true Ease (F *originally*)
The inserted passage is from H, *replacing the word* now *in* F. *In* H *an* x *is pencilled over the passage, evidently marking it for omission. The* F *version is so much longer than that in* H *that another manuscript version (now lost) may have been used. The inserted passage is from* H, *a conflation not entirely satisfactory.*

540. F 246 L 26 N 406 S 211 M 285. *Date from* L (H *mistakenly gives* Sept?).
best time for] best way of (F *originally*)
L *is in note form and reverses the order of the two sentences.*

541. F 243 H 350 L 26 S 217. *Date from* L (H *mistakenly gives* Sept?).
The anecdote is crossed out in F, *so it was not copied in* N.
Minerva . . . by the hand] Minerva with Folly pulling her? by the sleeve; & Folly is but a child of about 3 foot high (L)
stultitiam consiliis] consiliis stultitiam (MSS.)

542. L 27.

543. F 249 H 360 L 27 N 414 S 216 M 288. *Date from* L (H *mistakenly gives* Oct?).
Insertion from H 359, *opposite the text of* H 360.

544. F 250 H 362 L 27 N 414 S 217 M 288. *Date from* L (H *mistakenly gives* Oct?).

F *divides the two parts as two anecdotes.* F *and* H *give the source of the quotation as* Ecl: 8; 88.

545. F 250 H 362 L 27 N 414 S 217 M 289. *Date from* L (H *mistakenly gives* Oct?).

evidently] certainly (H, L). *The inserted sentence from* H *and* L.

546. F 249 H 360 L 27 N 412 S 215 M 287. *Date from* L (H *mistakenly gives* Oct?).

H *and* L *begin:* Virgil very vain. *Though marked* Omitted *in the margin of* F, *it appears in* N.

547. F 249 H 360 L 27 N 414 S 216 M 288. *Date from* L (H *mistakenly gives* Oct?).

poet] Hesiod (ascr: carm:) (L)

Parenthetical quotation is from the margin of F*; Spence intended it for the notes.—The different MS. versions show Spence struggling to organize his material. In some ways* H *is the most satisfactory text; Singer obscured the meaning by omitting the key phrase,* what we now have for

548. F 249 H 360 L 27 N 412 S 215 M 287. *Date from* L (H *mistakenly gives* Oct?).

Hesiod] Hesiod, dit: Ascraeum carmen (L)

He never . . . anachronism] Homer, never: bec: his subj. did not necessitate him to do it (L)

549. F 7 L 3 p. 1 N 19 S 9. *Date from* L (F *omits query*).

Polyclitus] Polyclete (MSS.)

Insertion from L.

550. F 239 H 344 W 6 L 24 p. 1 N 394 S 204. *Date from* L (H *mistakenly gives* July 1739*;* F, 1739).

Spence's comment is from F *and* N.

Tarquinius Priscus] *note in the margin of* F *reads:* See Polymetis; Dial: 6 Note 52 & 54.

551. F 350 H 438 L 31 p. 2 N 512 S 273 M 43. *Date from* L.

Where] F *is not easy to read, for* 'r' *is written over* 'nc'*; thus* S *reads* Whence, *and* M, *following* N, *gives* Where.

F *is considerably expanded. The initial query is not in* H *or* L, *where the anecdote opens with Pope's early marking Politian with a cross. Both end with the reference to the Meles line* from his old reading—L *lacks the part about Statius;* H *has a note on the opposite page:* y[e] remains of a mistake or two, in his first setting out.

552. H 338 L 25 p. 4. *Date from* L.

In H *crossed out in pencil and hence does not appear in* F *and* N.

552a. L 3 p. 4.

553. F 18 L 15 p. 5 L 4 p. 11 N 83 S 22 M 88. *Date from* L 4.

first-rate] very first rate (L 4, L 15)

The inserted phrase is from L 4 *and* L 15.

554. F 233 H 332 L 25 p. 3 N 382 S 199 M 276. *Date from* L.

555. L 22. *Date inferred from* F.

556. L 2.
first] *since the figure* 1 *occurs in the MS., perhaps the text should read* one.
worth . . . reading him] *deleted in* MS.
know nothing of him] *written in the margin*

557. F 238 H 344 W 5 L 24 p. 1 N 392 S 204 M 25. *Date from* L (H *mistakenly gives* July 1739; F, 1739).
There is . . . us] Anything will delight us (L, W); Anything capable of delighting us (H)
How true] how soon (L, W)

558. F 9 L 3 p. 4 N 23 S 12 M 195. *Date from* L (F *omits query*).

559. F 9 L 3 p. 4 N 23 S 12 M 194. *Date from* L (F *omits query*).
three or four] two or three (L, F *originally*)

560. F 9 L 3 p. 4 N 23 S 11 M 194. *Date from* L (F *omits query*).

561. F 239 H 344 W 6 L 24 p. 2 N 394 S 210. *Date from* L (H *mis takenly gives* July 1739; F, 1739).
favola !] *in the margin of* F.
The first insertion is from L *and* H. F *reads* that it was so. *The second insertion is from* H, *where it is lightly crossed out in pencil.* L *has substantially the same, and follows* §567.

562. L 15 p. 5 L 4 p. 11. *Date from* L 4.
The text is taken from L 15 *as* L 4 *is briefer.*
the . . . these] they have had this (L 4)

563. L 4 p. 11.

564. F 164 N 285 S 170. *Date from* F.

565. S 332.
Singer gives no indication of source or date, but it should perhaps be dated '1729?' as a transcript occurs in his 'Supplemental Ancedotes', p. 4 (see p. lxvi).

566. F 238 N 392 S 203 M 281. *Date from* F.

567. F 238 H 342 L 24 p. 1 N 392 S 203 M 281. *Date from* L (H *mistakenly gives* July 1739; F, 1739).
chooses] approves (L)
Spence was puzzled about the punctuation, and pencilled in F: W[ithou]t breaks: only dashes.

568. F 238 H 342 L 24 p. 1 N 392 S 203 M 281. *Date from* L (H *mistakenly gives* July 1739; F, 1739).
For Spence's note pencilled on H 341, *see explanatory note* §575.

569. F 238 H 342 L 24 p. 1 N 392 S 204 M 281. *Date from* L (H *mistakenly gives* July 1739; F, 1739).

570. L 4 p. 9 S 336. *Date from* L.
At the end L *reads:* Q? frō Mr Sav:

571. F 235 H 336 L 25 p. 4 N 386 S 200 M 280. *Date from* L.
taste] judgement (L)
not fit for the crowd] not so proper for them (L)
Insertion from L.

572. F 237 H 342 L 24 p. 1 N 390 S 203 M 281. *Date from* L (H *mistakenly gives* July 1739; F, 1739).
some phenomena] some Phaenomenons (F); the (Phaenomenons) (H, L, F *originally*)

573. F 348 H 434 L 31 p. 1 N 510 S 271. *Date from* L.
other stages] our three or four next stages (L)
Spence's comment is from H *and* L.

574. F 374 H 486 L 34 p. 1 N 551 S 301 M 300. *Date from* L.

575. F 237 H 342 L 24 p. 1 N 390 S 203 M 280. *Date from* L (H *mistakenly gives* July 1739; F, 1739).
Insertion from H *and* L. *For Spence's pencilled note on* H 341, *see explanatory note.*

576. F 143 L 22 N 253 S 145. *Date from* F.
L *reads:* Our own Self-Love necessary as y[e] Scale for y[e] love to our neighb[r].

577. H 412.
The anecdote is crossed out in pencil and so does not occur in later manuscripts.

578. F 351 H 440 L 31 pp. 2–3 N 514 S 274 M 45. *Date from* L.
First insertion from L, *the second from the margin of* F.
from about . . . twenty-one] (from 14 to 20 &c) (H, L); *it occurs in the margin of* F *and was intended for the notes.*
opportunity] H *and* L *add:* etc.

579. F 385 H 514 L 35 pp. 1–2 N 576 S 315 M 302. *Date from* L.

580. F 375 H 492 W 9 L 34 p. 2 N 553 S 303 M 300. *Date from* L.

581. L 3 p. 1 F 12 N 29 S 15 M 196. *Date from* L.
was . . . etc.] was very useful, & necessary, in Erasmus, & the earlier Revivers of Learning; (F)
only . . . text], by the later Critics, has only served to puzle the text (F)
Bassano] Bassan (MSS.)
F *omits the bracketed sentence.*

582. F 169 N 295 S 176 M 258. *Date from* F.

583. F 151 N 265 S 155. *Date from* F.

584. F 349 H 436 L 31 p. 2 N 510 S 272 M 299. *Date from* L.
L *and* H *begin:* We have never had an honest Minister, I think one may say, since L[d] Clarendon.
the Stuarts] *written in the margin of* F
F *has a partially erased* M[r] L *as the source, replaced by* Mr. Pope. L *shows that* Mr. Legg *was the source for the following anecdote.*

585. F 373 H 480 L 33 p. 3 N 549 298 S M 271. *Date from* L.

586. F 362 H 464 L 33 p. 3 N 534 S 286 M 273. *Date from* L*; in* F *the anecdote is the last under* 1743, *in* H *the page is dated* Mar: 1743.
and a friend] & anothers (L)*; marginal note in* H. *In dating this anecdote in* F *Spence overlooked the reminder in margin of* H*:* See Original Paper Jan: 10 = 14, 1744.

587. H 464. *Date inferred from preceding anecdote* (H *has* Mar: 1743).

588. F 360 H 460 N 532 S 284 M 127. *Date from* H.
(Sheffield)] *written in the margin of* F

589. F 169 N 293 S 175 M 160. *Date from* F.

590. H 488 L 34 p. 1 S 300. *Date from* L.
Singer tidied up this anecdote and reversed the order of the sentences.

591. H 418.
Royal] R (*pencilled in* H)

592. L 3 p. 2.

593. H 490 L 34 p. 1 S 300. *Date from* L.
In H *crossed out in pencil.*

594. F 142 L 22 N 251 S 143. *Date from* F.
Count . . . me] *omitted in* L

595. F 245 H 354 L 26. *Date from* L (H *mistakenly gives* Sept?).
Spence crossed the anecdote in F *and wrote* omit? *in the margin; it does not appear in* N.
The first . . . voice] & the manner, & voice with wch it was spoken (H)*;* Short strong answer; with a particular air (L)

596. N 406 F 245 H 354 L 26 S 210 M 285. *Date from* L (H *mistakenly gives* Sept?).
the . . . Chiswick] his (Odelschalchi?) Pope (L)*;* Ld Burlington's Pope, Odelscalchi? (H)*;* the Pope (F)
Odescalchi?] *inserted from* H *and* L
Maratta] Marat (MSS.)
The N *text is used here since it is clearer than any earlier* MS.

597. L 4 p. 11.
Maratta] Marat (MSS.)

598. L 48. *Date inferred from* L 3.

599. H 488 L 34 p. 1. *Date from* L *and* H.
The version in L *is more telegraphic:* The Shit^n^ story of Ste: Fox & Ld Craven: sent to Court. The brown dishonours of ye race etc

600. F 341 H 422 L 30 p. 1 N 496 S 264. *Date from* L.
Spence's remark (*quoted in explanatory note*) *is not in* L *and* H, *only in* F.

601. S 264. *No. MS. source has been found; both text and date from Singer.*

602. G 39–40.

603. G 34–35.
Southcote's last sentence is actually a marginal note keyed to Pope's name. Spence's notes are pencilled in the margin opposite the end of Southcote's remarks.

604. G 53.

605. 1758 MB p. 7.

606. L 22 F 143 N 251 S 144. *Date from* F.
Spence wrote only the first sentence in F*; Singer copied a more finished version of the remainder in the margin of* F *from an undisclosed source* (MS. B?) *which contained the words* at Oxford.
For Shenstone's remark see explanatory note.

607. F 244 H 352 L 26 N 404 S 209 M 284. *Date from* L (H *mistakenly gives* Sept?).

608. L 22. *Date:* L 22 *is headed* 1735 *but seems to date from 1734. This remark may have been made after Pope's visit to Bevis Mount in August and September 1734* (Corresp., *iii. 421, 431*)*, or it may belong to the last week in August 1735, when Peterborow lay seriously ill* (*see* §260). *In view of the other textual evidence* (*see list of MSS.*)*, 1734 seems the more probable date.*

609. F 9 L 48 N 23 S 12 M 195. *Date inferred from* L 3 (F *gives* 1728).
because . . . variety] pour varieté, because his situation is all a Plain (L)

610. F 244 H 352 L 26 N 404 S 209 M 284. *Date from* L (H *mistakenly gives* Sept?).
that obelisk] his obelisk (L)
L *has at the end:* The darkest things appear nearest?
Insertion from H*;* F *has a marginal note instead:* In the same [*i.e. Pope's garden*]

611. F 244 H 352 L 26 N 404 S 209 M 284. *Date from* L (H *mistakenly gives* Sept?).
grove-work] wood-work (L)
eye . . . judge] *not in* L *or* H

612. F 340 H 418 N 492 S 260 M 298. *Date from* H.
The two lines from Horace (Ars Poetica, *ll. 343–4*) *are given in the margin of* F.
all points] all ends (F) *Spence repeated this mistake in the* Letter to Wheeler*; see p.* 650.

613. L 3 p. 2 S 11. *Date from* L.

614. L 3 p. 2.
The text is preceded by the inscrutable jotting, Quote (applyd to a Man or House L[or]d B[olingbroke]. *Another occurs following the text:* As luce, the Environ, L[or]d B[olingbroke]. *The speaker is listed as* P[ope] & un:, *perhaps meaning that an unknown person* (*to Spence*) *participated in the conversation.*

615. G 35.

616. F 9 L 3 p. 2 N 21 S 11 M 194. *Date from* L (F *omits query*).
L *begins more simply:* A Tree as great an object as a Prince.
at a birthnight] *crossed out in* L

617. L 3 p. 2 S 11. *Date from* L.
[on the]] *Singer inserted* looking

618. F 243 H 350 L 26 N 402 S 208 M 283. *Date from* L (H *mistakenly gives* Sept?).
Dinocrates] Dinochares (MSS.)
of forming . . . of that prince] *in the margin of* F, *to go to notes.*
and pay the workmen] *not in* H *or* L
The first insertion is in H *and* L, *the second in* L *only.*

619. F 10 L 3 p. 4 N 25 S 12 M 195. *Date from* L (F *omits query*).
L *has only a brief hint:* Temple with its Isles in Trees.
aisles] isles (MSS.)
or rather . . . temple] L*; written in* F *and then deleted; not in* N.

620. F 349 H 438 L 31 p. 2 N 512 S 273 M 43. *Date from* L.
grove-work] woodwork (L)
H *has Spence's parenthetical remark, but omits the anecdote itself:* L *also omits the anecdote, and contains only rough notes of Spence's comment.*

621. F 342 H 426 L 30 p. 2 N 498 S 266 M 36. *Date from* L.
exclusive of the Iliad and Odyssey] Beside w[ch] all Homer (L, H)

622. F 371 H 480 L 33 p. 3 N 545 S 295 M 61. *Date from* L.

623. 1755 MB p. 17 S 367. *Date from* MB.

623a. L 34 p. 3 S viii. *Date from* L.

624. F 366 H 466 N 537 S 289 M 57. *Date from* H.
The inserted sentence is from H.

625. H 478 L 33 p. 3. *Date from* L.
L *has substantially the same in a telescoped form.*
Hales] L *has the initial only.*
therefore] *underscored in* H.
Seville orange] Civil-Orange (H)

626. F 374 H 488 W 9 L 34 p. 1 N 553 S 301 M 64. *Date from* L.

627. F 369 H 472 L 33 p. 1 N 541 S 293 M 59. *Date from* L.
Of the inserted words he quoted *is pencilled on the opposite page in* H, *followed by* Pectora nostra duas &c. L *lacks* he quoted, *but gives the full Latin quotation.*

628. H 488 L 34 p. 1 *Date from* L.
The words] The word (L)

629. F 374 H 486 L 33 p. 1 N 551 S 301 M 63. *Date from* L.
to leave this world] to leave this body (L)

630. F 387 H 510 W 12 L 36 p. 1 N 569 S 317 M 74. *Date from* L.
W *and* L *begin:* 'I have not changed', *&c., as did originally* H, *where the introductory remark was later superscribed in pencil.*
our Church] the Church of Rome (L *originally*)

631. F 387 H 518 W 12 L 36 p. 2 N 571 S 318 M 75. *Date from* L *and* H *dated* 10–17 May 1744. *This is the first anecdote under those dates.*
In F *and* W *two anecdotes are made of this* (L *not clear*), *but not in* H. *On the opposite page in* H, *Spence recorded for himself the plan for the end of the*

volume: ye thing rel^g^ to his illness tog^r^, at last, & then 'may our end &c' [§658]

several times] *not in* L, H, W, *which read:* when I was last at Twitnam

was apt . . . look] look'd (L, H, W)*; in* H, *however, the later version is pencilled interlineally.*

That . . . present] Ay but I can say very little thats wise to you now (L, H, W)*; again* H *has the later version pencilled interlineally.*

632. L 33 p. 1.

the?] *superscribed over* those? *Spence was not sure which was correct.*

Miss L^m^] *badly blotted; impossible to tell whether Miss, Mrs. or Mr. was meant.*

633. F 388 H 518 W 12 L 36 p. 2 N 571 S 319 M 75. *Date from* L *and* H.

I had any,] *omitted in* L, W *and* H

my mind] my senses (L *originally*)

634. F 388 H 518 L 36 p. 2 N 571 S 319 M 75. *Date from* L *and* H.

H *begins:* It was between that [*i.e. the sixth*] & the 10th*; in* L *is the note* (before ye 10th)

The inserted phrase is from L, *which reads:* as if he had had a curtain before his eyes, & seeing everything in the room thro' it.

635. L 36 p. 2. *Date inferred from position in* L.

636. F 388 H 518 L 36 p. 2 N 571 S 319 M 76. *Date from* L *and* H.

637. F 388 H 518 W 12 L 36 p. 2 N 571 S 319 M 76. *Date from* L *and* H.

Mr. Lyttelton's] *so originally in* F, *but crossed out in favour of* a friend's*; omitted in* L, W

⌜Dr. Thomson⌝] *from* H *and* W. *Crossed out in pencil in* H*;* F *reads* the Doctor*;* L *has the initial only.*

638. F 388 H 518 W 12 L 36 p. 2 N 571 S 319 M 76. *Date from position in* L *and* H.

639. F 389 H 518 W 12 L 36 p. 2 N 573 S 320 M 76. *Date from position in* L *and* H.

W *has this anecdote as an addition to* §633. *With no justification Singer made this anecdote follow* §646.

640. L 36 p. 2 H 518 W 12. *Dated from the position in* L *where it precedes* §643.

641. 1755 MB p. 17. S 367. *Date from* MB.

The order of the sentences is here reversed. In the MS. Warburton's precedes Spence's.

very . . . month] *evidently an interpolation, is found on p. 16*

642. 1755 MB p. 17 S 365. *Date from* MB.

643. F 389 H 518 W 13 L 36 p. 2 N 571 S 319 M 76. *Date from* L *and* H*; in* L *the anecdote is preceded by* (17) *which gives the precise date.*

Longus'] Longus his (MS.)

Daphnis and Chloe] *omitted in* L

got in my hand] brought in my pocket (F *originally*)
so infected a mind] so corrupted a life (L *originally*)

644. H 526 W 14 L 36 p. 4 S 319. *Date from* L *and* H.
pointing up in] pointing into (L, W)
pleasure] great pleasure (L *originally*)
sweetness and complacency] softness (L, W)

645. F 389 H 522 L 36 p. 3 N 573 S 320 M 76. *Date from* L *and* H.

646. F 389 H 522 W 13 L 36 p. 3 N 573 S 320 M 76. *Date from* L *and* H.
meanness] *not in* L, W, H*; inserted in* F
The passages in the explanatory notes are quoted from H*; they are also in* L *with minor differences.*

647. F 389 H 522 W 13 L 36 p. 3 N 573 S 321 M 77. *Date from* W*;* L *and* H *have* May 19–29
several times] often (L)

648. H 526 W 13 L 36 p. 4 S 320. *Date from* L *and* H.
The inserted phrase is from W, *which alone does not attribute the anecdote to Hooke.* W *reads:* Mr P—S'
having been] being (L *originally*)

648a. W 13.

649. H 526 W 14 L 36 p. 4 S 320. *Date from* L *and* W.
Singer 'improved' the text here.

650. H 526 W 14 L 36 p. 4. *Date from* L *and* W.
mortify] humble (*superscribed in* H)

651. H 522 F 389 L 36 p. 3 S 321. *Date from* L *and* H.
The text is from H, *since* F *has only the last sentence,* We can ... possibilities, *and even that is crossed out.*

652. F 389 H 522 W 13 L 36 p. 3 N 573 S 321 M 77. *Date from* L *and* H.
Spence's note is from H, *and the Italian also occurs in* L.
Pencilled in H*:* 'To add some instances'
Che'l] che il (H)
di Sciro] de Sciro (H)

653. F 390 H 522 L 36 p. 4 N 573 S 32 M 77. *Date from* C *and* H.

654. F 390 H 524 W 13 L 36 p. 4 N 573 S 321 M 78. *Date from* L *and* H.
the soul's] the truth of the Soul's (H)
Singer added to the beginning, with no authority: A short time before his death, *&c.*

655. F 390 H 524 W 13 L 36 p. 4 N 575 S 322 M 78. *Date from* L *and* H.
⌜Mr. Hooke⌝] *from original in* H, L, *and* W. *Other MSS. have the initial only.*

it will be right] F *read originally*, it will look right, *as in* L, W, *and* H, *then emended into* be very right, *and* very *crossed out. Hence Ruffhead who used* W *printed* look right (p. 54), *but Dr. Johnson who saw* N, *printed* be right. *Singer chose* look right, *following the original reading in* F, *perhaps influenced by Ruffhead or Warton.*

656. F 390 H 524 W 13 L 36 p. 4 N 575 S 322 M 78. *Date from* L *and* H.
In . . . them] The morning that the priest had been with him (L, H *originally*)
given him . . . them] performed the last ceremonies (W)

657. H 524 L 36 p. 4 S 322. *Date from* L *and* H.
told this very low] whispered this (L)
at dinner] at table (L)

657a. W 14.

658. F 390 H 526 W 14 N 575 S 322 M 78. *Date from* W *and* H.
in the evening] after 11 at Night (W, H)

659. 1755 MB p. 17 S 365. *Date from* MB.
The anecdote is marked with vertical parallel lines in red ink.

660. F 55 L 15 p. 4 L 9 p. 10 N 115 S 67 M 206. *Date from* L 9.
L 15 *has only the first sentence, in briefer form.*

661. L 9 p. 6.
valuable] val:

662. F 62 L 16 N 129 S 75 M 213. *Date from* F *and* L. *In* L *the anecdote precedes some anecdotes dated 25 August 1730.*

663. F 55 L 9 p. 2 N 115 S 67 M 93. *Date from* L.
L *reads:* He spoke of Farquar as a mean poet: & of Suckling as a first-rate. *This is apparently the source of this anecdote as well as for* §683.

664. F 49 L 9 p. 1 N 103 S 59 M 107. *Date from* L.
'tis my *Mac Fleckno*e] L *adds:* (that indeed the best thing he wrote)
how long . . . dealer in poetry] How long have you been a poet? (L)
borrowed some strokes] taken some lines (L)
Insertion from L, *which omits* especially . . . published

665. F 51 L 9 p. 1 N 107 S 61 M 103. *Date from* L.
greater] est *superscribed over* er (L)
F *has a pencil note in the margin:* Note, of ye Custom *referring to Buckingham's capping of Dryden's line.*

666. F 52 L 9 pp. 6–7 N 109 S 63 M 102. *Date from* L.
fencing] at ye Sword (L). L *adds:* ye irony of Quartir salt (*which may have been an addition to the present* § 718).

667. F 52 L 9 p. 7 N 109 S 63 M 102. *Date from* L.
Insertion from L.

668. F 53 L 9 p. 2 N 111 S 63 M 103. *Date from* L.
was)] *followed in* L *by:* ye H & P^r^ transprosd full of Wit but a Servile Copy.

669. F 51 L 9 p. 1 N 105 S 61 M 109. *Date from* L.

670. F 51 L 9 p. 1 N 107 S 61 M 111. *Date from* L.
Absalom and Achitophel] L *adds:* (Mot: si quis tamen haec quoque si quis Captus amore leget). *This, of course, is the motto of Tate's poem.*

671. F 55 L 9 p. 10 N 115 S 67 M 115. *Date from* L.
best hands] top men (L)

672. F 51 L 9 p. 1 N 107 S 61 M 111. *Date from* L.

673. F 53 L 9 p. 7 N 111 S 63 M 128. *Date from* L.
as his own] L *adds:* In y^e^ 3 Vols of State Poems before?
indeed . . . those] D^r^ often repeated y^e^ Alterations wch were (L)
Insertions from L. *For Lockier's opinion of the poem in* L *see explanatory note.*

674. L 9 p. 3.

675. L 9 p. 3.
For [considered] *the text has the* = *sign.*

676. L 9 p. 3.
Duke of Bucks] id. (*meaning* ibid.) *referring to the Duke.*
[new territories]] L *reads* etc.

677. F 52 L 9 p. 2 N 109 S 62 M 101. *Date from* L.
Trinity College] *Originally* our College (L), *meaning* New College, *then* our *deleted and* Trin? *inserted.*

677a. *As reported by Warton; see explanatory note.*

678. F 52 L 9 p. 2 N 109 S 62 M 116. *Date from* L.
Insertion from L.

679. L 9 p. 2.

680. L 9 p. 3.

681. L 9 p. 10 F 54 (*transcribed by Singer from* MS. B) S 66 (*from* MS. B). *Date from* L.
lies] lays (MSS.)
That . . . yesterday] In the coffee house yesterday I received (F, S *as from* MS. B)*: this is clearly Singer's rewriting of his MS. source for in* F *he at first began the sentence after* day *with* That. *However, he deleted the word and wrote the present text on the next new line, thus making a new anecdote.*
four] three (S): *the transcript in* F *reads* four *correctly*
False . . . it:] *omitted in Singer*
Another . . . latter] *omitted in Singer*
Singer split it into two anecdotes, suggesting that 'it is not clear whether Swift or Lockier said this', *and somewhat altering the text.* L *makes it clear that it is one anecdote and that Swift was the speaker.*

682. L 9 p. 5.

683. F 55 L 9 p. 2 N 115 S 67 M 143. *Date from* L.
See textual note on § 663.

684. F 59 L 15 p. 4 L 9 p. 11 N 123 S 72 M 159. *Date from* L 9.

685. L 9 p. 11.
Islay] Ila (MS.)

686. L 9 p. 7.

687. L 16.

688. F 60 L 15 p. 3 L 9 p. 7 N 125 S 73 M 168. *Date from* L 9.
Marishal] Marshal (MSS.)
strong opposition] brisk opposition (L 9)

689. F 61 L 9 p. 8 N 127 S 73. *Date from* L.
freethinker] Heretic (L, F *originally*)
Insertions from L 9. *The second insertion follows* now *in* L 9. *Both were transcribed by Singer in the margin of* F *as from* first MS. *and printed in* S *as from* MS. B. *The identification of the Queen in* S *is an editorial addition.*

690. L 9 p. 8 L 15 p. 3 F 61 (*transcribed by Singer from* first MS. [MS. B?]). *Date from* L 9.
better cleared] *followed by a question mark in* L 9 *which is omitted in* L 15. L 15 *omits the last sentence.*

691. L 9 p. 12 F 49 (*transcribed by Singer* from MS. Book [MS. B?]) S 58 (*from* papers). *Date from* L.
See textual note to § 692.

692. L 9 p. 12 F 49 (*transcribed by Singer* from MS. Book [MS. B?]) S 58 (*from* papers). *Date from* L.
The text of §§ 691–2 *as copied by Singer from* [MS. B?] *is a shortened and re-ordered version of the material in* L 9, *omitting 'Mr. Nic''s remarks and the sentence on Lord Molesworth's daughter. It presumably represents a conflation of the two anecdotes by Spence.*

693. L 9 p. 7.
as that Lord . . . accused] *The reading is difficult because of crowding between the lines.*

694. L 9 p. 7.

695. F 61 L 9 pp. 11–12 N 129 S 75 M 212. *Date from* L.
Insertion is from L.

696. F 61 L 9 p. 11 N 127 S 74 M 212. *Date from* L.
L *supplies the information that Lockier was referring to Locke.*

697. F 60 L 9 p. 11 N 125 S 72 M 211. *Date from* L.
the Irish and Scotch] ye Germans, Scotch, etc. (L)
get the air of the natives] look as if they were naturalized (L)

698. F 59 L 9 p. 11 N 125 S 72 M 211. *Date from* L.
as he can] as they can (MSS.)

699. L 9 p. 11.

700. L 9 p. 11 L 15 p. 4 F 60 (*transcribed by Singer from* MS. B) S 72 (*from* MS. B). *Date from* L 9.
Singer's slight variations may be his own wording.

701. F 62 L 16 p. 1 N 129 S 75. *Date from* F *and* L.
Insertion from L, *which reads also* Petit *for* petty.
There are question marks after Munich *and* the Duke of Bavaria's.
Fleming] Flemyng (MSS.)

702. L 16 p. 3.

703. L 16 p. 2.
il più magnifico capriccio] il piu magnifique Caprice; magnifique *is changed to* magnifiquo, *and there is a question-mark over* Caprice.

704. F 54 L 15 pp. 2, 3 L 9 p. 6 N 113 S 65 M 205. *Date from* L 9.
In F *Spence combined two elements that appear separately* (*with other anecdotes between them*) *in* L 9 *and* L 15. *Insertion from* L 15.
very good] excel[t] (L 9, L 15)

705. F 54 L 15 p. 2 L 9 pp. 6, 10 N 113 S 65 M 205. *Date from* L 9.
In L 9 *the first sentence is on p. 10, the rest on p. 6.*
Sadolet] Marino *follows in* L 9, L 12 *and* F, *but deleted in* F.

706. F 54 L 15 pp. 2–3 L 9 p. 6 N 113 S 65 M 158. *Date from* L 9.
L 9 *begins:* Yes, S[r], I have it, (of Sannazarius' Arcadia)
have given the hint] have been a pattern (L 9); be a copy (L 15)

707. L 9 p. 5.

708. F 54 L 15 p. 2 L 9 p. 6 N 113 S 64 M 205. *Date from* L 9.

709. F 54 L 15 p. 2 L 9 p. 6 N 113 S 65 M 205. *Date from* L 9.
Aminta] Amyntas (MSS.)

710. L 9 p. 3 L 15 p. 1. *Date from* L 9.

711. F 55 L 15 p. 1 L 9 p. 3 N 115 S 67. *Date from* L 9.
the Greek poets] L 9 *adds:* Major & Minor
printed in Holland] L 9 *and* L 15 *continue:* y[t] [*i.e. the illegibility*] stopt his design
The insertion is from L 9 *and* L 15. *Singer transcribed it from* MS. B *in the margin of* F *and printed it in his edition.*

712. F 54 L 15 p. 3 L 9 p. 7 N 115 S 65 M 206. *Date from* L 9.
Lope] Lopez (MSS.)
what Lord Bolingbroke said] F'*s first reading, then altered to* what is said. L 15 *reads:* he b'lieved w[t] Dryden said of them to be true.
Mariana] *underlined in the MSS.*
The cross-reference in F *is to* Cent. 1, 28, *Spence's number for* §781.

713. F 53 L 9 p. 3 N 111 S 64. *Date from* L.
Lazarillo] Lazarello (MSS.)

714. L 9 p. 3.
The omitted passage forms the first draft for §713.
Buscón] Bruscôt (MS.)

715. L 9 pp. 3–4.
Lockier's comment on the Theatre Italien ? (*given in the explanatory note*) *also occurs in* L 15 p. 3.

716. F 54 L 15 p. 3 L 9 p. 6 N 113 S 64 M 205. *Date from* L 9.
Insertion from L 9.

717. F 54 L 15 p. 3 L 9 p. 6 N 113 S 64 M 205. *Date from* L 9.

718. L 9 p. 6 L 15 p. 3. *Date from* L 9.
See textual note on §666.

719. L 9 p. 3 L 15 p. 1 F 54 (*transcribed by Singer from* [MS. B?]) S 65 (*from* papers). *Date from* L 9.
Régnier] *spelled* René *in* L 9; *so originally in* L 15 *but corrected.*
It is not altogether certain that §§719–21 *derive from* MS. B. *Singer gives their source simply as* from papers. *His transcription in* F *follows that of* §681 (*given in both* F *and* S *as from* MS. B) *with no indication that they came from a different source. In transcribing the anecdotes Singer wrote over a pencil note by Spence: the note reads,* Addend? B: 1, [100?], 102, 104. *As* B: 1 *presumably means* B[ook] 1, *i.e.* MS. B, *the note strongly suggests that all four anecdotes derive from* MS. B.

720. L 9 p. 3 F 54 (*transcribed by Singer from* [MS. B?]) S 66 (*from* papers). *Date from* L.
exceeds . . . this] very much improves on his (MS. B?)
For the probable derivation of Singer's version from MS. B, *see textual note to* §719.

721. L 9 p. 6 L 15 p. 3 F 54 (*transcribed by Singer from* [MS. B?]) S 66 (*from* papers). *Date from* L 9.
Moses] *Singer gives a footnote to this: Ειπεν ὁ Θεος φηοι τι γενεθω φως, και ἐγενετο:- γενεθω γη, και ἐγενετο* (sic). *This example does not occur in Singer's transcript of* MS. B *into* F.
necessity . . . matter] greatness of the thing spoken of (MS. B?)
Any Jew . . . sublime] *omitted in* MS. B?
of the] of it in the (MS. B?)
For the probable derivation of Singer's version from MS. B, *see textual note to* §719.

722. F 58 L 9 p. 11 N 121 S 71 M 210. *Date from* L.

723. F 58 N 123 S 71 M 210. *Date from* F.
Orientals] Orientalists (MS.)

724. F 58 L 9 p. 4 N 121 S 70 M 209. *Date from* L.
The insertion is from L. *It is also transcribed by Singer in the margin of* F *and printed in* S *as from* MS. B.
This . . . answer] This sense of the passage is plain from the context (F, S, *as from* MS. B)

725. F 57 L 9 p. 4 N 121 S 70 M 209. *Date from* L.
the Hebrew] S. phrase (L), Scripture Phrase (F *originally*)
equivalent] synonymous (L)

726. F 58 L 9 p. 8 N 121 S 70 M 209. *Date from* L.
call by their names *and* have dominion over anything] *underscored in* L
Singer changed cattle *to* animals; L *has* beasts.

727. F 57 L 9 p. 4 N 119 S 69 M 208. *Date from* L.
The insertions are from L.

728. F 63 L 15 p. 3 L 9 p. 8 N 131 S 77 M 214. *Date from* L 9.

729. F 64 L 15 p. 3 L 9 p. 9 N 133 S 77 M 215. *Date from* L 9.
long gallery] *underlined in pencil, with question-mark in the margin of* F
Rycaut] Ricaut (MSS.)
every Christian man's duty] our duty (L 9)
their falseness and meanness] L 9 *continues:* & villanies evn to y[e] stories of crucifying Children &c.
L 15 *has only a brief note:* Cromwell's artful behaviour w[n] he allowed em a Synagogue. 60 th[d] p[d] for it.

730. L 9 p. 3.
Nini] Nenni (MS.)

731. F 62 L 16 p. 1 N 131 S 76 M 214. *Date from* F *and* L.
Our Gothic] Our Gothic & Ostrogothic (L)

732. L 16 p. 2.

733. F 56 L 15 p. 1 L 9 p. 5 N 117 S 69 M 207. *Date from* L 9.
L 9 *and* L 15 *open with:* I verily believe . . .
celebrated] *not in* L 9, L 15

734. F 57 L 15 p. 2 L 9 p. 5 N 119 S 69 M 208. *Date from* L 9.
a comet] the last Comet (L 9, L 15, F *originally*)*; Spence pencilled in the margin of* F*:* an Eclipse (or else Tycho Brahe is wrong-natur'd)
the learned] Scavans (L 9, L 15)
Peking] Pequin (MSS.)

735. L 9 p. 5 L 15 p. 2. *Date from* L 9.

736. F 56 L 15 p. 2 L 9 p. 5 N 119 S 69 M 207. *Date from* L 9.
The quotation in the explanatory note is from L 9*;* L 15 *has basically the same.*

737. F 55 L 15 p. 1 L 9 p. 4 N 117 S 68 M 206. *Date from* L 9.
sad fellows] poor fellows (L 9)*;* poor ones (L 15)
250,000 men] L 9 *and* L 15 *add:* (or a Million)*; in* L 15 250,000 *is crossed out*
have ever since been] are still (L 9, L 15)*;* are now (F *originally*)

738. F 61 L 9 p. 12 F 49 (*transcribed by Singer from* MS. Book [MS. B?]) N 127 S 74 M 212. *Date from* L.
Singer transcribed the anecdote on F 49 *but apparently crossed it out when he found it in the text at* F 61.
is but] can be but (F 61 *originally*, F 49 [*from* MS. B?])
most] best (F 49 [*from* MS. B?])

739. S 74 (*transcribed by Singer as* Addition from papers [MS. B?]) F 61 L 15 p. 4 L 9 p. 12 N 129 M 212. *Date from* L 9.
L 15, F, N, *and* M *give only the final sentence of the anecdote*. L 9 *is much fuller, but Singer's text, which almost certainly derives from* MS. B, *is more*

finished. Consequently, in this instance, Singer's version has been adopted as the copy text.

He . . . very] Very (L 9)
used] always usd (L 9)
and . . . reason] his Reason (L 9)
that . . . done?] I convers'd with Ladies, y[t] I might as soon think of marrying as y[e] Princess Ann: & I was to get a Competency to keep as Good Company as I had been usd to; t'will do as it is, but a family &c. (L 9)

740. F 61 L 9 p. 11 N 127 S 74 M 212. *Date from* L.
teaches] makes (L)
Spence's comment is from L. *Singer's version is substantially the same, but has frequent minor variants.*

741. F 61 L 9 p. 11 L 15 p. 4 N 127 S 74 M 211. *Date from* L 9.
fine] good (L 9, L 15)
The inserted quotation is from L 9.

742. L 9 pp. 10–11.

743. F 278 H 380 L 28 p. 3 N 452 S 232 M 29 *and* 179. *Date for this group of anecdotes* (§§743–65) *is inferred from Spence's and Lady Mary's correspondence. She arrived in Rome* c. *12 January and left by the middle of February 1740/1; Spence's conversations with her must have taken place during this period.* Dec[r]: 1740 *in* H *is clearly a mistake.* L *has* 5 January, *which also is too early. In* F *the anecdotes are placed at the head of the year 1741. Singer writes:* I have the original notes of this conversation, which took place, January 5, 1740–1, at Rome. *Singer's date comes from* L 28 *which, as noted above, is too early.*
Spence's comment ([1]) *is from* L, *which has only the first sentence of the anecdote.*

744. F 278 H 384 L 28 p. 3 N 450 S 232 M 29 *and* 154. *Date: see* §743.
The inserted sentence is in H, *where it is enclosed in square brackets.*

745. F 279 H 372 L 28 p. 2 N 452 S 234 M 30. *Date: see* §743.

746. F 278 H 374 L 28 p. 2 N 452 S 233 M 30 *and* 155. *Date: see* §743.

747. F 280 H 382 L 28 p. 3 N 456 S 237 M 32. *Date: see* §743.

748. F 280 H 382 L 28 p. 3 N 456 S 237 M 32. *Date: see* §743.

749. F 280 H 382 L 28 p. 3 N 454 S 236 M 32. *Date: see* §743.
that he is . . . disrepute] that he will make even Good Verse scandalous (L, H *originally*)

750. F 279 H 374 L 28 p. 2 N 452 S 233 M 30. *Date: see* §743.
but . . . in it] *omitted in* L, H

751. F 280 H 374 L 28 p. 2 N 454 S 235 M 31. *Date: see* §743.
Insertions from L *and* H.

752. F 279 H 380 L 28 p. 3 N 454 S 234 M 31. *Date: see* §743.
though . . . writings] tho' he us'd me so cruelly (L, H)

printed] F *has a marginal note against this:* [to Notes] Mr Pope's Letters: the 121st, in the Qto Edition*;* H *also gives the reference marginally.*
Insertions from H.

753. F 279 H 376 L 28 p. 3 N 452 S 234 M 140. *Date: see* §743.

754. F 279 H 376 L 28 p. 2 N 454 S 234 M 132. *Date: see* §743.

755. F 279 H 376 L 28 p. 2 N 454 S 234 M 180. *Date: see* §743.

756. H 380 L 28 p. 3. *Date: see* §743.

757. H 374 L 28 p. 2. *Date: see* §743.

758. F 277 H 382 L 28 p. 3 N 450 S 231 M 182. *Date: see* §743.
L *begins:* How angry with those . . . *;* H*:* With what anger she expres'd herself against those . . .
ladies] Young Ladies (L)

759. H 372 L 28 p. 2. *Date: see* §743.

760. H 382 L 28 p. 3. *Date: see* §743.
Wise William] *Spence was somewhat confused and wrote:* Wise Thomas (or William? Pierrepont). *William is correct, and has been adopted in the text.*

761. F 277 H 374 L 28 p. 2 N 450 S 231 M 182. *Date see* §743.
Insertion from H *and* L.

762. F 275 H 376 L 28 p. 2 N 448 S 230 M 180. *Date: see* §743.

763. F 275 H 376 L 28 p. 2 N 448 S 230 M 180. *Date: see* §743.
bosom] breasts (L, H)
Insertion from H.

764. F 276 H 378 L 28 p. 3 N 448 S 230 M 180. *Date: see* §743.
L *has a bare reminder:* the stays.
baths. When] baths; & when (MSS.)
how cruelly . . . husbands] how much crueller the husbands in Europe are than ours (H)

765. F 277 H 378 L 28 p. 3 N 450 S 231 M 181. *Date: see* §743.
It . . . Turks] The ease of Divorce in Turky (L, H)
Insertion from H.

766. L 7 p. 6 S 331. *Date from* L.
Colet] Collet (MS.)
in his notes] *a query follows* (L)
Aristotle] (Ar?) (L)

767. L 4 p. 19.
Camden] Cambden
Cateau-] Chasteau
1559] 1658 (*by mistake*)
Over Mr *in signature there is a* 'D' *in pencil, which makes it read* Dr

768. L 4 p. 19.

769. L 4 p. 19.
His papers . . . Prussia] *added in pencil*

770. F 11 L 3 p. 1 L 15 p. 6 N 27 S 14 N 158. *Date from* L 3 (L 15 *and* F *omit query*).

771. L 6 p. 1 S 334. *Date from* L.
concordet] *the last two letters not clear*
In L (Stylus) *is in brackets and* colours *is underscored.*

772. 1757 MB p. 6.

773. L 1 p. 1.

774. L 1 p. 1.

775. L 4 p. 19.

776. L 6 p. 1.

777. L 49. *Date inferred: Spence met Holdsworth* c. *May 1732* (*see headnote before* §1416). *Further, the MS. also gives material for* Polymetis, *which Spence did not start work upon until his stay in Florence in 1732* (*Wright, p. 85*). *For a reference by Spence to Crashaw's burial see* §445, *textual note.*

778. L 6 p. 1.

779. L 16 p. 4.

780. L 2 S 339. *Date from* L.

781. F 11 L 15 p. 6 L 3 p. 1 N 29 S 14 M 106. *Date from* L 3 (F *omits query*).

782. 1756 MB p. 14 S 371. *Date from* MB.

783. L 13 S 171. *Date from* L.

784. L 3 p. 4.
Lady Bolingbroke] Lady B^{k}

785. F 36 L 5 p. 2 N 93 S 45 M 106. *Date from* L *and* F.
TONSON] Old Jacob Tonson (F)
In F *the anecdote is crossed out in pencil, and a marginal note reads:* Addend: Chub's Pap: N^{o}, 4. 2^{d} p^{t}.

786. L 4 p. 19 F 36 (*transcribed by Singer from* MS. B) S 45 (*from* MS. B). *Date from* L.
Insertions from MS. B *version preserved by Singer.*

787. L 2.

788. L 6 p. 2 S 334. *Date from* L.
The same] *preceded in* F *by* Neg^{r}
Among some sheets of notes in Singer's hand (*Spence Papers*) *is a comment on this anecdote:* This inference is hardly a fair one, for Dryden only translated part of Juvenal, and does not prefer Persius to Horace, though he translated the whole of him. *It is not clear whether this is Singer's own note, or a copy of one by Spence from some source now missing.*

789. L 16 p. 4.
Flatman] *underscored in* MS.

790. F 34 L 4 p. 19 N 91 S 43 M 115. *Date from* L.
that . . . cheats themselves] y^{t} were made use of often to hide cheats (L)
DENNIS] Old Mr Dennis, the Critic (F)

791. F 34 L 4 p. 17 N 91 S 44 M 121. *Date from* L.
Bath or Tunbridge] Bristol or Tunbridge? (L)
Col. Brett] Col^{n} (L), *originally in* F *but deleted:* Col. Brett, (I think it was)

792. F 34 L 4 p. 17 N 91 S 44 M 100. *Date from* L.

793. F 352 H 442 L 31 p. 3 N 516 S 275 M 175. *Date from* L. H *has the anecdote under February.*
at Lambeth] *not in* H *or* L
The text is condensed in L. *The source of the anecdote is unidentified. In* L *it is signed* Mr N. *In* F *and* H *it is unsigned, and Singer printed it as coming from* P, *or* Pope.

794. L 1 p. 2.

795. L 16 p. 2.

796. L 7 p. 6.

797. H 410.
The anecdote is lightly crossed out in pencil, and there are faded brackets round Dell: *which may have been blotted or added later.*

798. 1757 MB p. 11 S 376. *Date from* MB.

799. L 7 p. 3.
Mallet] Mallack
The phrase from Mrs. Rogers, most of it illegible, is interpolated above the last sentence.

800. F 111 L 11 p. 10 N 207 S 114 M 141. *Date from Letters.*
sincerely] his opinion sincerely (F *originally*)
MR. TOWNLEY] F *originally added* (of Townley, in Lancashire)
L *is condensed.*

801. F 337 H 410 N 488 S 256 M 298. *Date from* H.
H *has a note on the page opposite:* This is said to be mention'd in Hume's History of England. Q.
broke in] quite spoil'd (H)
he was forced to insert them] it was done (H)

802. L 7 p. 4 S 329. *Date from* L.

803. L 7 p. 3 S 342. *Date from* L.

804. L 11 p. 5. *Date from Letters.*
The anecdote is crossed out in L*; the immediately surrounding anecdotes were collected abroad in 1732.*

805. 1756 MB p. 1 S 367. *Date from* MB.
Cowper] Cooper (MS.)

806. L 7 p. 2 S 326. *Date from* L.

807. L 7 p. 4 S 329. *Date from* L.
Dr. Walton] *followed by question mark*
The insertion occurs in brackets after CHEYNEY *in* MS.

808. L 7 p. 4.
Zuylenstein] Zulestien?

809. F 151 N 265 S 155 M 173. *Date from* F.
[Penn]] *for* Penn *Spence wrote* Sir William, *a common error.*

810. L 21.
Though the anecdote is unsigned, Lord Peterborow was responsible for the preceding one (*i.e.* §811), *and the subject matter argues his authorship.*

811. F 136 L 21 N 241 S 136 M 131. *Date from* L.

812. L 2.

813. L 2 S 339. *Date from* L.

814. F 37 L 5 p. 2 N 97 S 47 M 114 *and* 147. *Date from* L.
L *has a question mark after Steele's name.*

815. F 186 N 311 S 184 M 151. *Date from* F.
Singer printed the following footnote from MS. B, *since it followed this anecdote in that text, but questioned any connexion with Addison:* The strange story that the Abbé Morei told, as the cause of redness in his cheeks;—a blow from an invisible hand, in an old castle in Normandy. *Because Addison's known route did not include Normandy and his attitude towards superstition was later so strongly expressed* (Guardian 48 *and* Spectator 110) *it seems best to leave this strange story at the door of the otherwise unknown Abbé Morei.*

816. F 79 N 163 S 93 M 151. *Date from* F.

817. F 36 L 5 p. 2 N 95 S 46 M 146. *Date from* L.
The statement by Young appears in the margin of F *in Singer's hand, and as a footnote in* S (*where it is headed* Note by Mr. Spence). *This was probably a marginal note in* MS. B, *in which case it is likely to date from 1759, as in the case of* §857.

818. L 6 p. 2 S 335. *Date from* L.

819. L 6 p. 1.

820. L 6 p. 2 S 335. *Date from* L.

821. L 14 S 343. *Date from* L.

822. L 6 p. 2 S 335. *Date from* L.

823. 1756 MB p. 17 S 372. *Date from* MB.

824. F 188 N 315 S 186 M 152. *Date from* F.

825. L 7 p. 2 L 47 S 325. *Date from* L 7.
reputation] fame (L 7 *originally*)
friend] *in* L 7 *followed by* & *and* §826.
Spence originally reversed the order of the two periodicals, but corrected it by marking them (b) *and* (a). *Singer's version differs from* L *in emphasis though not substantially. The major differences occur in the second half. It is not clear whether these changes derive from* MS. B *or from an attempt by Singer to clarify the anecdote.*

826. L 7 p. 2 S 326. *Date from* L.

827. L 6 p. 2 S 335. *Date from* L.

828. L 38 p. 1 S 348. *Date from* L.

829. L 6 p. 2 S 334. *Date from* L.

830. L 42.
At the bottom of L *is the following jotting:* Welling in 30; ye Dr had =. *undoubtedly referring to Dr. Young's benefice at Welwyn, received in 1730. It paid £300 a year.*

831. F 189 N 315 S 186 M 132. *Date from* F.

832. S 355.
Since the original MS. is not among the Spence Papers there is no evidence to date the anecdote. However, the date 1759 might be inferred (p. lxiv).

833. L 43 p. 1 S 335. *Date from* L.

834. TN 4f. 183.
It is not clear from the MS. *how the beginning of this anecdote should be divided between the speakers. It is arranged as follows:*

Dit: [*i.e. Mr. Jones*] from Budgell;—
(Name Adns best friend—Letter X—— Sr. . . .

835. L 43 p. 2 TN 4f. 183 S 350. *Date from* L.
There . . . situation] & kept him swinging on one of the High-Gates (TN)
TN *is briefer, omitting much of the detail.*

836. L 43 p. 2 TN 4f. 183 S 351. *Date from* L.
The Doctor . . . Genius] A miraculous Genius (TN)
Following this anecdote in TN *are some jottings:* Harrison—his Sister—in what distress Congreve, Bracegirdle, Ds of M.

837. L 44 S 351. *Date from* L.
Harrison] Harrison (Willm) (L)

838. L 44 S 351. *Date from* L.

839. L 44 S 351. *Date from* L.

840. L 44 S 352. *Date from* L.

841. TN 4 f. 183 S 354. *Date from* TN.
After this anecdote in TN *Spence added in pencil:* wt Look? Any picture of him.

842. L 44 TN 4 f. 183 S 352. *Date from* L.

843. L 44 S 352–4. *Date from* L.
Addison *and* Lord Strafford *are followed by queries in* L.
turned] L *has* brought on *interlineally, which is, however, deleted*

844. 1757 MB p. 11 TN 4 f. 183 S 375. *Date from* MB.
TN *has only a brief note.*

845. TN 4 f. 183.

846. F 337 H 410 N 486 S 255 M 145. *Date from* H.
Universal Passion] H *has a query after the title.*

847. F 337 H 410 N 486 S 255 M 145. *Date from* H.
H *is much briefer.*

848. S 355. *Since no manuscript version of this anecdote is among the* Spence Papers, *there is no evidence to date it. However, the date* '1759' *might be inferred* (*p.* lxiv)

849. L 6 p. 1 S 333. *Date from* L.

850. L 6 p. 2 S 334. *Date from* L.

851. L 6 p. 1.

852. 1758 MB f. 24 S 377. *Date from* MB.
Accept] *Singer's emendation: Spence wrote* Except

853. F 1 (*transcribed by Singer as* note by Mr Spence [MS. B]) S 2 (*from* MS. B). *Dated by Singer in* F.
tell] ask (S)

854. 1757 MB p. 10 S 374. *Date from* MB.

855. 1757 MB p. 10 1758 MB f. 24 S 375. *Date from* 1757 MB.
Milton's] *Spence wrote* Milton (1758 MB)
are] were (1758 MB)
The anecdote is unsigned but probably comes from Young. The couplet and final sentence occur in 1758 MB.

856. L 6 p. 1.

857. L 43 p. 1 S 356. *Date from* L.

858. L 6 p. 2.

859. S 174 (*from* MS. B.) *Date from* S.
On the significance of this anecdote in an account of MS. B, *see p.* lxxiv.

860. 1758 MB f. 24ᵛ S 378. *Date from* MB.

861. 1758 MB f. 26.
deleting] delating (MS.)

862. S 354. *No date or source in Singer. However, the date 1759 might be inferred* (*p.* lxiv).

863. L 16 p. 4.

864. L 16 p. 4.

865. L 16 p. 4.

866. L 16 p. 3.
Oldisworth *and* He *are underscored, evidently to show the antecedent.*

867. 1758 MB f. 23 S 378. *Date from* MB.

868. L 7 p. 6 S 331. *Date from* L.
OLDISWORTH from DR. METCALF] Medcalf frō Dʳ Oldisworth (MS.)

869. L 7 p. 5.

869a. L 3 p. 1.

870. F 339 H 416 N 490 S 257 M 143. *Date from* H.
pretty personage] *Singer prints* comely personage

871. L 14.

872. L 7 p. 3 S 326. *Date from* L.

873. F 337 H 410 N 486 S 255 M 184. *Date from* H.
Cheyne] Cheney (MSS.)
H *has a shorter form.*

874. 1756 MB p. 1.
The anecdote is signed 'S^r^ Is^c^', *but the next one has a note:* '(All frō Ld Radnor)'

875. 1756 MB p. 1 S 368. *Date from* MB.

876. L 7 p. 2 L 47 S 325. *Date from* L 7.
those gentlemen but as enemies to classical studies] *The words are difficult to read; Singer has:* I can't imagine the utility of such studies, *which is clearly wrong*

877. 1756 MB p. 1 S 368. *Date from* MB.

878. 1755 MB p. 9 S 362. *Date from* MB.
Colsterworth] Coldsworth (MS.)

879. 1755 MB p. 1 S 362. *Date from* MB.
south] *originally:* SW
Colsterworth] Coldsworth (MS.)
Ponton] Polton (MS.)

880. L 1 p. 3.

881. L 1 p. 1.

882. F 11 L 15 p. 6 L 3 p. 1 N 27 S 13. *Date from* L 3 (L 15 *and* F *omit query*).
Two pencilled comments in the margin of F: no body living, y[t] does not allow it *and* unless w[t] any mark for their names.

883. F 11 L 15 p. 6 L 3 p. 1 N 27 S 14 M 160. *Date from* L 3 (F *and* L 15 *omit query*).
Insertion from L 3. L 15 *omits final sentence.*

884. F 12 L 3 p. 4 N 29 S 15 M 196. *Date from* L (F *omits query*).
Spence's pencilled marginal notes read: See loose paper B 1, 16 [*not among Spence Papers; perhaps a reference to* MS. B]; Addend? Pap: N° 3 [*a reference to* §885 *which does not occur in* F]; Hence, at No. 52 [*a reference to* §1208 *which Spence intended, with other anecdotes, all for the year 1729, to follow this one*].

885. L 15 p. 6 L 3 p. 4. *Date from* L 3 (L 15 *omits query*).
in Rome] L 3 *has:* V.C. (*i.e. ab urbe condita*)
Insertions from L 3.

886. L 3 p. 4.

887. F 12 L 3 p. 1 N 29 S 15 M 196. *Date from* L (F *omits query*).
L *has the following comment by Spence:* certain, tho' set down Aug[t] 1729.

888. S 355. *No date or source in Singer. However, the date 1759 might be inferred* (*p.* lxiv).

889. L 3 p. 1 S 340. *Date from* L.

890. L 3 p. 1.

891. F 11 L 15 p. 6 L 3 p. 1 N 29 S 14 M 163. *Date from* L (F *and* L 15 *omit query*).
to be able to read and answer] even to write letters (L 3, L 15)
in it] L 3 *adds:* &c

892. 1756 MB p. 11 S 370. *Date from* MB.

893. F 11 L 3 p. 1 N 27 S 14 M 169. *Date from* L (F *omits query*).
should break] should *lightly deleted in* F, *with* might perhaps *superscribed. The comment in the explanatory note is from* L.

894. S 314.
Singer found this anecdote among Mr Spence's papers, *but it is not among those in the Spence Papers.*

895. 1756 MB p. 9 S 369. *Date from* MB.

896. L 38 pp. 1–2 S 349. *Date from* L.

897. L 38 p. 1 S 348. *Date from* L.

898. L 38 p. 2 S 349. *Date from* L.

899. L 38 p. 2.

900. L 38 p. 1.

901. L 42 1757 MB p. 12 S 376. *Date from* L.
a sad dog] a wretched fellow (L *originally*)
The earlier version in 1757 MB *has several variants:* 1) Old Cibber's Brother? at Winch^r Coll: in ye D^rs time: recond ingenious, as well as loose. His varying; Quàm pulchrũ est digito monstrari, & dicier, *Hic est:* Hei Mihi, quàm maestè vox sonat, *Ille fuit*—A Vile Rake afterw^ds; & in ye greatest distress. Told Dr Sim: Burton, on a Visit, 'that he did not know any sin he had not been guilty of but one; wch was Avarice; & if the D^r w^d give him a Guinea he w^d endeavour his utmost to be guilty of y^t. D^r Y^g. *Singer conflated the two texts, using that in* 1757 MB *as his basis, but gave the* '*Fourth Memorandum Book. 1758.*' *as his source.*

902. L 37 p. 3.

903. L 4 p. 19 S 337. *Date from* L.
the . . . Portsmouth] *in* S *this, in expanded form, opens the anecdote:* when the Prince of Orange was landing at Portsmouth he began to harangue the populace, and said. . . . *It is not clear whether Singer introduced an alteration or took this from* MS. B.

904. L 4 p. 19.

905. L 6 pp. 7–8 S 342. *Date from* L.
[liberty, liberty]] *not in* L, *but given in* S, *which differs in minor details from* L *and may be based upon* MS. B. *The sense requires the triple repetition.*

906. 1758 MB f. 23.

907. L 4 p. 19.

908. S 342. S *gives no indication of source or date.*

909. Supplemental Anecdotes, p. 11 'Addition' S 343. S *gives no indication of source or date.*

In Singer's Supplemental Anecdotes the speaker was originally recorded as Richardson Junior, *but* Junior *was deleted.*

910. F 30 L 7 p. 1 N 49 S 37 M 202. *Date from* L.

911. 1755 MB p. 17 S 37. *Date from* MB.

912. L 7 p. 3 S 342. *Date from* L.

913. L 48. *Date inferred from* L 3.

914. L 48. *Date inferred from* L 3.
Sir —] Sir,

915. L 7 pp. 2–3.

916. L 7 p. 4 S 329. *Date from* L.

917. L 37 p. 1.
Goodman's Fields *and* there *underlined.*

918. L 3 p. 4.

919. L 3 p. 4 S 340. *Date from* L.

920. L 3 p. 4.
Job] Job[s]

921. L 3 p. 4.

922. F 240 H 346 L 24 p. 2 N 398 S 205. *Date from* L (H *mistakenly gives* July 1739*;* F, 1739).

In F *there is a marginal note in pencil to the second couplet:* M[r] Benson that studied versification so particularly usd to call this 'The softest couplet that ever was writ.'

923. F 239 H 344 L 24 p. 2 N 396. *Date from* L (H *mistakenly gives* July 1739*;* F, 1739).

BENSON] M[r] A B.' *in* F, *over which is superscribed in pencil* Auditor Benson. *A pencil note below the anecdote reads:* To be new worded, *because of the many corrections. The quotations in* F *are in the margin.*

reckoning] blaming (L, F *originally*)

The first is picturesque *and* And the second, very particular (*see explanatory note*) *crossed out in* F

924. F 239 H 344 L 24 p. 2 N 396. *Date from* L (H *mistakenly gives* July 1739*;* F, 1739).
pavidae] timidae (MS.)

925. F 240 H 344 L 24 p. 2 N 398 S 205. *Date from* L (H *mistakenly gives* July 1739*;* F, 1739)

The passage in brackets, both in F *and in* N, *is in marginal notes.*

926. F 240 H 346 L 24 p. 2 N 398 S 205 M 97. *Date from* L (H *mistakenly gives* July 1739*;* F, 1739).

927. F 240 H 346 L 24 p. 2 N 400 S 206 M 282. *Date from* L (H *mistakenly gives* August 1739*;* F, 1739).

H *and* L *read simply:* Has seen English Verse of Havillan's. Q?
Vives, in his treatise] F *has a marginal note,* Lib: 3 p. 542. *The edition Spence used has not been identified.*
one of the most celebrated men] one of the best poets (F *originally*)

928. F 240 H 346 L 24 p. 2 N 400 S 205 M 282. *Date from* L (H *mistakenly gives* August 1739; F, 1739).

929. L 48. *Date inferred from* L 3.
of a lens] *originally followed by* & focus (*deleted*)

930. L 48. *Date inferred from* L 3.

931. L 48. *Date inferred from* L 3.
prey] preys

932. L 48. *Date inferred from* L 3.

933. L 48. *Date inferred from* L 3.

934. L 48. *Date inferred from* L 3.
Borelli] Brunelli?
right] *preceded by an illegible sign.*

935. L 48. *Date inferred from* L 3.

936. F 387 H 520 L 36 p. 3 N 569 S 318. *Date from* L, *where it follows* §643 *and is the last anecdote in 10–17 May section.*

937. L 3 p. 1.
In the margin is written, Youw Myn Heer, *apparently unrelated to this anecdote.*

938. L 7 p. 5 L 15 p. 8. *Date from* L 7 *and* L 15.
The first sentence only is in L 15.
The spelling of the titles is mixed, French and English.

939. L 7 p. 4.

940. L 7 p. 4 S 327. *Date from* L.
Speaker] *followed by a query* (L).

941. L 7 p. 4 S 328. *Date from* L.

942. L 2 S 339. *Date from* L.

943. L 7 p. 3 S 327. *Date from* L.

944. L 48. *Date inferred from* L 3.
THOMSON] Tom.

945. L 13.

946. L 38 p. 2 S 349. *Date from* L.

947. L 38 p. 2 S 349. *Date from* L.

948. L 38 p. 2 S 349. *Date from* L.
studium] *Horace has* ludum

949. L 38 p. 3.

950. 1757 MB p. 12.

951. 1756 MB p. 11.

952. L 34 p. 4.

953. F 382 H 504 L 34 p. 4 N 563 S 311 M 70. *Date from* L.
Insertion from H *and* L.

954. F 382 H 506 L 34 p. 4 N 563 S 311 M 71. *Date from* L.
The insertion is from H*; L has it in briefer form.*
excess] vitious excess (L)

955. 1756 MB p. 11.

956. F 382 H 508 L 34 p. 4 N 563 S 311 M 71. *Date from* L.
Insertions from the margin of H.

957. L 34 p. 4.

958. 1756 MB p. 10 S 370. *Date from* MB.

959. F 380 H 502 L 34 p. 3 N 561 S 309 M 301. *Date from* L.

960. F 381 H 500 L 34 p. 3 N 561 S 309 M 302. *Date from* L.
as such] L *adds:* after losing them*;* H *adds* as Benefactors after their Deaths

961. F 381 H 502 L 34 p. 3 N 561 S 310 M 302. *Date from* L.

962. H 500 L 34 p. 3. *Date from* L.

963. 1756 MB pp. 10–11 1755 MB p. 15 S 363. *Date from* 1755 MB.
S *differs in order from* 1756 MB.

964. L 4 p. 25.
There are query marks after 1712, 1714 *and* grocer. *The order of these Chubb anecdotes has been altered in the interest of clarity and narrative flow, the manuscript order being* §§ 970–3, 968–9, 976, 974, 964, 965–7, 975.

965. L 4 p. 27.

966. L 4 p. 27.

967. L 4 p. 27.

968. L 4 p. 25.

969. L 4 p. 25.
'Tis very true] *preceded in the MS. by* 'Wh: ='

970. L 4 p. 23.

971. L 4 p. 23.

972. L 4 p. 23.

973. L 4 p. 23.

974. L 4 p. 25.

975. L 4 p. 27.

976. L 4 p. 25.

977. L 16 p. 2.

978. L 37 p. 2 S 346. *Date from* L.
Elders] *followed by a query* (L)

979. L 37 p. 2 S 346. *Date from* L.

980. L 37 p. 1 S 345. *Date from* L.

981. L 37 p. 2 S 346. *Date from* L.

982. L 37 p. 2 S 346. *Date from* L.

983. L 14 S 344. *Date from* L.

984. L 14.

985. L 14.

986. L 14.

987. L 1 p. 2.

988. L 14. *Date conjectural: see list of* MSS.

988a. L2.

989. L 14.
Mill] Mills

990. L 14.

991. L 1 p. 4.

992. L 14. *Date conjectural: see list of* MSS.

993. L 14. *Date conjectural: see list of* MSS.

994. L 2.
The jotting given in the explanatory note is taken from L 14.

995. L 14.

996. L 14.

997. L 7 p. 7 S 333. *Date from* L.
absolute desire] command (L *originally*)
effects] good (L *originally*)

998. L 7 pp. 6–7 S 332. *Date from* L.

999. L 1 p. 4.

1000. L 1 p. 2.

1001. L 1 p. 3.

1002. L 1 p. 3.

1003. L 1 p. 4.

1004. L 1 p. 3.

1005. L 1 p. 3.

1006. L 1 p. 4.

1007. L 1 p. 4.

1008. L 1 p. 4.
The D. de Rochf. *in the* MS. *perhaps indicates that Spence considered some of the maxims analogous to La Rochefoucauld's.*

1009. L 1 p. 4.

1010. L 7 p. 6 S 330. *Date from* L.

1011. L 2 S 340. *Date from* L.
Because it is signed 'W' *in the* MS., *Singer mistakenly assigned this anecdote to Walter Harte. But Spence used* 'H' *for Harte.*

1012. L 14.

1013. L 14.
The two anecdotes are not together in L, *but an asterisk with each indicates that Spence meant them to be associated.*

1014. L 1 p. 2.

1015. L 1 p. 1.

1016. L 14.

1017. L 1 p. 1.

1018. L 1 p. 1.

1019. L 1 p. 4.

1020. L 1 p. 1.
attracting] *followed by a query in* MS.

1021. L 1 p. 1.

1021a. L 4 p. 21.

1021b. L 4 p. 21.

1022. L 48 S 340. *Date inferred from* L 3.
[Some . . . a]] The (L): *the text here is taken from* S.
Spence spelled Kircher *as* Kircherus *on its first appearance.*

1023. L 7 p. 5.
generally] (generally?)

1024. L 7 p. 5 S 330. *Date from* L.
ilarità] Hilarità (MS.)

1025. L 7 p. 6.

1026. L 7 p. 6.
part with] sell (*originally*)
METCALFE] Medcalf

1027. L 7 p. 7.
some say] *followed by* ?
METCALFE] Medcalf

1028. L 7 p. 5.

1029. L 7 p. 4 S 328. *Date from* L.

1030. L 7 p. 6 S 330. *Date from* L.

1031. L 7 p. 6 S 330. *Date from* L.
one in a thousand] $\frac{1}{1000}$ (MS.)

1032. L 7 p. 7 S 333. *Date from* L.

1033. L 7 p. 5.

1034. L 7 p. 5 S 330. *Date from* L.

1035. L 47. *Date and author are inferential* (*see list of* MSS.).
Let. Pers. No. 83] *Spence mistakenly wrote* No. 81.

1036. L 7 p. 3.

1037. L 7 p. 2 L 47 S 326. *Date from* L 7.
S *does not print the last sentence as part of* §1037, *but as it has no connexion with the succeeding anecdote in* L, *it must stand here.* L 43 *confirmed it. The complete text there reads:* Ld Cowper ow'd all ye reasoning he was master of to reading Chill:th—Mr Nic: = ye Speaker = Ld Cr.
From both L's *it appears that the anecdote came from Chute.*

1038. L 7 p. 4 S 328. *Date from* L.
was . . . Lockier?] *Spence originally wrote:* it seem'd to be Dr Clark of St James'. *He later deleted this and wrote the present text interlineally. Singer simplified the situation, and merely printed* Dean Lockier.

1039. L 7 pp. 3–4 S 328. *Date from* L.

1040. L 7 p. 4 S 328. *Date from* L.

1041. L 12.
This is followed by a note which probably belongs with this anecdote (*see explanatory note*).

1042. F 216.

1043. F 308 H 400 N 480 S 248. *Date from* F.
H *supplies insertion and Chesterfield's name. Born in September 1694, he had had his forty-seventh birthday in 1741.*

1044. F 308 H 400 N 480 S 249. *Date from* H.

1045. H 400.
The manuscript indicates that Spence was uncertain of the identity of the speaker. But since he recorded it in Paris, Lord Chesterfield (*source of the following anecdote in the MS.*) *seems likely.*

1046. L 31 p. 3.

1047. H 434 L 31 p. 1. *Date from* L.
The Huntington MS. has query marks: 6? pound *and* 6? hours.

1048. F 375 H 490 L 34 pp. 1–2 N 553 S 303. *Date from* H.
of Abscourt] *from* H
L *has a shorter form.*

1049. F 375 H 490 L 34 p. 2 N 553 S 303 M 300. *Date from* L.
In L *the anecdote is the last but one under date of 21–24 February: this dates the preceding anecdote,* §1048.

1050. 1755 MB p. 27.

1051. 1756 MB p. 2.

1052. F 349 H 364 L 31 p. 2 N 512 S 272 M 299. *Date from* L.
The insertion is from L. H *read instead:* (Inst: in a very bad spr. in genl.)
I scarce ever heard] I never knew (F *originally*)

1053. 1756 MB p. 1.

1054. 1756 MB p. 11 S 370.

1055. 1756 MB p. 15.

1056. 1755 MB p. 7.

1057. 1757 MB p. 10.

1058. 1755 MB p. 9.

1059. G 38.

1060. 1757 MB p. 14.

1061. 1756 MB p. 9.

1062. G 55.

1063. G 54.

1064. G 39.
Wright] Right

1065. G 37–38.
What Le Nôtre] *preceded by a query in MS.*
The two sentences occur as queries in G*; they have been run together here and the* Q *preceding the second sentence omitted.*

1066. G 39.

1067. G 38.

1068. G 38.

1069. 1758 MB f. 18.
The fuller version of the third aim given in the explanatory occurs in L 46 p. 3.
'beautiful Nature'] *not in inverted commas*
extend . . . call in] call in . . . extend (*but marked for reversal*)

1069a. L 41.

1070. G 58.
The deleted jotting mentioned in the explanatory notes is on p. 3.

1071. G 57.

1072. 1758 MB f. 17^{v}.

1073. G 57.

1074. 1757 MB p. 9.

1075. 1756 MB p. 11 S 370. *Date from* MB.

1076. 1758 MB f. 18.

1077. G 61–62.
Briggs] Brigg
Opthalmo-Graphia] Ophthalm:

1078. G 58.
expressing thoughts] talking (*originally*)

1079. G 58.

1080. G 55.

1081. G 51.

1082. G 51.

1083. G 51.

1084. G 59.

1085. G 59.

1086. G 53.

1087. 1757 MB f. 2^{v}.
in the horizontal line] on an absolutely rated line (*originally*)

1087a. L 54.

1088. 1757 MB f. 2^{v} S 373. *Date from* MB.

1089. 1758 MB f. 17^{v}.

1090. 1758 MB f. 17^{v}.

1091. 1758 MB f. 17^{v}.

1092. 1758 MB f. 18.

1093. G 61.

1094. G 56.

1095. G 61.

1096. G 56.

1097. G 56.

1098. G 55.

1099. G 35.

1100. L 50.

1101. L 52.

1102. L 52.
This . . . 200] *written in the margin*

1103. L 52.
Directed . . . world] *written in the margin. At the foot of the anecdote is:* Q (Di[stre]ss of his excel^{t} Nephew)

1104. G 62.

1105. G 57.
A note in the margin reads: Solid Openings

1106. G 46.

1107. G 46.
consider] *an asterisk after this refers to a note:* S^{r} G: Lyttleton's Hint: as in ye Close of Crito (*presumably a reference to Dodsley's* Fugitive Pieces, *i. 54–58*).
humane;] *in the* MS. §1108 *occurs after this word, set off from the anecdote in brackets.*

1108. G 46.
The Latin in the MS. reads simply: adde quod ingenuas &c.
See also textual note §1107.

1109. G 47.

1110. 1757 MB p. 13 S 377. *Date from* MB.

1111. 1758 MB f. 17.

1112. 1755 MB p. 25.

1113. 1758 MB f. 17^{v}.

1114. G 37.

1115. G 37.
The final parenthetical sentence is pencilled in the margin.

1116. G 38.

1117. G 37.

1118. G 36.

1119. 1755 MB p. 11.

1120. 1758 MB f. 18^{v}.

1121. G 34.

1122. G 37.

1123. G 54.

1124. G 39.

1125. G 34.

1126. G 37.

1127. G 34.

1128. G 37.

1129. G 53.

1130. G 52.

1131. G 35.
Marked to go to Rules

1132. G 52.

1133. G 52.

1134. G 38.

1135. G 57.

1136. G 54.

1137. 1755 MB p. 3 S 361. *Date from* MB.

1138. G 35–36.
Marked to go to Rules

1139. G 34.
A note says: See 1750, Feb: 11, *probably referring to a letter or a memorandum book not among the Spence Papers.*

1140. G 35.
Marked to go to Rules

1141. 1755 MB p. 3 S 361. *Date from* MB.

1142. G 54.

1143. G 53.

1144. L 51. *Date inferred.*

1144a. L 51 G 51. *Date from* L *and* G.
Every . . . pleasing] *Southcote's correction; Spence wrote:* The reason of the first is very evident
makes] *Southcote's correction; Spence wrote:* looks like
a level . . . it] *Spence originally wrote:* the top of the rising
blanks all] *Southcote's correction; Spence's words following are deleted and illegible.*
For the text in G *see explanatory note.*

1145. G 35.
Marked to go to Rules

1146. 54.

1147. G 60.

1148. 1755 MB p. 19.
After M^r^ Bl^k^ *follows* (see H†)

1149. 1755 MB p. 19.

1150. 1755 MB p. 21.

1151. 1755 MB p. 21.

1152. 1755 MB p. 21.

1153. 1755 MB p. 19.

1154. 1755 MB p. 9.

1155. 1755 MB p. 9.

1156. 1755 MB p. 23.

1157. 1755 MB p. 21.

1158. 1755 MB p. 27.

1159. 1755 MB p. 9.

1160. 1758 MB f. 18.

1161. 1758 MB f. 20^{v}.

1162. 1756 MB p. 7.

1163. 1755 MB p. 30.

1164. 1758 MB f. 20^{v}.

1165. 1758 MB f. 19^{v}.
Holdeston] Hoddesdon

1166. 1755 MB p. 5 S 362. *Date from* MB.

1167. 1755 MB p. 27 S 367. *Date from* MB.

1168. L 1 p. 1.
weight or concern] *followed by a colon in the* MS.

1169. L 1 p. 2.

1170. L 1 p. 2.

1171. L 1 p. 2.

1172. L 1 p. 4.
547] 547–441, *apparently a slip of the pen.*

1173. L 1 p. 4.

1174. L 1 p. 4.

1175. H 366.

1176. L 39.
turned into English] given in English (*originally*)
for there is . . . to us] but that is only w[t] one may imagine, for all y[e] works of Prodicus's are lost (*originally*)
as plainly] as justly (*originally*)

1177. L 53 p. 3. *Date inferred from* L.

1178. L 1 p. 1.

1179. 1755 MB p. 3 S 361. *Date from* MB.
Written in pencil immediately after this and the following anecdote are the following jottings: Atfield of Chatham?—Miller's affair, Smith paymaster: *followed in ink by* The Grand S[g] [i.e. Signor]. *No connexion with this anecdote is clear.*

1180. 1755 MB p. 3 S 361. *Date from* MB.

1181. 1757 MB p. 3 S 374. *Date from* MB.

1182. 1756 MB p. 11 S 370. *Date from* MB.
nineteen in twenty] MS *reads:* $\frac{19}{20}$ths

1183. 1756 MB p. 16.

1184. 1755 MB p. 16.

1185. 1756 MB p. 12 S 371. *Date from* MB.

1186. G 46.

1187. H 388.
Date by inference from letters; H *has only the year. The anecdote is unsigned* (*the preceding was by Giacomo Frey, the following by Abbé Grant*).

1188. 1755 MB p. 5.

1189. 1756 MB p. 15.

1190. *Anecdote cancelled.*

1191. L 45 p. 1.

1192. 1757 MB p. 2 S 373. *Date from* MB.

1193. L 1 p. 2.
argues] argue
show] *written over* Grandeur

1194. 1756 MB p. 4.

1195. 1755 MB p. 25.

1196. 1757 MB p. 13.

1197. 1757 MB p. 17.

1198. 1758 MB f. 19^v.

1199. 1757 MB p. 14.

1200. 1756 MB p. 4.

1201. 1755 MB p. 5.

1202. 1757 MB p. 4 S 374. *Date from* MB.

1203. 1755 MB p. 35.

1204. 1755 MB p. 33.
Thorowgood] Thoroughgood (MS.)
MRS. SPENCE] Mother (MS.)

1205. 1755 MB p. 35.

1206. F 40 L 8 p. 3 N 59 S 51. *Date from* L 8.
Ramsay . . . twenty] R: was 22 (L).
went to the Archbishop's] *written interlinearly* in L*:* (or w^n under Facio)

1207. F 41 L 15 p. 8 L 8 p. 3 N 61 S 51. *Date from* L 8.
interpreters] interpretations (L 8, L 15)
Insertion from L 8, L 15.

1208. F 22 L 15 p. 6 L 6 p. 2 N 31 S 26 M 197. *Date from* L 6 (F *and* L 15 *give year*).
Protestants] Protestants in distress (L 15)

1209. F 40 L 15 p. 7 L 8 p. 3 N 59 S 51. *Date from* L 8.
Insertion from L 8, L 15.

1210. F 49 L 8 p. 3 N 67 S 57 M 204. *Date from* L.
have disarmed . . . doctrine of] *at first in* L*:* weakend (quoad hominem) by*; this was replaced interlineally by:* lose half their argts ag^{st} ye great point of

1211. L 7 p. 1 L 15 p. 7 F 32 (*transcribed by Singer from* MS. B) S 38 (*from* MS. B). *Date from* L 7 (F *and* L 15 *give year*).
The version copied in F *and* S *was apparently put into direct speech by Spence.*
first] beginning of the (F, S, *from* MS. B)*; this may be Singer's silent emendation of the* MS. B *text.*

1212. L 8 p. 3.
The manuscript begins with the word W[he]n, *here omitted as redundant. Fénelon's exclamation is not in quotation marks and Spence's comment is run on with the rest of the anecdote.*

1213. F 22 L 15 p. 6 L 6 pp. 2–3 N 31 S 27 M 197. *Date from* L 6 (F *and* L 15 *give year*).
the Bishop of Meaux] *originally* another eminent Prelate *with a pencilled query in the margin:* (Pere le Tellier? only to avoid the Confessor)
L 6 *has a much abbreviated form;* L 15 *only a reminder.*

1214. F 23 L 6 p. 4 N 33 S 28. *Date from* L.
continued . . . him] was ever fond of his Tutor; w^{n} they took his book from him (L)

1215. L 6 p. 3.

1216. F 24 L 8 pp. 3–4 L 6 p. 3 N 37 S 29. *Date from* L 6.
This anecdote is based on a conflation of the material in L 8 (*re-ordered*) *with that in* F. L 8 *reads:* T'was to Rochel y^{t} Mr Fenelon (then Head of ye converted Hugonots College in Paris) was sent as a *Missionaire* to bring them to ye Church; & it was on y^{t} Occasion he said he w^{d} not go unless ye King w^{d} recall his Dragoons: The K^{g} did so frō those parts: Fenelon went & in his 3? Years there, had very great Success among them. L 6 *has a briefer version of the text in* L 8, *though adding the details noted below.*
unpolitic as well as unchristian] not only impolitic, but absolutely contrary to ye Spirit of ye Gospel (L 6)
Insertions are from L 6 *and* L 8.

1217. F 26 L 6 p. 4 N 41 S 32. *Date from* L *and* F.
opened . . . use] receiv'd several of them at Cambray, & kept them there, at his own expence (F *originally*)

1218. L 6 p. 4 S 30 (*from* MS. B). *Date from* L.
lies] lays (L)
often wrote] wrote several letters (S)

1219. F 28 L 15 p. 6 L 6 p. 4 N 45 S 35. *Date from* L 6 (F *and* L 15 *give year*).

1220. L 6 p. 5 S 33 (*from* MS. B). *Date from* L.

1221. L 6 p. 5 S 33 (*from* MS. B). *Date from* L.
[asked Hooke]] Hooke *is conjectural. Since he is Ramsay's interlocutor throughout the anecdote, the question was most likely asked by him.*
The use . . . bush] *in* L *enclosed in brackets*

1222. L 8 p. 4.

1223. F 25 L 6 p. 5 N 37 S 30 M 199. *Date from* L.
Insertions from L 6.

1224. L 6 p. 4.
sing] *followed by an illegible word or abbreviation*

1225. L 7 p. 8 S 53 (*from* MS. B). *Date from* L.

1226. F 24 L 6 p. 8 N 35 S 28. *Date from* L.
so far moved . . . knees] so charmd wth y^{t} Prelate y^{t} he fell down on his knees, begd his pardon, *&c.* (L)
take care . . . last] take care of himself that he did not come to some misfortune from his enemies (L)

1227. F 26 L 6 p. 4 S 32. *Date from* L.
L 6 *reads simply:* His civil behaviour to ye two Germans at his table: standing up —'

1228. F 23 L 6 p. 4 N 33 S 28. *Date from* L.
a panegyric] a very handsome panegyric (L)
ran] run (MS.)

1229. F 25 L 15 p. 7 L 7 p. 1 H 39 S 31. *Date from* L 7 (F *and* L 15 *give year*).
In L 7 *and* L 15 *half of the quotation is in French.*
Swiss] Sweed (L 7, F); F, *however, has a note in the margin:* Q Swiss (Muralt? in a Book Letters of ye Fr & Engl:); L 15 *reads:* who spoke yt of ye Arch Bp of C? *in place of* is . . . better.

1230. F 25 L 6 p. 2 N 39 S 31 M 200. *Date from* L.
after a visit to] us'd to say that (F *originally*)
was never] was flung away & never (F *originally*)
delicious] exclusive (*superscribed in* L)
pious] religious (*pencilled in the margin of* F)

1231. F 34 L 6 p. 5 N 57 S 43. *Date from* L.
Cellamare] Celamar (MSS.)
In the margin of F *a* Q *pencilled next to this anecdote; a query follows in* L.

1232. F 24 L 6 p. 3 N 37 S 29 M 199. *Date from* L.
Lightly deleted in F. *The opening sentence is from* L.

1233. L 6 p. 4.
Laws] *underlined*

1234. F 26 L 15 p. 6 L 6 p. 3 N 39 S 32. *Date from* L 6 (F *and* L 15 *give year*).
dangerous book] *in* L 6 dangerous *deleted,* pernicious *superscribed, then again changed to* dangerous

1235. F 49 L 7 p. 6 N 67 S 57. *Date from* L.
one of the completest politicians] ye greatest man yt ever was (L)
The preceding anecdote in L *is attributed to* Oldisworth fro Dr Medcalf. *The order indicates that Dr. Metcalfe was in both cases the transmitter.*

1236. F 26 F 49 (*in both instances copied by Singer from* MS. B) L 6 p. 3. *Date from* L.
Insertions from L 6*; the final insertion is separated from this anecdote by* §1234, *but clearly belongs here.*

1237. L 8 p. 1.

1238. F 41 L 8 pp. 1–2 L 15 p. 7 N 61 S 52. *Date from* L 8.
Desfontaines] de Fontaine (MSS.)
irritate] provoke (L 8); L 15 *reads:* urgd on . . . agst R
[He]] I (F). *Spence often shifted from first to third persons*
one of her sons] her 2d? Son (L 8)
disgust] distaste (L 8)
Count d'Agénois] Count of Genoa (*a phonetic slip on Spence's part*)
gallant. Indeed] gallant: & indeed (MS.)
later Roman historians] Historians of ye bas-empire (L 8, F *originally*); L 8 *concludes:* Who has told it of two people yt did not live near one another in time. L 15 *is in note form; insertions from* L 8.

1239. L 7 p. 5.

1240. L 7 p. 1.

1241. L 6 p. 6.
Spagnoletto's] Spanolet's (MS.)

1241a. L 6 p. 7.

1242. F 29 L 6 p. 7 N 47 S 36 M 183. *Date from* L.
Cheyne's] Cheney's (MS.)
and went . . . next] L *continues:* ye Writer left an Hiatus
The insertion was pencilled in the margin of F *by Spence; Singer inked it over in his own hand, headed it as* (note from papers) *and printed it as such.* L *does not contain Spence's comment.*

1243. L 6 p. 6.

1244. L 6 p. 6 S 42 (*from* MS. B). *Date from* L.

1245. L 6 p. 6.

1246. F 189 N 315 S 186. *Date from* F.

1247. F 33 L 15 p. 6 L 6 p. 3 N 55 S 42. *Date from* L 6 (F *and* L 15 *give year*).
Marshal] Mareschal (MSS.)
Insertion from L 6. L 15 *has only a hint:* The Duke of Vendosme's good nature
(Nightcap. Stockings). *In* L 6 *also,* Duke of Vendosme *is given instead of* Turenne.

1248. F 124 L 19 N 235 S 132. *Date from* L.
Marshal] Mareschal (MSS.)
Following this anecdote in L *is an unrelated remark:* The feminine Rhime's demanding a masculine to follow it. Do you remark on ye Language? No: there one must quote their Countrymen authorities.

1249. F 30 L 6 p. 6 S 38. *Date from* L.
Insertion from L. *The anecdote is crossed out in* F, *but Spence's pencilled note in the margin says* To be printed.

1250. F 31 L 6 p. 6 S 38. *Date from* L.
Insertion from L. *The anecdote is crossed out in* F, *but Spence's pencilled note in the margin says* To be printed.

1251. L 12.

1252. F 31 S 39. *Date from* F.
The anecdote is crossed out, but Spence's pencilled note in the margin says To be printed.

1253. L 6 p. 6 F 32 (*transcribed by Singer as* addn from MS. B.) S 38 (*from* MS. B). *Date from* L.
livre] *supplied from the transcript in* F*:* L *has* shilling?

1254. F 31 L 7 p. 1 N 51 S 39. *Date from* L *and* F.
sort of man] sort of Govr (L)
and . . . spirit] without considering ye Soul (L)
The first sentence is underlined in F.

1255. F 125 N 237 S 132. *Date from* F.
A French version of Alberoni's speech appears in S 133, *probably taken from* MS. B.

1256. F 28 L 15 p. 7 L 7 p. 1 N 47 S 35 M 93. *Date from* L 7 (F *and* L 15 *give year*).
contents . . . French] naked plan of yᵉ Paradise Lost (like our Contents before each Book) (L 7)
In F *the two clauses of the opening sentences are transposed, but Spence's superscript numbering indicates that he intended the order adopted here* (*and in* N *and* M) *to be followed. Singer gives the earlier arrangement.*

1257. F 30 L 7 p. 1 N 49 S 37. *Date from* L.

1258. F 42 L 7 p. 8 S 53. *Date from* L.
L *is briefer.*

1259. F 42 L 15 p. 7 L 7 p. 8 N 63 S 54 M 158. *Date from* L 7 (F *and* L 15 *give year*).
diverting . . . ordinary] playing about and breaking a few pebbles & shells (L 7, L 15)

1260. F 47 L 8 p. 2 N 63 S 55. *Date from* L 8.
The great aim] The great Centre (L)
Faccio] Fatio (MSS.)
Insertions from L.

1261. F 27 L 15 p. 7 L 6 p. 6 N 43 S 33 M 200. *Date from* L 6 (F *and* L 15 *give year*).

1262. L 8 p. 1.
Arabian *and* They *underscored in* L.
Dr. Clarke] Mr. Clarke *with* Dr. *superscribed*

1263. L 8 p. 4 L 15 p. 8. *Date from* L 8.
Insertion from L 15.

1264. F 48 L 7 p. 8 N 67 S 57 M 204. *Date from* L.
Insertion from L.

1265. F 32 L 7 p. 2 N 51 S 39. *Date from* L.
consequently . . . Church] it strikes at yᵉ Root, the Infallibility of the Catholic Church (L)

1266. L 7 p. 1.

1267. L 7 p. 1.

1268. F 31 L 7 p. 1 N 51 S 39 M 202. *Date from* L.
The second sentence is in L 7 *only, but is separated from the anecdote by* §1267.

1269. F 32 L 7 p. 2 N 51 S 40 M 203. *Date from* L.
L *is a brief reminder.*

1270. L 6 p. 7 S 53 (*from* MS. B). *Date from* L.
S *arranges the materials slightly differently, putting the first sentence in direct speech and giving its source as Hooke.*
against] that could be written against (S)

1271. L 6 p. 6 F 27 (*transcribed by Singer from* MS. B) S 34 (*from* MS. B). *Date from* L.

The last sentence is superscribed at the end of the anecdote, and marked to y^s^ (*i.e.* '*to this add the following comment*').

The insertion is from F *and* S. L *has only a mark indicating the missing letter.*

1272. L 6 p. 5.

1273. L 7 p. 7.

1274. F 27 L 6 p. 5 N 43 S 34 M 200. *Date from* L.

Insertion from L. F *is much condensed; it reads:* His favourite point seem'd to be that of all things being good at first; that there has been a great degeneracy & disorder in the world; & that there will be a general Restoration.

1275. F 28 L 6 p. 8 N 45 S 35 M 201. *Date from* L.

In L *the anecdote begins:* He is to prove in his book that . . . .

what he said] *in brackets in* F, N

In the margin Spence pencilled: in ye Pref: to Cyrus

Spence's comment is crossed out.

1276. F 27 L 6 p. 8 N 45 S 34. *Date from* L.

Mr. Hooke] *deleted in* F

That] They (L)

1277. L 6 p. 8.

1278. L 6 p. 8.

1279. F 40 L 15 p. 8 L 8 p. 3 N 59 S 50. *Date from* L 8.

Clement XI] King William's Pope (L 8, L 15)*;* F *originally read* Innocent the 11th *but Spence corrected it.*

1280. L 7 p. 8 S 343. *Date from* L.

The second sentence is separated from the first by §1264 *in* L.

1281. L 6 p. 4 L 15 p. 7 S 43 (*from* MS. B). *Date from* L 6 (L 15 *gives year*).

L 15 *is briefer.*

gran filosofo] grande philosopho (MS.)

his . . . etc.] in Italy (S)

The . . . Deist] *omitted in* S

The order of the exchanges in the conversation is different in the version from MS. B *given by* S.

1282. F 47 L 7 p. 8 N 63 S 55. *Date from* L*;* F *has* 1730.

The anecdote is crossed out in N *and marked* to be omitted.

annual orbit] L *continues:* frō its place in Each of ye Solstices 2 Angles & ye Diameter of ye Ellipsis known, gives ye other angle.

Insertion from L.

1283. F 29 L 15 p. 7 L 6 p. 8 N 49 S 37. *Date from* L 6 (F *and* L 15 *give year*).

L 15 *has a condensed version.*

1284. L 7 p. 8.

1285. F 33 L 6 p. 7 N 55 S 41. *Date from* L.
Bernini] ye great Cavalier Bernini (R thought was ye person who) (L)
undertook] endeavourd (L)
hollowed] hallowd (L)
a staircase] a pair of stairs (L)
Insertions from L.
Mr. L's comment was originally written in pencil in the margin of F *by Spence; Singer rubbed it out, inked in the note in his own hand and printed it in* S *with no indication of its source.*

1286. L 6 p. 8 S 43 (*from* MS. B). *Date from* L.

1287. L 6 p. 8.

1288. L 6 p. 8.
Pont du Gard] d *in* Gard *underlined and followed by query* (*presumably Spence was not sure about the spelling*)

1289. L 6 p. 7.
Medici] Medicis
study] study?

1290. L 6 p. 8 F 28 (*transcribed by Singer as* note from MS. B) S 35 (*from* MS. B). *Date from* L.
The first sentence in L *is separated from the rest by* §1275. *The two parts seem to have been joined together in* MS. B.

1291. L 7 p. 8.

1292. L 11 p. 14 S 341. *Date from Letters.*
concetti] concetti's (MS.)

1293. L 12 p. 1.

1294. L 19 F 124 N 235 S 132. *Date from* L.
For the shorter version in F, *see explanatory note; Singer followed this but omitted* Ramsay; (at Paris)

1295. L 19 L 12. *Date and text from both.*
The second half of the anecdote, Du Bos . . . taste, *is from the fuller* L 12 *version.*
In L 19 *some of the names are underlined.* L 12 *is preceded by the query:* Who ye Author of ye Reflec: on Painting & Poetry?

1296. L 12.

1297. L 12.

1298. F 28 L 15 pp. 6–7 L 6 pp. 3–4, 6 N 45 S 35 M 202. *Date from* L 6 (F *and* L *give year*).
In both L 6 *and* L 15 *the first sentence is a separate anecdote.*

1299. F 124 L 19 S 132. *Date from* L.
The anecdote is crossed out in F. *Insertion from* L.

1300. L 19.
Le Sueur] La Souer
Du Fresnoy] Fresnoy

1301. L 19.

1302. F 69 N 143 S 83 M 219. *Date from* F.
In the margin of F *Spence wrote:* Add: Pr; No, 10 & No, 11.

1303. F 67 L 11 p. 1 TN 3 f. 102 N 139 S 80 M 217. *Date from Letters*
their head] their governour (L)
man of letters] savant (L, TN)
The side of TN *is covered, making it difficult to read without the aid of the other MSS.*

1304. TN 3 f. 102. *Date from Letters.*
of Gauls] TN *reads* des Gaulles

1305. F 67 L 11 p. 1 TN 3 f. 102 N 139 S 80. *Date from Letters.*
In . . . of] His character of the Pope (F *originally*)
Immediately after this anecdote is the following jotting: Ld Islay's obj: & his Criticism on Sæpe sinistra cavâ (id:)—The other Jesuit there, of Bayle. *The story behind this memorandum is given in Holdsworth, and repeated in* The Monthly Review, xxxviii (1768), 417–18.

1306. F 66 L 11 p. 1 TN 3 f. 102 N 139 S 80. *Date from Letters.*
religieux . . . grands et *petits*] *not underlined in* F, *but in* L: *Religieux . . . Chanoins . . . Curés . . . Vicairs . . . Abbés*
particular churches] their churches (TN)
without cure] L *and* TN *add:* or business

1307. F 66 L 11 p. 1 L 17 N 137 S 79. *Date from Letters.*
Except for a few verbal omissions, L 17 *is almost the same as* L 11, *and neither differs substantially from* F. *The* present Pope *is identified by* F *as* Clement 12.

1308. F 66 L 11 p. 1 L 17 N 137 S 79. *Date from Letters.*
some years ago] in 1730? (L 11); (in 1730) (L 17)
mortmain . . . clergy] Mortmain. They can leave nothing more to the Clergy (L 11, L 17)
as bold] F *reads* the same *with* as bold *written above. It appears that Spence was thinking of* as bold *as an alternative phrase, and since it is his second thought it has been used in the text. The copyist of* N, *however, included everything not cancelled, so that the reading there is* the same steps (as bold, at least). *Both the earlier manuscripts conclude simply,* he wd probably have done ye same.
Insertions from L 11 *and* L 17.

1309. L 11 p. 1 TN 3 f. 102. *Date from Letters* (L *has* 1732).
Duke of] D: de (L)

1310. L 11 p. 2. *Date from Letters* (L *has* 1732).

1311. L 11 p. 1. *Date from Letters.*
Immediately after this anecdote are the following jottings: The three punishments for Sod: & ye Mamalukes, Possessi ab homine (P: Vincent, ye Sp: Minim)—Arragon, Catalogne/ye Capt: his friend/& Valentia, as well cultivated, & as free mannered as Lyons.

1312. L 11 p. 14. *Date from Letters.*
Istoria . . . Storia] *Spence spelled* History
Mr. Gr.] *pencilled in the margin is* Dr. Gr.

1313. L 7 p. 3.

1314. F 67 TN 1 f. 4 N 139 S 80. *Date from Letters.*
At the end of this group (§§1314–17) *Spence pencilled a marginal note in* F: Add? From Geneva Paper 20 . . . 30 Articles: or rather to be flung in together in a Note? *Among the Spence Papers is a MS. entitled* State, of Geneva *to which this probably refers. There Spence gives his source as* From y^e^ État présent du governement de Génève, 1730. MSS. M^r^ Sh ——. *possibly Dr. Shaw? Written in the margin of the letter is:* +Mr Stanyan acct of Switzerl. (*i.e. Abraham Stanyan,* An Account of Switzerland written in the year 1714, *1714*).
is partly] is a Medium between that of ye 7 Aristocratic, & 6 democratic Cantons: 'tis partly (TN) *A note to* 7 *reads:* Mr Stanyan's acc^t^ of Switzerl^d^. ye 7 Arist: are Zurich, Berne, Lucerne, Basle, Fribourg, Solerne & Schaffôuse (TN)
whom we] which we (TN)
give our consent] ourselves consent (TN)

1315. F 67 TN 1 f. 4 N 139 S 80–81. *Date from Letters.*
nominate twenty- . . . elect] choose out of themselves the Council of 25: out of which 25, the Assembly of Bourgeois again nominate (TN)
A note above Assembly *reads:* 200 *and* wch was originally nominated out of themselves (TN)
elect] nominate (TN)

1316. F 67 TN 1 f. 4 N 141 S 81 M 217. *Date from Letters.*
small] little (TN)
any] a (TN)
these] this (TN)

1317. F 67 TN 1 f. 4 N 141 S 81. *Date from Letters.*
amongst us] with us (TN)
small] no (TN)
Our pay] *omitted in* TN
republic] TN *adds:* (to be a Syndic or even of ye Council of 25? &c?)

1318. L 11 p. 1 *Date from Letters.*

1319. F 68 L 10 N 141 S 81 M 218. *Date from Letters* (L *has* 1732).
L, *apart from unimportant variants is the same. It begins:* From Monsr Soyer's acc^t^ of ye Ecclesiastical Polity in Holland, it excells ours perhaps in five Articles.
brigues] *Singer silently changed to* intrigues
£240] 240 (F)
at Geneva] *deleted in* F

1320. F 69 L 11 p. 2 N 143 S 82 M 218. *Date from Letters.*
The secretary saw . . . but] 'Twas a Livy: & after examining it you may imagine how overjoyd he was to find it was entire. He showd his eagerness;

however after raising ye price very high, ye man agreed to carry it home after him (L)

long robe] gown (F *originally*)

1321. L 11 p. 2. *Date from Letters.*

1322. *Anecdote cancelled.*

1323. *Anecdote cancelled.*

1324. F 69 L 11 p. 1 N 143 S 83. *Date from Letters.*

The French General] Fr: Brig^{r}, in ye Sp: service, y^{t} we met upon ye Alps (L)

L *has a briefer version.*

1325. L 11 p. 1. *Date from Letters.*

1326. L 20. *Date from Letters.*

1327. F 123 L 20 N 235 S 131. *Date from Letters.*

Spence intended the French section for the notes as is indicated by F. L *has rough notes only, but the final sentence is from* L.

1328. F 182 TN 2 f. 63 N 305. *Date from Letters.*

The last sentence is slightly revised from the original.

1329. F 181 TN 2 f. 63 N 303. *Date from Letters.*

numerously taxed] *Spence underlined part of the first word in pencil and put a query in the margin.*

1330. F 182 TN 2 f. 63 N 303. *Date from Letters.*

1331. F 182 TN 2 f. 63 N 305. *Date from Letters.*

1332. F 183 TN 2 f. 63^{r-v} N 305. *Date from Letters.*

1333. F 183 TN 2 f. 63^{v} N 307. *Date from Letters.*

1334. F 181 TN 2 f. 62 N 303. *Date from Letters.*

They...in it] TN *gives a source for this information; it reads:* 400000 souls in it. (M^{r}. Tronchir). *A marginal note contains Millings's rebuttal of the higher figure.*

1335. F 184 TN 2 f. 68 N 307 S 182 M 259. *Date from Letters.*

This and the two following anecdotes were originally combined in F (*and Singer printed them as one*), *but Spence indicated that he intended to separate them. For important variants in* TN *see explanatory note.*

1336. F 185 TN 2 f. 68^{v} N 307 S 183. *Date from Letters.*

The F *version was written from notes in* TN*:* The Roof & Sides of the Gallery, are (the elements & Virgil Stories) by Coypel: they are in a bad neighbourhood (as ye person who showed it said:) & though they might do very well in any other Pallace in Paris they look but very poor & unaffecting; after the company one has been in, before one comes to ye Gallery. *A note to* Roof *reads:* The Roof is better y^{n} ye Sides Pictures. he took to drinking eau de vie, before he began ye latter: before he us'd to drink nothing but water. Several Coypels, this, ye best. Tis very true ils ont des mauvais voisins.

1337. F 184 TN 2 f. 68 N 307 S 182 M 260. *Date from Letters.*
TN *is in note form:* The Sign (by Correggio) 12^{thd}. A Muletier, &c: he told ye story differently (about his being obligd to a Muletier on ye Road) & making an Albergiste of him. It has been doubled in; by ye upper corners. *Note the difference in prices: 12,000 francs was worth* c. *£250.*

1338. F 185 TN 2 f. 69 N 309 S 183. *Date from Letters.*
TN *is in note form:* The best of Masters: I w^{d} willingly give him 10 y^{rs} out of my Life (abt. 73). You have 200 Servts, all of wch w^{d} dye to save y^{r} Life; That may be but I w^{d} not have anyone of 'em dye to save it.

1339. F 186 N 309. *Date from Letters.*
two . . . livres] *a marginal note in* F *reads:* to Notes 87500^{L}. Sterling.

1340. F 187 N 311 S 185 M 260. *Date from Letters.*

1341. F 188 N 313 S 185. *Date from Letters.*

1342. F 188 N 313 S 185 M 261. *Date from Letters.*
in his particular tenets] at heart (F *originally*)
Spence indicated that the second sentence was to go into the notes.

1343. F 189 N 315 S 187. *Date from Letters* (F *has* 1737).

1344. F 188 N 313 S 186 M 262. *Date from Letters* (F *has* 1737).

1345. F 188 N 313 S 186 M 261. *Date from Letters* (F *has* 1737).

1346. F 190 N 317 S 187. *Date from Letters.*

1347. F 190 N 317. *Date from Letters.*

1348. F 190 N 317 S 187 M 186. *Date from Letters.*

1349. F 309 H 404 N 482 S 250 M 188. *Date inferred from* H. H *gives year only but the preceding page gives the month: Spence stayed at Paris from* c. *30 August until (mid-?) November 1741.*
The text in H *combines* §1350 *with this anecdote.*

1350. F 309 H 404 N 482 S 251 M 188. *Date: see* §1349.
Montmenil] *A note in* H *reads:* Mont*m*enil? (Tis *so* spelt, in the Article L'Arbitre des differens; in the Biblioteque des Teatres.)(A Pocket-Companion, to the Play-Houses: For Mr Dodsley.) *Spence originally spelt the word as* Mominie *in* H.
plain, easy comedy] genteel comedy (F *originally*)
At first, Spence intended this to be inserted after the preceding anecdote; then he consigned it to Notes. *Here it seems worth separate notice.*

1351. H 400. *Date from* H.

1352. F 309 H 400 N 482 S 250 M 188. *Date from* H.

1353. F 308 H 402 N 480 S 249 M 186. *Date from* H.
In H *the French appears in the text, while the English is in a note.*

1354. F 308 H 400 N 482 S 249 M 186. *Date from* H.
For additional details in the description of the garden see the explanatory note.

1355. F 308 H 402 N 480 S 249 M 186. *Date from* H.

1356. H 402. *Date from* H.

Inserted above the anecdote is the note: Ent[ere]d, In poet[ical] Coll[ectio]n.

1357. F 309 H 402 N 484 S 251 M 188. *Date from* H.

1358. F 309 H 402 N 484 S 251 M 188. *Date from* H.

good country] charming (H, F *originally*)

In F *Spence made the mistake of substituting his own observation for Le Sage's concise one, which appears in* H *and is here given in half-brackets.*

1359. F 304 H 394 N 480 S 248. *Date from* H.

H *does not mention the site of the Tuileries.*

1360. F 304 H 394 N 480 S 248 M 297. *Date from* H.

The French translation of the lady's remark is marked for Notes *in the margin of* F.

1361. F 71 L 11 p. 2 N 147 S 84 M 220. *Date from Letters.*

It is impossible to determine the exact date as Spence post-dated a number of letters. The first letter in which Maffei is mentioned was written in January or February 1732 from Venice (reaching Winchester 21 February 1731/2), but dated 'Verona, November 10, 1731'. This must be fairly accurate, for Spence spent four days in Verona between being in Turin on 24 October and Venice on 21 December 1731.

Infida] infidele (L)

Spence's final remark is from L.

1362. F 70 L 11 p. 2 N 145 S 84. *Date: see* §1361.

L *begins:* The French have no taste for our Music, yet is their Music a feuille de nôtre arbre.

Some of our musicians. . . .] L *continues:* studied their taste, & found it out to please them (L)

Insertion from L.

1363. F 70 L 11 p. 2 N 145 M 220. *Date: see* §1361.

in the fourteenth century] in 1400 (L)

1364. F 70 L 11 p. 2 N 145 S 83 M 220. *Date: see* §1361.

1365. F 97 L 11 pp. 8–9 N 183 S 98 M 234. *Date from Letters.*

1366. F 75 N 155 S 89. *Date from Letters:* F *has* 1731–2*;* N, 1731.

1367. F 77 N 159 S 91. *Date from Letters:* F *has* 1731–2*;* N, 1731.

1368. F 81 N 167 S 96 M 224. *Date from Letters:* F *has* 1731–2*;* N, 1731.

1369. F 78 N 161 S 92 M 222. *Date from Letters:* F *has* 1731–2*;* N, 1731.

Domenichino] Dominiquin (MS.)

1370. F 78 N 161. *Date from Letters:* F *has* 1731–2*;* N, 1731.

Maratta] Marat (MS.)

1371. F 77 N 159 S 91 M 222. *Date from Letters:* F *has* 1731–2*;* N, 1731.

Maratta] Marat (MS.)

1372. F 81 N 167 S 95 M 224. *Date from Letters:* F *has* 1731–2; N, 1731.

1373. F 79 N 163 S 93. *Date from Letters:* F *has* 1731–2; N, 1731.

1374. F 77 N 159 S 90. *Date from Letters:* F *has* 1731–2; N, 1731.

1375. F 73 N 151 S 87. *Date from Letters:* F *has* 1731–2; N, 1731.

1376. F 73 N 151 S 87. *Date from Letters:* F *has* 1731–2; N, 1731.

1377. F 75 N 153 S 89. *Date from Letters:* F *has* 1731–2; N, 1731.
can never be unsuccessful] must allways be succesful (F *originally*)
The first two sentences of this anecdote occur in Spence's letters (2 Aug. 1732).

1378. F 79 N 163 S 93. *Date from Letters:* F *has* 1731–2; N, 1731.

1379. F 80 N 165 S 94. *Date from Letters:* F *has* 1731–2; N, 1731.
Preceding this anecdote in F *is a deleted fragment:* Old Trevisone was an apartment in the Palazzo dei [*word illegible*]

1380. F 71 N 147 S 84. *Date from Letters:* F *has* 1731–2; N, 1731.
Spence's pencilled marginal note reads: These from the Travelling Papers: Q Art: Rome. *Another pencilled note reads:* Ficoroni (from his Lead^{n}. Med^{ls})

1381. F 71 N 147 S 84. *Date from Letters:* F *has* 1731–2; N, 1731.
'Tis since . . . Capitol] *this is a later marginal addition by Spence in pencil and was intended to go* To Notes

1382. F 81 L 11 p. 9 N 167 S 96 M 224. *Date from Letters.*
ancient . . . tables] solid antique Pillars still remaining entire there, beside so many that have been cut for Tables (L)
When . . . glory] With all these, in their beauty, w^{t} a figure must Rome have made! (L)

1383. F 71 N 149 S 85. *Date from Letters:* F *has* 1731–2; N, 1731.
the fatal] that celebrated (F *originally*)
A pencilled marginal note in F *by Spence reads:* Q: in Vacca's acc^{t} (Harding?[)] p. 11 Art: 57 & the Roman History for ye place [*or* plans?].

1384. F 72 N 149 S 86. *Date from Letters:* F *has* 1731–2; N, 1731.
lies] lays (MS.)

1385. F 73 N 151 S 86. *Date from Letters:* F *has* 1731–2; N, 1731.

1386. F 77 N 159 S 91 M 221. *Date from Letters:* F *has* 1731–2; N, 1731.

1387. F 77 N 159 S 91. *Date from Letters:* F *has* 1731–2; N, 1731.
Spence deleted his own parenthetical remark at the end, so that it does not appear in N.

1388. F 74 N 153 S 88. *Date from Letters:* F *has* 1731–2; N, 1731.

1389. F 76 N 157 S 90. *Date from Letters:* F *has* 1731–2; N, 1731.

1390. F 78 N 161 S 92. *Date from Letters:* F *has* 1731–2; N, 1731.

1391. F 81 N 167 S 95 M 223. *Date from Letters: F has* 1731–2; N, 1731.

1392. F 78. *Date from Letters:* F *has* 1731–2.
The anecdote was crossed out by Spence and so does not appear in N.
the Invincible Messalina] Messalina the Unconquerable (*originally*)

1393. F 81 N 165 S 95. *Date from Letters:* F *has* 1731–2*;* N, 1731.

1394. F 80 N 165 S 94. *Date from Letters:* F *has* 1731–2*;* N, 1731.
large equestrian statues] Colossal statues (F *originally*)

1395. F 76 N 155. *Date from Letters:* F *has* 1731–2*;* N, 1731.

1396. F 76 L 11 p. 8 N 157 S 90. *Date from Letters.*
This is a revised version of the anecdote which Spence wrote in the margin of F *after crossing out the first somewhat shorter version.*

1397. F 71 L 11 p. 8 N 147 S 85. *Date from Letters.*
In L *the anecdote is attributed to the painter Knapton, following, and in the same paragraph as, the preceding anecdote. Spence was probably mistaken when, in transcribing in* F, *he assigned it to Ficoroni. However, the last sentence, which does not appear in* L, *might have come from Ficoroni.*
According to L, *Knapton named three Egyptian pieces, the third being* a Basso Relievo at Pal: Maffei.
Hercules . . . head] Hercules of Basalto (F *originally*)
were his own words] as he expressed it *pencilled above this phrase by Spence* (F).

1398. F 79 N 163 S 93 M 223. *Date from Letters:* F *has* 1731–2*;* N, 1731.
exclusive of] without (F *originally*)

1399. F 110 L 11 p. 9 N 205 S 112. *Date from Letters.*
The addition from Ficoroni was marked for the notes by Spence. L *has a significant variant. It begins:* Marforio usd to stand in y[e] Forum of Mars; he has now a good while been imprison'd in y[e] Capitol. The same Pope wou'd have imprison'd Pasquin too. . . .

1400. F 295 N 464 S 239. *Date from* F.

1401. F 298 N 470 S 243. *Date from* F.
Spence put the last sentence in a marginal note, replacing a briefer one which originally closed the anecdote.

1402. L 11 p. 8 S 342. *Date from Letters.*

1403. F 78 N 161 S 92 M 222. *Date from Letters:* F *gives* 1731–2*;* N, 1731.
F *indicates that Spence could not decide who the speaker was, for both names are deleted several times: see explanatory note.*

1404. F 80 N 165 S 94 M 223. *Date inferred from Spence's list of people met on the tours.* F *gives* 1731–2*;* N, 1731.
Spence at first attributed the anecdote to Ficoroni. He then deleted the name and wrote M[r] Philips.

1405. L 22. *Date inferred from* F (*see list of* MSS.).
L *is marked* P—— 1735 *but Pope is not involved in this, the first anecdote on the sheet.*

1406. F 95 L 11 pp. 5, 7 N 179 S 97 M 230. *Date from Letters.*
dissertation on their funerals] L *gives the Latin title:* De Funeribus Sinensium: Dissertatio Praelusoria
a treatise . . . God.] L *gives the French:* Que le charactere, Taô, signifie Le Dieu.
Spence's comment was written in the margin of F *and intended for the notes.*

1407. F 89 L 11 p. 6 N 171. *Date from Letters.*
several of them] many (L)

1408. L 11 p. 6 N 171. *Date from Letters.*

1409. F 90 L 11 p. 6 N 173. *Date from Letters.*
the most perfect system of morality] ye best regulation for ye mind of man (L)
and that . . . teach] (Plusieurs des plus grandes verités et misteres de notre Religion) That, & their other sacred writings, if we may believe this Missionary teach (F *originally*)
For the text of the letter in French given in F, *together with the introductory sentence, see Appendix to* §*1409.*

1410. F 96 L 11 p. 7 N 181. *Date from Letters.*
from the top . . . left] de droit en gauche; & de haut en bas (L)
A pencilled note in the margin of F, See ye Specimen of this, p: , *probably referred to the characters in the preceding anecdote.*

1411. F 96 L 11 p. 6 N 181. *Date from Letters.*

1412. F 96 L 11 p. 7 N 181. *Date from Letters.*

1413. F 97 L 11 p. 7 N 181. *Date from Letters.*
ninety years] *a pencilled note in the margin of* F *calls attention to the fact that* This was s^{d} in ye Year 1732.

1414. F 97 L 11 p. 7 N 183. *Date from Letters.*
the overseer of] ye man who had laboured at (L)
before . . . era] Ante X^{tum} (L)

1415. F 97 L 11 p. 7 N 183. *Date from Letters.*
carried] design'd (F *originally*)

1415a. L 11 p. 7. *Date from Letters.*

1416. F 121 N 231 S 130 M 257. *Dates for the following group* (§§1416–20) *from Letters:* F *and* N *have* 1733.
four stories] 4 story (MSS.)

1417. F 120 L 11 p. 9 N 229 S 128. *Date from Letters:* F *and* N *have* 1733.
Insertion from L.

1418. F 121 N 231 S 129 M 256. *Date from Letters:* F *and* N *have* 1733.

1419. F 121 N 231 S 129 M 257. *Date from Letters:* F *and* N *have* 1733.
ornamented] borrow'd (F *originally*).

1420. F 120 L 11 p. 4 N 229 S 129. *Date from Letters:* F *and* N *have* 1733.
The version in L *is in note form.*

1421. F 212 H 404 N 364 S 189. *Date from* F *and* N. *There is some confusion over the dating of this and the following anecdotes from Holdsworth*

(§§1421–8). *While* H *dates them* 1741, *both* F *and* N *give* 1738. *Both dates are possible ones: Spence met Holdsworth once more at Turin in 1741* (*Wright, p. 59*), *and Holdsworth, judging by Pope's letter to him in December 1737* (Corresp. *iv. 90*), *seems to have visited England* c. *1737–8. Consequently Spence's revised date in* F (1738) *has been accepted as correct.*

it. Others] it: & others (MSS.)

the country of the Taurini] H *continues:* but nearer Milan (He himself thought 'twas to the left, but not so far to the left.) *The parenthetical remark must be Spence's;* he himself *refers to Holdsworth.*

1422. F 212 H 406 N 364 S 189. *Date from* F *and* N*:* H *has* 1741.
[He]] who (MSS.)
In F *Spence pencilled in the margin:* Add? his obs[ervatio]ⁿ on Livy's acc[oun]ts

1423. H 406. *Date inferred from* F *and* N*:* H *has* 1741.
that . . . Polybius] H *read at first:* that translated Livy. *The present reading was pencilled on the opposite page as a correction from Lockier, who also identified the officer as* Folard.

1424. F 211 H 404 N 364 S 189. *Date from* F *and* N*:* H *has* 1741.

1425. F 213 H 406 N 366 S 190 M 298. *Date from* F *and* N*:* H *has* 1741.
on Monte Mario] *deleted in* F
one of his epigrams] F *and* H *both cite:* Lib. 1: Ep. 64. Ed: Mattaire *in a note;* H *adds a sentence after* epigrams *not in* F*:* The Epigram is addresd to one of his own name who had a Villa there.

1426. F 213 H 408 N 368 S 190 M 269. *Date from* F *and* N*:* H *has* 1741.
Insertion from H.

1427. F 213 H 408 N 368 S 190 M 269. *Date from* F *and* N*:* H *has* 1741.
Fucinus] H *continues:* (where he caught his Rheumatism)
invidia . . . intermissum] *Spence's note cites:* Suetonius; in Claud: C: 21.
thirty miles round] H *concludes with this sentence, which is attributed there to Holdsworth.*

1428. F 215 H 408 N 366 S 191 M 269. *Date from* F *and* N*:* H *has* 1741.
The Greeks] The Greeks of old (H)
turn] Genius (H)
F *has a note pencilled in the margin by Spence:* [to be Transposed.] before yᵉ 2 former arᵗˢ. *In* H *not the book but the author was unknown.*

1429. F 241 H 346 L 24 p. 2 S 206. *Date from* L (H *mistakenly gives* August 1739*;* F, 1739).
having shifted] misunderstanding (H, F *originally*)*;* mistaking (L)
In F *the anecdote is marked for omission. Insertion from* H *and* L. *The source of the anecdote is questionable.* F *read* Mr. T *originally. Then Spence crossed it out and wrote in pencil,* Mr. H?*; Spence apparently overlooked the* De Pr *which appears in* L *before the anecdote* (*instead of after, as is more usual*) *and which certainly belongs with this anecdote.* H *gives no source.*

1430. F 241 H 348 L 24 p. 2 S 207. *Date from* L (H *mistakenly gives* August 1739; F, 1739).

the blacks] ye Indians (L)

slashing their faces] L *adds* & limbs *which is, however, deleted.*

In F *the anecdote is marked for omission. Insertion from* H *where it is deleted.* L *has an earlier form. As in* §1429 *the source in* L *seems to be* De Pr. H *gives no source, and* F *again gives Holdsworth* (*i.e.* Dit. *referring to* Mr H? *in* §1429).

1431. F 283 H 386 L 28 p. 4 N 460 S 239 M 295. *Date from Letters.*

1432. F 283 H 388 L 28 p. 4 N 460 S 239 M 295. *Date from Letters.*

1433. F 283 H 386 L 28 pp. 3–4 N 460. *Date from Letters.*

L *opens with a jotting omitted from the text:* Sweat of my Brows; Action, of Costerna; *this is apparently unrelated to the exchange that follows. For the text in* H *see explanatory note.*

1434. F 283 H 388 N 460. *Date from Letters. In* H *this anecdote immediately precedes the section dated* June 1741.

the boys] the scholars (H)

Spence has a note opposite the text in H*:* The Printed List, if found, to Notes *It is missing in* N.

Insertions from H.

1435. F 300 TN 1 f. 22 N 472 S 245. *Date from Letters.*

Majesty] *underlined in* F

In TN *the anecdote runs:* The King has a pretty House & Garden at Portici (wch he likd & took from one of the Noblemen of Naples)

1436. TN 1 f. 22. *Date inferred from* §1435, *to which it forms a marginal note.*

For reference to a version of this, apparently derived from Spence, see explanatory note.

1437. H 392 L 29. *Date from* H.

a future life] something more (L)

1438. F 281 H 384 L 28 p. 3 N 456 S 237 M 292. *Date from Letters.*

devotion] *In* H *and* L *the French is used in the text: in* F *it is given as a marginal note* (*here put in brackets*)

bis, bis] F *has a marginal note:* The same as our, Encore!

Insertion from H *and* L. F *attributes the anecdote to* Sign^r N; Ab: Nicolini *occurs in* H *with a query.* L *attributes it to no-one.*

1439. F 281 L 28 p. 3 N 456 S 238 M 293. *Date from Letters.*

1440. F 281 H 386 L 28 p. 3 N 456 S 238 M 293. *Date from Letters.*

Perdona . . . quernos] *in* F *removed to margin.*

1441. F 281 H 384 L 28 p. 3 N 458 S 238 M 293. *Date from Letters.*

ombre] huomini *in margin of* H; uomini (F). *In* F *the Italian sentence is removed to the margin.*

1442. F 282 H 386 L 28 p. 3 N 458 S 239 M 294. *Date from Letters.*

The insertion is from H *and* L; *in* H *the first sentence reads:* The Spanish Ladies how warm, & how apt to take fire. *In* L *it reads:* The women how fiery & passionate.

1443. F 282 H 386 L 28 p. 3 N 458 S 239 M 294. *Date from Letters.*
Sono . . . her words] *this occurs in the margin of* F*;* H *and* L *give it instead of the English*

1444. F 282 N 458. *Date inferred from Letters.*
Mr. Coventry . . . *Hydaspes.*] *pencilled in the margin of* F

1445. F 283 H 386 L 28 p. 4 N 460. *Date from Letters.*
H *has a query after the word* first*;* L *reads simply* ye H Week. F *attributes this to* Signor N, *which is, however, deleted in pencil.*

1446. F 283 N 460. *Date inferred from Letters.*
F *attributes this to* Signor N, *which, is however, deleted in pencil.*

1447. H 386 L 28 p. 4. *Date from Letters.*
L *shows that the speaker was addressed as* '*Abate*'—Ab. Nicolini.

1448. F 295 N 464 S 240. *Date from* F.
at top] *to this Spence added a marginal note given here as the last sentence of the text.*
[. . .]] This (F, N)

1449. F 295 N 466 S 240. *Date from* F.

1450. F 295 N 464 S 240. *Date from* F.

1451. F 296 N 466 S 240. *Date from* F.

1452. F 296 N 466 S 241. *Date from* F.
of Hades] of the Hades (MS.)

1453. F 297 N 468 S 242. *Date from* F.
basin] bason (MS.)
giallo antique] *this semi-anglicized form was common in the eighteenth century* (OED).

1454. F 297 N 468 S 242. *Date from* F.

1455. F 298 N 470 S 243. *Date from* F.
holes in each] *followed in* F *by* for spiracula, *which Spence deleted*

1456. F 299 N 470. *Date from* F.
St. Peter's] *originally in* F *followed by* at Rome (*deleted*)
The court . . . Silvester] The Court, building & all, is not so much as 84f by 72 (F *originally*)
circuit of it should be] outline of it is (F *originally*)

1457. F 299 N 472 S 244. *Date from* F.
but ten oars] *originally followed by* on each side (F, *deleted*)

1458. F 301 N 474 S 244. *Date from* F.

1459. F 275 N 446 S 229. *Date from* F.
Coypel] *Spence spelled* Coypell*; he at first wrote* Rubens. *In the margin of* F *he pencilled* Q Coypell. *Then* Rubens *was deleted and* Coypell *written above in the text.*

1460. F 267 TN 2 f. 80^v^ S 221. *Date from* F.
The anecdote is crossed out by Spence, and a marginal note reads: Omitt^d^ here; to Travel^g^ P:^rs^. *In* TN 2 *the anecdote reads:* T'was at Pianoro, the first

Post House from Bologna, that there were those fine Remains of the Deluge: the great square stone all coverd with Shells in ye Chemin du Torrent: but falln from the sides of the Hill.

1461. F 301 N 474 S 245. *Date from* F.

1462. F 267 TN 2 f. 80v S 222. *Date from* F.
First sentence not in TN
saw the largest] could see the Principal (TN)
sun . . . foot] sun & appeard there, first like a great Candle thro' the Trees, & afterwards (as above the ground) about 3 ft (TN)
At the place . . . say] As they told us (TN)
ten feet long] TN *adds:* (half the Room)

1463. F 273 N 442 S 227. *Date from* F.

1464. F 273 N 444 S 228 M 29. *Date from* F.

1465. F 270 N 438 S 225. *Date from* F.
de' Medici] of Medici (MS.)
Victorious. If] victorious: & if (MS.)

1465a. F 274 N 444 S 228. *Date from* F.

1466. F 271 N 438 S 225. *Date from* F.
that at Rome] F *originally continued:* neither good, nor of certain authority.

1467. F 272 N 440 S 226 M 290. *Date from* F.
brought into Italy] *Spence has a marginal note in* F*:* In the year 1013, accg to Felibien. Vol: 1. p: 157.

1468. F 273 N 442 S 227 M 290. *Date from* F.

1469. F 98 L 11 p. 2 N 183 S 98 M 234. *Date from Letters.*
He is . . . similes] The beauty & particularity of his Similies. (L)
Insertion from L.

1470. L 11 p. 3. *Date from Letters.*

1471. F 98 L 11 p. 2 N 185 S 99 M 235. *Date from Letters.*

1472. F 99 L 11 p. 3 N 185 S 99. *Date from Letters.*
L *begins:* Petrarch the Top of the Lyrics. The dispute about preferring him or Chiabrera wholly on ye Lyric account.

1473. F 107 L 11 p. 12 N 201 S 109 M 245. *Date from Letters.*
The inserted passage is from L.

1474. F 99 L 11 p. 3 N 185 S 99 M 235. *Date from Letters.*

1475. F 103 L 11 p. 4 N 193 S 105 M 240. *Date from Letters.*
Spence's pencilled marginal note in F *reads:* Reference to his Letter Harln Miscy 1 (or Quotations from it, if not in his works.) Rather, to Appx?

1476. F 103 L 11 p. 4 N 193 S 105 M 241. *Date from Letters.*
Machiavelli] *spelled throughout* Machiavel

1477. F 103 L 11 p. 4 N 193 S 105 M 241. *Date from Letters.*

1478. F 99 L 11 p. 3 N 187 S 100 M 236. *Date from Letters.*

1479. F 99 L 11 p. 3 N 187 S 100 M 236. *Date from Letters.*
the greatest wits] ye cleverest people there (L)
In L, *which has a number of additions in the margin, later incorporated into* F, *a note reads:* These additions, inserted when it was read over to ye Dr?

1480. F 100 L 11 p. 3 N 187 S 100 M 236. *Date from Letters.*

1481. F 106 L 11 p. 11 N 199 S 108 M 243. *Date from Letters.*
For differences in L *see explanatory note.*

1482. F 106 L 11 p. 10 N 197 S 108 M 242. *Date from Letters.*
by Tirsi] *pencilled in the margin of* F *against this is:* (or, of?) Q

1483. F 100 L 11 p. 3 N 187 S 101. *Date from Letters.*

1484. F 100 L 11 p. 3 N 189 S 102. *Date from Letters.*
Insertion from L. *After the Italian in* L (*where the anecdote occurs as a marginal note*) *is the jotting:* March: look his des: of Trg all Lucr: &c.

1485. F 100 L 11 p. 3 N 187 S 101. *Date from Letters.*

1486. F 100 L 11 p. 3 N 189 S 101 M 237. *Date from Letters.*
mixed language] strange language (L); L *continues:* Fol: calls himself Merlin Coccrius.
the *Fidenzian*] *above this in* L *is inserted:* invented by Camillo Stroga Coll. V. 73.

1487. F 100 L 11 p. 3 N 189 S 102 M 237. *Date from Letters.*
L *begins:* There's a late Heriocomical Poem, by Lippi, the Painter, very good.

1488. F 108 L 11 p. 12 N 201 S 111 M 245. *Date from Letters.*
Insertion from L.

1489. F 108 L 11 p. 12 N 201 S 109. *Date from Letters.*

1490. F 101 L 11 p. 3 N 189 S 102 M 237. *Date from Letters.*
L *has in the margin:* il Mauro a scritto di cose basse in stilo gentile mediocre
Spence pencilled in the margin of F: Q *Il.* Mauro
The final sentence is from L.
Remark in explanatory note from L 11 p. 12.

1491. L 11 pp. 11–12. *Date from Letters.*

1492. L 11 p. 12. *Date from Letters.*
For the Italian dialogue see explanatory note.

1493. F 101 L 11 p. 4 N 189 S 102 M 238. *Date from Letters.*
For an added detail given in L, *see explanatory note.*

1494. F 102 L 11 p. 4 N 191 S 103 M 239. *Date from Letters.*

1495. F 104 L 11 p. 4 N 195 S 106. *Date from Letters.*

1496. F 106 L 11 p. 5 N 197 S 108 M 242. *Date from Letters.*

1497. F 104 L 11 pp. 4–5 N 195 S 106 M 242. *Date from Letters.*

1498. F 105 L 11 p. 5 N 195 S 107. *Date from Letters.*
L *adds* Urb. 8 *at end.*

1499. F 104 L 11 p. 5 N 195 S 107. *Date from Letters.*
further] farther (MSS.)

1500. F 105 L 11 p. 5 N 197 S 107 M 159. *Date from Letters.*
judiciary] judicial (L, F *originally*)
L *has the sentence about Newton first, and the opening sentence there reads:* Bad things may have a good effect (L).

1501. F 105 L 11 p. 5 N 197 S 107 M 160. *Date from Letters.*
in any other country] *deleted in* L, *and replaced by* in other countrys
F *has a marginal note in pencil by Spence:* Q w^{n} ye D^{r} was in Engl^{d}? for Notes.

1502. F 105 L 11 p. 5 N 197 S 107 M 160. *Date from Letters.*
[Cocchi]] who (MSS.)
The comment by Spence is crossed out in F *and* Omit *written in the margin.*
for the matter] for any great matter (F *originally*)
In the margin of L *is written:* His Phys: Adversaria in C's hands, given him by Coste. The only Recipe I saw there of his own was a Cure for ye C^{bs}.

1503. L 11 p. 5 *Date from Letters.*

1504. L 11 p. 5. *Date from Letters.*
I'm] I'me only (*originally*)

1504a. L 11 p. 5. *Date from Letters.*
think] *originally followed by* Dr Clarke *but deleted*

1505. F 108 L 11 p. 14 N 201 S 111 M 245. *Date from Letters.*
She is] they are (F)
her] their (F)
L *gives a reminder only.*

1505a. F 107 L 11 p. 10 N 201 S 109. *Date from Letters.*

1506. F 108 L 11 p. 14 N 203 S 111. *Date from Letters.*
barbarous Latin translation] Latino-Barbaro translation (L)
five or six] abt 6 (L)
Insertion from margin of F.

1507. F 107 L 11 p. 9. *Date from Letters.*
as infections] being catching (L)
woman . . . herself] woman takes, infects, & escapes (L)
epigram] Cotemp: Gr: Epigram (L)
providing for] helping (L)

1508. F 106 L 11 p. 9. *Date from Letters.*
L *begins:* There's no dispute but that the greatest Physicians in Italy (some time after ye discovery of America) looked on the Pox as a New Thing: The only Question was . . ., *etc.* (L)
Insertion from L.

1509. F 109 L 11 p. 4 N 203 S 112 M 246. *Date from Letters.*
any passage] several passages (F *originally*)
L *contains the additional information that the paraphrase was written* in Theod: Gaza's own hand

1510. F 109 L 11 p. 14 N 203 S 111 M 246. *Date from Letters.*
catenas] *as often, Spence anglicizes the plural. The Italian is* '*catene*'.

1511. L 11 p. 4. *Date from Letters.*

1512. F 108 L 11 p. 12 N 201 S 110 M 245. *Date from Letters.*

1513. F 102 L 11 p. 12 N 191 S 104 M 239. *Date from Letters.*

1514. F 102 L 11 p. 12 N 191 S 104 M 240. *Date from Letters.*
Hill's comment was originally written in pencil in the margin by Singer; Singer erased it and inked in the note in his own hand (Spence's note is now virtually illegible). Singer printed it as a Note by Mr. Spence from papers *which in this instance refers to* F. *The comment must have been added after 1753 when Spence first met Hill.*

1515. F 103 L 11 p. 5 N 193 S 104 M 240. *Date from Letters.*
In L *this and the following anecdote occur together, under the heading:* Derivations of some Engl: Phrases.

1516. F 102 L 11 p. 5 N 193 S 104 M 240. *Date from Letters.*

1517. L 11 p. 10. *Date from Letters.*
Spence does not make clear whether the last sentence was spoken by Shaw or Cocchi.

1517a. L 11 p. 10. *Date from Letters.*

1518. F 101 L 11 pp. 3–4 N 191 S 103 M 238. *Date from Letters.*
Perfetti *is not mentioned by name in* L.

1519. F 114 N 213 S 117 M 249. *Date from Letters* (F *gives* 1733).
as I could think of] as I pleasd (F *originally*)
guitarers] *Singer inserts* (*Suonatori*)*; his source may have been* MS. B.
what he calls] F *has a pencilled marginal note by Spence:* Virgil's Ecl: 7, 18

1520. F 113 L 11 p. 12 N 211 S 116 M 248. *Date from Letters.*
Spence deleted his comment after Vanneschi's name in F.

1521. F 116 L 11 p. 12 N 215 S 119 M 251. *Date from Letters.*
Tuscany . . . poetry] Tuscany is the great Place for Improviso: (they call it ye only one.) (L)

1522. F 116 L 11 p. 12 N 215 S 120 M 251. *Date from Letters.*
Perfetti . . . and] L *begins:* Perfetti di Sienna, a Cavalier of S. Stefano
improvvisatore] improvisoer (MSS.)
in the Capitol] in the Campidoglio (L)
the Pope] the late Pope (L)
He had . . . language] A una grande infarinatura di tutte le scienze: una fluidità struordinaria (L)
The last sentence was added in the margin of F. *In* L *it occurs in connexion with the following anecdote, and is preceded by a passage which reads:* They always improviso to Music, (wch hides ye breaks, & gives 'em time,) but Perfetti. . . ., *&c.*

1523. F 116 L 11 p. 13 N 215 S 120 M 252. *Date from Letters.*
Insertions from L.
L *adds a further detail:* The Folia di Sienna is a late tune

1524. F 115 L 11 p. 12 N 211 S 119 M 251. *Date from Letters.*
Settignano] Settimiano (MSS.)
When . . . particular] When they want to get the better much, they do it (something like our Crambo) by flinging in a very hard rhime (L)

1525. F 118 L 11 p. 13 N 217 S 122 M 253. *Date from Letters.*
Manfredi *is mentioned in* L *only.*
VANNESCHI] L *shows by the use of* Id. *that he was the source of this anecdote, but in* F *Spence attributed it to Crudeli. His mistake may have been due to the fact that another remark by Crudeli is quoted in the margin of* L *just at this point.*

1526. F 118 L 11 p. 13 N 217 S 122. *Date from Letters.*
low and tasteless] low, secs, & indifferens (L)
Like the preceding anecdote, the speaker may have been Crudeli instead of Vanneschi.

1527. F 117 L 11 p. 12 N 217 S 122 M 253. *Date from Letters.*
F *attributes this to Crudeli, but* L *shows that it comes from Vanneschi.*

1528. F 117 L 11 p. 12 N 217 S 122 M 253. *Date from Letters.*
F *attributes this to Crudeli, but* L *shows that it comes from Vanneschi.*
The insertions are from L.

1529. F 118 L 11 p. 13 N 219 S 122 M 254. *Date from Letters.*
F *attributes this anecdote to Crudeli, but* L *shows it to have come from two sources.* L *reads:* Salvini's Absences, Slovenlyness, & Notes on ye Sides of his Classics. Id. [*Vanneschi*]. *In the margin is written:* Je ne veux pas mourir absolument. Crud:)
odd sort] negligent sort (F *originally*)

1530. F 116 L 11 pp. 12–13 N 215 S 120 M 252. *Date from Letters.*
F *attributes this to Crudeli, but* L *shows that it comes from Vanneschi.*
Montanto] Montaiuti (MSS.)

1531. F 117 L 11 p. 13 N 217 S 121. *Date from Letters.*
F *attributes this to Crudeli, but* L *shows that it comes from Vanneschi.*
Montanto] Montaiuti (MSS.)

1532. F 117 L 11 p. 3 N 217 S 121. *Date from Letters.*
a constant] everywhere (F *originally*)
The second sentence reads in L*:* He is an Imitator of Chiabrera par tout. Plus gracieux; mais non pas avec tant de Grandeur, ni tant de Majesté, ni tant d'esprit.
The source of this anecdote is not clear. In L *Vanneschi is given as the speaker for the preceding anecdotes. This and* §1534 *form the beginning of a new paragraph, and are followed by* §1526*: this is followed by* Crud:, *which, however, seems to refer to the ensuing anecdotes, beginning with* §1546. F *gives both* §§1532 *and* 1534 *to Crudeli, but Spence had already erred in* §1525 (*which immediately precedes this anecdote in the* MS.).

1533. F 117 L 11 p. 13 N 217 S 121 M 253. *Date from* F.
L *gives the insertion and attributes the anecdote to Vanneschi.* F *gives it to Crudeli.*

1534. F 118 L 11 p. 13 N 219 S 122 M 254. *Date from Letters.*
A gentleman of Florence] A Florentine (L)
cried out] F *originally continued:* in great wrath against the author (*deleted*)
Oh . . . barbarisms!] Oh ho!, ces sont des Lombardismes! (L); *see explanatory note for alterations to* F.
The source of the anecdote is not clear.
See textual note §1532.

1535. F 111 L 11 p. 10 N 207 S 113 M 247. *Date from Letters.*
Querno . . . couplet] L *omits, and following the couplet has:* Was ye beginning? of an Epigram made by him

1536. F 113 L 11 p. 11 N 209 S 116 M 248. *Date from Letters.*
In L *Spence's comment begins:* I was offered at Venice to have a Gondolier brought me, who cd. . . .

1537. F 113 L 11 p. 11 N 211 S 116. *Date from Letters.*

1538. F 117 L 11 p. 11 N 217 S 120 M 253. *Date from Letters.*

1539. F 117 L 11 p. 11 N 217 S 121. *Date from Letters.*
Spence garbled the first line, and wrote it as: Ed il guerrier, qui non s'en era accorto.

1540. F 111 L 11 p. 10 N 207 M 248. *Date from Letters.*
study . . . things] don't understand *things* (L)

1541. F 109 L 11 p. 13 N 205 S 112 M 246. *Date from Letters.*
There were] MSS. *read* There was
for acting] for singing (L)
This is the first anecdote in F *for the year 1733.*
L *gives the source of the anecdote as* Co., *and after it comes Spence's query,* S[houl]^d^ be Cr? *Below this is another note,* for Cocchi bef[ore] is alw[ay]^s^ D^r^. C &c. *Spence decided on Crudeli when he wrote the anecdote in* F.

1542. L 11 p. 13 F 117 N 217 S 122 M 253. *Date from Letters.*
The text is based on the earliest MS. *to preserve the original dialogue. The insertion is from* F *which reads:* Metastasio, tho' much the best for Operas, blames that way of writing; but shrugs up his shoulders, & says; "You know, One must get Money!' *Vanneschi's remark occurs in* L *in the body of anecdotes attributed to him: Crudeli's remark* (*signed* Crud:) *is written as a marginal note.*

1543. F 112 L 11 p. 11 N 209 S 115 M 185. *Date from Letters.*
wore the *petit collet*] *so in* L; *in* F *Spence drew a line through it and substituted the words in pencil,* was an Abbé

1544. F 110 L 11 p. 10 N 207 S 113 M 247. *Date from Letters.*

1545. F 110 L 11 p. 10 N 207 S 113. *Date from Letters.*
by the best judges] by Connoisseurs (L)

1546. F 119 L 11 p. 13 N 219 S 123. *Date from Letters.*

1547. L 11 p. 13. *Date from Letters.*

1548. L 11 p. 13. *Date from Letters.*
Stosch] *Spence spells* Stosche

1549. F 119 L 11 p. 13 N 219 S 123 M 255. *Date from Letters.*
knowledge] Virtù (L)

1550. F 119 L 11 p. 14 N 221 S 123. *Date from Letters.*
L *begins:* The Etymological Dictionary, written by a Spanish Abbé. . . .

1551. F 127 N 221 S 124 M 255. *Date from Letters.*
See explanatory note.

1552. F 119 L 11 p. 13 N 219 S 123 M 254. *Date from Letters.*
The opening sentence is from L.

1553. F 271 N 438 S 225. *Date from* F.

1554. F 110 L 11 p. 9 N 205 S 112 M 247. *Date from Letters.*
L *reads:* The good Taste for Building, continu'd frō Augustus to Septimius Severus. Fic.—In Medals, to Adrian. B^{n} Stoche.

1555. L 11 p. 9. *Date from Letters.*

1556. F 269 H 368 L 28 p. 1 N 434 S 223. *Date from* L.
nobleman] Gentleman (L)
on his travels] in his Tour (L)
a man] an agreeable man (H, L)
agreeable fools] an agreeable Fool (H, L)
On Singer's false ascription of this and following anecdotes to 'Lady Oxford', *see explanatory note.*

1557. F 269 H 372 L 28 p. 2 N 436 S 223. *Date from* L.

1558. H 368 L 28 p. 1. *Date from* L.
be coward] have cowardice (L)

1559. F 270 H 370 L 28 p. 1 N 436 S 224. *Date from* H.
Lady Mary's] that lady's (F)*;* H *and* L *give her name, though in* H *it is pencilled out and* most Ladies *substituted.*
romances and novels] *in* F *this is in the margin and is marked for the notes; in* H *and* L *it is in the text.*
The second paragraph is a separate anecdote in F. *The combination of the two, however, occurs in* H *and* L.

1560. H 370 L 28 p. 1. *Date from* L.

1561. F 269 H 368 L 28 p. 1 N 434 S 223. *Date from* L.

1562. F 268 H 370 L 28 pp. 1–2 N 434 S 222. *Date from* L.
Insertion from H. *It also occurs in* L. *In* F *Spence made it a separate anecdote which he changed to read,* One can't be sensible in this Country with impunity (Speaking of Italy in general). *Singer tacked on the deleted version at the end of this anecdote, but the logical context of* H *and* L *is preferable.*
When one . . . knowledge] With all this, I rather wonder how there comes to be so much knowledge (H *and* L)

1563. F 268 H 368 L 28 p. 1 N 434 S 223. *Date from* L.

1564. F 270 H 368 L 28 p. 1 N 436 S 224 M 289. *Date from* L.

1565. F 270 H 368 L 28 p. 1 N 436 S 224. *Date from* L.
Singer combined this and the preceding anecdote without any justification.

1566. F 269 H 372 L 28 p. 2 N 436 S 224 M 289. *Date from* L.

1566a. F 270 H 370 L 28 p. 1 N 438 S 224. *Date from* L.
such] so (L)

1567. F 270 H 368 L 28 p. 1 N 436 S 224. *Date from* L.
Boccaccio] Boccace (MSS.)
novelle] novell (F *and* H); novel (L)

1568. H 372 F 269 L 28 p. 2. *Date from* L.
F *is so heavily deleted as to be illegible without the assistance of* H *or* L. *The text seems to be identical with* H.

1569. L 11 p. 10. *Date from Letters.*

1570. L 11 p. 10. *Date from Letters.*

1571. F 274 N 446 S 229 M 291. *Date from Letters* (*see headnote to* §1571).

1572. F 274 N 444 S 228. *Date from Letters* (*see headnote to* §1571).

1573. F 275 N 446 S 229 M 292. *Date from Letters* (*see headnote to* §1571).

1574. F 275 N 446 S 229 M 292. *Date from Letters* (*see headnote to* §1571).
taste] good taste (F *originally*)
pretty good] *in* F *followed by faint superscript* one

1575. F 275 N 446 S 229. *Date from Letters* (*see headnote to* §1571).

1576. F 274 N 444 S 228. *Date from Letters* (*see headnote to* §1571).
head] *this or some other word was omitted in* F; *some pencil scribbling between the lines is illegible. In* N *the copyist inserted* head.

1577. F 274 N 444 S 228. *Date from Letters* (*see headnote to* §1571).
Sansovino] Sansovin (MS.)

1578. F 274 N 444 S 228. *Date from Letters* (*see headnote to* §1571).

1579. F 273 N 442 S 227 M 291. *Date from Letters* (*see headnote to* §1571).
Maratta] Marat (MS.)
Correggio's] *for Spence's marginal note to this word* (*printed in* M *but not in* S), *see the explanatory note.*

1580. F 129 N 227 S 127. *Date from* F.
Spence's pencilled marginal note at the beginning cites: Aen: 8, 603.
Caere] Caeris (MS.)
Cerveteri] Cervetere (MS.)

1581. F 129 N 227 S 127. *Date from* F.

1582. F 129 N 225. *Date from* F.

1583. L 20.

1584. L 20.

1585. L 20.
The text reads: Fr Pol. gr^{t}. Mon. Lew 11 & establisht by L 14.

1586. F 263 TN 2 f. 74v–75v N 426. *Date from* F.
For additional details given by TN, *see explanatory note.*

1587. F 264 TN 2 f. 75v N 428. *Date from* F.
dilatoriness] delay (TN)
in order for] as intending (TN)
deferred . . . summer] drew off their troops for the present (TN)
In that interval] On this Notice (TN)
drew the siege] run out the Siege (TN)
join him] beat them (TN)
together again] TN *adds:* in their Entrenchments

1588. F 264 TN 2 f. 75v–76 N 428. *Date from* F.
In TN *the anecdote is preceded by the following sentence:* The Spirit that is ye most general in Turin at present is that of War. Their Situation has almost always oblig'd them to be on their Guard; & the late Reign . . ., *&c.*
Greater Powers] TN *adds:* out of Italy
Or . . . Greater Powers] *In* TN *the original wording is:* As so many of the States in Italy are either in the Possession or under the Protection of the Greater Powers; they must watch their occasions, when the Greater Powers are embroil'd; & join with one, to gain ground on the other.

1589. F 265 TN 2 f. 76 N 430 S 220. *Date from* F.
It was to have . . . to this day] *These two sentences are in a marginal note in* F
taste . . . chilled] Taste for these sort of things was quite lost among them (TN)
this . . . Statues'] *a marginal note in* F*:* TN *has* which the gentleman who told me of it called, Le Cimitiere des Statues

1590. F 265 TN 2 f. 77v N 430 S 219. *Date from* F.
It was . . . who] 'Twas . . . that (TN)
the Cardinal of Savoy] TN *continues:* & is now safe in this place: tho' Montfaucon, it seems, did not happen to meet with it whilst he was at Turin.
relievos at Rome] rilievos that I have seen at Rome (TN)
compartments] compartiments (MSS.)
you see . . . sell it] there would have been more had not the soldiers cleard several places of it to sell it (TN)

1591. H 366.

1592. H 366.

1593. H 366.
guardi] *Spence wrote* guarde *with a question mark over the* 'e'.

1594. H 366.
Opposite the anecdote Spence wrote: the Queries ansd by Dom Villa, Richa, & Mr Villette?—to Letters. *Above this, in pencil, he added:* Many things here from them, etc.

1595. F 259 H 366 N 418. *Date from* H.
'La . . . words] *in* F *this is given as a marginal note.* H *does not identify Richa, and the French takes the place of the first sentence.*

1596. F 259 N 420. *Date from* F.
Spence's source of information was given at first as: C. R. – M^r V— & M^r D V. *This was cancelled and* Count Richa —&c. *substituted.*

1597. F 260 N 420. *Date from* F.
The list of provinces appears in Spence's marginal note.

1598. F 259 N 418. *Date from* F.
[Count Richa]] who (MSS.)
The first . . . 1729.] *Spence wrote this as a note in the margin*
Piedmont] *here and hereafter Spence spells* Piemont

1599. F 260 N 420. *Date from* F.
The bracketed sums are marginal notes in F.

1600. F 260 N 422. *Date from* F.

1601. F 261 N 424. *Date from* F.

1602. F 261 N 422. *Date from* F.

1603. F 266 N 432 S 221. *Date from* F.
The parenthetical phrase is from Spence's marginal note.

1604. H 366.
For Spence's interlinear annotation, see explanatory note.

1605. L 20.
L *has* Neg^r? *in parentheses preceding the anecdote.*
security] *followed by a query in* L.
when they came to sign] L *uses the present tense. The present tense is retained by the editor when it adds colour to a story, but not when it is disconcertingly bad grammar.*

1606. H 366.

1607. 1756 MB p. 16.
Singer added this inscription to that quoted in §1608.
Placentia] *Piacenza in modern Italian*

1608. 1756 MB pp. 9 *and* 16 S 368. *Date from* MB.
The first part from Massingberd appears on p. 9 of the MB, *while Dr. Lowth's translation is on p. 16.*
MASSINGBERD] (Mr Mass^ds Mss Travels. conf[irme]d by Dr Lowth.) (MB)
all the Trinity] *the* MB *has, tautologically,* all the whole Trinity

1609. F 302 H 390 L 29 N 476 S 246 M 297. *Date from* H.
malinconico] melanconico (MSS.)
Insertion from H. L *has brief hints of the anecdote, including the passage in* H.

1610. F 302 H 390 N 476 S 246 M 297. *Date from* H.

1611. F 302 H 390 L 29 N 476 S 246 M 297. *Date from* H.
For details added at the beginning of H, *see explanatory note.*
L *has brief hints of the anecdote.*

1612. H 392 L 29. *Date from* H.

1613. F 303 H 392 L 29 N 478 S 247. *Date from* H.
si valentuomini] F *has* si valenthuomini *in the margin,* H *and* L *in the text.*

1614. F 303 H 392 L 29 N 478 S 247. *Date from* H.
The French is in the margin of F, *and marked* To Notes. H *usea he French in the text itself.*

1615. F 303 H 392 L 29 N 478 S 247. *Date from* H.
a very good piece] F *has* brave *in the margin: this is in the text of* H *and* L.

1616. F 303 H 392 L 29 N 478 S 247. *Date from* H.

1617. F 303 H 392 L 29 N 476 S 247. *Date from* H.
H *has only the equivalent of the first sentence.* L *reads:* Miniature: imitative in everything: first Opera; Concerto.

1618. H 392 F 303 L 29 N 478 S 247. *Date from* H.
For variants see explanatory note.

1619. F 302 H 390 L 29 N 476 S 246. *Date from* H.
F *omits the lady's name, but it appears in* H.
Insertion from L *and* H.

LIST OF CONTRIBUTORS TO *ANECDOTES*

[New anecdotes are numbered in italics]

Anon.: *Anecdotes from*, *951*, *996*, *1053*, *1605*.

A., Dr. (unident.; for three possible candidates see 1042 n.): *Anecdote from*, *1042*.

A., Mr. R. (possibly Robert Arbuthnot, brother of Dr. John): *Anecdote from*, 344.

Addison, Joseph, 1672–1719, essayist and critic: *Anecdote from*, 853 (or Thomas Tickell, reported by Dr. Young).

Allen, Catherine, wife of Edward: *Anecdote from*, *1436*.

Allen, Edward, British Consul at Naples *c.* 1737–53: *Anecdote from*, 1435.

Annesley (? Martin, 1704?–49): *Anecdotes from*, *773–4*, *881*.

Arbuthnot, Anne, daughter of Dr. John, close friend of Pope: *Anecdotes from*, 328, 371, 375, *917*.

Arbuthnot, Dr. John, 1667–1735, physician and wit: *Anecdote from*, 916.

Arbuthnot, Robert: *see* A., Mr. R.

Arles, Archbishop of: *see* FORBIN-JANSON, Jacques de.

Armstrong, Dr. John, 1709?–79: *comment upon anecdote*, 503.

Atwell, Joseph, *fl.* 1733; *Anecdote via*, *996* (from Mr. —, recorded by John Conybeare).

B., The: *see* WILLIS, Richard, Bishop of Winchester.

Baillardeau, ?, *c.* 1655– still living 1727, Huguenot antiquary: *Anecdotes from*, *1023*, 1024.

Bathurst, Allen, 1684–1775, 1st Earl of Bathurst, friend of Pope: *Anecdotes from*, *784*, *918–21*.

Benson, William, 1682–1754, minor politician and patron of poetry: *Anecdotes from*, 922, *923–4*, 925–8.

Betterton, Thomas, 1635?–1710, actor: *Anecdotes from*, 475 (? reported by Pope), 783 (reported by Dr. Joseph Trapp).

Bianchi, Francesco, 1670–1752, br. of Sebastian: *Anecdotes from*, *1569–70*; *comment upon anecdote*, 1463 (?).

Bianchi, Sebastian, 1662–1738, a keeper in the Grand Duke's Gallery (i.e. the Uffizi), Florence: *Anecdotes from*, 1571, 1572 (with Baron Stosch), 1573–9.

Blacklock, Dr. Thomas, 1721–91, blind poet of Dumfries: *Anecdotes from*, *1148–54*, *1156–7*.

Blount, John Pope (1707–34): *Anecdotes from*, *208–208a*, *351*, 872.

Blount, Martha, 1690–1762, Pope's friend: *Anecdotes from*, 12, 13, 101, 284, 287, 355 (with Spence), 358–61, 409; *comments upon anecdotes*, 6, 44.

Boileau, Abbé at Blois (unident.): *Anecdotes from*, 824, 831, 1246, 1343–5.

Bonvalet, M., of Blois (unident.): *Anecdote from*, *1339*.

Bowman, Walter, d. 1782, Scottish traveller and antiquarian: *Anecdotes from*, *1583–5*.

Brandreth, John, 1695–1765, Fellow of Trinity College, Cambridge: *Anecdote recorded by*, 1034 (from Pr[io]r Greg).

Brideoak, Rev. Ralph, Archdeacon of Windsor: *Comment upon anecdote*, *1013*.

Browne, Patrick, 1720?–90, naturalist: *Anecdotes from*, 1048–9.

Budgell, Eustace, 1686–1737, journalist: *Anecdote from*, *834* (reported by Rev. John Jones).

C.: *see* CONYBEARE, John.

Carriera, Rosalba, 1675–1757, Venetian pastel portraitist: *Anecdotes from*, 1609–11, *1612*, 1613–19.

Ch.: *see* CHUBB, Thomas.

Cheselden, Dr. William, 1688–1752, surgeon: *Anecdotes from*, 252, *326*, *488a* (with Pope), 639, *929–35*, 936, *937*.

Chesterfield, 4th Earl of: *see* STANHOPE, Philip Dormer.

Cheyney, Thomas, 1694–1760, Fellow of New College, later Dean of Lincoln and Winchester: *Anecdotes from*, 807, *808*.

Chubb, Thomas, 1679–1747, self-taught deist: *Anecdotes from*, *965*, *967–76*, *977* (?).

Chute, Francis, d. 1745, minor poet and friend of Spence: *Anecdotes from*, 806, 825–6, 876, *1035–6*, 1037 (from William Nichols).

Cibber, Colley, 1671–1757, dramatist and actor: *Anecdotes from*, 235, 253, 896–8, *899–900*, *902* (recorded by Dr. Gilbert West).

Clark, Mr.: *see* CLARKE, Thomas.

Clarke, Dr. Alured, 1696–1742, chaplain-in-ordinary to George II: *Anecdotes from*, 1038–9.

Clarke, Charles, d. 1750, brother of Dr. Alured, later judge of the Exchequer: *Anecdote from*, 1040.

Clarke, Thomas, Esq., subscriber to *Polymetis* (otherwise unident.): *Anecdote possibly from*, 1302.

Cocchi, Dr. Antonio, 1665–1758, Florentine physician and friend of Spence: *Anecdotes from*, *804* (from Edward Holdsworth), 1399, 1469, *1470*, 1471–90, *1491–2*, 1493–1502, *1503–4a*, 1505–6, *1507–8*, 1509–16, *1517–17a*, 1518.

Cole, Capt. [? William, d. 1769]: *Anecdote from*, *1326*.

Colonia, Père Dominique de, 1660–1741, Jesuit librarian and author of Lyons: *Anecdotes from*, 1303, *1304*, 1305.

Colvil, Abbé, of Tours (otherwise unident.): *Anecdotes from*, 1346, *1347*, 1348–50.

Congreve, William, 1670–1729, dramatist: *Anecdote from a letter of*, 242.

Conybeare, John, 1692–1755, Fellow of Exeter College, later Bishop of Bristol: *Anecdotes from*, 983, *984–6*, *987* (?), *988a–90*, *992–5*, *996* (from Joseph Atwell from Mr. —), 997, 998 (recorded by Francis Hare, Bishop of Chichester).

Cotterell, Sir Clement, 1685–1758, courtier: *comment upon anecdote*, 492.

Cowper, Spencer, 1713–74, Dean of Durham: *Anecdote from*, 805.

Cramer, Jean, 1701–87, law professor of Geneva: *Anecdotes from*, 1314–17.

Cristoferi, Pietro Paolo de', 1685–1743, mosaic artist at St. Peter's: *Anecdote from*, 1376 (with Francesco Ficoroni).

Crudeli, Tommaso, 1703–45, Italian poet: *Anecdotes from*, 1535–41, 1543–6, *1547*; *comments upon anecdotes*, 1529, 1542.

Curé at a *bastide* near Nice (unident.): *Anecdote from*, 857 (reported by Dr. Young).

Dennis, John, 1657–1734, critic: *Anecdotes from*, 786, 790–2.

De Pr. (unident.), Oxford acquaintance of Spence: *Anecdotes from*, *999–1009*, 1031 (with Dr. William King), 1429–30 (or Edward Holdsworth).

Derham, William, 1702–57, Fellow and later president of St. John's College, Oxford: *Anecdote from*, 766.

Dodsley, Robert, 1703–64, bookseller, dramatist, poet, and friend of Spence: *Anecdote from*, *1155*.

Dorset, 2nd Duke of: *see* SACKVILLE, Charles.

Drummond, Mary, d. 1777, Quaker preacher: *Anecdotes from*, 979–82.

Drummond, Robert Hay: *see* HAY, Robert.

Fanshaw, Rev. John, d. 1763, later Regius Professor of Greek, Oxford: *Anecdotes from*, 1033, *1239* (? this may derive from Simon Fanshawe, q.v.).

Fanshawe, Simon, d. 1765, a subscriber to *Polymetis*: *Anecdote possibly from*, *1239* (? this may derive from John Fanshaw, q.v.).

Felton, Dr. Henry, 1679–1740, divine and Principal of St. Edmund Hall, Oxford: *Anecdote from*, 1032 (recorded by John Hudson).

Stanhope, Charles, 1673–1721, 1st Earl: *Anecdotes from*, *1020–1* (?).

Stanhope, Philip Dormer, 1694–1773, 4th Earl of Chesterfield, statesman: *Anecdotes from*, 1043–4, *1045*.

Stosch, Baron Philip von, 1691–1757, collector and British secret agent in Rome and Florence (*see* Walpole, *Corresp.* xvii, 9 n. 31): *Anecdotes from*, *1548*, 1549–53, 1554 (with Francesco Ficoroni), *1555*, 1572 (with Sebastian Bianchi).

Swift, Dr. Jonathan, 1667–1745, satirist: *Anecdote from*, 387.

T., Mr. (unident.; *see* pp. 660–1): *Anecdotes from*, 1448–55, *1456*, 1457–68; for further remarks by Mr. T. on Horace see Appendix (pp. 662–79), Nos. *1–46*.

Thomson, James, 1700–48, poet: *Anecdotes from*, *789* (?), *944*(?)*–5*.

Tickell, Thomas, 1686–1740, poet: *Anecdote from*, 853 (or Addison, reported by Dr. Young).

T^k^, Mr. (unident.): *Anecdote from*, *880*, *1014*.

Tonson, Jacob, sr. (1656 ?–1736), publisher: *Anecdotes from*, 118 (with Pope), 120, 155–6 (with Pope), 184 (with Pope), 185, 785, 814, 817.

Towneley, Mr.: *Anecdote from*, 800.

Trapp, Dr. Joseph, 1679–1747, poet and pamphleteer: *Anecdote from*, 783 (from Betterton).

Vanneschi, Abbé Francesco, *fl.* 1732–56, *improvvisatore*, and later, opera impresario in England: *Anecdotes from*, 1520–34, 1542.

Venuti, Cavaliere Niccolò, 1700–55, antiquarian: *Anecdotes from*, 1580–1.

Villa, Dom, archivist of Royal Academy, Turin (otherwise unident.): *Anecdotes from*, *1586–8*, 1589–90, *1591*, *1596* (with Count Richa and Arthur Villette).

Villette, Arthur, 1702–76, British Secretary at Turin, in 1741 Resident: *Anecdote from*, *1596* (with Count Richa and Dom Villa).

W.: *see* WALTER, William.

W., Monsieur (unident.): *Anecdote from*, *1437*.

Walpole, Lady: *see* ROLLE, Margaret.

W[alter, William, 1707–51]: *Anecdotes from*, 813, 1011, *1012*.

Warburton, Dr. William, 1698–1779, Bishop of Gloucester, Pope's friend, editor and executor: *Anecdotes from*, 111, 140, 254, 285–6, 290, *291*, 317 (with Spence), 324, 338, 352, 357, 364–5, 367, 376, *379* (reported by), 623, 642 (from Hooke), 659, 892, 895, 911, *952*, 953–4, *955*, 956, *957*, 958–61, *962*, 963; *comment upon anecdote*, 641.

Wavell, Daniel, b. 1676, rector of Winchester St. Maurice and St. Mary Calendar and friend of Spence family: *Anecdotes from*, *1017–19*.

West, Dr. Gilbert, 1703–56, author: *Anecdote from*, *902* (from Cibber), 947–8, *949*.

Whood, Isaac: *Anecdote possibly from*, *see* WOOD, John.

Willis, Richard, 1664–1734, Bishop of Winchester: *Anecdote from*, 795 (?).

Wilson, Thomas, of Evesham (attended Balliol College, Oxford): *Anecdotes from*, *207*, *869*.

Winton, Dean of: *see* NAYLOR, Charles.

Wood, [? John, 1705 ?–54, architect]: *Anecdotes from*, *1021a–b* (the source of these anecdotes might have been the Revd. Thomas Wood or Isaac Whood).

Wood, Revd. Thomas: *Anecdote possibly from*, *see* WOOD, John.

Wright, Stephen, d. 1780, assistant to William Kent: *Anecdote from*, *1064*.

Yarborough, Francis, 1695–1770, later Principal of Brasenose College, Oxford: *Anecdote from*, *1013*.

Young, Dr. Edward, 1683–1765, poet: *Anecdotes from*, *194*, 507, 771, 788, 798, 818, 820, 822, 827, 829, *830* (with Rev. John Jones), 832–3, 835–8, 839(?), 840–4, 848–50, 853 (from Addison or Thomas Tickell), 854–5, *856*, 857 (from a *curé* near Nice), *858*, 859–60, *861*, 888, 901: *comment upon anecdote*, 817.

INDEX

The index includes references to the text, to the explanatory and textual notes, and to the appendixes and the preliminaries, though the last are minimized. It omits most modern writers cited in the notes and Mr. T's remarks on Horace, pp. 662–79.

The numbers are those of anecdotes unless preceded by 'p.' or 'pp.', when they refer to pages of the preliminaries or Appendixes. 'n.' following an anecdote number indicates an explanatory note, 'tn.' a textual note, and 'head.' a head-note.

This index was begun by Slava Klima; thereafter the main task was performed by John Barnard. References to preliminaries and appendixes were added by the editor, who is responsible for any shortcomings.

The Pope section of the index is divided into two parts.

I. General Section: Most of the entries for major figures concerned with Pope or about whom the poet gives information, are entered in the main index with only a cross-reference. This part of the index contains the following important sub-headings: — Beliefs and opinions. — Books owned by Pope. — Catholicism. — Dogs. — Editing. — Education of Pope, and his opinions on Education. — Financial Affairs. — Gardening. — Habits. — Health. — Last Illness. — Lost MSS., etc. — Manuscripts.

PRINTED IN GREAT BRITAIN
AT THE UNIVERSITY PRESS, OXFORD
BY VIVIAN RIDLER
PRINTER TO THE UNIVERSITY